PRACTICAL

Microsoft® Windows® 2000 Server

Robert Reinstein

Dave Bixler

Contents
at a Glance

A Division of Macmillan USA
201 W. 103rd Street
Indianapolis, Indiana 46290

i

Practical Microsoft® Windows® 2000 Server

International Standard Book Number: 0-7897-2141-4

Library of Congress Catalog Card Number: 99-65441

Printed in the United States of America

First Printing: February, 2000

02 01 00   4 3 2 1

Trademarks

Warning and Disclaimer

Publisher
Jim Minatel

Acquisitions Editor
Tracy Williams

Development Editor
Valerie Perry

Managing Editor
Matt Purcell

Project Editor
Natalie Harris

Indexer
Becky Hornyak

Proofreader
Rachel Lopez Bell

Technical Editor
Doug Klippert

Team Coordinator
Vicki Harding

Interior Designer
Anne Jones

Cover Designer
Rader Design

Editorial Assistant
Angela Boley

Production
Dan Harris
George Poole

Contents

About the Author

Robert Reinstein has worked in the computer industry since 1984. He began alpha testing Windows NT® in 1992, the same year he became a Microsoft Certified Professional. He is a Microsoft Certified Systems Engineer, Citrix Certified Administrator, and a Compaq Master Accredited Systems Engineer. Robert is a major contributing author for the best-selling *Windows NT Server 4.0 Unleashed* and is the lead author for *Windows NT Troubleshooting and Configuration*.

Dave Bixler manages a consulting services team for a Fortune 500 systems integrator. He has been working in the computer industry since the mid-1980s. Dave has been focused on Internet technologies, including DNS and Web servers, information security, firewalls, VPNs, and Windows 2000. His industry certifications include Microsoft's MCP and MCSE, as well as Novell®'s MCNE, and a number of others.

Acknowledgments

This book would not have been possible without the hard work, dedication, and support of many people.

I'd like to extend a debt of gratitude to the folks at Macmillan Publishing who helped get this project off the ground, and worked hard to see it get to this final stage. To my editors: Tracy Williams, Valerie Perry, Jill Hayden, Natalie Harris, and Doug Klippert, I offer my sincerest thanks. And to Dave Bixler for his fine writing contribution, and helping round out the book you now hold in your hands.

When writing a book, additional support is also necessary. That is why I'd like to acknowledge the people who have been allowing me to focus on Microsoft technologies, and for providing support for my endeavors. To all of my co-workers, customers, and friends, thank you for allowing me to do what I enjoy the most: exploring the evolution of information technologies.

Dare I omit the people that *really* make this all possible? To everyone at Microsoft, especially all the great people at the Microsoft New York/New Jersey/Connecticut regional office. Great job guys! Your vision never fails to excite me and astound me.

This book could have never been completed if it wasn't for the love and support from my family. To Lisa, Justin, Kevin, and Stephen: Thank you for your patience and understanding. I love you all dearly.

And finally, my thanks to you, the reader. Your quest for information is really what this is all about.

Robert Reinstein

Tell Us What You Think!

As the reader of this book, you are our most important critic and commentator. We value your opinion and want to know what we're doing right, what we could do better, what areas you'd like to see us publish in, and any other words of wisdom you're willing to pass our way.

As an Associate Publisher for Que, I welcome your comments. You can fax, email, or write me directly to let me know what you did or didn't like about this book—as well as what we can do to make our books stronger.

Please note that I cannot help you with technical problems related to the topic of this book, and that due to the high volume of mail I receive, I might not be able to reply to every message.

When you write, please be sure to include this book's title and author as well as your name and phone or fax number. I will carefully review your comments and share them with the author and editors who worked on the book.

Fax: 317-581-4666

Email: office_que@mcp.com

Mail: Associate Publisher
Que
201 West 103rd Street
Indianapolis, IN 46290 USA

part

PLANNING AND INSTALLING
AN NT SERVER 2000
NETWORK

What's New in Windows 2000 Server?

Active Directory

Backward Compatibility

Automation Tools

Troubleshooting and Maintenance Tools

Microsoft Active Directory Services

Active Directory is Microsoft's first entry into the enterprise directory service arena and positions it well to compete with more established directory services, such as Banyan Vines or Novell Directory Services. Active Directory is a scalable directory service leveraging Internet standards such as LDAP (Lightweight Directory Access Protocol) and DNS (Domain Name Service) and fully integrates these standards into the Windows 2000 operating system. The directory services, which had been handled previously as NetBIOS names, have been replaced by a combination of LDAP, DNS, UNC names, HTTP URL names, X.500 names, and the Active Directory Service Interface (ADSI). Some of the benefits of the new Active Directory Service include the following:

- *Interoperability*. To ensure interoperability with other standards-based directories, Microsoft designed Active Directory as a native LDAP server. With the introduction of Active Directory, Microsoft has embraced DNS, in order to provide a scalable enterprise solution. Backward compatibility is still available through NetBIOS naming, but a purely native Windows 2000 network environment will adhere to DNS naming standards. By moving away from NetBIOS, Microsoft has been able to alleviate some of the overhead associated with the NetBIOS method, which rode on top of any of the Microsoft protocols, such as NetBEUI, IPX/SPX, and TCP/IP.

NetBIOS naming

NetBIOS naming has been the primary method of accessing and identifying resources that are available on Microsoft-based networks. When you had installed a Microsoft networking client, running on Windows 95, for example, you would have had to give that computer a name. The computer name was its NetBIOS name. This NetBIOS name would be translated to a computer address by using Microsoft WINS (Windows Internet Naming Service).

- *The Global Catalog*. The Global Catalog that is created for the enterprise is capable of holding ten million objects, more than enough for very large companies. It also uses advanced indexing and replication technologies to speed performance. By implementing LDAP and DNS, Windows 2000's Global Catalog can now easily interface with other operating systems and platforms that also use the LDAP protocol.

- *Active Directory Service Interface (ADSI)*. The ADSI is an interface that programmers can easily write to. By the time of this printing there should be numerous applications and utilities that use ADSI. It also allows for interaction with competitive directory services, such as NDS (Novell Directory Services).

- *Extensibility*. The objects that are contained within Active Directory can be either predefined by Microsoft or have custom properties added. New types of objects can also be created, thus making Active Directory an extensible directory schema. These objects can even be data, giving easy access to any or all resources on a network.

- *Improved Manageability*. Active Directory provides a hierarchical information repository that simplifies management tasks. Unlike the previous domain architecture, under Active Directory you can delegate administrative privileges. It even simplifies locating and managing resources such as servers or printers.

- *Improved Security*. Active Directory supports authentication protocols such as Kerberos version 5, Secure Sockets Layer (SSL) version 3, and X.509 certificates.

- *Improved Support for Internet Standards*. The directory services, which had been handled previously as NetBIOS names, have been replaced by a combination of LDAP, DNS, UNC names, HTTP URL names, X.500 names, and ADSI. By implementing LDAP and DNS, Windows 2000's Global Catalog can now easily interface with other operating systems and platforms that also use the LDAP protocol.

No proprietary protocols needed

A DNS-compatible name can be resolved to an IP address through DNS services, which can run on a Windows 2000 Server, or on another platform, such as a UNIX server. Because DNS is a standard—whereas NetBIOS has been used almost exclusively by Microsoft—it is now possible to have Microsoft networks integrate with legacy networks without introducing proprietary protocols.

Simply put, Active Directory provides a mechanism for locating, managing, and effectively using enterprise resources in a secure, scalable manner.

Global Catalog

The Global Catalog holds all objects from all domains in Active Directory. It allows for fast searches, no matter where the objects physically reside. In addition, the

Global Catalog allows for the concept of a multimaster domain and multimaster replication. Multimaster replication takes the former PDC (Primary Domain Controller) and BDC (Backup Domain Controller) and puts them both at the same level. No longer is one physical computer responsible for holding a master database. With multimaster replication, changes can be made on any domain controller in the domain. The domain controller then replicates the changes to its replication partners. Using multimaster replication results in 100 percent availability of the directory for changes, even if single domain controllers are unavailable. No more promoting a Backup Domain Controller when the Primary is down so you can add a user. In addition, by providing multiple copies of the directory across multiple servers, the Windows 2000 Server directory is able to scale to meet enterprise needs. This was a serious drawback under the old domain model.

Backward Compatibility

If needed, Windows 2000 servers can also mimic the older Microsoft Directory Services and provide NetBIOS names, allowing legacy systems that are not Active Directory–aware to access the network as if the servers were running Windows NT 4.0. This feature allows existing Windows 4.0 networks to migrate over to Active Directory at a pace as slow or fast as you want. This mode is referred to as "mixed." When you have migrated entirely to Windows 2000, you can remove the backward compatibility and run in "native" mode. One word of caution: When you migrate to "native" mode, there is no going back to mixed, so be sure you're ready.

Security Configuration Manager

Network security features have been enhanced as well. The Security Configuration Manager gives quick access to many security features that were available to Windows NT 4.0 users but had to be implemented as registry hacks. This tool allows administrators to define templates of varying security levels, making it easier to implement a strong security model on your network.

NTFS File System

The NTFS file system has been enhanced to allow for encryption of files, making all Windows 2000 computers safe for keeping sensitive data. This feature prevents NTFS-hacking tools from penetrating data.

The new NTFS is more efficient at storing files. And finally NTFS supports disk quotas. This allows administrators to restrict disk space usage by user, by application, or any way they see fit. Thresholds are placed on disk space, and policies can be set for when these thresholds are passed.

What about FAT?

Windows 2000 continues to support the FAT file system, and also supports the FAT32 file system introduced in Windows 95.

SEE ALSO

➤ *For information on NTFS, see page 223.*

Kerberos Authentication

First introduced in 1988 by S. P. Miller, B. C. Neuman, J. I. Schiller, and J. H. Saltzer, Kerberos is a network authentication protocol developed at the Massachusetts Institute of Technology (MIT). Kerberos is designed to enable two parties to exchange private information across an otherwise open network. It works by assigning a unique key, called a *ticket*, to each user that logs on to the network. The ticket is then embedded in messages to identify the sender of the message. The default security protocol that had been used in earlier versions of Windows NT has been replaced by Kerberos v5 authentication, yielding a much more secure logon environment.

The Kerberos protocol requires that a client can prove its identity to a server (and vice versa). After a client and server have used Kerberos to prove their identity, they can also encrypt all their communications to assure privacy and data integrity. One benefit of Microsoft's adoption of Kerberos is that you do not need to use a Windows 2000 Kerberos server for authentication. Microsoft supports any standards-based Kerberos server that supports version 5 for authentication. This greatly enhances flexibility and can save a lot of time creating IDs if you already are using Kerberos for a different purpose.

Distributed File System (DFS)

Microsoft's Distributed File System (DFS) allows administrators to make shared hard drive resources on the network easier to find for the end user. By creating a virtual share that includes pointers to one or more shares, it eases administration by allowing permissions to be assigned to these virtual directories.

Improved Virtual Private Networking

If you have worked with the PPTP protocol supported by Windows NT 4.0, you have some familiarity with what a VPN is. If not, a Virtual Private Network (VPN) enables you to send data securely between two computers across a public network (such as the Internet) so that it appears to the users that they exist on the same private network. Although earlier incarnations of Microsoft's VPN technology suffered from criticism from some parts of the industry, due to their proprietary protocol and some perceived security issues, the VPN capabilities of Windows 2000 enhance security while also supporting standard protocols. The supported protocols include the following:

- Point-to-Point Tunneling Protocol (PPTP)
- Layer Two Tunneling Protocol (L2TP)
- Internet Protocol Security (IPSec)

Point-to-Point Tunneling Protocol (PPTP)

The Point-to-Point Tunneling Protocol (PPTP) encapsulates Point-to-Point Protocol (PPP) frames for transmission over an IP-based network such as the Internet. Because PPTP encapsulates PPP, PPTP can support multiple protocols, including TCP/IP, IPX, and NetBEUI. Windows 2000 supports PPTP version 2.

Layer Two Tunneling Protocol (L2TP)

Layer Two Tunneling Protocol (L2TP) is a combination of PPTP and Layer Two Forwarding (L2F), a tunneling protocol championed by Cisco Systems. At the outset, the need to support competing protocols was an issue for third-party VPN vendors who were forced to either choose or try to support both. To solve this problem, the Internet Engineering Task Force, the standards body chartered with maintaining Internet standards, mandated that the two technologies be combined into a single tunneling protocol that represents the best features of PPTP and L2F. L2TP was the result and is fully supported by Windows 2000. For more information you can reference Request for Comment (RFC) 2661, "Layer Two Tunneling Protocol 'L2TP'."

Internet Protocol Security (IPSec)

Internet Protocol Security (IPSec) is a framework of open standards for ensuring private, secure communications over Internet Protocol (IP) networks. This protocol is rapidly becoming the underlying framework for secure communications using Virtual Private Networks (VPN). IPSec manages this by taking advantage of many of the industry-standard cryptographic security services. Windows 2000 implementation of IPSec is based on standards developed by the Internet Engineering Task Force (IETF) IPSec working group. However, Windows 2000 supports IPSec in two modes; the IETF version, which Microsoft refers to as "Pure IPSec," and the Microsoft variant on IPSec, which it refers to as "L2TP/IPSec Tunnel Mode." For more information on IPSec, you can always reference RFC 2401, the IPSec specifications document.

SEE ALSO

➤ *For information on VPNs, see page 433.*

Microsoft Certificate Services

If you have ever had to go to VeriSign or Entrust for a certificate for your Microsoft Internet Information Server 4 server so you can use the Secure Socket Layer (SSL) protocol, you have dealt with an X.509 certificate. The problems with this model are that you have to pay for each of these certificates, and that you have to trust a third party with a copy of your certificates. Windows 2000 changes that model by allowing you to use your Windows 2000 server as a fully standards-compliant X.509 certificate server. Although this had been included in Microsoft Internet Information Server 4, the Windows 2000 version is completely integrated into the Windows 2000 operating system and leverages the security technologies included as part of Windows 2000 and Active Directory. Microsoft Certificate Services allows for the creation of X.509 certificates and also integrates the resulting public keys with Active Directory. This technology also extends to the use of Smart Cards, which are also supported by Windows 2000.

Public key encryption

Each person gets a pair of keys: the public key and the private key. Messages are encrypted using the intended recipient's public key and can only be decrypted using his private key. All communications involve only public keys, so the need for sender and receiver to share private key information through a secure channel is eliminated.

The Microsoft Management Console

Although some users might have already gotten their feet wet with the Microsoft Management Console (MMC) by implementing the latest versions of Systems Management Server, Microsoft SQL Server, or Internet Information Server, the MMC is now the primary tool for managing your Windows 2000 computers, clients, resources, and networks.

What is the MMC? First, it is not a management application. The MMC is an integral part of the Windows 2000 operating system. This provides the next-generation management framework for managing Windows 2000 servers and services. Using applications known as snap-ins, the MMC provides a single interface for all Windows 2000 management applications. All the old management tools, such as User Manager For Domains and Server Manager, have been replaced by snap-ins that allow you to create customized management consoles. The other BackOffice products as well as third-party software vendors offer their own snap-ins, which allow you to have one screen that permits you to, for example, manage user accounts, tape backup software, software distribution tasks, network performance, and free disk space.

With the MMC, your imagination and the size of your monitor are your only limits.

Windows 2000 Server ships with many predefined snap-ins, including the following:

- The Directory Service Migration Tool, which allows you to migrate data from NDS or from a NetWare bindery.
- The Computer Management snap-in gives you a view of any computer on your network. This is similar to what used to be Server Manager, in that you are able to look at running services, maintain shares, and view event logs.

SEE ALSO

➤ *For information on the Computer Management snap-in, see page 81.*

- The Disk Management snap-in is the replacement for Disk Administrator. This update includes many wizards that allow you to easily create volume sets, stripe sets, and mirror sets. Adding and initializing new drives are done through this tool. The great thing is that not all these tasks require a reboot, which is a feature that you'll find throughout Windows 2000: *fewer reboots*.

SEE ALSO

➤ *For information on the Disk Management snap-in, see page 239.*

- The System Service Management snap-in is the new version of the Services applet from the Control Panel. Through this snap-in you can start and stop services on both the local and remote computers. An exciting new feature is the ability to specify how to handle a failed service. Some options you have are to restart the service, run a batch or script file, or restart the computer.

- The Device Manager is already familiar to Windows 9x users. Windows 2000 implements the Device Manager as an MMC snap-in. This snap-in includes the same functionality that users are used to, such as changing the hardware resources for a given piece of hardware or resolving IRQ and address conflicts. A new feature for Device Manager is the ability to add new hardware through the Hardware Wizard.

- A Group Policy snap-in allows for easy management of setting policies for groups of objects. This can include the ability to distribute software, as well as the usual "user profile" tasks.

If you will spend any time with either Windows 2000 Server or Windows 2000 Professional on your desktop, you can expect to become very familiar with the Microsoft Management Console.

Advanced Automation Services

With earlier versions of Windows NT, administrators had to depend on a third-party program or the command-line AT command to perform automation of utilities. The Task Scheduler in Windows 2000 is the same that is found in Windows 9x with some enhancements. Task Scheduler lets you specify a script, a program, or any type of action, to run at a predetermined time, such as at boot time, at logon, or at regular intervals.

Another advanced service is the ability to install the Windows 2000 Professional operating system on Windows 2000 Server clients. This ability has been added to Windows 2000 with Remote Operating System Installation. If a PC has remote-boot capability, it can connect to a Windows 2000 Server and upgrade to Windows 2000 Professional or you can even configure it to format the hard drive and then perform a complete installation from scratch, with no user intervention required.

IntelliMirror

Microsoft has been leading up to IntelliMirror for quite some time. One common misconception exists regarding IntelliMirror. It is not an application. IntelliMirror is a set of features built into the Microsoft Windows 2000 operating system, designed for desktop management. Building on earlier technologies such as Policy Manager and roaming profiles, IntelliMirror provides users with seamless access to the network, applications, and data. Whether the user is online or offline, IntelliMirror creates a standard computing environment from which she can work.

Client-side caching allows data synchronization to be performed at regular intervals or in the background while a user is working at her PC. When users save data to the network, they are also saving the data locally, allowing them to work offline. When they connect to the network again, the data is automatically synchronized.

This technology also gives user data fault tolerance by allowing data to be replicated between server and workstation. A user's data, personal computer settings, and computing environment are consistently available and based on policy definitions. IntelliMirror can deploy, recover, restore, or replace user's data, software, and personal settings in a Windows 2000–based environment, providing a powerful incentive for companies to move to a fully integrated Windows 2000 environment.

SEE ALSO

➤ *To learn more about IntelliMirror, see page 122.*

Windows Terminal Services

Formerly Windows NT Server Terminal Server Edition, Windows 2000 now has the Terminal Server's functionality available as an installable service as part of the core operating system. Using the much-abused concept of "thin" clients, Terminal Services allows any computer to act as a Windows 2000 client, with the ability to run Windows-based applications on the server itself. This includes not only Windows PCs, but also Macintosh and UNIX clients.

Troubleshooting and Maintenance Tools

Windows 2000 now incorporates the Windows 9x Safe Mode startup option. This allows you to start Windows 2000 loading only the drivers that you are sure are not causing the problem that prompted you to start in Safe Mode. This option alone prevents you from performing some of the tasks that were required under previous versions of Windows NT, most notably the need to reinstall the operating system.

Another option carried over from Windows 9x is the ability to boot into command mode. On Windows 2000, this is called the Repair Command Console. The types of tasks that can be performed from the Repair Command Console include FDISK, FORMAT, and restoring the master boot record (MBR). By having this option available it is no longer a troubleshooting requirement to format the system partition as FAT to allow booting from a diagnostic disk.

Some of the utilities available include the following:

- *FDISK.* By using the FDISK utility, which is a character-based utility used to define logical drives on physical drives, you can see what partitions have been defined on the system. When you are prevented from booting in to the Windows 2000 GUI and running Disk Management Console, the FDISK program might be your only way to regain access to the system volume.
- *FORMAT.* The FORMAT option is similar to FDISK, in the sense that the only way to format a partition through Windows NT had been from within the GUI mode of Windows NT. The FORMAT utility allows you to take a partition defined by FDISK and then format it using the file system you choose.
- *FIXMBR.* The FIXMBR utility will replace an existing master boot record (MBR) with a proper Windows 2000 Server master boot record. A master boot record is located on all hard drives in a location that is not directly accessible by a user. A special MBR is required to allow Windows 2000 to load its boot loader, which results in the menu that you see when booting your server.

Applying Service Packs under the previous versions of Windows NT required reinstallation of the Service Pack if you had overwritten any of the system files. This usually happened if you installed a service or drivers off the original pre-Service Pack Windows NT CD-ROM. Windows 2000 introduces a technology that Microsoft calls *Slip-Streaming*. At boot time, the Windows 2000 Server inspects its system files. If there are any system files that have been downgraded to an older version, a self-repair process is automatically run in the background, allowing you to continue the boot process.

The Windows 2000 Service Packs can be installed to a network share, allowing any Windows 2000 computer on the network to automatically update the necessary files when adding older services or drivers.

And finally, a disk defragmentation utility has been embedded into Windows 2000. Previously only available as a third-party add-on, disk optimizing is now a part of the operating system, allowing you to keep disk access at its optimum speed. The disk defragmentation utility works on FAT16, FAT32, and NTFS.

The Windows 2000 backup utility is still based on Seagate's Backup Exec. The good news is that not only does this application support backup to tape devices, it also has support for other recording media, such as CD-R(W), Zip drives, and external hard drives.

Network Protocol Support

Microsoft is fully integrating Internet and security technologies by building support into Windows 2000 Server. Some of the most familiar protocols that are new for Windows 2000 Server include CHAP, MS-CHAP, PAP, EAP, RC4 Encryption, RADIUS (both client and server support), IP packet filtering, and IPX packet filtering.

Additional TCP/IP Support

Windows 2000 now supports (in fact, requires) the use of Dynamic DNS (DDNS). By integrating DNS with DHCP, there is hardly a need to manually modify the Microsoft DNS Server. Active Directory also ties into the dynamic DNS, making it easier than ever to maintain a TCP/IP network.

SEE ALSO

➤ *To get an introduction to TCP/IP concepts, see Chapter 9, "Introduction to TCP/IP"*

➤ *For a look at advanced TCP/IP concepts, see Chapter 14, "Advanced TCP/IP Concepts."*

Network Address Translation, a feature previously available only in Microsoft's Proxy Server, is included in Windows 2000 Server. This allows for internal IP addresses to be hidden by translating private addresses to public addresses.

Reliability and Robustness

Windows 2000 Server includes many features that take it to the next plateau of networking.

Windows 2000 Server can address up to 64GB of RAM on supported platforms. And Windows 2000 Server right out of the box can support SMP servers with eight processors.

IP service load balancing is built into Windows 2000 Server. A group of servers running an IP service, such as Web services, can share resources and distribute workloads automatically. This is a separate service from the Clustering Services formerly

available on Windows NT Server Enterprise Edition, that are now part of
Windows 2000 Advanced Server and Windows 2000 DataCenter Server.

In general, everything is faster on Windows 2000 Server. Even blue screen crash file
dumps write faster, and CHKDSK runs faster.

There are far fewer reasons for blue screens to occur because many more preventa-
tive diagnostic routines are built in to Windows 2000 Server, and development
guidelines are stricter for the Windows 2000 platform.

The greatest complaint about previous versions of Windows NT was the number of
reboots that had to be performed during system configuration. This has been greatly
reduced in Windows 2000.

So, there really are many major upgrades in Windows 2000 that will have seasoned
Windows NT administrators learning a few new tricks.

Planning Your Windows 2000 Server Network

Determine your server requirements

Establish hard drive requirements

Determine memory requirements

Establish processor requirements

Evaluate fault tolerance methods

Examine the Active Directory
architecture

Understand the relationships between
Organization Units (OU), Domains, and
Forests

Understand Trust relationships

Identifying Your Goals

Planning for a Windows 2000 Server requires a great deal of thought in advance. Luckily, there are tools that can assist you in doing this, and this chapter can serve as your guide.

When thinking about planning your Windows 2000 Server configuration, you need to figure out the number of users on your network. Next, think about the amount of disk space you require. Be sure to plan for growth. It is easier to add drives before the server is deployed than it is to take down a production server to add disk capacity. It is also important that you think about your growth, which can include multiple servers, and plan for your bandwidth, which includes (depending on the scope of your network) multiple segments, routers, bridges, remote access, and other basic networking considerations.

Before you can come up with a plan, you should first identify your goals. You need to explore what exactly you are looking for in a Windows 2000 network, and identify the overall purposes of this network—file and print services, application servers, remote access, access to other networks (such as mainframes or minicomputers), communications, Internet access, or other considerations.

Look ahead at the next 12 to 24 months and make sure you account for as much future growth as possible. Although it is impossible to know precisely what your requirements will be in two years, an educated guess can frequently save you time down the road. You should evaluate whether you are thinking about only a LAN environment, or if you will be working with a WAN environment. Your goals should dictate the initial hardware that you use for your Windows 2000 Server network, so that you do not find yourself outgrowing that hardware in too short a time.

Ideally, you should plan for the following goals:

- High availability
- Sufficient resources (disks, printers, and other services)
- Optimal user response time

The following sections can help you define the type of configuration that would suit your environment. Don't forget to plan for growth!

Meeting Minimum Hardware Requirements

When you're thinking about implementing a Windows 2000 network, there are some minimum requirements that need to be met, even before you think about the growth of your network. One thing you should be absolutely sure of is that the hardware you select for your Windows 2000 Server is on Microsoft's *Hardware Compatibility List (HCL)*. By ensuring that your hardware is contained on the HCL, you know it has been tested by Microsoft and will function with Windows 2000. Microsoft has also been known to be reluctant to provide support for hardware not on the list, so if you have an issue on that server your friend built in his basement, you are probably on your own. The HCL is located on the Web at `http://www.microsoft.com/hcl/default.asp`.

The other component of hardware requirements is to make sure you have the right hardware. The minimum requirements for Windows 2000 Server follow:

- 200MHz Pentium or higher microprocessor. Multiple processors are supported. Pentium II, Pentium III, or Xeon processors are included. Equivalent processors such as Cyrix or AMD processors are included.

- 128MB RAM minimum; 256MB recommended, 4GB maximum (expandable to 64GB on Intel-based PAE platforms running Windows 2000 Advanced Server or DataCenter Server).

- 2GB hard disk with a minimum of 900MB of free space. If you are upgrading an existing domain controller and implementing Active Directory, be sure to allow for additional disk space for the domain database upgrade. Windows 2000 uses a lot of temporary storage to accomplish this upgrade. The actual amount is wholly dependent on the size of your domain.

- VGA or better resolution monitor.

- Keyboard.

- Mouse or other pointing device is optional, but with a graphical user interface (GUI), trying to install Windows 2000 from the keyboard can be a frustrating exercise. If you want to do it once to see how frustrating, go ahead. Then run down to the computer store and buy yourself a mouse.

- For a CD-ROM only installation you need an El Torito–compatible CD-ROM drive. That's not something you pick up at Taco Bell but is in fact a bootable CD-ROM, allowing the Windows 2000 CD to start Setup without benefit of a floppy or hard drive boot process.

- For a floppy disk and CD-ROM installation, you need a CD-ROM drive, preferably at least 12X speed, and a 3.5 inch disk drive.

- For network installations, you need a network card that's on the HCL and access to a network share with the installation files.

These are the minimum required configurations, per Microsoft's specifications. For optimum performance, starting with more than the minimum is usually a good idea.

Number of Servers

Although a smaller group of users with limited networking needs might require only one Windows 2000 Server, most network implementations can benefit from a multi-server environment. This allows you to not only provide some level of fault-tolerance (discussed later in the chapter) but also to be flexible in the deployment of the servers. Making a single server your Domain Controller, SQL Server, Web server, and file and print server is certainly possible, but can be ill-advised.

Obviously, a network with multiple offices in multiple locations provides an excellent candidate for multiple servers. Applications that have require a lot of capacity and resources are also good examples of when multiple servers would best serve the network, even if the network exists within one physical location.

Domain Controllers

One consideration for multiple servers is domain planning. Allowing for optimum uptime and logon response might dictate the minimum number of servers necessary to get your network off the ground. Planning a domain requires identifying your network client's requirements, such as access to applications, printers, and other network resources. Based on your bandwidth availability, user distribution, and requirements for availability, you might need to implement more than one domain controller.

Load Balancing

Load balancing is another potential reason to have more than one server. For instance, if your clients heavily use a word processing program that is installed on a server, you might find that having that application installed on two servers gives the clients faster access to some of the features of that application.

Certain software might have recommendations to exist on its own server, thus overall load balancing is supplied by dedicating a server for that application. A good example of this could be for a Remote Access Services (RAS) server. Although RAS can certainly exist on a single server network, it does create overhead that might affect other network services. Placing RAS on its own server will ensure that your production applications such as file and print, mail, and so on are not negatively affected by the overhead of supporting RAS and dial-in users.

Server-based applications, such as Microsoft Exchange Server, have been designed to allow one application to run across multiple servers, for purposes of load balancing. This means that if you have a large number of users and need multiple servers, the application can actually be used to balance the load across a group of servers, rather than manually load balancing by assigning certain users to one machine and a different group to another.

Clustering

Microsoft's Cluster Services for Windows 2000 requires a minimum of two servers. If this is the approach that you want to take with your network, you must check Microsoft's Hardware Compatibility List (HCL) for its Clustering Services, which is a subset of the list for Windows 2000.

To check the Cluster Services HCL, go to this Internet URL:
`http://www.microsoft.com/hcl/default.asp`.

To view validated cluster configurations, choose the category called "Cluster."

Clustering might be something you need to consider in your enterprise network storage strategy when you are looking for high availability coupled with ease of administration. Microsoft's clustering technology provides a mechanism that can keep systems and applications available even in the event of an entire server failure. Windows 2000 Clustering Service allows two servers to form a "cluster" of servers working together as a single system. For those of you familiar with Novell NetWare, this provides a similar functionality to the old SFT III software used with NetWare 3.x. Each server operates independently of the server in the cluster but continues to provide services even when the other server is unavailable.

In the Microsoft clustering model, each server has its own memory, system disk, operating system, and subset of the cluster's resources. When one server fails, the other server takes over all the resources and adds the failed server's addresses to its own. Client traffic is then routed to the system that is available. When the server that crashed is back and available, redistribute resources and client requests as needed. In fact, you can also replace the failed server and add it to the cluster to assume the role of the original server.

One other note about clustering: This is an advanced technology and will generally not be used by smaller networks. This technology is extremely well-suited to high-availability environments where server down time translates to an immediate loss of revenue (that is, a stock exchange or online broker) or to an application that requires not only high availability but also load balancing, like a high-traffic Internet or intranet site (for example, Amazon.com or Yahoo). In any event, the specifics of clustering are well beyond the scope of this book. If you reach a point where you need to deploy Windows 2000 Server in an environment such as the ones just described, clustering could provide an excellent solution.

Server Fault Tolerance

Fault tolerance is another reason to extend your network beyond a single server. Usually the determining factor here is the amount of downtime you are willing to tolerate or that your business can endure without pain.

The average server can come with a 48-hour on-site warranty that can be upgraded to a 24-hour response or even a 4-hour response. In some cases even this is not enough protection, and that's when a second server is required. Third-party solutions, such as Vinca Systems' StandbyServer, provides real-time server mirroring that has a server mirror kick in whenever the main server fails. The downtime here would be minimized to only a few moments and would be transparent to the network clients.

Another approach that I have used was having an extra server, identical to two other servers we installed, but lacking hard drives, which stood in a closet. If one of the two live servers had a problem other than a hard drive problem, for which RAID solutions should handle recovery, we would remove the hard drives from the failed server and put them into the spare server. This would provide a live server within minutes, but with a noticeable absence from the network that might affect network clients. The extra server method also requires manual intervention (such as swapping drives), which the real-time server mirroring solutions handle automatically.

SEE ALSO

➤ *For more information about RAID, see page 293.*

Number of Processors

Increasing the number of processors on a Windows 2000 server can greatly improve performance, depending on the other software that is running on the computer.

A single processor computer running Windows 2000 Server is capable of handling the network traffic and internal processes created by hundreds of users. Usually, simple file and print services will not make the purchase of multiple processors for your computer cost effective.

However, a single processor is limited to handling one process at a time. Windows 2000 Server was designed to perform load balancing when running on multiple processors.

Right out of the box, Windows 2000 Server can accommodate eight processors. If the hardware manufacturer provides the necessary drivers, Windows 2000 Server can take advantage of a computer with up to 32 processors.

If the computer running Windows 2000 Server is also running a processor-intensive program, such as Microsoft SQL Server or Microsoft Exchange Server, and is handling a large amount of requests, a second processor can boost the power of the computer almost 90%. A Web server is another example of a server that can get overburdened with requests. As you add each additional processor, the return is lessened.

If you have the resources to test your production conditions in a lab and can set up a server with multiple processors, the results can be measured, which can allow you to decide on whether the investment in a multiprocessor server would be cost-justified.

A low-cost method to set up a lab

We often procure evaluation hardware from hardware manufacturers. You might want to speak to your systems integrator about setting up evaluation equipment at little or no cost to you.

Also, Microsoft offers their Corporate Solutions Pilot Program which gives end-user evaluation copies of all of Microsoft's business software for a 120-day trial period, through Microsoft Certified Solution Providers, usually at no cost.

You might want to see about engaging a Microsoft Certified Solution Provider to help you kick-start your evaluation process.

Memory Requirements

The memory requirements for Windows 2000 Server are a minimum of 128MB. I'd rather see a minimum of 256MB RAM, which should give most file and print servers ample memory for caching among other performance concerns. For a small work-group, which I consider to be 10 users or fewer, you should be able to get by on the 128MB minimum.

Applications that reside on the server dictate additional memory requirements for your server. Using Microsoft BackOffice as an example, loading a copy of Microsoft SQL Server onto your Windows 2000 server can easily bring the minimum RAM requirement up to 256MB. Adding Microsoft Systems Management Server can drive that up to 384MB RAM, depending on the number of users.

Running Microsoft BackOffice components on the same server

Ideally, using this scenario, there would be more than one server. One would run the Microsoft Systems Management Server and the other could have Microsoft SQL Server installed on it. Although Microsoft licenses its BackOffice suite to run on a single server, running the individual programs on their own server guarantees improved performance and also makes troubleshooting these programs much easier.

Disk Requirements

Predicting the amount of disk space needed for a Windows 2000 server is difficult, as the size of applications grow at an alarming rate. Luckily, the cost of adding disk space has been decreasing, making it easier to aim high and avoid running out of disk space.

The base Windows 2000 Server package can use 1GB of disk space. Each user directory can easily become hundreds of megabytes, depending on how you implement user directories. Email packages, such as Microsoft Exchange Server, can also occupy a large amount per user, plus a defined amount of disk space for public folders.

Megabytes to gigabytes

One gigabyte of storage is the equivalent of 1,000 megabytes. That's one thousand million bytes of information.

Expansion

Luckily, today's servers are built to accommodate a large number of hard drives. For example, both Compaq and Hewlett Packard have server models with more than 12 hot-swap drive bays. External expansion units can allow for terabytes of data to be stored online.

Special disk array controller cards, such as the Compaq SmartArray II, allow for disk expansion without requiring the server be powered off.

And in addition to using hard drives for storage, optical media, such as CD-ROM, can be used to house unlimited amounts of data.

Verify that external hardware is on the HCL

If you plan to use external units for storing data, be sure to check that these units are compatible with Windows 2000. Go to `http://www.microsoft.com/hcl/default.asp` on the Web to check your hardware for compatibility.

Drive Fault Tolerance

Besides the base requirements for hard drive capacity, you should be thinking about a fault-tolerant system.

Disk mirroring, also known as RAID Level 1, requires you to double the amount of drive capacity that you want to have usable. Disk volumes that use disk striping with parity, also known as RAID Level 5, use one drive in addition to the other drives that are part of the volume.

Decreasing your server downtime

Hot-swappable drives are hard drives that are enclosed in a shell that allow for quick removal from the server or housing and can be installed without the need to down the server. It is strongly advised that this type of medium is used whenever possible.

SEE ALSO
➤ *To learn how to protect your network using RAID, see page 235.*

Directory Services

The last several sections discussed the hardware requirements you need to consider when planning your Windows 2000 Server deployment. This section discusses some of the software planning you need to do in order to have a smooth installation or upgrade. In order to begin planning your Windows 2000 Server, you need to be able to look at the big picture. Creating a Windows 2000 network requires a design for the Active Directory architecture.

This chapter introduces you to the building blocks of Windows 2000 Server architecture. Even if you have experience working with previous versions of Windows NT, the domain strategy has changed quite a bit.

Key to any network operating system is the *Directory Service*. This is the repository of information about all the entities that make up the network. This can include users, computers, printers, shared drive space, applications, routers, and gateways, among others. Both administrators and network clients use the directory. Administrators use the directory to assign permissions to items in the directory.

The Directory Service used in previous versions of Windows NT, was known as NTDS. With Windows 2000 Server, the Directory Service is called *AD*, or *Active Directory*.

The Active Directory Architecture

Windows 2000 Server introduces a new architecture for Microsoft networking. It is important to understand this new architecture in order to decide how you will implement it in your environment. The Active Directory can scale from a single server environment, where there might be only a hundred objects, to a multidomain environment with millions of objects.

Two elements of Active Directory are *Domains* and *Organizational Units*. These two entities define your enterprise. Domains are further broken down into *Trees* and *Forests*, which allow you to define the cohesiveness between different parts of your organization.

Remember that Active Directory uses DNS (Domain Name System) as its locator service to take advantage of the namespace that DNS supports. By using the Internet-based namespace, both administrators and network clients can easily recognize objects that belong to their domain. All the examples I give in this section have their related DNS name given. Understanding how DNS works and how to interpret DNS names will help you interpret the names that Windows 2000 Server will generate for your servers and resources.

SEE ALSO

➤ *For more information on DNS, see page 410.*

Sites

A *Site* is a group of domain controllers connected by a high-speed connection. A Site can contain one or more Domains, but does not span a wide area network connection. A Site is a boundary, within which are one or more Windows 2000 Server domains. When a user logs on to his Windows 2000 Server domain, he will seek a domain controller to authenticate him. The domain controllers that are queried will exist within the same site as the user. Site boundaries are usually dictated by slow links or by the separation of IP subnets.

Domains

Domains are the highest-level unit within the Active Directory structure. You can think of Domains as a boundary that permits you as the administrator to set policies and security within your domain. This has been the case with previous versions of Windows NT; however, with this latest incarnation of domains, we are introduced to the domain name as a DNS entry, not just a single word.

For example, if my organization is the Acme Ipso-Facto Company and has a registered Internet domain name of `aif.com` (which will now be the site name) and I choose to call my Windows 2000 domain `ipso-facto`, the fully qualified domain name would be `ipso-facto.aif.com`.

The domain entry in the Active Directory can contain up to 10 million objects under it. This number should be sufficient for most organizations. Unfortunately, not all companies have the luxury to work with a single domain, due to politics or security reasons. But the easiest type of Active Directory to maintain is one that contains only one domain.

A single domain keeps its own *Access Control List (ACL)*. The ACL, administrative rights, and other security settings are restricted to their own domain. From a design standpoint, you should strive towards using a single domain.

The domain controllers within a domain all replicate information with each other. This is called multimaster replication.

In previous versions of Windows NT, a single domain meant a flat structure. That is not necessarily the case with Active Directory. A single domain can have different containers within it. These containers are *Organizational Units (OUs)*.

Organizational Units (OU)

The implementation of the OU allows for the further breakdown of domains creating new boundaries for administration and security. This takes the former flat organization of a Windows NT domain into a new dimension with a hierarchy.

By defining different organizational units, say by department, you can assign administrators that only control users and resources that belong to that department. Figure 2.1 demonstrates the typical OU model.

Less need for multiple domains

This type of granularity was unavailable in previous versions of Windows NT and might have prompted the creation of multiple domain models; however, it might no longer be necessary to go beyond the single domain in order to achieve the same results.

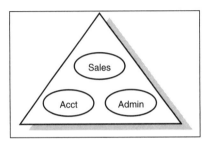

FIGURE 2.1
Organizational Units (OUs) exist within a domain.

When designing a Windows 2000 Server domain, it is important to ensure that the hierarchy reflects the actual company organization. OUs should be created only where necessary though. It is also acceptable to create an OU within an OU, if this clearly defines your organizational structure *and* it will be used to clearly set a boundary regarding security and policies.

An OU is a container that can have group policies applied, among other security settings. The beautiful part here is that business rules can be applied to these individual containers, which can then be filtered by User Group membership. In fact, resources can be placed in their own container within a departmental OU, allowing for restrictions to be applied only to those resources. The combinations are limitless; however, Microsoft does recommend a limitation of no more than 10 levels of OUs for manageability and performance purposes.

Trees

A Windows 2000 *Server Tree* is a one or more domains within a site. To create a tree, a root domain must first be created. This root domain would be the same as a domain for a single domain environment. For instance, using the aif.com site again, the root domain would be aif.com. Two child domains would be created. One domain could be ipso-facto.aif.com. If another domain were created because another area of the company needed its own domain, there could be an `acme.aif.com` domain. Figure 2.2 illustrates this tree.

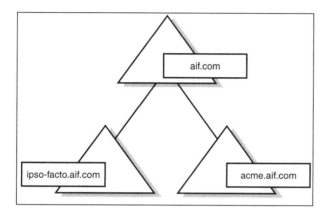

FIGURE 2.2
The `aif.com` tree includes a root domain and child domains.

What makes trees different than just a series of domains is that as members of the same tree, these domains already have a two-way trust. A *trust* is the availability of resources between one domain and another. By having more than one domain in a tree, each domain gives access of its objects to the other domains. This type of trust is called a *Kerberos transitive-trust* relationship. In other words, if Domain1 trusts Domain2 and Domain2 trusts Domain3, Domain1 automatically trusts Domain3 (see Figure 2.3).

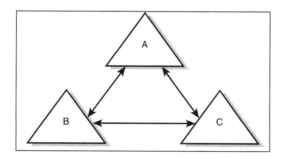

FIGURE 2.3
Transitive trusts are created within a tree.

A domain can also have a child domain, which can inherit configuration and security from its parent domain. In Figure 2.4 the `acme.aif.com` domain has a child domain: `manufacturing.acme.aif.com`. Note the DNS name that explicitly tells you that manufacturing is a child of acme, which is a member of the `aif.com` site.

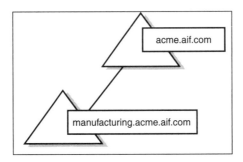

FIGURE 2.4
The `acme.aif.com` domain has a child domain: `manufacturing.acme.aif.com`.

All the domains within a tree share the *Global Catalog*. These domains also share a common *schema*. The *schema* is the way that objects are defined within the Active Directory. The *Global Catalog* allows for lookup of objects that are contained within the tree. As a new domain joins an existing tree, it automatically has the two-way trust relationship enabled with all domains within the same tree, and its objects are added to the Global Catalog.

Actually, only a subset of information about each object exists in the Global Catalog. The Global Catalog actually exists on all domain controllers within a tree. Each domain controller holds only its domain's portion of the Global Catalog, therefore the growth of the catalog only occurs in the domain where the growth is actually taking place. When a user requests an object, the first domain controller to get the request looks in its subset of the Global Catalog and then either goes the next domain or, if the information is found, turns over the translation to the user. This allows users anywhere to get fast results when looking for objects that might reside outside of their own domain.

Forests

A Windows 2000 Forest is a collection of two or more trees. These trees are connected through a communications line. Although the schema is the same across the forest, no trust relationships are automatically set up, although trust relationships can be manually set up. By joining the same forest, the Global Catalog and schema for each tree might be replicated. It is not possible to replicate a schema or Global Catalog across separate forests.

Creating a successful Windows 2000 network takes careful planning. Determining your requirements helps ensure that the proper hardware is implemented. If you find that after the network has been installed, there are noticeable lags (which usually come to light when users complain about applications running slowly off of the network), a number of tools can help you diagnose or fine-tune the existing network.

It might actually pay to have a consultant who is experienced in setting up these networks help you get off the ground. If this is not an option, you are sure to get off to a good start, using the methods and tools I've introduced in this chapter.

chapter

3

Installing Windows 2000 Server

Before You Start

The installation process for Windows 2000 Server can be achieved in a few different ways. This chapter reviews the steps necessary to perform an install from scratch. The upgrade process is discussed later in the chapter.

You might recall that hardware compatibility and hardware specifications are very important for a proper Windows 2000 server. The installation routine for Windows 2000 depends on your knowledge of the hardware you are installing it on. Although the software itself uses hardware recognition, you'll need to be able to verify the settings that the setup program determines.

Even before you insert the Windows 2000 Server CD-ROM into your CD drive or place the Windows 2000 Server boot floppy into your floppy drive, I recommend that you check the Web sites for the manufacturers of any hardware you have installed in your server. They might have posted drivers that are newer or not included on the Windows 2000 Server CD-ROM.

You should also check the maker of the server itself to see if there are any ROM BIOS upgrades that are required for the installation of Windows 2000 Server.

Installing Windows 2000

The installation of Windows 2000 Server uses four floppy disks and a single CD-ROM. Depending on the type of hardware you are using, you might also need updated driver disks. If you are using a server that has a bootable CD-ROM drive, you will not need to use the four floppy disks. I highly recommend just installing from the CD-ROM because the floppy swap process makes the installation take that much longer.

1. Put the CD-ROM into your CD-ROM drive, and if you are using the floppies, place the disk marked Setup Boot Disk into the floppy drive. Power on your server, and the installation begins.

2. The first part of the setup program is a character-based program. The underlying operating system that you boot up on is actually MS-DOS. If you're using the boot floppy, you will be prompted to insert Setup Disk 2 and then press Enter to continue.

3. At this point, many device drivers are loaded. This enables the setup program to determine what hardware you have installed. After drivers are loaded for the keyboard, serial ports, and other system-level drivers, you will be prompted to

insert Setup Disk 3 and then press Enter. If you are installing from the CD-ROM only, you will not get this prompt.

Mass storage drivers

Perhaps the most delicate part of the installation is the recognition of mass storage devices. This is accomplished by the Windows 2000 installation program loading a series of SCSI and IDE drivers. These drivers represent the hard drive controllers that Windows 2000 natively will recognize. In some cases, Windows 2000 will not ship with a driver that is appropriate for your hardware.

---

4. Next, on a floppy based install, you will be prompted to insert Setup Disk 4 and then press Enter.

5. Next, Windows 2000 Server Setup welcomes you and gives you three options on how to continue. The first option is to simply press Enter to continue with the installation. The second option is to repair a previous Windows 2000 installation. By pressing R you can recover a damaged Windows 2000 installation. The third option is to abort the installation by pressing the F3 key. Press Enter to continue.

6. Now the Windows 2000 Licensing Agreement is displayed. After carefully reading this information, press the F8 key to indicate that you agree to abide by the license. If you choose to abort the installation at this time, you can press the Esc key.

7. The next step in the installation process is one of the most crucial. You need to determine where you are going to install Windows 2000 Server. A list of existing partitions and free space is displayed. You have the option to choose an existing partition for the install or create a new partition for the installation in an area of free space. You can also delete existing partitions and create new ones in their place.

Which file system should you use?

If indeed you are installing Windows 2000 Server from scratch, the choice should be to format a partition as NTFS and install the operating system on that partition. It is important to make sure that the system partition is large enough to accommodate not only the operating system but other drivers and files that might be required to reside on the system partition as well. This decision should be made with consideration to the life of the server; as programs are added, the requirement for the size of the system partition can increase.

This exercise demonstrates installing Windows 2000 Server onto the C drive, which is a new partition on a new hard drive that does not contain any existing partitions.

But there's already a partition there

Some server hardware might have already placed a partition on the primary hard drive that contains information required by the hardware for diagnostic, fault tolerance, and configuration purposes. Do not remove any existing partition without first knowing exactly what you are removing. When you remove a partition and install a new partition for Windows 2000, you might not be able to reinstall that partition without removing Windows 2000 first.

The hard drive requirements for Windows 2000 Server should force you to make this partition at least 2GB. This includes room for the operating system and the dump file, should you choose to have one. The more RAM you have installed, the more room you will need to allow for the dump file.

What is a dump file?

The dump file is one of the options for dealing with server crashes, which would allow for the system memory to be written to a file for debugging purposes. Generally that means sending the file to Microsoft for analysis. As an administrator you should not be looking at a hex dump of the contents of memory as part of your day-to-day job.

---

8. To create the new partition, press C. Next enter the size for this partition (in megabytes) and press Enter. The new partition shows up on the list of existing partitions as unformatted. Highlight this new partition and press Enter to indicate that you want to install Windows 2000 Server on that partition.

9. Next, you are asked for the file system you want to use to format the partition. NTFS is the preferred file system for all Windows 2000 Server installations. If you decide that you want to use the FAT file system, the installation program will let you know that a FAT partition cannot be greater than 2GB. If you choose the partition to be greater than 2GB, the program lets you know that FAT32 must be used. In this case, select NTFS and press Enter.

When formatting is complete, the partition is scanned for defects. Setup then copies several folders from the CD-ROM to temporary installation folders that it has created on the installation partition. It also lays the groundwork for the Windows 2000 operating system by installing the boot files onto the system partition. The speed of your computer's CPU, CD-ROM drive, and hard drive determines how long this step takes. When the files are copied, your configuration is saved to disk.

10. Now you are prompted to remove any floppy disks or CD-ROMs from the drives because the system automatically restarts in fifteen seconds. You can press the Enter key to reboot immediately.

This completes the character-based portion of the installation. The next phase of this process will be the GUI configuration portion of the installation.

The First Windows 2000 Boot

When your computer restarts it boots Windows 2000 in graphical mode. This portion of the setup program resembles the Windows 9x setup program.

1. After initialization, the Windows 2000 Server Setup Wizard starts by displaying its Welcome screen. If you selected NTFS as your file system, the conversion will take place at this time. Click the Next button to allow Windows 2000 to start detecting your hardware. Hardware detection usually takes several minutes because it's poring through its extensive database of hardware and checking BIOS strings and other plug-and-play information that it can find in RAM. This procedure can take a lot of the guesswork and manual installation of hardware away, which is why it is important to use hardware that is supported by the Windows 2000 operating system. If you are using any older hardware, such as non–Plug-and-Play boards, you will have an opportunity to manually install these. It is important to note that this process has been significantly improved because the Windows NT 4.0 operating system does a much better job accurately detecting your hardware.

2. The Regional Settings dialog box is next. This lets you specify the system locale and user locales, which enable your Windows 2000 Server to display items such as time, currency, and numbers in the proper format for those locales. You can also change the way the keyboard is handled. By default, Windows 2000 Server derives the locale from the actual software package. Therefore, my Windows 2000 Server package assumed English for the United States. Click the Next button to continue.

3. Now you are prompted for your name and organization. This is the usual personalization routine that is included in most Microsoft software. Fill in your name and organization and press Next to continue.

4. Now you should see the Licensing Mode dialog box. As with previous versions of Windows NT Server, you need to specify whether you will run the server in Per Server mode or in Per Seat mode. For this exercise, select Per Server and give yourself an adequate number of concurrent users. As with Windows NT Server 4.0, when you select Per Seat, you cannot switch back to Per Server mode. You can however switch from Per Server to Per Seat at any time. Click Next to continue.

Licensing users

Windows 2000 Server clients must be licensed using Client Access Licenses (CALs). These CALs are required when users are connecting to the server for file or print services. Users that are attaching to a Windows 2000 Server only for access to an application, such as Microsoft SQL Server, would be required to have a Windows 2000 Server CAL.

Check with your application vendor to see whether you are required to also purchase a Windows 2000 Server CAL, as in some cases it might be required.

Per Server versus Per Seat

Per Server mode refers to the number of concurrent connections that will be allowed to that specific computer. For instance, if you have 500 computers in your organization, but you expect that only 300 users will be on the server at the same time, you can license your server for 300 users. This does not prevent you from installing the Microsoft networking client onto all 500 computers.

Per Seat mode is used when you want to assign a CAL to each computer in your organization. The reason you would do this is because when Per Seat licensing is used, the CAL allows for connection to as many Windows 2000 Servers you have in your organizations. Therefore, using the 500-computer example again, if you were to license 500 CALs, all 500 computers could access every Windows 2000 Server you have.

If Per Server mode is chosen, you have to specify the number of CALs you have purchased. This licensing mode may be changed from Per Server to Per Seat once during the lifetime of the server. Microsoft licensing prohibits taking a server that has been installed using Per Seat licensing and then changing it to Per Server mode after the initial installation.

5. Now it's time to name your Windows 2000 Server. This name must be unique to your network. Enter the name you want and click Next.

A Windows 2000 computer by any other name

The computer name you select for your new Windows 2000 Server will be used as a NetBIOS name (should you decide to run your server using the now-legacy Microsoft NetBIOS naming conventions) and it will also be used as part of the qualified name for the computer as defined in the Active Directory Global Catalog. So, for example, if you give the server a name of `w2k`, your domain is named `windows2000`, and the public domain name for your network is `manchesterequipment.com`, the computer's entry in the Active Directory will be `w2k.windows2000.manchesterequipment.com`. Computers that are not Active Directory–enabled will see this server as `w2k` through Microsoft networking. By the way, choosing clever names such as `w2k` will inevitably get you into trouble in a larger network. The name that you give the computer should be descriptive because a list of computers can become very cluttered, when that list is shown to a user browsing the network, or to administrators managing a computer.

6. The next step prompts you for the administrator's password. By default, Windows 2000 Server creates two user accounts. One is the GUEST account, which is used for anonymous access to the server, and the other is the ADMINISTRATOR account, which holds administrative permissions. In this dialog box, you need to enter the password you'll use for the default ADMINISTRATOR account. Enter the password twice to confirm that the password you have entered is correct. Note that passwords are case-sensitive, so be aware of what you are entering. As you type the password it will not be displayed. Click Next to proceed.

Please select a password

You can proceed past this dialog box without specifying an ADMINISTRATOR password; however, this would leave your server, and possibly your domain, open to all intruders; it is generally understood that the default user ID for Microsoft networks is ADMINISTRATOR. Because of this I highly recommend that you enter a password here.

7. The next dialog box allows you to select and deselect different components for your Windows 2000 Server. These optional components are

- *Certificate Services*. Allows you to create a Certification Authority on your server for issuing digital certificates.

- *Internet Information Services (IIS).* Installs the Microsoft Web Server component. Optional subcomponents for IIS include FrontPage 2000 Server Extensions, FTP services, NNTP services, SMTP services, and Visual InterDev RAD Remote Deployment Support.

- *Management and Monitoring Services.* These four tools include the Connection Management components, the Directory Service Migration Tool (from NDS to Active Directory), the Network Monitor program, and SNMP support.

- *Message Queuing Services.* Allows applications to communicate over potentially unreliable networks using "Push" style delivery.

- *Microsoft Indexing Service.* This can index all the files on your server in order to perform fast full-text searches.

- *Microsoft Script Debugger.* Includes both server-side and client-side debugging tools for VBScript and JScript.

- *Networking Services.* The many networking services offered by Windows 2000 Server include the following:

  - *The COM Internet Services Proxy.* Allows DCOM to travel over HTTP connections.

  - *DNS (Domain Name System).* Provides name-to-address resolution for IP hosts and is essential if you are going to use Active Directory and do not have another Microsoft DNS server on your network.

  - *DHCP (Dynamic Host Configuration Protocol).* Allows for the dynamic distribution of IP addresses across a network, improving address management.

  - *The Internet Authentication Service.* Allows authentication through the RADIUS protocol.

  - *The QoS Admission Control Service.* Allows you to specify the quality of the network connection for each subnet.

  - *Microsoft Simple TCP/IP Services.* Character Generator, Daytime Discard, Echo, and Quote of the Day.

  - *The Site Server LDAP Services.* Scans TCP/IP stacks and updates directories with current user information.

  - *The Windows Internet Name Service (WINS).* Allows TCP/IP clients to resolve NetBIOS names to IP addresses.

- *Other Network File and Print Services.* These include
  - *File and Print Services for Macintosh.* Allows Macintosh clients to use resources on your Microsoft network.
  - *Print Services for UNIX.* Offers UNIX clients access to printers on the Microsoft network.
- *Remote Installation Services.* Allows for remote installation of Windows 2000 Professional onto network clients that have remote boot capability.
- *Remote Storage.* A Hierarchical Storage Management (HSM) service that can move infrequently used files off to magnetic media.
- *Terminal Services.* A whole other topic in itself, Microsoft Terminal Services allows network clients to run Windows-based on the server itself. You also have the option to install the Terminal Services License Service which enables license pooling for multiple Windows 2000 Servers running the Terminal Services.

Which services should you install?

Each service carries certain overhead on the server. It is unwise to unnecessarily install services onto the server that will not be used. In some cases, these services should each run on its own dedicated server. For the primary server in a new domain a good selection of these options would be to include DNS, DHCP, and WINS from the Networking Services. IIS should be deselected if you do not want to use your server as a Web server. SNMP should be enabled if you plan on monitoring this server from a systems-monitoring tool, such as HP Open View. The Network Monitor is a good tool to use on your server for troubleshooting purposes.

The other services and tools should be individually evaluated. Remember that you can always add these options at any time after you have successfully completed your Windows 2000 Server install.

---

8. After selecting the components you want to install, you are prompted for Modem Dialing Information. This happens only in the event Windows 2000 Server's hardware detection routing detects a modem during installation. In the event that you are going to be using this server to connect to other servers or other networks, the installation program prompts you for your country and area code, a number to dial to get an outside line, and whether your phone system uses tone or pulse dialing. Press Next to continue.

9. Finally, you need to specify the date and time, the time zone for where the server will reside, and whether Windows 2000 Server should automatically adjust the clock for daylight savings time changes. Click Next to continue.

The installation program copies the files necessary for the networking options you have chosen. During this operation, a status line displays exactly what services are being installed or configured or are having files copied.

10. When the components have been copied, installed, and configured, the final installation tasks take place. First, all the shortcuts on the Start menu are created. Next, the registry is modified to include the files that need to be registered, among other settings. When all the registry changes have been made, the temporary installation folders are removed.

11. This ends the Windows 2000 Server Setup Wizard. You are prompted to click the Finish button to restart your server.

When your server restarts you will need to log on to the server as the administrator. Based on which additional components you chose to install, you might be faced with additional configuration options. One such option is for the NetWare gateway, which will require you to choose a preferred server or a default tree and context in order to log on to NDS.

Windows 2000 Configure Your Server

For this first actual boot into Windows 2000 Server, the Microsoft Windows 2000 Configure Your Server application will start. Based on your choices during installation, you can have additional configuration. Assuming you have selected additional components that need to be configured, you need to do the following:

1. As seen in Figure 3.1, "Windows has detected that you have selected components that require additional setup and configuration before they are fully functional." Click the "Finish setup" hyperlink to continue with this configuration.

2. Figure 3.2 shows the Add/Remove Programs dialog box for Windows 2000. The components that still require configuration will be displayed along with a Configure button. Click the Configure button to start the configuration for the respective component.

3. The Windows Component Wizard will then start configuring the appropriate components, as shown in Figure 3.3. When these components have been configured you will be able to proceed to configuring your server.

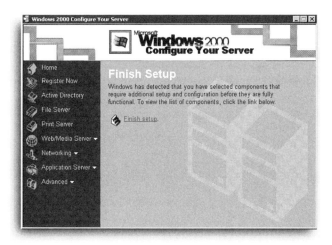

FIGURE 3.1
The Finish Setup screen allows you to configure the components you selected during installation.

FIGURE 3.2
The Add/Remove Programs dialog box is where you can configure the components. Just click the Configure button.

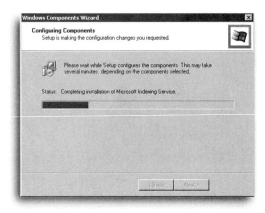

FIGURE 3.3
Configuring the Microsoft Indexing Service.

4. Finally, it is time to configure your server so that its role in your domain is defined. Figure 3.4 shows the configuration screen that appears after you have successfully configured the optional components for your server; or if you had not chosen any components that required additional configuration, this screen would appear after your initial reboot. Select This Is the Only Server in My Network and click Next.

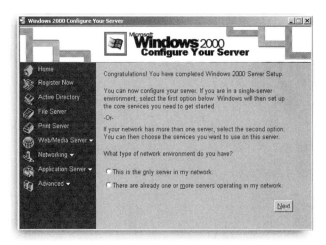

FIGURE 3.4
Selecting your server's role in the network.

Which option should I choose?

There are two options. Choose the first option if this is your first server on the network. This choice presumes that this server will be set up as a domain controller; therefore, it will install and configure the Active Directory. It will also set up and configure DNS and DHCP services.

Choose the second option if you will be integrating this server into an existing Windows 2000 network. This option allows you to choose whether this server participates in the domain as a domain controller. This option also presumes that DNS and DHCP services are already installed on your network; you will, however, be given the chance to add these components to your server if they are part of your requirements.

For this exercise, you will want to select This Is the Only Server in My Network because it will expose you to all the possible steps involved in this installation.

Creating the first server on your network

5. After you select the option to make this server the first server on your network, the dialog box shown in Figure 3.5 is presented. This confirms your choice to allow the setup program to automatically install and configure Active Directory, DNS, and DHCP. As the confirmation screen reads, you should not continue with this step if there are already servers on your network running DNS, DHCP, or Active Directory.

FIGURE 3.5
Setting up Active Directory, DNS, and DHCP.

6. After you accept the confirmation screen by clicking the Next button, the Active Directory setup screen is displayed (see Figure 3.6). The entries that are required here are the Windows 2000 domain name and the public domain name. If you are already registered with Network Solutions, that is the public domain name that you should use. In my example, I have put in my public domain name at work, which is manchesterequipment.com. The Windows 2000 domain name will be used as a NetBIOS name for any clients on the network that does not know how to talk to the Active Directory. This Windows 2000 domain name will be used to create a fully qualified domain name for the Active Directory. In this case, I have named the Windows 2000 domain as windows2000. Therefore, the fully qualified domain name for this domain is windows2000. manchesterequipment.com. The NetBIOS name that will be used for this domain is windows2000.

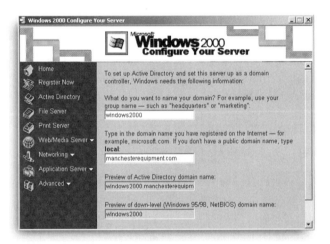

FIGURE 3.6
The Active Directory setup screen.

7. If you do not have a registered public domain name, enter the word local instead of a .com entry. This helps identify the DNS entries that are created as being strictly for a local network. Had I used local, the Active Directory domain name would have been windows2000.local. When you have confirmed these entries and click the Next button, the creation of the Active Directory takes place. Another confirmation screen is displayed, as shown in Figure 3.7. Click the Next button to continue the setup process.

Picking your domain name

Ideally, the name that you use for the domain reflects the purpose of the domain. For instance, if you had been installing this server to create a domain for the Human Resources department, you might want to call the domain `humanresources`, which would have made the fully qualified domain name `humanresources.manchesterequipment.com`.

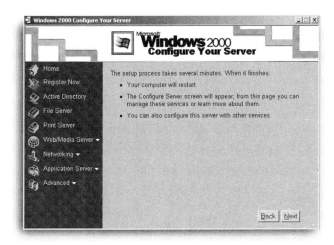

FIGURE 3.7
This status screen lets you know what is happening during the setup process.

8. The Active Directory creation runs as a background task. This is the Active Directory Installation Wizard running in unattended mode. Several dialog box and confirmation screens will be shown, such as the ones shown in Figure 3.8. None of these dialog boxes requires any input from you. The creation of thousands of objects within the Active Directory, such as the schema, is taking place at this point. The appropriate entries into the DNS service is also being created, which initializes the DNS service to be used by Active Directory and the rest of your Windows 2000 network. When the Active Directory has been created, you need to configure TCP/IP.

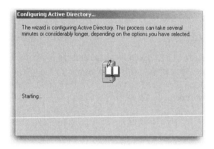

FIGURE 3.8
Creating the Active Directory generates status and confirmation screens, so you know the progress of the installation.

9. As the wizard in Figure 3.9 instructs, TCP/IP can be configured by using your mouse to right-click the *My Network Places* desktop icon and choosing *Properties* from the context menu. The resulting display (Figure 3.10) shows icons for the existing Local Area Connection and the icon that is used to create a new network connection. Double-click the Local Area Network icon to continue.

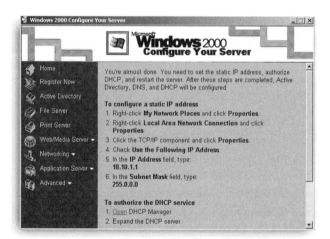

FIGURE 3.9
This portion of the setup process gives you detailed instructions on setting up your TCP/IP protocol stack.

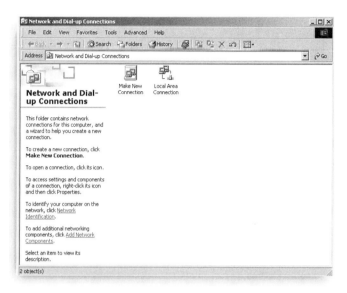

FIGURE 3.10
Network and Dial-Up Connections is where you configure new and existing network connections.

10. The properties for the network connection include the network adapters that were found during the installation routine, the file and print services for Microsoft networking, the Network Monitor driver if you had chosen to install the Network Monitor component, and the TCP/IP protocol. It is here (Figure 3.11) that you will highlight the protocol and click the Properties button to configure TCP/IP.

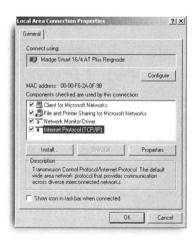

FIGURE 3.11
Clicking the Properties button allows you to configure the TCP/IP protocol.

11. The Internet Protocol (TCP/IP) Properties dialog box, shown in Figure 3.12, lets you specify whether to use DHCP services that might already be available on your network or specify a static IP address. Because this is a server, even if you already have DHCP services available, I highly recommend that you use a static IP address for your server. It makes it easier for you to manage your server and find it on the network. For this example, enter an IP address, subnet mask, and DNS server address, and click OK. Close the dialog box to save the information. Then you can close or minimize the My Network Places window.

SEE ALSO

➤ *For more information on configuring TCP/IP, see page xx [Essential TCP/IP Concepts], ch 9]*

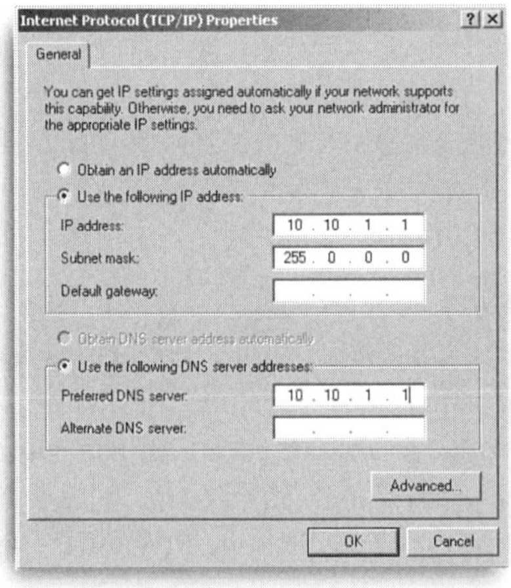

FIGURE 3.12
The TCP/IP Properties dialog box.

Using the Default Gateway

You have the option to enter a Default Gateway for your server. This can be the IP address of a router or other type of gateway that will take you out of the local subnet. If you do not need the gateway, you do not need to make an entry for the Default Gateway. If you are specifying a static IP address and have not manually entered a DNS server address, you are notified that the local server, which is running the DNS service, will be placed automatically as the Preferred DNS server.

12. Return to the Windows 2000 Configure Your Server dialog box. (Refer to Figure 3.9.) It's time (if applicable for your environment) to start the DHCP service. If you already have DHCP services enabled on your network, you do not need to proceed with this step, which is called DHCP Service Authorization. To proceed with authorization, click the hyperlink to open the DHCP Manager.

13. When the DHCP Manager starts, right-click the name of the server (in this case it is w2k.windows2000.manchesterequipment.com) and select All Tasks from the context menu. Next, choose Authorize from the resulting menu, as shown in Figure 3.13. When the DHCP service has been authorized, after a reboot, the server will be prepared to hand out IP addresses to network clients. The authorization process still has not configured a range of addresses to give out to clients.

SEE ALSO

➤ *For more information on how to set up a scope of address, see page 389.*

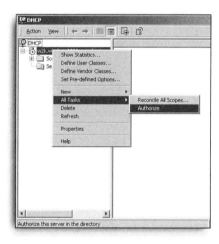

FIGURE 3.13
Authorizing the DHCP service to start.

14. The next time you reboot your server, the Windows 2000 Configure Your Server dialog box will be displayed again, as shown in Figure 3.14. This time you can choose to not display this dialog box whenever logon occurs at the server console, by removing the checkmark from the box that is labeled Show This Screen at Startup.

Congratulations! You have just installed and configured Windows 2000 Server.

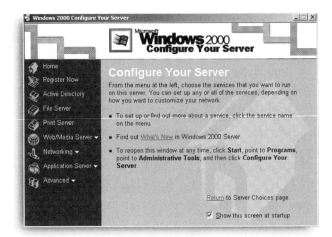

FIGURE 3.14
The Configure Your Server dialog box can be disabled from automatically starting at this point.

This section discussed the base install for Windows 2000 Server. Of course, selecting different options will vary the installation procedure. Now it's time to look at how to upgrade from an existing server.

Preparing for the Upgrade

When the upgrade process begins, there is no turning back. Therefore, it is a good idea to do at least two full backups of your existing system before attempting to upgrade the operating system.

Not only will you upgrade the base operating system, but also you will upgrade the administrative tools that you have gotten used to. When the Windows 2000 Server boots for the first time, you might be faced with a learning curve because of the new tools. Although I hope that this book helps you through that phase, it might be a good idea to practice the upgrade on a test machine first.

Performing a full backup

Remember that a full backup includes backing up any open files, which will require the use of an open-files agent for your tape backup software.

How much space?

The upgrade from Windows NT Server 4.0 to Windows 2000 Server requires around 700MB of free drive space on the system drive.

If you want to preserve user accounts, shares, print queues, and other configuration settings, you should choose to upgrade the existing installation. You also have the option to perform a fresh install to a separate directory, which would allow you to dual-boot your server between Windows NT and Windows 2000; however, that type of installation will not migrate any settings.

This chapter steps you through the upgrade of an existing Windows NT 4.0 Server Primary Domain Controller (PDC). The computer name is NT4, and the domain is W2K.

For this installation, the C drive was formatted as FAT. As you will see, the upgrade suggests converting the C drive to NTFS. The Users defined to the W2K domain are migrated to the new Active Directory format (discussed later in this chapter), as are User Groups.

SEE ALSO

➤ *For an explanation of the FAT and NTFS file systems, see Chapter 7, "Managing Resources."*

Updating Installed Drivers and Server Hardware

The Windows 2000 Server upgrade process should update your installed drivers; however, it might be a good idea to jump over to the hardware manufacturer's Web site for any hardware installed in your server and check to see whether drivers are available for Windows 2000 that are newer than the drivers that might have been included on the Windows 2000 Server CD-ROM.

In the case of the server hardware itself, you should check with the server manufacturer to determine whether there are updated ROM BIOS patches that you need to successfully upgrade to Windows 2000 Server.

SEE ALSO

➤ *For more considerations before you install Windows 2000 Server, see Chapter 2, "Planning Your Windows 2000 Server Network."*

Performing the Upgrade

When you're ready to begin the upgrade, follow these steps:

Starting the upgrade

1. Place the Windows 2000 Server CD into the CD-ROM drive. If Autostart is turned on, the upgrade program should start by itself. Otherwise, run SETUP from the root directory of the CD-ROM.

2. The upgrade program lets you know that you are running an older version of Windows and asks whether you would like to install a newer version, Windows 2000. Confirm that you want to install Windows 2000 by clicking the Yes button.

3. The Welcome to the Windows 2000 Setup Wizard dialog box, shown in Figure 3.15, asks whether you want to upgrade the current operating system to Windows 2000 or whether you want to install a fresh copy of Windows 2000 into another directory. Choose to upgrade the existing operating system if you want to retain all your Windows NT Server 4.0 settings. If you choose to install a fresh copy of Windows 2000 Server, Windows 2000 Server is installed into its own directory and does not carry over the settings from the existing Windows NT Server 4.0 installation.

FIGURE 3.15
Upgrade or install a fresh copy?

4. Accept the Microsoft License Agreement (after you have read it, of course!)

5. Click the Next button

Installing from FAT partitions

If your installation of Windows NT Server 4.0 was on a FAT partition, the upgrade program asks if you want to upgrade this partition to NTFS (Figure 3.16). In order to use Active Directory, you must have an NTFS partition to host the Active Directory. In general, if you have a dedicated Windows 2000 Server computer, you should take advantage of the benefits that NTFS has to offer. So, choose Yes, Upgrade My Drive and then click the Next button.

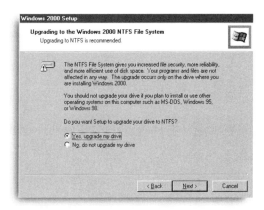

FIGURE 3.16
If the previous operating system was installed on FAT, you are asked to upgrade to NTFS.

6. When the files are copied, your server restarts and the setup program resumes in character mode.

Character Mode of the Upgrade

7. Just as the character mode setup begins, you will be prompted to press the F6 key if you have a third-party disk driver to be loaded in order for you to install Windows 2000 Server.

8. Unless you have chosen to install a third-party driver that requires you to insert a disk containing the driver, the setup program continues to run without requiring any manual intervention on your part.

9. When it's finished copying files to the Windows NT directory, it restarts your computer automatically in fifteen seconds. You can press Enter to reboot immediately. When the system starts again, it will be to the graphical portion of the upgrade.

Introducing the Windows 2000 Server Boot Menu

The next time the server boots, the boot menu will have changed to Windows 2000 Server. Notice that there is no longer a VGA Mode menu item for you to choose. Now the F8 key allow you to choose different modes to boot into if necessary. This includes the ability to boot without loading any drivers other than ones that are absolutely required in order to boot the operating system. This is handy when it comes to troubleshooting a failed Windows 2000 Server installation.

The Windows 2000 Advanced Options Menu gives you the options shown in Table 3.1.

Table 3.1 Windows 2000 Advanced Options Menu Choices

Menu Item	Description
Safe Mode	Boots the server without loading any drivers that are unnecessary to start the Windows 2000 Server graphical user interface. Especially useful for trouble-shooting.
Safe Mode with Networking	Similar to the previous option, but will also attempt to load network adapter drivers and start networking services.
Safe Mode with Command Prompt	Enables you to boot to a command prompt, where commands can be run to recover your server.
Enable Boot Logging	Boot logging creates a text file that describes drivers that are attempting to load and services that are attempting to start. The inability to load a driver or start a service will either be written to the file, or the last attempt shown in the file will indicate which service or driver caused the system to halt.
Enable VGA Mode	Boots the server normally; however, a generic VGA video driver will load instead. Use this if you suspect your video driver is causing you problems.
Last Known Good Configuration Menu	Automatically restores the registry settings that were used during the last time Windows 2000 Server was booted successfully.
Directory Service Restore Mode	Allows you to restore the Directory Service from a backup copy. Available only for Domain Controllers,
Debugging Mode	Displays verbose status information when booting.
Boot Normally	Press the Esc key to continue booting normally.

> **Autodotootion of hardware in Windows 2000 Server**
>
> Windows 2000 Server can identify thousands of hardware devices. This depends on the cooperation of hardware manufacturers to provide Microsoft with ways of identifying their hardware. In some cases it is possible that a manufacturer did not provide this information to Microsoft or possibly submitted their data to Microsoft too late for the release of Windows 2000 Server.
>
> *Legacy hardware,* such as ISA cards or peripherals that are pre–plug-and-play, might not be identified. And even if they are identified, Windows 2000 Server might be unable to determine the settings, such as IRQ and DMA.
>
> You should know the settings for legacy hardware and know the availability of drivers before you install Windows 2000 Server.

Preparing to run for the first time

1. The setup program detects and installs devices attached to your server. This step uses the new plug-and-play functions that Windows 2000 Server has.

2. The networking components are upgraded.

3. A status line keeps you informed of which services the upgrade program is copying. You should see that services beyond what you had installed on Windows NT Server 4.0 will be installed. This is mainly because of the new reliance that Windows 2000 Server has on TCP/IP.

4. Also installed are the core components for the new Terminal Services, the COM+ framework, and the Microsoft Fax service.

5. The Start menu is created.

6. The new components are registered.

7. The temporary directory that was created on your hard drive for the upgrade process is removed.

8. When this is completed the computer restarts automatically in fifteen seconds.

Running the Active Directory Installation Wizard

When your computer restarts, Windows 2000 Server is fully functional. The first task is setting up the Active Directory. The Active Directory Wizard prompts you through the creation of your new environment. The next step for the wizard is to find out if you want to create a new tree (see Chapter 2, "Planning Your Windows 2000 Server Network"), or join an existing tree as a child domain, as shown in Figure 3.17.

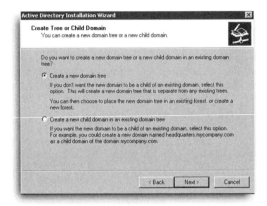

FIGURE 3.17
Will you create a new tree or add a child domain to an existing tree?

To run the Active Directory Installation Wizard

1. In the Create Tree or Child Domain window, create a new tree for your domain, which will be the root domain for this tree.

2. Next, in the Create or Join Forest window, you need to place the tree into a new forest, or add the tree to an existing forest. In this instance, as shown in Figure 3.18, this new tree is also in its own forest.

Trees in the same forest

As Chapter 2 explains, trees in the same forest share a common schema and allow for trust relationships to be set up.

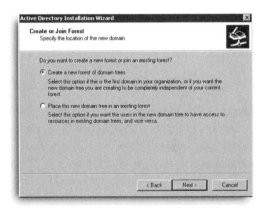

FIGURE 3.18
You must choose to create a new forest or join an existing forest.

DNS

DNS (Domain Name Service) is an integral part of Active Directory. Therefore when the Active Directory Wizard sees that DNS has not been configured on a server yet, DNS needs to know if you want to set it up on a server, or if you will use DNS services elsewhere on your network (Figure 3.19). When this is the only server on the network, that server requires DNS.

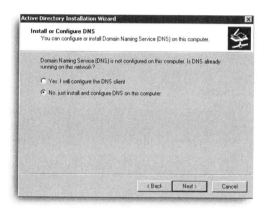

FIGURE 3.19
If DNS is already running on your network, you do not need to install it on your server.

3. If DNS had already been running on the network, you would need to manually configure Active Directory to work with DNS server.

4. You must create a new domain name, unless you are registered with the InterNIC and already have a name. Windows 2000 Server uses DNS-type naming; therefore, the name must not include any special characters except a dash.

Considerations for storing the Active Directory

The Active Directory must reside on an NTFS partition. For the best performance it should have its database on logs stored on different physical hard drives.

5. The Database and Log Locations dialog box prompts you for the location for the Active Directory database and for the Active Directory log files.

6. The Shared System Volume dialog box (Figure 3.20) prompts you for the location for the SYS volume.

The SYS volume

The SYS volume is a public folder that will be replicated automatically to other domain controllers in the e-manchester.com domain. This too needs to reside on an NTFS partition.

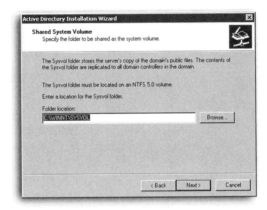

FIGURE 3.20
A location for the system volume must be specified.

Backward compatibility

If you have a network with both Windows NT 4.0 servers and Windows 2000 Server, you need to be aware of a caveat of backward compatibility.

Although backward compatibility is sometimes a useful method of migration, you must keep in mind that the new security features of Windows 2000 Server will not carry over to any older versions of Windows NT.

Windows NT/Windows 2000 Remote Access Services

The Windows NT Server 4.0 Remote Access Services (RAS) allowed users to log on to a domain through a modem or other type of remote connection. RAS also allowed servers to attach to each other when the availability of high speed or leased lines were not available.

In Windows 2000 Server, RAS is replaced by Routing and Remote Access Services (RRAS). This upgrade to RAS includes many more functions. The new RAS is described in more detail in Chapter 17, "Configuring a Remote Access Server."

7. The Windows NT 4.0 RAS Servers dialog box, shown in Figure 3.21, asks whether any users in this domain will access the domain though Remote Access Services (RAS) in Windows NT 4.0. If this is the case, the permissions set on all user objects should be weakened. If no Windows 4.0 RAS servers are used, choose No, do not change the permissions.

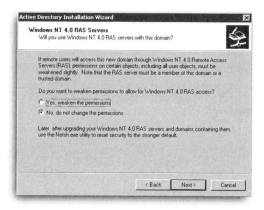

FIGURE 3.21
Active Directory needs to know whether Windows NT 4.0 Remote Access Services will remain on the network.

8. The Summary screen, shown in Figure 3.22, recaps the choices you made for setting up Active Directory in your new domain. Verify these choices, and use the Back button if you need to modify any of these. Otherwise, proceed by clicking the Next button.

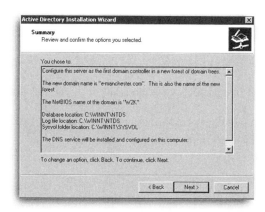

FIGURE 3.22
Active Directory Installation Wizard Summary screen.

SEE ALSO

➤ *For more information about the Active Directory, see page 26.*

➤ *For detailed information about the function of DNS, see page 410.*

Active Directory Creation

Migrating from your existing Windows NT 4.0 Directory Services to Windows 2000 Server's Active Directory can be a lengthy process.

Every object in your current Windows 4.0 Server domain must be read and converted to an Active Directory object. Luckily the Active Directory Installation Wizard makes it easy to define your new Windows 2000 Server environment.

Creating the Active Directory

1. First, the wizard stops the NETLOGON service. This prevents any users from logging on to the domain while this migration is taking place.

2. Next, the wizard creates the shared system volume (SYSVOL).

3. The wizard then copies the initial directory service database from the SYSTEM32 directory to the new location for the Active Directory database, as shown in Figure 3.23. In this case it is on the same drive.

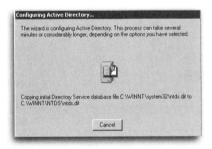

FIGURE 3.23
The initial database file is copied to the new Active Directory location.

4. The Active Directory service configuration is then finalized so that the Active Directory may be used by the domain controller.

Identifying partitions

Because each domain in the tree keeps its own information separate from the other domains in the tree, its own part of the Global Catalog is called a *partition*.

5. A partition is identified in Figure 3.24.

CN and DC

The DNS standards CN and DC are abbreviations for container and domain component, respectively. The number of objects for the domain shown in Figure 3.24 has been calculated as only 1585 (this test domain only had a handful of users and minimal resources).

FIGURE 3.24
The partition for the new domain is created.

6. After all the objects are created, the DNS root is created (Figure 3.25). In this example, the DNS root is e-manchester.com, so all the objects belonging to this domain will use suffix e-manchester.com.

FIGURE 3.25
Creation of the DNS root entry.

7. Security is then applied to the Active Directory files and registry entries and the DNS service is ready to start servicing the domain.

8. The Active Directory service has been created and is ready for use by Active Directory–enabled clients and servers.

9. The final step for the Active Directory Installation Wizard is to install the short-cuts in the Administrative Tools folder in the Programs option of the Start menu.

10. Now the server must restart so that this Active Directory–enabled computer can start its Active Directory services for the first time. Click the Restart Now button to allow the server to reboot.

Be sure to restart!

This restart of the server is a very crucial one. Hopefully you will not be notified of any services not being able to start. If you see the Configure Your Server application after you log on to the server console (Figure 3.26), you have successfully installed Active Directory into your new domain.

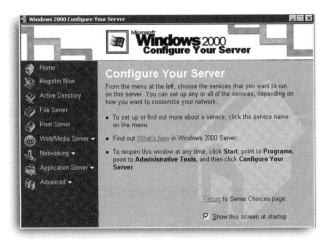

FIGURE 3.26
The Configure Your Server application signals a successful completion of setting up Active Directory.

Congratulations! You have just completed the upgrade of your server to Windows 2000 Server. Now that your server is running Windows 2000, move on to Chapter 4, "Configuring Your Server."

chapter

4

Configuring Your Server

Working with the `BOOT.INI` file •

Modifying and configuring security
on your Windows 2000 Server •

Adding optional components to your
Windows 2000 Server installation •

Specifying Operating System Startup with the Startup and Recovery Options

By default, a BOOT.INI file is created in the root of your C drive and is assigned the Read Only and Hidden attributes. This text file contains entries that define what will be shown on the boot menu and for how long the boot menu will be displayed before the default selection is made.

Under normal circumstances you will not need to manually edit the BOOT.INI file; however, a configuration change, such as adding a new disk drive, might require that you perform a manual alteration to BOOT.INI.

This section does not discuss disaster recovery using the BOOT.INI file but does discuss using the Startup and Recovery option to alter the contents of the BOOT.INI file.

By default, Windows Explorer does not show hidden files. In order to complete the task to edit the BOOT.INI file you must configure Explorer to show hidden files.

Configuring Windows Explorer to show hidden files

1. Open Windows Explorer.
2. From the Tools menu, select Folder Options.
3. On the View tab, under the item Hidden Files and Folders, select Show hidden files and folders.

Opening the *BOOT.INI* file

1. Open Windows Explorer.
2. Navigate to the root of the C: drive.
3. Select the BOOT.INI file.
4. Double-click the file to load the file into Notepad.

Displaying the Startup and Recovery options

1. From the context menu for the My Computer icon, select Properties.
2. Select the Advanced tab, shown in Figure 4.1.
3. Click the Startup and Recovery button.
4. Note the System Startup values shown in Figure 4.2.

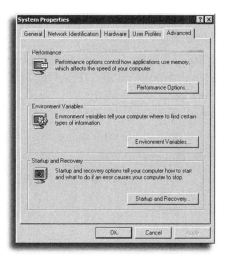

FIGURE 4.1
The Advanced tab for your server permits you to access the Startup and Recovery options dialog box.

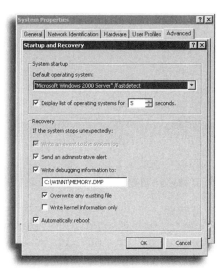

FIGURE 4.2
The two values that you can choose for Startup options will actually modify the BOOT.INI file.

5. The Default Operating System drop-down box lists the different entries that are in the BOOT.INI file. If only one operating system is installed on your Windows 2000 Server, that will be the only value in this drop-down list, as well as the only value shown in the Windows 2000 boot menu.

If another operating system is installed, such as a copy of Windows NT Server, this would also be listed in the drop-down box and on the boot menu.

6. By default, the boot menu will be displayed for 30 seconds before the default operating system is automatically booted. The Display List of Operating Systems for xx Seconds option determines whether there is a timeout before the default operating system is booted.

When you uncheck this option, the boot menu will be shown for an indefinite time until the Enter key is pressed.

If you want to have the default operating system automatically started after a timeout period, leave this option enabled.

Choosing the timeout period

In Figure 4.2 I have changed the timeout value to five seconds. By minimizing the timeout, you can reduce the time it takes for a restarted system to start the default operating system. If you do have multiple operating systems installed on your Windows 2000 Server, or if you want to allow yourself time to select F8 for displaying the Advanced Options Menu, be sure to leave yourself adequate time before the default operating system is started.

By assigning a value of 0 seconds, you can actually bypass the boot menu and immediately start the default operating system.

Configuring Security

One of the first things you can do is tweak the security on your server. There are some standard tasks that I like to do with a new server.

Renaming the Logon Name for the Default Administrator Account

Perhaps the most critical manual change that you make to your server is renaming the logon name for the Administrator account. Although you or your company might feel that making this change is a symptom of being too paranoid, keep in mind that *everybody* knows that the default administrative account on a Windows 2000 Server is Administrator. Now, for someone to break in with administrative rights all they need is the password. Doesn't it make sense that by changing the logon name for the Administrator account you can make it that much more difficult for an outsider to infiltrate your network?

Logon name versus user ID

In previous versions of Windows NT, the logon name was the same as the user ID. This is not the case in Windows 2000 Server. The logon name can be changed without changing the account name.

Changing the logon name for the Administrator account

1. Open the Active Directory Users and Computers Console from the Administrative Tools program group on the program menu. The Administrator user account is defined as the first User on the list (see Figure 4.3).

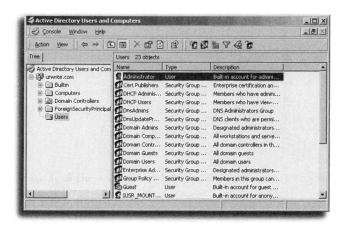

FIGURE 4.3
Active Directory Users and Computers.

2. Double-click the Administrator entry in order to show the properties for the Administrator account.

3. Switch to the Account tab, shown in Figure 4.4.

4. You can now type a new logon name that you want to give to the Administrator account.

5. Put the new name into both User Logon Name and Downlevel logon name, as shown in Figure 4.5. In this case, the DNS logon name will now be SecureName@urwrite.com. The Downlevel logon name is used by non–Active Directory-enabled clients (for example, being prompted for a user ID and password from a Windows NT 4.0 computer when trying to access a resource in the Windows 2000 Server domain).

6. Click the Apply or OK button to save the change. Now the user list will still show the Administrator account, but no one will be able to log on to the domain as Administrator.

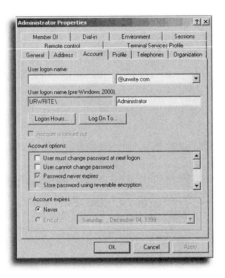

FIGURE 4.4
The Account dialog box offers the ability to modify default Windows 2000 Server account properties.

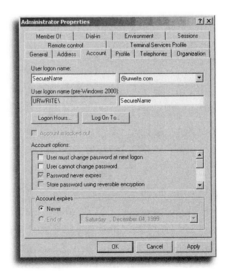

FIGURE 4.5
The two changed Account Name fields.

> **Additional oonfiguration**
>
> Additional configuration can include setting up a tape backup device, creating user groups, creating Organizational Units, defining printers, setting up policies, and many other customization and configuration choices that you have. Later chapters discuss each of these in detail.

SEE ALSO

➤ *To learn about the Microsoft administration framework extensively used by Windows 2000 Server, see page 10.*

➤ *For a better understanding of the Active Directory Users and Computers Console, see page 105.*

Configuring Your Server

The Configure Your Server application is an administrative tool that helps you get a quick start at configuring your servers' services and resources. It is automatically launched the first time Windows 2000 Server boots.

The Configure Your Server application has a shortcut that is located in the Administrative Tools program group on the Start/Programs menu.

Launching the Configure Your Server application

1. Click the Start button.

2. Select Programs.

3. Choose Administration Tools.

4. Select Configure Your Server.

5. On the home page you are given two options: You can find out what's new in Windows 2000 Server, or return to the Server Choices dialog box. You have already seen it if you did a clean install. You might not have seen it if you upgraded an existing server.

6. Choose the Register item from the left column to register your copy of Windows 2000 Server over the Internet.

7. The Active Directory choice (Figure 4.6) will let you know the status of your Windows 2000 Server and whether Active Directory is installed locally. Use the Manage hyperlink to start the Active Directory - Users and Computers console, or access documentation about Active Directory by clicking on Learn More.

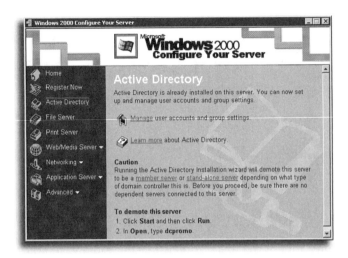

FIGURE 4.6
Configuring Active Directory.

8. The File Server option shown in Figure 4.7 allows you to run the Shared Folders Wizard. It's helpful in creating shared drive space on the server, opening the Computer Management console, or just reading about sharing folders.

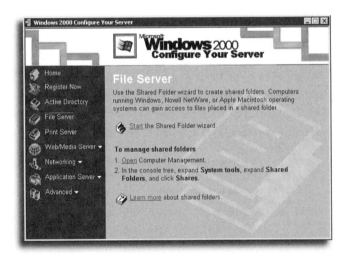

FIGURE 4.7
Options for accessing tools to configure shared folders.

9. The Print Server option, shown in Figure 4.8, gives you hyperlinks to run the Add Printer Wizard, manage existing printers through the Microsoft Management Console, or read about setting up and configuring print services.

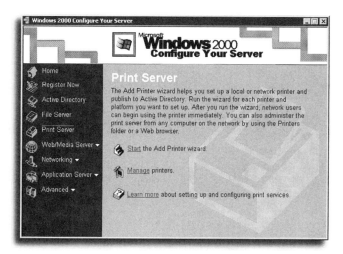

FIGURE 4.8
These hyperlinks give you direct access to tools that allow you to manage, create, or learn more about creating a Print Server.

10. The Web and Media Server options offer suboptions that allow you to install the Microsoft Internet Information Server (IIS), which gives you Web services and FTP services. The Web Server option, shown in Figure 4.9, allows you to install, manage, and learn more about IIS.

11. You can install IIS by running the Windows Components Wizard, through the Start hyperlink shown in Figure 4.10.

12. The Networking option permits you to view your existing network connections, or simply view the server's identity on the network, as shown in Figure 4.11.

13. The first of many suboptions for Networking Configuration is DHCP (see Figure 4.12). The Windows Component Wizard allows you to add DHCP services to your server (if you don't already have it installed) or permits you to configure DHCP services.

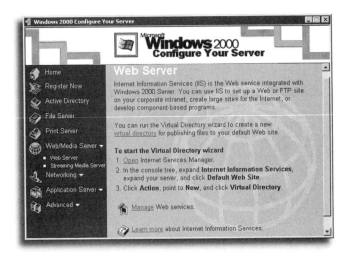

FIGURE 4.9
The Web Server configuration dialog box offers hyperlinks to manage and learn more about IIS.

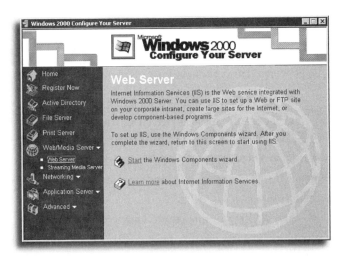

FIGURE 4.10
You can click the hyperlink to run the Windows Component Wizard in order to install IIS.

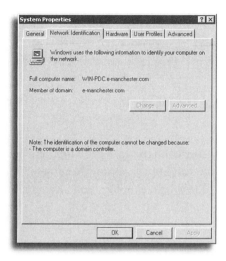

FIGURE 4.11
Select the Network Identification hyperlink to display the System Properties Network Identification tab.

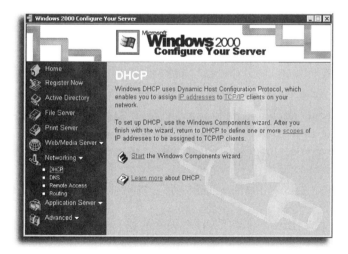

FIGURE 4.12
The DHCP dialog box offers a quick way to install DHCP services, configure DHCP, and learn about DHCP.

14. DNS is already installed on our server, but if you do not have DNS configured on your server, the DNS configuration dialog box allows you to run the Configure New Server Wizard from here to reconfigure your server in order to run DNS.

Remote Access and Routing

The Remote Access and Routing suboptions for Networking are tightly related. In previous versions of Windows NT, Remote Access Services (RAS) was available without routing capabilities. Only by installing a standalone upgrade could you add the routing functionality to RAS. Selecting either of these options brings you to choosing a hyperlink that will guide you to the Routing and Remote Access Configuration Wizard.

15. The Application Server configuration page first lets you read about different technologies that you can implement on Windows 2000 Server. You can read about the new IntelliMirror technology and also gain an understanding about group policy.

Introducing IntelliMirror

IntelliMirror technology allows Windows 2000 Server to interact with Windows 2000 Professional in a way that previous versions of Windows NT never could. Implementing IntelliMirror allows users to have their data, applications, and settings follow them to any computer.

IntelliMirror also allows network administrators to perform remote installations of Windows 2000.

SEE ALSO
➤ *For more information on IntelliMirror, see page 122. (IntelliMirror, Chapter 5.)*

16. The first suboption for Application Server is Component Services (Figure 4.13). This page gives you a brief overview of eight of the many Component Services available to you, along with a hyperlink to start the Component Services management console.

17. Next, you can start the Terminal Services Installation Wizard to set up Terminal.

The Database Server and E-mail Server options

The Database Server and E-mail Server options simply are a reminder that Windows 2000 Server makes a great platform for both hosting a database engine and for running a messaging service.

18. The Advanced Options main page gives you information on installing Windows 2000 Server administration tools that can run on client computers. It also has a hyperlink to a help file about setting up these tools.

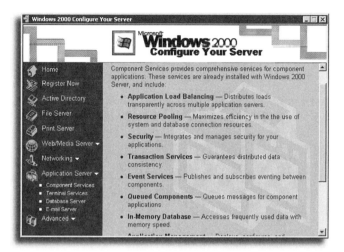

FIGURE 4.13
Manage and learn about Component Services from this dialog box.

19. The first suboption under Advanced is for the Microsoft Message Queuing Service. This component is installed via the Windows Component Wizard.

> **Resource Kit Support Tools**
>
> The Microsoft Windows 2000 Server Resource Kit Support Tools were included on the copy of Windows 2000 Server that I used during this writing. In previous versions of Windows NT Server, the resource kit tools were available as a separate purchase along with the Resource Kit book.

20. The Optional Components screen links you to the Windows Component Wizard, so that you can install or configure any of the remaining Windows components that were not explicitly mentioned in the previous dialog boxes in the Configure Your Server application.

SEE ALSO

➤ *To learn more about the Active Directory architecture, see page 26.*

➤ *For information on sharing folders and managing shared folders, see page 154.*

➤ *To create and manage Windows 2000 Server print queues, see page 168.*

➤ *To learn more about DHCP services, see page 391.*

➤ *For information on DNS, see page 410.*

➤ *Installing and managing Internet Information Server is detailed starting on page 464.*

➤ *Routing and Remote Access are discussed in detail starting on page 492.*

part

II

BUILDING YOUR WINDOWS 2000 NETWORK

5

Managing Users and Groups

Naming Conventions

Besides needing to know the first and last name of the user, you will need to give the user a logon name. This should be a name that follows some type of convention, such as first initial followed by last name, or first name followed by last initial. In some cases, where even user IDs are to be kept secure, you might want to follow a naming convention such as a name followed by a phone extension, or another number that might only be known internally. Also bear in mind that the account name can be used as an Internet mail address.

Using my name as an example, see Table 5.1 for possible naming conventions.

Table 5.1 Windows 2000 Server Account Naming Conventions

Convention	Result
First initial followed by last name	Rreinstein
First name followed last initial	Robertr
Initials followed by telephone extension	Rr8414

Because a user account is simply another object in the Active Directory, it is important to know where you want to place the user in the Active Directory hierarchy. This might require the creation of Organizational Units (OU) or User Groups in advance.

SEE ALSO

➤ *For a discussion of Organizational Units, see page 27.*

In my example, I have already created an OU for each of the departments in my organization.

Adding a User Account

Figure 5.1 shows where you can find the MMCs that will allow you to work with objects in the Active Directory.

User accounts can be added through the Active Directory Users and Computers Console. To start the Active Directory Users and Computers Console, do the following:

1. Click the Start button.

2. Select Programs.

3. Select Administrative Tools from the Programs folder.

4. Choose Active Directory Users and Computers from the Administrative Tools folder.

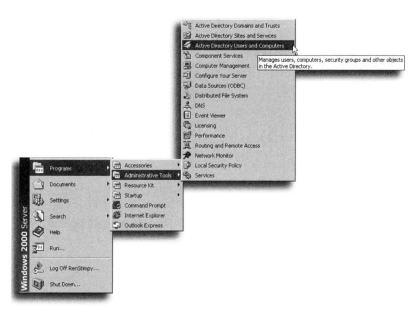

FIGURE 5.1
Start menu path to Active Directory Users and Computers Console.

Figure 5.2 shows the Active Directory Users and Computers Console, with my domain (e-manchester.com) displayed on the left column, with containers listed underneath.

The containers

The different OUs listed here are Admin, Consulting Services, and Sales. The Windows 2000 Server installation program had already predefined the Builtin, Computers, Domain Controllers, and Users containers.

To add a new user object, you need to do the following:

1. In the Active Directory Users and Computers console, select the container that you want to create the new user object in.

2. Click the Add User Object icon on the toolbar, as shown in Figure 5.3 to display the New Object - User dialog box.

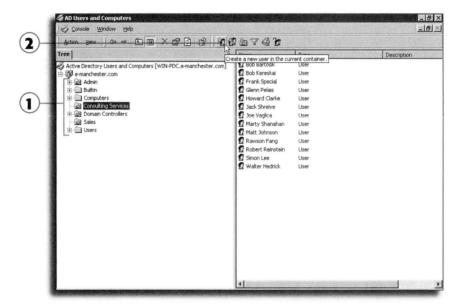

FIGURE 5.2
The Active Directory User and Computers Console.

1 Hierarchy of the Active Directory in this domain

2 Click to add a user object

FIGURE 5.3
Adding a new user object.

3. Enter a first name and a last name, which generates the full name.

4. Next, enter the user logon name according to the naming conventions that you have adopted for your domain.

Domains in the Active Directory

Note that the drop-down box that reads @e-manchester.com would list any domains that belong to this Active Directory. In this case, e-manchester.com is the only domain. Also note that the dialog box shows the name of the container in which this object is being created: e-manchester.com/ Consulting Services.

5. Click the Next button to continue adding the user object.

6. Enter the user's password in each field of the New Object dialog box shown in Figure 5.4.

FIGURE 5.4
Creating the password and other options for the new user object.

7. You might also choose to force the user to change the password during the first domain logon.

8. If you do not want to enable this user account yet, you can check the Account Is Disabled checkbox.

9. Click the Next button to display a summary of the information that you entered for the new user object (see Figure 5.5).

FIGURE 5.5
Adding a New User Object Verification dialog box.

10. Click the Finish button to create the new user object.

The resulting list of user objects in the current container will reflect the new user object that you just added, as seen in Figure 5.6.

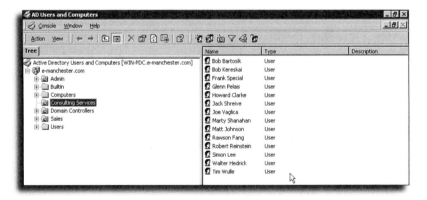

FIGURE 5.6
Updated list of user objects.

SEE ALSO

➤ *To learn more about the Microsoft Management Console, see page 10 (The Microsoft Management Console, Chapter 1).*

Modifying a User Object

After user objects have already been created, you might need to modify their properties. To modify an existing user object, do the following:

1. Open the Active Directory Users and Computers Console.

2. Select the container in which the user object you want to modify exists.

3. Locate the user object and bring up its context menu (as shown in Figure 5.7).

FIGURE 5.7
Context menu for user objects.

4. Select the option that you want to modify.

To disable a user account, do the following:

1. Locate the user object and bring up its context menu (as shown in Figure 5.7).

2. Select Disable Account.

3. A confirmation dialog box will tell you that the user object has been disabled. Click the OK button. Note that the user object will now reflect this change by showing an **X** in the user icon next to the user object's name, which means that the user object has been disabled.

A disabled user object can be enabled by following the same procedure; however, select Enable from the user object's context menu.

Why not delete a user object instead of disabling it?

When you delete a user object you not only rid the Active Directory Users and Computers Console of that object, but you also erase any other configuration information attached to that user object, which can include permissions. This is because each user object has a unique identifier attached to it, which was generated at the time of creation of the object. Had you deleted the user object and then re-created the user object, the unique identifier would be a totally new identifier.

By disabling the user object you preserve those settings. By simply enabling the user object you also restore all configuration settings that were associated with that user object, because its original unique identifier has been preserved as well.

You can also send an email easily to a user object that has had an email address defined within its properties. See Figure 5.8.

FIGURE 5.8
Choosing to send mail to a defined user object.

Configuring User Object Properties

A user object can be much more than just a name. The Windows 2000 Server Active Directory schema has dozens of predefined entries that allow you to add more information about user objects. These entries are easily accessible within the user object's Properties dialog box. To view the Properties for a user object, do the following:

1. Open the Active Directory Users and Computers Console.

2. Locate the user object for which you would like to work with its properties.

3. Display the user object's context menu.

4. Select Properties from the context menu.

5. The resulting dialog box will appear. A Properties dialog box is shown in Figure 5.9.

FIGURE 5.9
The User Object Properties dialog box.

6. In the General tab, you can add information about the user object.

7. The Address tab, shown in Figure 5.10, lets you store address information about the user object.

Searching for users

While this information is all optional, keep in mind that these fields are all defined within the Active Directory schema. This means that you can easily search for users based on the city they reside in, if you have properly defined all the cities for the user objects.

8. The Account tab (see Figure 5.11) provides you with additional information regarding the user object. You can modify the account's logon name, the NetBIOS logon name, and other restrictions.

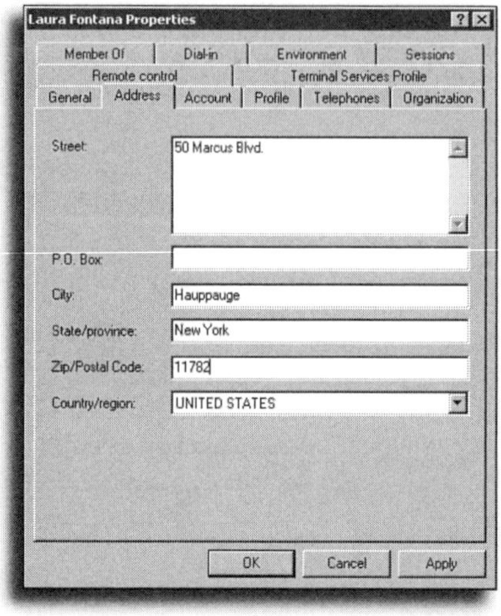

FIGURE 5.10
The Address tab.

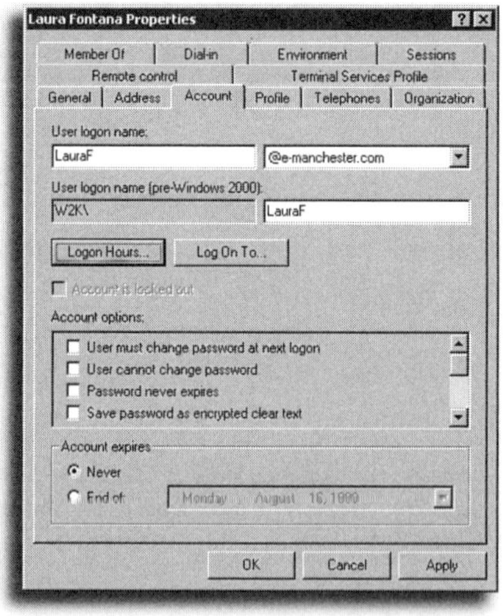

FIGURE 5.11
The User Object Account tab.

To change or create a NetBIOS-specific logon name, do the following:

1. Open the Active Directory Users and Computers Console.

2. Find the user object for which you want to set a NetBIOS logon name.

3. From the user object's context menu, select Properties.

4. Select the Account tab.

5. Enter a NetBIOS logon name in the entry field where it says User Logon Name (Pre–Windows 2000).

6. Click either the Apply or OK button.

To set specific times of the day and days of the week that a user can log on to the domain, do the following:

1. Open the Properties dialog box for the user object as previously described.

2. Select the Account tab.

3. Click the Logon Hours button to display the Logon Hours dialog box shown in Figure 5.12.

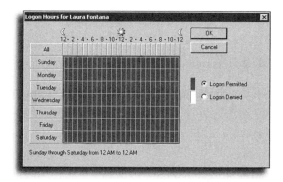

FIGURE 5.12
The time of day in which a user can log on to the domain can be limited by using the Logon Hours dialog box.

4. Drag the mouse to highlight the hours and days that you want to toggle between Logon Permitted and Logon Denied and set the permissions accordingly.

5. Repeat Step 4 until all hours and days have been permitted or denied as you want.

6. Click the OK button.

7. After you return to the Account tab, click either the Apply or OK button to save these settings.

To limit a user's domain logon access to specific computers, do the following:

1. Open the Properties dialog box for the user object as previously described.

2. Select the Account tab.

3. Click the Log On To button to display the Logon Workstations dialog box shown in Figure 5.13.

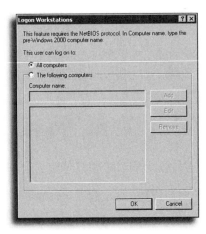

FIGURE 5.13
The Logon Workstations dialog box allows you to specify which computers a user can log on to the domain from.

4. Click the radio button to change the setting from All Computers to The Following Computers.

5. Enter a computer name in the Computer Name field.

6. Click the Add button.

7. Repeat steps 5 and 6 until all computers from which the user is allowed to log on have been added to the list.

8. Click the OK button.

9. After you return to the Account tab, click either the Apply or OK button to save these settings.

A few other items of some interest include

■ The Profile tab, shown in Figure 5.14, allows you to specify a path to a User Profile and a path to a logon script.

■ The Remote Control tab, shown in Figure 5.15, gives you control over whether or not that a user can have permission to take control of this account's Terminal Services session. Other options on this tab configure the remote control further.

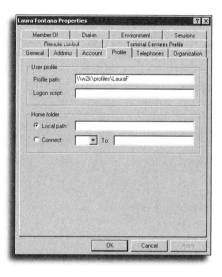

FIGURE 5.14
The User's Profile location is specified on this tab.

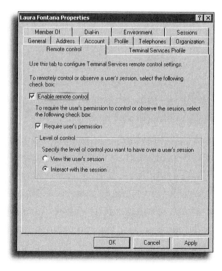

FIGURE 5.15
Remote Control options for Terminal Services sessions.

■ The Terminal Services Profile tab, shown in Figure 5.16, lets you specify whether this user object has permission to use Terminal Services, and if so, when the account logs on through Terminal Services. You can also decide whether a specific profile and logon script is used and whether a different home directory will be used. Leaving any of these options blank will automatically make the entries on the Profile tab valid during Terminal Services sessions.

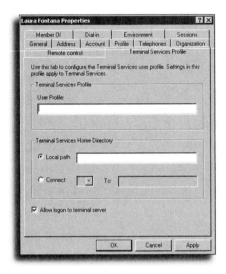

FIGURE 5.16
The Terminal Services Profile tab.

- The Member Of tab (see Figure 5.17) shows the Group objects that this User object is a member of. By default, all user objects are placed in the domain users group. From this tab you can add or remove the account from group objects.

- The Dial-In properties tab shown in Figure 5.18 defines whether the user object can use Windows 2000 Server's Remote Access Services (RAS) and Virtual Private Network (VPN) capabilities. If this user object has been permitted access by selecting Allow Access in the Remote Access Permission (Dial-In or VPN) area, you can specify whether the account will require a callback for security purposes, and how an IP address will be assigned to the remote user.

- The Environment tab (see Figure 5.19) dictates whether this user, when connecting through Terminal Services, will have a specific program start automatically at logon. If this is the case, exiting the program will release the session.

- The Sessions tab (see Figure 5.20) defines additional properties for the Terminal Services session for this user.

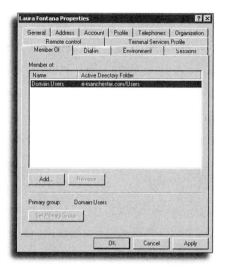

FIGURE 5.17
User objects can become members of Group objects through the Member Of tab.

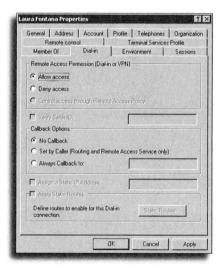

FIGURE 5.18
Properties for accessing the domain through Windows 2000 Server's Remote Access Services and VPN Services are defined in the Dial-in tab.

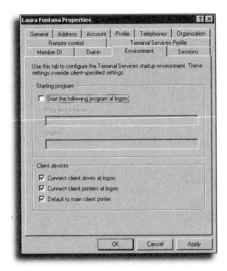

FIGURE 5.19
Setting the environment for a Terminal Services client.

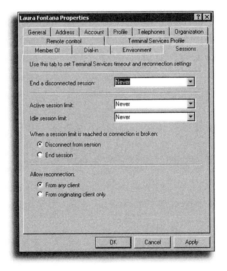

FIGURE 5.20
Terminal Services Sessions Parameters.

Logon scripts

Logon scripts are basically **.cmd** files (Windows 2000 batch files) that run whenever the account logs on to the domain. The Home Folder specifies a default folder that can exist on the local computer or on another computer and that the user can use to save documents. This setting is also used by the Terminal Services of Windows 2000 Server for storing registry settings and application settings that are specific to the user (if they are working on the server through Terminal Services).

None of this information is required, unless you are using Terminal Services for this account.

The Telephones and Organization tabs

Information for the Telephones and Organization tabs is not mandatory. Again, this information is part of the Active Directory schema, which can be used to perform searches.

Windows 2000 Server Terminal Services

This is an advanced component that is not discussed in this book. However if you are using this feature, these properties tabs are essential for the configuration of Terminal Services clients.

The Environment tab

If the Start the Following Program checkbox is left unchecked, the user will receive a full Windows 2000 desktop. The client devices checkboxes determine whether this user, connecting through Terminal Services, will have local hard drives or local printers available as part of the Terminal Services session.

Moving a User Object to Another Container

A user object can be moved to another container by using the context menu (which is displayed by clicking the right mouse button on the user object, as shown in Figure 5.21).

FIGURE 5.21
Moving a user object.

To move a user object to another container, do the following:

1. Open the Active Directory Users and Computers Console.

2. Locate the user object that you want to move between containers.

3. Display the context menu for the user object you want to move.

4. Select Move from the context menu to display a list of the containers available to move the user object to.

5. Highlight the container you want to move the user object to, shown in Figure 5.22, and then click the OK button. The user object will then appear in the target container.

FIGURE 5.22
The list of target containers.

Filtering the Objects Shown in the AD User and Computers Console

Depending on the size of your organization and the design of your Active Directory, an Active Directory Users and Computers Console can get cluttered and difficult to navigate. That is why the ability to display only relevant information has been implemented in the form of filters. To limit the data that is displayed in the Active Directory Users and Computers Console, do the following:

1. In the Active Directory Users and Computers Console, click the Set Filtering Options icon (see Figure 5.23).

FIGURE 5.23
The Set Filtering Options icon is represented by a funnel.

①   Set Filtering Options

2. Select the object that you want to display within the console by checking off the types you want to see. For example, if you select only Users in the Filter Options dialog box, shown in Figure 5.24, the Active Directory Users and Computers Console will show user objects exclusively. This filter also applies to searches that are performed while the filter is active.

To create a custom filter, do the following:

1. In the Active Directory Users and Computers Console, click the Set Filtering Options icon, which is represented by a funnel. The funnel icon is used to set filtering options for the Active Directory User and Computers Console.

2. Click the radio button labeled Create Custom Filter.

3. Click the Customize button to display the Find Customer Search dialog box.

4. Click the Field button to select a type of object you want to filter on.

FIGURE 5.24
Setting the filtering options.

5. Further select a property for that object that you want to query.

6. Now you need to select an operator, such as Starts With, Ends With, Is (exactly), Is Not, Present, or Not Present. In the example shown in Figure 5.25, I am querying for computer objects that do not have an operating system noted in the Active Directory.

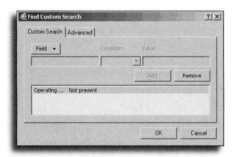

FIGURE 5.25
Building search criteria for a custom filter.

7. If a value is required for this type of query, enter it.

8. Click the Add button.

9. Repeat steps 4 through 8 until you have finished building your query.

10. Click the OK button to save the search criteria. If you want to limit the number of objects that are displayed within a folder, you can enter that in the Maximum number of objects displayed in a folder field.

11. Click the OK button and the filter will be activated.

Finding Objects in the Active Directory

After your user list grows along with the number of containers (OUs, domains, and so on) it might become a tough task to locate particular objects. This does not have to be a difficult task, as long as you have taken advantage of the Active Directory and its schema. To find objects in your Active Directory, do the following:

1. Click the Find Objects icon shown in Figure 5.26.

FIGURE 5.26
Click here to start Find Objects.

2. From the Find drop-down box, select the appropriate type of object.

3. Select the domain you want to search in from the In drop-down box.

4. Enter the search criteria in the appropriate fields.

5. Click the Find Now button.

6. The results are displayed at the bottom of the dialog box.

7. The example shown in Figure 5.27 creates a subset of the Active Directory objects by searching with the filtering options set to user objects only. Entering *bob* as a search argument returns the list shown in Figure 5.28, which includes the two user objects that have the name *bob*.

These are just the basics when it comes to working with user objects. Because the Active Directory has an extensible schema, it is possible to include almost any type of information about your users, and have the ability to search them out.

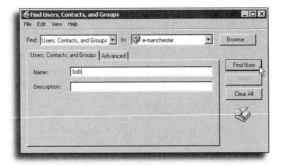

FIGURE 5.27
The Find Users, Contacts, and Groups search form lets you develop quick queries.

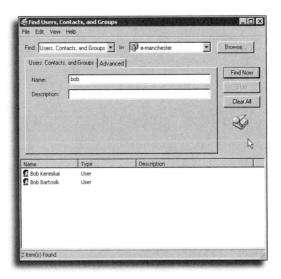

FIGURE 5.28
Results from performing the search.

Creating User Groups and User Profiles

We have spent a lot of time looking at how to create users. Now let's spend some time discussing some of the methods for managing them.

Creating a User Group

Groups allow user accounts to be assigned or denied, permissions to access a resource, or groups to be used as distribution lists. Distribution groups do not carry security information, therefore they carry less overhead.

There are three types of group scopes:

- **Domain local groups** can only include users or groups from the local domain. They can only be granted permissions to access resources in their own domain.

- **Global groups** include only users or groups from their local domain; however, they can also be defined to access resources in any domain in the domain tree or forest.

- **Universal groups** can include any users or groups that are within the same tree or forest. Permissions can be assigned to any resource within the same tree or forest. Universal Groups are not allowed in mixed-mode domains.

Universal groups do not exist in mixed mode

You cannot define a Universal Security group when you are running in the hybrid NetBIOS/DNS mode of Windows 2000. Only native-mode domains can create Universal security groups.

You can create a Universal distribution group even if you are running in hybrid mode.

To create a group, do the following:

1. From the Windows 2000 Configure Your Server application, select Active Directory.

2. From the Active Directory screen, click the hyperlink that reads Manage This Will Start the AD Users and Computers Console.

3. Select the container in which you would like to define the group. Creating a group in a specific container means that users who can manage objects in that container can manage the group as well.

4. Right-click the container in which you want to create the group. Select New from the context menu and then select Group. The New Object - Group dialog box will be displayed (see Figure 5.29).

FIGURE 5.29
The New Object - Group dialog box.

5. Enter the name for the new group. If you are running in hybrid mode you can also specify a different group name for pre–Windows 2000 computers to see.

6. Select the type of group you want to create, whether it is local to the current domain or a global group, which can be used outside of the local domain. If you are running your domain in native mode, you also have the option to create a universal group.

7. Select whether to create a Security group or a Distribution group.

8. Click the OK button to create the group. The new group will be added to the chosen container (see Figure 5.30).

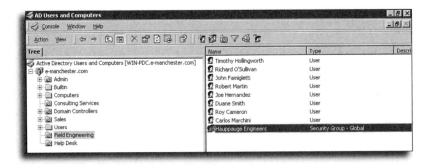

FIGURE 5.30
The current container reflecting the new group.

There are many methods of adding users to a group, but only two methods can be described in a straightforward way. The first method is good to use when you are adding members that are not all within the same container. The second method is the fastest way to add users that are in the same container to a group.

Adding Users to a Group

If you need to add users to a group, you can do the following:

1. Double-click the group to which you would like to add members.

2. The Properties dialog box for that group is displayed. Click the Members tab.

3. Click the Add button to display the Select Users, Contacts, Computers, or Groups dialog box (see Figure 5.31).

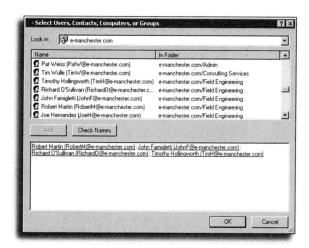

FIGURE 5.31
Select users from the top window, or type them in directly to the bottom window.

4. You can either type the names of the users you want to add to this group or you can select them from the upper window.

5. After you have finished selecting users, click the OK button. This will then display the Members tab again with the users you have chosen (see Figure 5.32).

FIGURE 5.32
The members you have added will now be shown in the Members tab.

6. Click the OK button to finalize the Member settings.

An alternative method for adding users to a group is to follow these steps:

1. Switch to the container that contains the users you want to add to the group.

2. Highlight the users that you want to add to the group.

3. Right-click the highlighted users to display the context menu (see Figure 5.33).

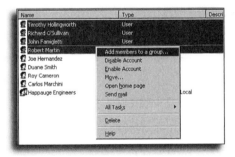

FIGURE 5.33
Select Add Members to a Group from the context menu.

4. From the context menu, choose Add Members to a Group. This will display a pick list of groups (see Figure 5.34).

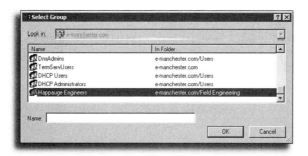

FIGURE 5.34
Choose the group to which you want to add the selected users.

5. Double-click the group you want to add these members to.

6. When the Confirmation dialog box appears (see Figure 5.35), click the OK button.

FIGURE 5.35
This dialog box verifies that the users have been added to the group.

You can also use both methods to add users from different containers into groups. Select whichever you find easier and try to use that, at least until you are comfortable with the process.

The Role of User Profiles

As you know, Windows 2000 retains your environment settings from one session to the next. When you log on, your desktop is restored to its state when you last logged off. Shortcut icons are in their accustomed positions, your Start menu has its familiar structure, your monitor has its accustomed settings, and your applications are configured as you like them. All this information is stored in a user profile created automatically and is identified with your user account.

Windows NT Profiles

Windows NT profiles are compatible with Windows 2000 profiles.

Table 5.2 summarizes the information stored in a user profile.

Table 5.2 Settings Stored in User Profiles

Source of Settings	Parameters in Profile
Accessories	User-specific settings for many Windows accessories (Clock, Calculator, Notepad, and so forth)
Control Panel	User-defined settings
Online Help	Bookmarks
Printer settings	Network printer connections
Taskbar	Personal program groups and program items with their properties, and all taskbar settings
Windows-aware applications	User-specific settings for applications that track settings on a per-user basis and update that information in the user profile
Windows 2000 Explorer	User-defined settings

Types of Profiles

All Windows 2000 computers, even isolated ones, support user profiles. *Local profiles* enable multiple users to share the same workstation while enabling them to regain their desktop settings when they log on. Windows 2000 maintains local profiles automatically, and little administrative oversight is required. When a Windows 2000 computer is connected to a network, it becomes possible to establish *roaming profiles* and *mandatory profiles*, both of which are stored on a network server.

Roaming profiles are a user's desktop settings that are stored on a server. Whenever the user logs on to the network, the profile is loaded into the workstation that the user is logging in from. When the user logs off, the profile is then updated with any changes the user might have made during the session.

A *mandatory profile* is similar to a roaming profile; however, no changes are saved back to the server. Use mandatory user profiles when you need a higher level of control than that of the standard user profile environment. Although the user can change items associated with the profile while logged on (such as screen colors or desktop icons), these changes are not saved when the user logs off.

Even after a network profile is established, a profile is maintained locally on the workstation, enabling the user to establish a familiar desktop when the network is unavailable. When you log off the network, Windows 2000 synchronizes your network and local profiles with copies of the current desktop configuration. This local profile is sometimes referred to as a locally cached profile. Regardless of the type of profile, all share a common database structure. Before putting profiles to work, it's important to examine the structure of a profile.

Profile Database Structure

The root folder for local profiles is `%SystemRoot%\Profiles` (by default, `C:\Winnt\Profiles`). After a newly created user logs on for the first time, a profile folder structure is created for the user in the `%SystemRoot%\Profiles` folder. Network profiles, on the other hand, can be stored in any folder. Figure 5.36 shows an example of a `%SystemRoot%\Profiles` folder. Each user is assigned a subfolder, named to match his or her username. Additionally there are two special profiles named Default User and All Users, which I'll get to later in this chapter.

To show all the contents of a user profile folder, Figure 5.36 was prepared after configuring Explorer to display hidden files and file extensions. The various folders in the profile directory store shortcuts and application preferences that define the user's desktop. Table 5.3 lists the folders together with the settings stored in each. It should be noted that some applications can add their own folders to a user's profile.

Table 5.3 Organization of Profile Folders

Profile Folder	What It Stores
Application Data	Application-specific data for some Windows applications, such as user preferences for Word.
Desktop	Non-system icons defined on the user's desktop, including shortcuts.
Favorites	Shortcuts to favorite programs and locations, such as favorites defined in Internet Explorer (used by some applications).

continues...

Table 5.3 Continued

Profile Folder	What It Stores
NetHood	Shortcuts defined in the user's Network Neighborhood.
Personal	Shortcuts to personal program items (used by some applications).
PrintHood	Shortcuts defined in the user's Printers folder.
Recent	Shortcuts to documents used recently by some applications, such as files recently edited under Word.
SendTo	Destinations available in the Send To option appearing in the context menus for files. Entries are defined by some applications.
Start Menu	Entries in the user's personal areas of the Start Menu.
Templates	Shortcuts to templates for some applications.

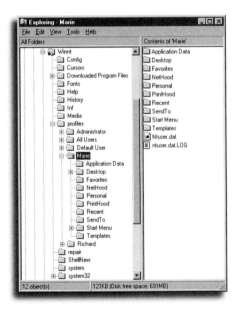

FIGURE 5.36
The structure of a profiles folder.

The Default Users Profile Folder

When a user logs on for the first time, he or she does not yet have a user profile (unless an administrator has copied one into the user's profile folder). So, where does the user's initial working environment come from? It is initialized from a default profile stored in the Default Users profile folder. When a user first logs on, NT creates a personal profile folder and initializes the user's environment from the Default Users profile. Consequently, all profiles begin as a copy of the Default Users profile. When the user logs off, any desktop changes that the user makes are stored in his or her personal profile.

The All Users Profile Folder

The All Users profile defines settings assigned to all users who log on locally to this computer and contains only two subfolders: a Desktop folder that contains desktop shortcuts displayed for all users and a Start Menu folder that defines common program groups and their shortcuts. Common program groups and shortcuts are the ones that appear below the line that subdivides entries on the Start menu.

Profiles and the Registry

The folders in the profile store much of the data that constitute a user profile, but a profile also includes other personal settings that have been established in the Control Panel. These settings are stored in the Registry, so a different mechanism is required to include the settings in the user's profile.

While working on a Windows 2000 computer, a user's personal settings are stored in the Registry under the HKEY_CURRENT_USER root key. Figure 5.37 shows the HKEY_CURRENT_USER Registry subtree. As you can see, the subtree contains several entries tied to configuration of the user's working environment.

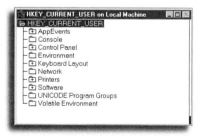

FIGURE 5.37
The HKEY_CURRENT_USER subtree.

The data file associated with HKEY_CURRENT_USER is named Ntuser.dat, and the transaction log file is Ntuser.dat.LOG. You will find an Ntuser.dat file in each user's profile directory. You will also find the associated log file, named `ntuser.dat.LOG`. In Figure 5.36, hidden files are turned on to show you the `Ntuser.dat` and `ntuser.dat.LOG` files in the example user's profile. When a user logs on to Windows 2000, the data in `Ntuser.dat` is used to initialize the `HKEY_CURRENT_USER` Registry subtree. When the user logs off, `Ntuser.dat` is updated from `HKEY_CURRENT_USER`.

As you can now see, a complete user profile consists of a folder structure in a profiles folder, together with numerous shortcuts and other files, and capped off with the `Ntuser.dat` Registry file. The `Ntuser.dat` file turns out to have a crucial role in determining how profiles will function after they are stored on the network.

Some of the Control Panel settings stored in the Registry are hardware dependent. An example is video display resolution. Consequently, profiles can be shared only among computers with similar hardware characteristics. It is unlikely, for instance, that you would be comfortable using the same profile on your 21-inch desktop monitor and your notebook. When profiles will be shared, they must be designed with consideration of the common capabilities of the workstations on which the profiles will be used.

Moving Profiles to the Network

Connecting a workstation to the network is a prerequisite to supporting network profiles, but it isn't the sole requirement. To support network-based user profiles, do the following:

1. Create a folder on the server in which users' network profiles will be stored.
2. Create a share for the profile folder.
3. Configure users' accounts with a profile path, which is found in User Manager for Domains by clicking the Profile button.

A user's profile folder can be located on any network server that is accessible to the user. You can create one or more profile folders. Often the best approach is to store profiles for groups of users, enabling you to distribute profiles across multiple volumes and servers, if necessary. You can store network profiles in the server's profile directory `%SystemRoot%\Profiles`, in which case users who are authorized to log on locally to the server will use their network profiles as local profiles. Or you can store each user's network profile in his or her network home directory, an approach that is complicated by the need to establish a network share for each profile directory.

To demonstrate network profiles, I'll use a separately created profiles folder, which will be named `C:\Profiles`. After creating the folder, grant the group `Everyone`

Change permissions for the folder, thereby enabling users to create and update their own profiles.

In this example, the profile folder is shared with the share name `Profiles$`. The `$` character makes this an administrative share that will not be advertised through network browsers. There is no reason users should connect to this share except through the profile mechanism.

The Universal Naming Convention

Windows 2000 makes extensive use of the Universal Naming Convention, which is also known as *UNC*. Using UNC allows for a folder to be referred to without having to specify a drive letter. Therefore, the UNC `\\manchester\profile$\PeterM` refers to a folder named `PeterM` contained within a shared folder named `profile$` which resides on the computer named `manchester`.

The next step is to configure the user's account with the profile path. This is done in the AD User and Computers Console, as shown in Figure 5.38. The UNC for the profile path specifies the server, share, and the name of the user's profile directory.

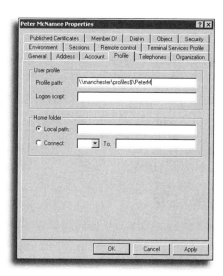

FIGURE 5.38
Setting a profile path.

You can specify the user's profile directory by name, but an alternative that is especially useful if you are defining profile paths for multiple users is to use the system variable %Username%, enabling AD User and Computers Console to supply the user-name for each user account being configured.

Logging On to a Network Profile

Assuming the previous steps have been performed to enable network profile support for a user, the events that take place when the user logs on depend on whether the user has previously logged on to the domain. Assume the user has never logged on, in which case neither a local or a network profile exists. When you log on for the first time, the following occurs:

1. The user logs on.
2. Because a profile does not yet exist, the user's working environment is initialized from the Default User profile on the user's local computer.
3. A profile folder is created in the %SystemRoot%Profiles folder on the user's local computer. The local profile folder is populated with the required folders and data files. The folders and data files are time-stamped with the logon date and time.
4. A profile folder is created in the server-based shared profiles folder. No folders or files are placed in the network profile folder at this time.
5. The user makes any desired changes to his or her environment.
6. The user logs off.
7. The profile is written out to the local profile folder. Changed files, including Ntuser.dat, are stamped with the logoff date and time.
8. The profile is written out to the network profile directory. All folders and files are stamped with the logoff date and time.

Logging On After the First Time

If the user has previously logged on to the network, things proceed a bit differently. The distinguishing factor is that if the user has previously logged on, a local profile has been created for the user on his or her local computer. Consequently, in step 2, the user's environment is initialized from the user's local profile.

Okay, now the user has logged on and has created both a network and a local profile. Which profile will be used the next time the user logs on? That depends on which profile is more recent, as determined by the "last write time" stamps of the

`Ntuser.dat` files. If the network profile time stamp is the same as or more recent than the time stamp of the local profile, the network profile will be used to initialize the user's environment. If the time stamp of the local profile is more recent, the local profile will be used.

The preceding procedures are all that are required to establish a roaming user profile. As you can see, it is not necessary for the network administrator to explicitly create the profile folders and files. All that is required is for the administrator to create the shared profiles folder, to establish the required security, and to add the path to the properties of the affected user accounts.

Identifying More Than One User Profile

Because it is possible for a given username to be associated with more than one profile, profile confusion can arise. Within Windows 2000, a user account is known not by the username but by a Security ID (SID). Each time a user account is created, it is assigned a unique SID. Now, consider a possible scenario:

Peter's computer is assigned to a workgroup, and he has diligently created a profile that suits him to a T. His company decides to implement Windows 2000 Server and assigns Peter a domain account, equipped with a roaming profile. Peter logs on to the domain and gets his default profile, not the beautiful profile he has labored over. What happened?

The problem is that Peter's workgroup and domain accounts, although they share a username, have different SIDs. As far as Windows 2000 is concerned, they are distinct accounts with distinct profiles. If Peter logs on to the domain, he gets his domain profile; if he logs on to the workgroup, he gets his workgroup profile. When an administrator creates Peter's domain user account, the SID for the domain account is different from the SID for the workgroup account. Consequently, when Peter logs on to the domain for the first time, Windows 2000 Server says, "Hmm, a new user. He doesn't have a profile, so he gets the default." Peter's desktop is initialized using the local Default User profile!

You can observe a user's various profiles in the System applet of the Control Panel. The User Profiles tab, shown in Figure 5.39 lists any profiles present on this computer. The Name column identifies the domain or workgroup the user belongs to. The Type column indicates whether the profile is Local (stored on this computer) or Roaming (stored on the network). We will return to this utility several times in the remainder of this chapter. Incidentally, although any user can view profiles in the

System applet, standard users see only their own profiles. Administrators see all profiles stored on the local computer.

FIGURE 5.39
Managing profiles in the System Properties applet.

Users often have several profiles and will access the appropriate profile depending on whether they are logging on to the domain or to the local machine. If they log on to the domain, they will access their roaming profile on the network server if it is available. Otherwise, they will access the locally cached copy of their network profiles.

Roaming Off the Network

A time-stamp issue comes into play if you work on a computer that is isolated from the network, either due to a network outage or to an intentional disconnection. Suppose that your Windows 2000 notebook is connected to the network and you are configured to use a roaming profile. You log off, disconnect the computer, and take a trip, during which the locally cached profile is used to set up your desktop. When you return and connect to the network, your local profile will have a time stamp that is more recent than the network profile. So, which profile will be accessed when you log on? To find out, take a look at the complete sequence of events.

Gina fires up her notebook in her hotel room. She wants to use her familiar network profile, so in the Logon Information dialog box she logs on to the office domain.

Here's what happens:

1. Because it takes too long for the workstation to connect with the network, Windows 2000 assumes a slow WAN link and displays a Slow Connection dialog box with the message A slow network connection has been detected. Would you like to download your profile or use the locally stored copy? Gina responds Use Local, which is also the default choice if Gina lets the counter expire. (The alternative is Download, which of course would fail in the instance. The Download option is provided for users who want to force downloading of a profile over a working but slow WAN connection such as a RAS modem connection.)

2. The next message informs Gina Your roaming profile is not available, the operating system is attempting to log you on with your local profile. Gina clicks OK.

3. Next a Logon Message box proclaims A domain controller for your domain could not be contacted. You have been logged on using cached account information. Changes to your profile since you last logged on might not be available.

4. Gina works remotely, during which time her profile is maintained locally.

5. Gina returns to the office and logs on to the network. After logging on, a Choose Profile message box proclaims Your locally stored profile is newer than your roaming profile. Would you like to use the locally stored profile?

6. Because Gina would like to retain profile changes she made on the road, she clicks Yes. She would respond No to revert to the network profile, losing any changes she made to the local profile.

7. While working in her hotel (step 4), if Gina looks at the User Profiles tab of the System Control Panel applet she will see that her domain profile is being accessed from the local copy.

Considering WAN Issues

In general, Windows 2000 profiles do not work well over slow WAN links. In fact, Microsoft does not recommend using roaming profiles across a slow network link. Not only does the profile maintenance traffic chew up scarce bandwidth, but it also can happen that local and roaming profiles get out of synchronization.

In one scenario, a user logs on through a WAN link slow enough to cause NT to time out. When that happens, Windows 2000 uses the local profile or initializes the user from the default profile, if necessary. If when the session ends the remote server has become available, the local profile is used to update the roaming profile.

If users change locations frequently and want to use roaming profiles, Microsoft recommends that copies of the roaming profiles be stored on servers at each site. You can use the directory replication capability of Windows 2000 Server to keep the various profile directories synchronized. Unfortunately, directory replication is one-way. You can update the remote profiles by copying the profile in the home office, but profile changes made at the remote site will not be replicated back to the main office.

Alternatively, you can switch users to mandatory profiles, which do not suffer from WAN update trouble because users cannot update them.

Even though you log on successfully through a slow link, such as a WAN or a RAS connection, it is usually preferable to switch from a roaming to a local profile. Doing so economizes on bandwidth utilization and eliminates synchronization errors. To switch to a local profile, open the User Profiles tab of the Control Panel System applet. Select your roaming profile in the profiles list and click Change Type. A roaming profile will revert to local, as reported in the Type column. If desired, you can switch back to a roaming profile at the end of the session so that your network profile will be updated.

Managing Administrator-Created Roaming Profiles

Suppose that you want to provide new users with predefined profiles. You could visit each workstation in the organization and modify user profiles, but there is a way to establish the user profile locally by copying a predefined profile to the new user's network profile directory. To create a predefined roaming profile, do the following:

1. Create a separate user account specifically for profile maintenance. (I call mine Profile Admin.)

2. Log on with this account on a workstation whose profile-dependent hardware characteristics are compatible with computers on which the profile will be used.

3. Design the profile as desired, such as by deleting or adding desktop shortcuts, changing wallpaper, and adding shortcuts to the programs folder.

4. Log off to save the profile.

While designing a profile, take care to ensure that any special files you incorporate into the profile, such as wallpapers, screen savers, and applications targeted by shortcuts, are present on the target computer. System files aren't usually a big deal because Windows 2000 knows where to find them and most are installed by default. Applications are a different matter. If the profiles you distribute include shortcuts to applications, the shortcuts must point to valid folders and files. Consequently, you should ensure that organization standards specify how and where applications will be installed.

The profile you create will be a local profile. After the profile is designed, it is copied from the profile administrator's profile to the profile folder of the target user—a task performed on the User Profiles tab of the System applet in the Control Panel (refer to Figure 5.39). This tab lists local profiles as well as roaming profiles that are associated with users logging on this computer. The procedure to copy a profile is as follows:

1. In the User Profiles tab of the System applet, select the profile to be copied and click Copy To.

2. In the Copy To dialog box, shown in Figure 5.40, specify the UNC pathname of the destination profile directory. The Browse button enables you to browse for a local folder or for a remote folder in the Network Neighborhood.

FIGURE 5.40
Specifying the destination folder and user when copying a profile.

3. In the Permitted to Use box, click Change and select the user who is permitted to use the profile. Although you can specify a group in this field, groups should not share roaming profiles (as you will see later). However, it is feasible for groups of users to share a mandatory profile.

4. Click OK to copy the profile.

You can use this procedure to modify the Default User profile on any workstation. But don't try to update the All Users profile, which has a different structure and serves only locally logged-on users. To modify the All Users profile, use Windows 2000 Explorer to create folders and shortcuts under the All Users folder.

When copying profiles for active users, the time stamps can get you into trouble. Suppose that you copy changes to Richard's profile while Richard is logged on. When Richard logs off, his profile will be saved, overwriting the profile you have copied.

Now, suppose that you update Richard's profile while he is working disconnected from the network. The profile you copy will be time-stamped at the time it is saved. Richard is working with a locally cached profile, which is time-stamped each time he logs off. Now Richard returns to the office and connects to the network. His local profile is now more recent than the network profile, and he will probably select the local profile, again discarding all the changes you put in his network profile. To prevent this sequence of events, you might need to update the time stamp on the profile you want to have precedence.

Sharing Roaming Profiles

In one word, the guideline on sharing roaming profiles is, "Don't!" Yes, it is possible to share roaming profiles, but all sorts of confusion can arise. Any user sharing the profile can make changes to the environment, which is confusing enough. If you ever shared a Windows 3.1 computer with someone who loved to mess around with the desktop, you know how much pain and suffering sharing can entail.

To complicate matters further, suppose Howard and Joe are logged on simultaneously with the same roaming profile. Howard logs off first. Because Joe still has the profile open, any changes Howard has made to the profile cannot be written out. When Joe logs off, only his changes are written to the profile. Given the difficulties, it is hard to imagine a solid reason for sharing a roaming profile among multiple users.

Working with Mandatory Profiles

Mandatory profiles cannot be permanently modified by the user. Although users can change their environments after logging on with a mandatory profile, the changes are not saved when the user logs off. Consequently, each time the user logs on, the exact same profile will be used. Because mandatory profiles cannot be modified by users, they can be shared. This is a great way to establish a standard desktop for large numbers of users, perhaps for dozens of employees who take telephone orders. Just assign the users the same mandatory profile in their user account properties. To create a mandatory profile, do the following:

1. Create a separate user account specifically for profile maintenance. (I call mine Profile Admin.)

2. Log on with this account on a workstation whose profile-dependent hardware characteristics are compatible with computers on which the profile will be used.

3. Design the profile as desired, such as by deleting or adding desktop shortcuts, changing wallpaper, and adding shortcuts to the programs folder.

4. Log off to save the profile.

5. Copy the profile to the desired directory.

6. In the Permitted to Use field, specify the user or a group of users permitted to use the profile.

7. Rename the `Ntuser.dat` file to `Ntuser.man`.

Managing Windows 95/98 Profiles

Although Windows 9x supports profiles, they are incompatible with Windows 2000 profiles and are considerably less capable. Windows 9x profiles include only shortcut (`.lnk`) and program information (`.pif`) files. Windows 9x profiles are also less robust than their Windows 2000 relatives because there is no fault tolerance mechanism similar to that provided by the `ntuser.dat.LOG` file. A file named `user.da0` provides a redundant copy of the `user.dat` file, which is the primary profile repository, but it does not provide fault tolerance through transaction logging and is used only when `user.dat` is lost or corrupted.

Windows 9x clients running the Microsoft Network Client or the Client for NetWare can access roaming user profiles, but these profiles must be stored in the users' home directories. The User Profile Path property of the user account is not used. Although mandatory profiles are supported for Windows 9x clients, mandatory profiles cannot be shared. It is necessary to create a separate profile for each user. To create a mandatory Windows 9x profile, rename the `user.dat` file to `user.man`.

IntelliMirror

We spent the last several sections discussing how to manage your user's environment through the use of profiles. If you have worked with profiles under the Windows NT 4 operating system, you might have noticed they have not changed significantly. But in Windows 2000, Microsoft has added a number of new tools and features that significantly enhance your ability to customize and control the end user environment. These tools, collectively known as IntelliMirror, are a set of powerful features built into the Microsoft Windows 2000 operating system. While not a single application, this suite of features is designed to give you full desktop configuration management. IntelliMirror uses features in both Windows 2000 Server and Windows 2000 Professional to allow users' data, software, and settings to follow them from building to building, computer to computer, and if your network is big enough, even country to country.

IntelliMirror increases the availability of a user's data, personal computer settings, and computing environment by intelligently managing information, settings, and software. This functionality is based on policy definitions and allows IntelliMirror to deploy, recover, restore or replace user's data, software, and personal settings in a Windows 2000–based environment. While you need to run a complete Windows 2000 environment, the amount of control these features give an administrator make a compelling case, and can significantly enhance any return-on-investment calculations surrounding a Windows 2000 rollout.

Essentially, IntelliMirror provides three features:

- User data management
- Software installation and maintenance
- User settings management

Although actually deploying IntelliMirror is a bit beyond the scope of an introductory book, be aware that it is available, and, after you are comfortable with Windows 2000 Server, is worth further investigation.

chapter

6

Adding Client Computers to Your Network

Configuring Windows 2000
Professional as a client

●

Configuring Windows NT
Workstation 4.0 as a client

●

Configuring Windows 95 and
Windows 98 as a client

●

Configuring Windows For
Workgroups 3.11 as a client

●

Windows 2000 Clients

Although Windows 9x has been available for about five years, the computer world still contains a broad mix of Microsoft operating systems. Windows For Workgroups remains in widespread use, often mixed with Windows 9x clients. Even last year's introduction of Windows 98 has not changed the product mix, because many organizations are hanging on to older hardware that won't run newer versions well. And some organizations just don't want the upgrade and training costs that an operating system upgrade entails.

At this point, though, the MS-DOS client for Microsoft networks (which is used for both MS-DOS and Windows 3.1 network clients) is no longer supported. Major changes in Microsoft Networking, due to Active Directory, render these older clients useless, unless you are running your Windows 2000 Server in NetBIOS-compatible mode. If this is the case, the Windows 2000 Server computer is acting as a Windows NT 4.0 server, not a Windows 2000 Server. Only the Windows 2000 Professional client will be able to "talk" to the Windows 2000 Servers in their native mode.

You need to know how to configure a wide variety of Microsoft network clients. This chapter covers four of them:

- Windows 2000 Professional
- Windows NT Workstation 4.0
- Windows 95 and Windows 98
- Windows For Workgroups 3.11

This discussion starts with the latest Windows version first and works back in time.

Enabling Windows 2000 Professional as Network Clients

I'll start by discussing using Windows 2000 Professional, Microsoft's latest desktop operating system as a network client. If you are installing Windows 2000 Server, the chances are high that you will have some Windows 2000 clients on the network.

In order to set up Windows 2000 Professional as a Windows 2000 Server client, you need to do the following:

1. From the Windows 2000 Professional desktop, select the My Computer icon and right-click. This opens the context menu. Select Properties and select the Network Identification tab, as shown in Figure 6.1.

Tip

If you right-click the My Network Places icon and select Properties, you will see a link to the Network Identification tab in the left pane. Click it and you will see the tab displayed in Figure 6.1. Windows 2000 contains a lot of these multiple methods for accessing utilities in an effort to simplify administration. Pick the one you are most comfortable with and use it.

FIGURE 6.1
The Network Identification tab is used to identify and modify the name and workgroup of the Windows 2000 Professional computer or to join a domain.

2. Click the Network ID button and start the Network Identification Wizard, which guides you through the network configuration. Click Next to continue.

3. The first option for the Network Identification Wizard is to identify whether it is necessary for the computer to participate in a network (see Figure 6.2).

4. Next, the wizard needs to know whether you require joining a domain or whether you simply participate on the network in a peer-to-peer relationship (see Figure 6.3).

5. The Network Information dialog box, shown in Figure 6.4, informs you that you need your user account and domain information to continue.

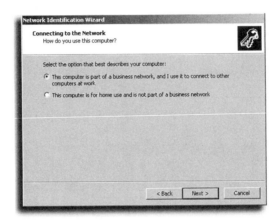

FIGURE 6.2
Determining whether you need to configure the network, based on your use.

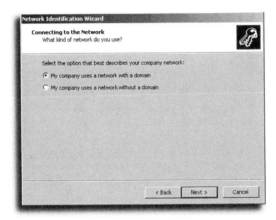

FIGURE 6.3
Determining the type of network you need, based on your use.

6. In the User Account and Domain Information dialog box, shown in Figure 6.5, you enter the information you gathered in the previous step. If you do not have an account within the domain, you need to add one. Because I'm logged on to the Windows 2000 Professional computer as the local Administrator, this dialog box already shows the User ID as Administrator. I now have to enter the password I use and the name of the domain that I want to join. Click Next to continue.

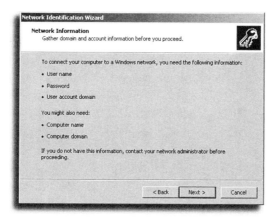

FIGURE 6.4
You need to have this information ready to continue joining the domain.

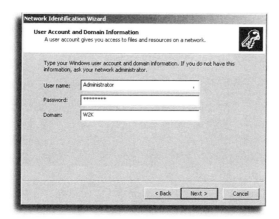

FIGURE 6.5
Enter your user account and domain information before continuing.

7. Next, the Computer Domain dialog box, shown in Figure 6.6, identifies my computer, W2KPROF, as not having a domain account in the W2K domain. If your computer already has an account in another domain, this is the place to enter the name of it. In this case, I want to create a computer account in the W2K domain, so I leave the information as it was presented to me, and click the Next button.

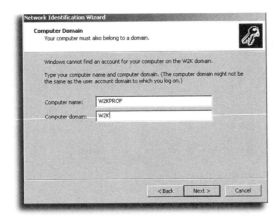

FIGURE 6.6
With Windows 2000 Professional, your computer must also be a member of the domain.

8. In order to join the domain, you must enter a user ID that has permission to add computers to the domain, along with the password, as shown in Figure 6.7. Click OK to continue.

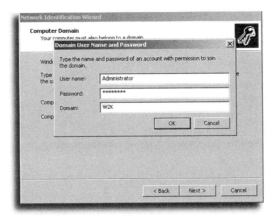

FIGURE 6.7
Domain User Name and Password screen.

9. Next, the Network Identification Wizard allows you to add a user account to the local computer. Because I want to set up an account for my own use, not as an Administrator, I choose to add a user, ROBERTR, to the W2KPROF computer and to the domain W2K. This is shown in Figure 6.8. Click Next to continue.

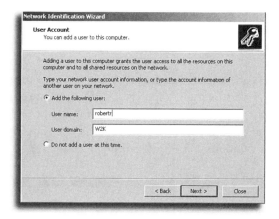

FIGURE 6.8
Adding a user account.

10. You can set the Access Level for the new user initially from the Access Level
dialog box, as shown in Figure 6.9. Click Next to continue.

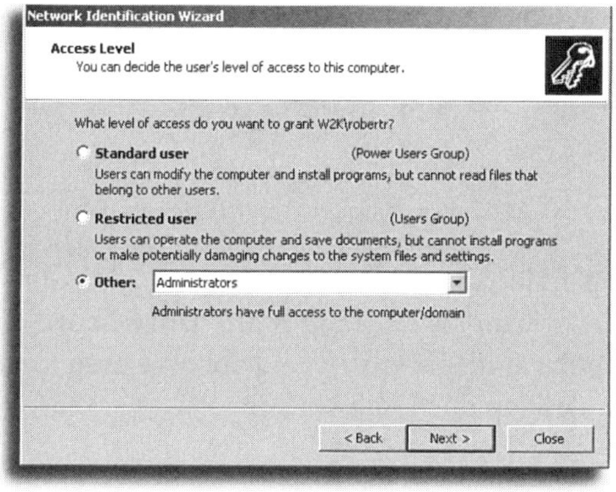

FIGURE 6.9
Setting the access level for the new user.

11. After setting the Access Level, you've finished the Network Identification
Wizard. Click Finish to close the wizard.

After you click the Finish button you will be reminded to reboot your PC to allow
the changes to take effect. Then the System Properties dialog box reflects the
changes that you have made. After you click OK, the wizard asks whether you want
to restart the computer, which you should do to allow you to log on to the domain.

Enabling Windows NT Workstation 4.0 as Network Clients

Any Windows NT Workstation, version 4.0 or earlier, sees your new Windows 2000 Server domain and servers by their respective NetBIOS names, appearing as an NT server and domain. In Figure 6.10, both a Windows NT Server 4.0 domain (REINSTEIN) and a Windows 2000 Server domain (W2K) are shown in the Network Neighborhood on a Windows NT Workstation 4.0 computer.

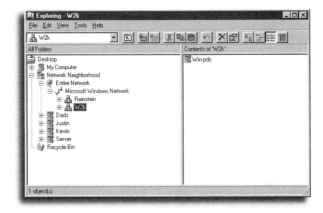

FIGURE 6.10
Windows NT Server 4.0 and Windows 2000 Server domains in Network Neighborhood

This backward compatibility is installed by default on a Windows 2000 Server; however, if your infrastructure is moving toward native Active Directory Service, this option might not be available to you, and you will need to install Windows 2000 Professional as your desktop operating system.

SEE ALSO

➤ For more information on the Active Directory Service, see page 26.

To add your Windows NT Workstation to a Windows 2000 domain, you need to do the following:

1. Install Microsoft Networking by opening the Network applet (Figure 6.11) from the Control Panel. Because installing Microsoft Networking involves installing the ethernet adapter and a protocol under Windows NT 4.0, it is a little out of scope for this book. I will assume the networking is already installed.

FIGURE 6.11
The Network applet in the Control Panel is used to configure all network components, including domains.

2. Double-click the Network applet icon and select the Identification tab. You should see the name and domain or workgroup you selected when you installed Windows NT Workstation 4.0.

3. Click the Change button. The resulting dialog box, shown in Figure 6.12, lets you change from an existing workgroup or domain name to the new Windows 2000 domain. Due to the backward compatibility of Windows 2000, the new Windows 2000 domain appears to the Windows NT Workstation 4.0 system as an NT 4.0 domain. In order to change domains, you need a user ID and password for an account that has permissions to add a computer to a domain. After you enter the new domain name, click OK. After the change is complete, you should receive a message welcoming you to the new domain. Press OK to clear it.

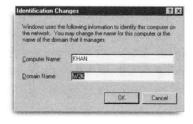

FIGURE 6.12
The Identification Changes dialog box allows you to enter the new information regarding the computer, identifies the name and domain of a computer, and is where you need to go to join a Windows 2000 domain.

4. Click OK on the Network properties dialog box, and then restart the computer so that it can log on to the new domain.

Enabling Windows 95 and Windows 98 as Network Clients

Windows 95 and 98 are intended to be plug-and-play operating systems. They are designed to detect the hardware in your computer and configure it appropriately. Self-configuration extends to networking. If either operating system detects a network card, it attempts to load the driver and get a network client running.

Windows 98 is particularly aggressive about self-configuration. It simply won't let you delete the driver for a network adapter. If an adapter is installed, it usually is detected and the drivers are reestablished when you restart the computer. So there's a degree to which it is unnecessary for me to cover client configuration for Windows 95 and 98. A lot is done for you, whether you want it or not.

Nevertheless, a time will come when you need to add an adapter driver, change a protocol, or reconfigure some network characteristic, so this section covers the procedures.

Installing Windows 95 and 98 Networking

If you have a network adapter installed, it probably is detected as you install Windows 95 or 98—unless it is a newer adapter that isn't in the software's repertoire.

Windows 95 gives you the option of detecting the network adapter. If you check the Network Adapter check box, the Setup Wizard scans your system for an adapter, which it will probably identify successfully. Windows 98 detects the adapter without prompting you.

Some network adapters have multiple personalities that can confuse the setup programs, making them latch on to the wrong personality. Be sure that you confirm the adapter setup during setup.

After setting up Windows 95 or 98, use the Network applet in the Control Panel to make changes to the network configuration. Figure 6.13 shows the Network applet as it appears in Windows 95 and 98.

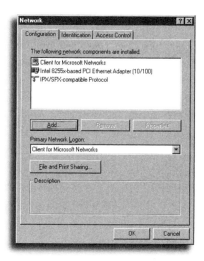

FIGURE 6.13
The Windows 95 and 98 Network Applet.

Configuring Network Components

Windows 98 is aggressive about setting up hardware, and it is unlikely that you will need to manually add a network adapter unless you use some very new hardware that Windows 98 can't recognize. Windows 95 is less aggressive and is older, so it is more likely that you will need to add network adapter drivers after installing new hardware.

If Windows 95 or 98 fails to detect a new adapter and to install the correct driver, or if you need to install updated drivers for an adapter, add the network driver as follows.

Adding a Network Adapter Driver

The first step in configuring Windows 9x networking is to install the network adapter:

1. Open the Network applet and select the Configuration tab.
2. Click Add to open the Select Network Component Type dialog box shown in Figure 6.14.

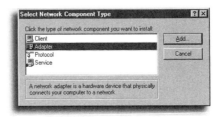

FIGURE 6.14
Selecting a network component to install.

3. Select Adapter in the list box labeled Click the Type of Network Component You Want to Install. Then click Add to open the Select Network adapters dialog box shown in Figure 6.15.

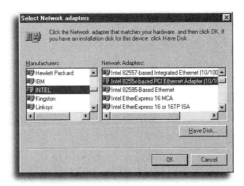

FIGURE 6.15
Selecting a network adapter.

4. In the Select Network adapters dialog box, do one of the following:

  • If you are installing a listed product, select an entry in the Manufacturer list box. Then select a product in the Network Adapters list box.

  • If you are installing an unlisted product or a product for which you have new drivers, click Have Disk. When prompted, specify a path where the drivers are located, typically on a floppy disk in drive A:.

Windows installs the driver for the network adapter, Client for Microsoft Networks, and default network protocols.

Configuring Adapters

The majority of plug-and-play adapters are completely self-configuring. Some network adapters, however, have configurable properties. If you double-click the network adapter in the list of installed network components, you open a dialog box that enables you to configure the adapter properties. The contents of this dialog box are specific to the network adapter being configured, so it is impossible to present a generic example here.

5. If you do not like the default protocols that Windows has selected, you can delete a protocol. Select a protocol in the list titled The Following Network Components Are Installed. Then click Remove.

6. To add a protocol to the configuration:

    a. Click Add in the Network applet dialog box.

    b. Select Protocol in the Select Network Component Type dialog box. Then click Add to open the Select Network Protocol dialog box shown in Figure 6.16.

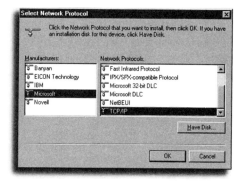

FIGURE 6.16
Selecting a network protocol to be installed.

    c. Select a manufacturer in the Manufacturers list.

    d. Select a protocol in the Network Protocol list.

If you select a protocol that requires configuration, you will see the required dialog boxes when you exit the Network applet. Enter the appropriate properties in the dialog boxes.

Multiple Network Clients

It is possible to install more than one network client on Windows 95 and 98. Windows 95 automatically installs Microsoft and NetWare clients. By default, Windows 98 installs the Microsoft client only. You can add or remove clients as you add or remove adapters or protocols.

7. If you have installed more than one network client, verify the selected client in the Primary Network Logon list box. When Windows 95 or 98 starts, it uses the client specified in this field to make an initial attempt to log on to the network.

8. Select the Identification tab, shown in Figure 6.17. This tab has the following fields:

- *Computer name.* Typically, this entry is the same as your network username.

- *Workgroup.* This value matches the name of the workgroup or domain the computer will log on to. If the computer will log on to a domain, this field must contain the name of the domain.

- *Computer Description.* Here you can enter a brief message that identifies or describes the computer in greater detail. This description appears with the computer name in browse lists.

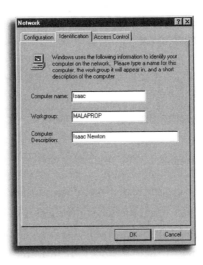

FIGURE 6.17
Configuring the computer's identification properties.

9. Return to the Configuration tab and check the properties of the Microsoft client. Double-click Client for Microsoft Networks to open the Client for Microsoft Networks Properties dialog box shown in Figure 6.18. This dialog box has the following fields:

   * *Log on to Windows NT Domain.* If you check this field, Windows 95 and 98 logs on to a domain rather than a workgroup.

   * *Windows NT Domain.* If the field Log on to Windows NT Domain is checked, this field must specify the name of the Windows 2000 Server domain the computer is to log on to. The value of this field must match the value of the Workgroup field on the Identification tab.

   * *Quick Logon.* If this radio button is selected, Windows 95 and 98 don't attempt to reestablish persistent connections when the user logs on. A persistent connection is reestablished only when the user attempts to access the shared resource. The logon process takes less time with this option, but the user experiences a delay when first connecting to a share.

   * *Logon and Restore Network Connections.* If this radio button is selected, Windows 95 and 98 attempts to reestablish all persistent connections when the user logs on. This option can prolong the logon process, but improves responsiveness when the user is logged on.

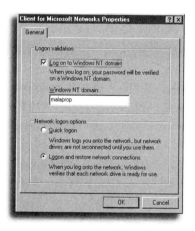

FIGURE 6.18
Configuring the Microsoft network client properties.

10. If this computer will share its files or printers on the network, click File and Print Sharing to open the File and Print Sharing dialog box. The following check boxes are available:

    - I Want to Be Able to Give Others Access to My Files
    - I Want to Be Able to Allow Others to Print to My Printer(s)

    If you check either option, the option File and Printer Sharing for Microsoft Networks is added to the list of installed network components.

11. After you have configured adapters, protocols, and clients as required, exit the Network applet. In most cases, you must restart the computer to activate changes.

Logging On

When Windows restarts, it attempts to connect to the network. If you specify a domain logon, you are presented with the logon prompt Type Your Password to enter the Microsoft network. Windows 95 and 98 remember your username from session to session, but you must enter your password with each logon attempt.

Mapping Drives to Shared Resources

If you are familiar with Windows 2000, there is little need to describe the browsing and connection management features of Windows 95 and 98. After all, Windows 2000 borrowed the Windows 9x user interface. To map a drive to a network file share, complete the following steps:

1. Browse network resources in the Network Neighborhood or in Windows NT Explorer.

2. After you find the share you want to connect to, right-click the share to open a context menu.

3. Choose Map Network Drive from the context menu to open the Map Network Drive dialog box. This dialog box has two data-entry fields:

    - *Drive.* Select the drive letter you want to map.
    - *Reconnect at Logon.* Check this box to establish a persistent connection. Depending on the settings in the Client for Microsoft Networks properties dialog box, persistent connections are reestablished when you log on (Quick Logon) or when you first attempt to connect with a resource (Logon and Restore Network Connections).

4. Click OK to map the drive.

Connecting to Shared Printers

Printer setup is managed by a wizard that is used to add a printer to your configuration. To add a printer, follow these steps:

1. Open the Printers folder in My Computer.

2. Double-click Add Printer to start the Add Printer Wizard.

3. When asked to specify how the printer is attached to your computer, select Network printer.

4. When asked to specify the network path or queue name, click Browse to open a browse box, where you can locate and select the shared printer.

5. Complete the printer setup as for a normal printer.

6. Windows 95 and 98 can identify the printer type by examining the printer share. If Windows 95 or 98 printer drivers were installed on the print server, they can be accessed by Windows 95 and 98, and it is unnecessary to install drivers on the local computer. If the required drivers are not installed at the print server, the required drivers are installed on the local computer.

Enabling Windows For Workgroups 3.11

Windows For Workgroups can be used by itself to build peer-to-peer networks that support file and printer sharing. The utilities included with Windows For Workgroups are network ready. Print Manager can share local printers and connect to shared printers elsewhere on the network. File Manager can share files and connect to shared files. Although you can network Windows 3.1, the utilities in Windows 3.1 cannot participate in the network with the same facility as the utilities in Windows For Workgroups.

Everything you need to configure a Windows For Workgroups 3.11 client is included with the product. This section shows you how to install networking software, connect to a domain, and access domain resources.

Installing Windows For Workgroups Network Software

When Windows For Workgroups is installed on a networked computer, Setup normally installs the network software and configures Windows For Workgroups to participate in a workgroup. If the Windows For Workgroups computer is already participating in a workgroup, the network software is already installed, and you can skip this section and go to the section titled "Connecting to a Domain."

This section contains step-by-step procedures for adding network software to an installed copy of Windows For Workgroups. To add network software to Windows For Workgroups, you need to do the following:

1. Run the Windows Setup utility. The icon for Windows Setup is normally stored in the Main program group. In the Windows Setup dialog box, the Network field indicates No Network Installed.

2. Choose the Change Network Settings command in the Options menu. The Network Setup dialog box is displayed as shown in Figure 6.19. This box is the focus for most Windows For Workgroups network configuration procedures. In Figure 6.19, no networking features are enabled.

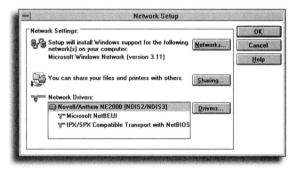

FIGURE 6.19
The Network Setup dialog box.

3. To install network support, click Networks to display the Networks dialog box shown in Figure 6.20.

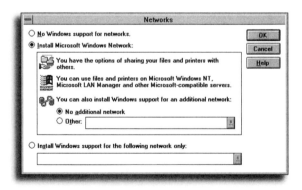

FIGURE 6.20
Selecting Network Support Options.

Use Microsoft's protocol stack

Although Windows For Workgroups can be configured with protocol stacks provided by other vendors, such as the Open Datalink Interface (ODI) stack from Novell, you should probably use the NDIS stack provided by Microsoft. NDIS supports multiple, simultaneous protocols including NetBEUI, NWLink (a transport compatible with Novell's IPX/SPX), and TCP/IP.

4. To install the protocols, click the radio button Install Microsoft Windows Network and click OK. (If your network includes NetWare or other supported networks, you also need to select Other and follow the required procedures for the other network type.)

You are returned to the Network Setup dialog box, which now indicates that Setup will install the Microsoft Windows Network (version 3.11). Click OK to continue.

5. Setup attempts to discover any network cards in the PC. It will be successful with many older network adapters, but it lacks the drivers required to support most modern adapters.

6. If you must manually select a network card driver, you do so from the list in the Add Network Adapter dialog box, shown in Figure 6.21. In the figure, an NE2000 has been chosen.

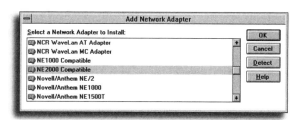

FIGURE 6.21
Choosing a network adapter.

7. Next, a series of boxes enables you to specify settings for your network card. In the case of the NE2000, the interrupt and the I/O port had to be confirmed.

If you select an interrupt that is normally dedicated to another resource, Setup warns you. Figure 6.22 shows the warning shown when Interrupt 3 is selected.

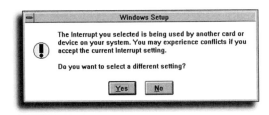

FIGURE 6.22
Setup warns you of potential resource conflicts.

8. After specifying card settings, Setup presents the Microsoft Windows Network Names dialog box shown in Figure 6.23. Here you must specify the following:

   - *User Name.* This entry should match a username recognized by the domain this user will access.

   - *Workgroup.* This can be a Windows For Workgroups workgroup (the default is WORKGROUP) or a domain. You should avoid using the default name WORKGROUP, especially if your network is connected to a WAN.

   - *Computer Name.* This name should uniquely identify this computer on the network.

     Workgroup and computer names can consist of up to 15 characters and can include the following characters:

     ! # $ % ( ) - _ . @ ^ ' ~

     Spaces are not permitted.

FIGURE 6.23
Specifying network names.

9. Click OK when network names have been specified. Setup will begin to install files. Insert disks and specify file locations when prompted.

You are notified that Setup will modify the files AUTOEXEC.BAT, SYSTEM.INI, and PROTOCOL.INI.

10. After files are installed, the computer must be rebooted to activate the network software. You are given the option Restart Your Computer Now?. Click Restart Computer to activate the network.

11. When you restart Windows, you see a Welcome to Windows For Workgroups dialog box. This dialog box has the following two fields:

    • *Logon Name.* This matches the name you specified in step 8.

    • *Password.* You should enter the password this user will enter to access the workgroup network.

12. Next you will see the message "There is no password list file for the user name. Do you want to create one now?". Respond by clicking Yes.

13. A Confirm User Password dialog box requests that you enter the password a second time. Type the password again in the Confirm New Password dialog box and click OK.

Windows For Workgroups encrypts the password you entered and stores it in a file named username.PWL in the Windows directory (where username matches the user's logon name). The next time this user logs on to Windows For Workgroups, a password is requested and checked against the password in the PWL file. If a blank password was entered, no password is requested when Windows For Workgroups starts.

The computer is now set up to participate on a network but cannot yet log on to a domain. The next section covers the steps to connect the computer to a Windows NT domain.

Connecting to a Domain

After a Windows For Workgroups computer has been configured to connect to a network, you can enable it to log on to a domain. Start the Network utility in the Control Panel. The Microsoft Windows Network dialog box that is shown can be used to reconfigure many Windows For Workgroups network settings (see Figure 6.24). To configure Windows For Workgroups to log on to a domain, do the following:

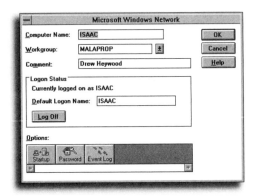

FIGURE 6.24
The Network applet for Windows For Workgroups.

1. Click the Startup button to display the Startup Settings dialog box shown in Figure 6.25. Several check boxes are included:

   - *Log On at Startup*. Check this box to have Windows For Workgroups log you on automatically when it starts.

   - *Enable Network DDE*. If you will use network DDE with your applications, check this box. Check the box only if network DDE is required because enabling this option uses about 50KB of memory.

   - *Ghosted Connections*. Selecting this option saves time at startup by not establishing connections to resources until they are actually placed in use. Drive letters are reserved for persistent connections, but connections are not established.

   - *Enable WinPopup*. WinPopup is a message display utility that displays network messages in Windows. If you will be broadcasting messages to users, enable this option. WinPopup also receives confirmation messages from domain print servers.

2. Check the box labeled Log On to Windows NT or LAN Manager Domain to enable Windows For Workgroups to log on to Windows NT Server when starting up.

3. Enter the logon domain name in the Domain Name box.

4. Click Set Password to enter the logon password at this time.

5. If you do not want to receive a message confirming a successful logon, check the box Don't Display Message on Successful Logon.

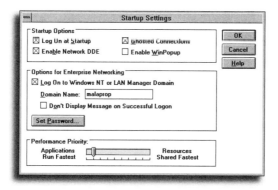

FIGURE 6.25
Specifying Windows For Workgroups startup settings.

6. Click OK. You are prompted to restart the computer.

7. When Windows For Workgroups restarts, you are presented with the Domain
Logon dialog box shown in Figure 6.26. Enter the password for the domain that
was selected. If desired, you can change the domain, or click Browse to search
for one.

FIGURE 6.26
Logging on to the domain.

8. If you check Save this Password in Your Password List, Windows For
Workgroups encrypts the domain password and stores it in this user's PWL file.

9. Following a successful domain logon, Windows For Workgroups displays a confirmation message similar to the one shown in Figure 6.27. (This box will not
display if Don't Display Message on Successful Logon was checked in step 5.)

After workgroup and domain passwords have been stored in a password file,
Windows For Workgroups will not request them when starting unless they are
refused by the workgroup or the domain.

FIGURE 6.27
Confirmation of a successful login.

Changing Your Password

Follow these steps to change your password:

1. Change your domain password by selecting the Set Password button in the Startup Settings window (refer back to Figure 6.25).

2. Change your workgroup password by selecting the Password button in the Microsoft Windows Network window, shown in Figure 6.24.

If you do not log on to a domain and attempt to browse domain resources, you are shown the logon message displayed in Figure 6.28, giving you the option of logging on to the domain.

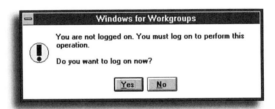

FIGURE 6.28
Logging on to the domain after the system has already booted.

Connecting to Shared Directories

One other thing you need to do after you have your networking configured is to connect to file shares on the server. In order to do this you need to

1. Run File Manager.

2. Choose the Connect Network Drive command in the Disk menu.

3. Specify a drive letter and browse the network for a shared directory.

4. Specify whether the disk should be reconnected at startup.

5. Click OK.

The disk connection can be used as a virtual hard drive.

Connecting to Shared Printers

Unlike Windows 2000, Windows For Workgroups computers cannot read print drivers from a print server. Before a Windows For Workgroups computer can use a printer shared by a Windows NT print server, the proper print drivers must be installed on the Windows For Workgroups computer. Because you should know how to install a print driver by now (the operating system has been out for over five years), I'll assume the driver is installed and jump right to connecting:

1. Open Print Manager and select the printer you want to connect. The printer is automatically installed to a local port when the driver is installed. Click Connect in the Printers window. This reveals the Connect dialog box.

2. Select an unoccupied port in the Ports list box.

3. Click OK. You are returned to the Printers dialog box. The printer is now installed on the port you have selected.

To enable an installed printer to print to the network, you must connect it to a shared printer. This is also done in Print Manager.

To print to a network printer, complete the following steps:

1. Start the Print Manager.

2. Select a printer that is labeled (not shared).

3. Choose Connect Network Printer from the Printer menu. This displays the Connect Network Printer dialog box in which you can browse for a network printer.

4. Browse for a shareable printer and select it to store the path in the Path box or enter the path manually.

5. Check Reconnect at Startup if the printer connection should be reestablished each time Windows For Workgroups starts up.

6. Click OK to return to the Connect dialog box. The Ports list box now shows that the port you specified is connected to the shared network printer.

7. Click OK to return to the Printer Manager. The printer list now indicates the resource path to which the printer is connected.

Print Manager need not be running to print to the network unless you are sharing a local printer with a workgroup. Windows For Workgroups opens Print Manager if it is required.

Using Network Client Commands

The NET command accepts several command arguments that control functions such as logon, logoff, and resource connections. These commands can be used interactively but are probably most valuable when included in logon scripts. See "A Sample Logon Script," later in this chapter.

I've described several of the most useful NET commands in this section. A complete list of NET commands can be found in Windows Help; however, not all the commands listed in Windows Help are supported by every client platform.

To list available NET commands at a command prompt, enter the command NET HELP. To obtain detailed help about a specific command, enter the command NET HELP COMMAND, where COMMAND is the specific command you want to learn about. From the command line you can also type NET /? to see the options.

The *NET HELP* Command

NET HELP displays a summary of the NET command options. You can display details about any command by including a command as an option. To see a help listing on the LOGON command, for example, type the following:

NET HELP LOGON

The *NET LOGON* Command

NET LOGON initiates a logon dialog box. Entered alone, NET LOGON prompts you for a username and a password. You can also enter the name and password as parameters. For example, isaac would log on to the default domain or workgroup with the password apple like this:

NET LOGON ISAAC APPLE

A different domain can be specified with the /domain:*domainname* option. For example,

NET LOGON MARIE RADIUM /DOMAIN:MALAPROP

The *NET LOGOFF* Command

NET LOGOFF breaks your logon connection with the network. If you include the /YES option, you will not be asked to confirm your logoff request.

The *NET USE* Command

Disks and printers are both connected and disconnected with the NET USE command. To connect drive C: to the APPS share on MALAPROP1, use this command:

```
NET USE C: \\MALAPROP1\APPS
```

The following command connects LPT1: to printer WIDGETS1 on server MALAPROP1:

```
NET USE LPT1: \\MALAPROP1\WIDGETS1
```

Add the option /PERSISTENT:YES to specify connections that should be made when the Workstation Connection starts up.

To see a list of your connected resources, enter the NET USE command without options.

The *NET VIEW* Command

Use the NET VIEW command to list computers and shared resources. Enter NET VIEW without options to list computers that are sharing resources in your domain.

Include a computer name to list shared resources on the computer. NET VIEW \\ MALAPROP1 lists shared resources on MALAPROP1.

The *NET TIME* Command

NET TIME provides a convenient means of synchronizing a computer's clock with the clock on another computer. It is generally preferable to synchronize clocks in a shared environment so that users can be assured that time and data stamps are meaningful.

To synchronize a client clock with the computer \\MALAPROP1, you would use this command:

```
NET TIME \\MALAPROP1 /SET /YES
```

The /YES parameter carries out the NET TIME command without prompting you for confirmation.

The *NET STOP* Command

The NET STOP command unloads services. To unload the pop-up, enter the following command:

```
NET STOP POPUP
```

You can stop the default redirector, which disconnects you from the network, by entering the following command:

```
NET STOP WORKSTATION
```

The *NET PASSWORD* Command

Change your password with the NET PASSWORD command. Remember that users can have passwords in several places, including the password list file on the client and the username database on a domain or workstation.

Entered without parameters, the command prompts you for old and new passwords. You can also include old and new passwords as parameters. To change the password in the client password list file, the command syntax is as follows:

```
NET PASSWORD oldpassword newpassword
```

To change a password on a specific computer, include the computer name as a parameter. A username is also required:

```
NET PASSWORD \\WIDGETS1 MABEL oldpassword newpassword
```

To specify a domain, use the /DOMAIN option:

```
NET PASSWORD /DOMAIN:MALAPROP oldpassword newpassword
```

A Sample Logon Script

Logon scripts don't need to be elaborate. The following is an example of a logon script that defines resources by department. It might be set up for Widgets Engineering:

```
@echo off
net time \\keystone1 /yes
net use g: \\keystone1\apps /yes
net use s: \\widgets1\status /yes
net use lpt1: \\widgets1\laser1 /yes
```

This script uses NET TIME to synchronize each client workstation to the clock of KEYSTONE. By synchronizing all clients to the same clock, you know that you can rely on the time and date stamps on files.

The /YES option is included with each command and has two effects. First, /YES eliminates the need for users to respond to any prompts. Second, /YES ensures that these settings replace any persistent settings that users have established.

Putting your network to work

You have now added the client part of your client/server network, and any computer running a Microsoft operating system can now participate in your network. That, of course, means that your major network administration headache—dealing with users and their complaints and problems—is just around the corner. Take the time to master the intricacies of each type of network client before you turn the client software loose on your users' desktops.

chapter

7

Managing Resources

Sharing Directories and Files

If you have networked any Microsoft product, from Windows for Workgroups to Windows 95, you are probably familiar with sharing, which is the Microsoft networking way of making resources (including folders) available to users on the network. But sharing is considerably more robust with Windows 2000 Server than with other Microsoft network-capable operating systems. You can establish very high levels of security and store files on centralized servers that are more reliable and better performing than most users' workstations.

It is easy to share directories and files. The trick is to share without compromising security. Windows 2000 Server supports four levels of security that enable you to tightly control user access to shares:

- *Abilities.* Users gain abilities by being assigned to built-in groups.
- *Rights.* Rights initially are assigned to built-in groups but can be assigned to groups or users by an administrator.
- *Shares.* Shares are directories that are shared on the network. Shares can be assigned share-level permissions. Shares extend the capabilities users gain as a result of their memberships in built-in groups.
- *Permissions.* Users and groups can be assigned permissions for directories and files on NTFS volumes. NTFS permissions are discussed in the next chapter.

Chapter 5, "Managing Users and Groups," discusses the capabilities that are assigned to built-in groups, capabilities that arise from the abilities, and rights held by the groups. It also covers how to establish users as members of groups. So, if you've read that chapter, you already know that users' memberships in built-in groups define much of users' access to network resources.

File Sharing Basics

Files can only be accessed through the network if they are shared. Figure 7.1 shows a server's file system as viewed in Windows 2000 Explorer.

You will probably find that Windows 2000 Explorer is your preferred tool for managing directories, files, and shares.

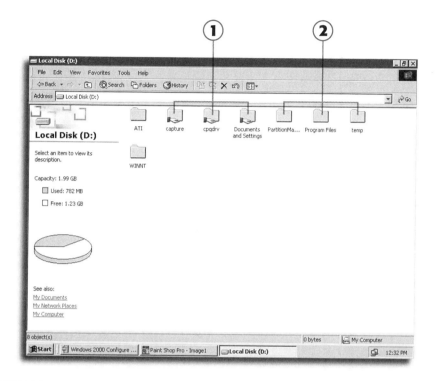

FIGURE 7.1
A folder in an outstretched hand indicates that the folder is shared.

(**1**)   Shared folders

(**2**)   Unshared folders

When Windows 2000 Server is installed, several shared folders are established:

- Each volume is assigned an administrative share. For example, D: is given the share name D$. Administrative shares are for use only by administrators.

- C:\Winnt is also shared as the administrative share ADMIN$.

- A share named NETLOGON is publicly available so that users can access the files they need to log on.

- Another share named SYSVOL appears only on domain controllers.

Most of the default shares are administrative shares and can't be used by ordinary users. The NETLOGON share isn't good for much besides logging on. So, before users can do anything useful with the network, you must create shares that give them access.

Every Windows 2000 computer has a Program Files directory. Suppose you have installed applications in Program Files that you want to share with network users. The following procedure assigns the share name Programs to Program Files. To share a directory, do the following:

1. Open Windows 2000 Explorer and expand the tree in My Computer, and then the C: drive until you can see Program Files, shown in Figure 7.2.

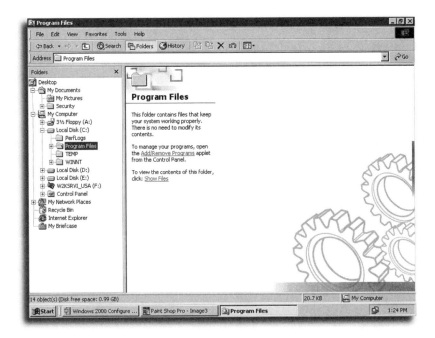

FIGURE 7.2
Expand the folder window to show folders in Windows 2000 Explorer.

2. Right-click the folder to be shared to open its context menu.

3. Choose Sharing from the context menu to open the Program Files Properties dialog box shown in Figure 7.3. Notice that the Sharing tab is selected.

4. Select the Share This Folder radio button to activate sharing for the folder.

5. In the Share Name field, enter the name that will be used to advertise the share on the network (in this case I have selected Programs).

6. If you want, you can include a description of the share in the Comment field. These descriptions appear in browse lists and help users identify shares.

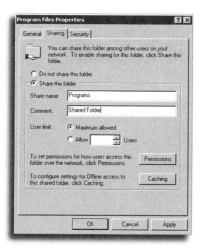

FIGURE 7.3
The Sharing tab from Folder Properties lets you specify the share name and permissions for accessing the share.

7. By default, the Maximum Allowed radio button is selected, indicating that the share can be accessed by an unlimited number of users.

8. To limit access to the share, select the Allow...Users radio button and indicate a maximum number of users in the spin box.

The Everyone group

By default, the special group Everyone is given Full Control permissions to the share. Because Everyone includes, well, everyone, all users who have been authenticated to access the domain, whether local or remote, can use the share.

---

9. Pressing the Permissions button opens the dialog box shown in Figure 7.4 where you can configure custom share permissions.

10. Click OK to save the share. The Program Files folder icon is now tagged with a sharing hand, shown in Figure 7.5.

SEE ALSO

➤ *To assign share permissions, see page 162.*

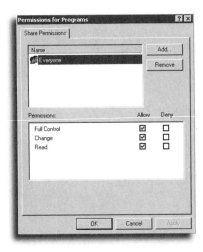

FIGURE 7.4
The Permissions for Programs dialog box permits you to add (or remove) users and groups.

FIGURE 7.5
Windows 2000 Explorer with the Program Files folder now shared.

Connecting with File Shares

Now that the folder has been shared, users can log on to the domain and access files in the shared folder. Shares are accessed differently from other network clients.

Windows 2000, Windows NT 4, Windows 95, and Windows 98 clients can access shares through Explorer or through the My Network Places/Network Neighborhood, tasks that are described in the next two sections. Shares can also be accessed from the command line by using the net use command.

Accessing shares with older clients

Older clients, such as Windows 3.x and Windows NT 3.x clients access shares through File Manager or the net use command.

MS-DOS users access shares through the net use command.

You can browse shares using Explorer, My Network Places, Network Neighborhood, or File Manager. After browsing, you will in most cases map a drive letter to the share, enabling you to use files in the share as though they are stored on a local hard disk.

Connecting Through My Network Places

Windows 2000 uses the My Network Places icon to represent resources available on the network. Windows NT 4.0, Windows 98, and Windows 95 use Network Neighborhood to represent network resources. This section uses Windows 2000 for its examples; however, wherever My Network Places is mentioned that information also applies to Network Neighborhood. To browse shares using My Network Places, do the following:

1. Double-click My Network Places. The resulting window (Figure 7.6) should show three icons by default (you can modify this, of course).

2. Double-click Computers Near Me to see computers that are part of the same domain that you have logged on to. In this case, the only server that exists is Win-pdc, shown in Figure 7.7.

3. Double-click the server that is hosting the share to display all the shared resources on that server. (See Figure 7.8.)

4. Right-click the Programs share to open its context menu.

5. Choose Map Network Drive from the context menu to open the Map Network Drive dialog box.

FIGURE 7.6
The default display for My Network Places shows three icons.

FIGURE 7.7
Computers Near Me shows the computers that are part of the same domain.

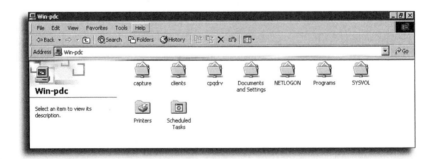

FIGURE 7.8
Opening a computer in Explorer shows shared folders among other properties for the computer.

6. In the Drive field, select a drive letter that will be used to access the share. Note that the Folder field is already completed with the UNC name of the share.

7. If this drive connection should be reestablished each time you log on to the network, check Reconnect at Logon.

8. If you don't have permission to access the share but you can use another user account that has the required permissions, you can specify the other user account by clicking the hyperlink that says Connect Using a <u>Different User Name</u>.

9. Choose Finish to create the connection.

The user can now access drive G: in My Computer or in Windows 2000 Explorer just as he or she would access a local drive. Figure 7.9 shows Explorer after a user has connected drive G: to \\Win-Pdc\Programs. Notice that the folder Program Files isn't visible to the user. The Program Files folder displays as the root directory of drive G:.

FIGURE 7.9
Windows 2000 Explorer with a newly mapped G: drive.

Connecting Through Explorer

To use the Windows 2000 Explorer, choose the command Map Network Drive from the Tools menu to open the Map Network Drive dialog box.

To map a drive using the Map Network Drive dialog box, do the following:

1. From the Tools menu in Explorer, select Map Network Drive.

2. The first unused drive letter will be selected. Use the drop-down box to select a different unused drive letter in the Drive field.

3. Complete the Folder field with the UNC name of the share. You can either enter the UNC manually or use the Browse button to drill down into a list of shared folders.

4. If this drive connection should be reestablished each time you log on to the network, check Reconnect at Logon.

5. If you don't have permission to access the share, but have use of another user account that has the required permissions, you can specify the other user account by using the hyperlink that says Connect Using a <u>Different User Name</u>.

6. Choose Finish to create the connection.

Assigning Share Permissions

You can fine-tune share access by assigning permissions to the share. Permissions establish upper limits on the operations a user can perform on files in the share. You can further limit the actions users can perform by assigning directory and file permissions on NTFS volumes, but users cannot perform any actions that are forbidden by the permissions of the share they are using to access the file.

Four types of permissions can be assigned to shared directories. Here they are, arranged from most to least restrictive:

- *No Access.* No permissions are granted for the share.
- *Read.* Share users can do the following:
  - Display subdirectory names and filenames.
  - Open subdirectories.
  - Display file data and file attributes.
  - Run program files.
- *Change.* In addition to actions permitted by Read permissions, users can do the following:
  - Create subdirectories and files.
  - Modify files.
  - Change subdirectory and file attributes.
  - Delete subdirectories and files.

- *Full control.* In addition to actions permitted by Change permissions, users can do the following:
  - Change permissions.
  - Take ownership.

Share permissions can be assigned to user accounts, groups, and the special identities Everyone, SYSTEM, NETWORK, INTERACTIVE, and CREATOR OWNER.

These permissions should not be confused with NTFS permissions, which are completely separate.

SEE ALSO

➤ *For more information on NTFS permissions, see page 223 (Understanding NTFS: The Windows 2000 File System, Chapter 10.)*

Assigning Share Permissions to Newly Created Shares

For a newly created share, Full Control permissions are assigned to the special identity Everyone. If the share is on an NTFS volume, you can leave the default share permissions in place. You can restrict effective user permissions using NTFS permissions.

Full Control for Everyone

It is important to note that unlike some other network operating systems, Windows 2000 gives full access to a share by default. If you want to control access to that share, you need to remove the permissions for the group Everyone, and add the appropriate permissions.

Some would say this is an inferior security model, but as long as you are aware of the requirements, this can be as secure as any other file sharing.

If the share resides on a FAT volume, share permissions are your only tools for limiting user access to files. (Remember that share permissions only restrict remote users!) Here are some suggestions for selecting share permissions:

- Users often need only Read permissions in application directories because they don't need to modify files.
- In some cases, applications require users to share a directory for temporary files. If that folder is the same as the application folder, you can enable users to create and delete files in the folder by assigning the Change permission to CREATOR USER.

- Users typically require the Change permission for a folder that contains shared data files.

- Often users will be assigned Full Control permissions only for their home folders.

- Permissions are cumulative. Suppose that user Justin belongs to the group Engineers. If Everyone has Read permissions to the Specs share but Engineers has Change permissions to Specs, Justin has Change permissions for the folder.

Changing Share Permissions

Now that you understand how share permissions work, you should probably look at how to view and modify them. To view and modify the permissions assigned to a share, do the following:

1. Choose the Permissions button in the Sharing tab of the folder Properties dialog box (see Figure 7.3).

2. This opens the Permissions for Programs (where Programs is the share name) dialog box shown in Figure 7.4. In this dialog box, you can examine the permissions that are assigned for the share.

3. Modify the permissions as required.

Adding a User or Group to the Share Permissions List

You can also add users or groups to the permissions list for the share as required. To add users or groups to the permissions list for a share, do the following:

1. Right-click the shared directory in Windows 2000 Explorer.

2. Choose the Sharing command in the context menu.

3. Click Permissions in the Sharing tab of the Properties dialog box. This opens the Permissions for Programs dialog box shown in Figure 7.4.

4. Click Add to open the Select Users, Computers, or Groups dialog box shown in Figure 7.10. In the figure, the group TermServUsers has been selected for addition to the share permissions list. By default this group will be given Read permission. Repeat this for each user or group that is to be assigned permissions to the share.

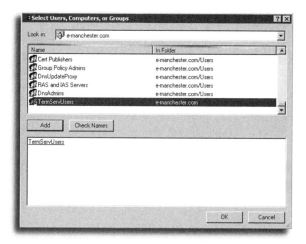

FIGURE 7.10
Assigning permissions to a folder by adding a group.

Adding objects manually to a permissions list

You can also just type the names of the User Objects, Computer Objects, or Group Objects into the entry field on the lower half of the Select Users, Computers, or Groups dialog box. Separate each object name by a semicolon. Then click the Check Names button, and if you have properly entered valid objects, those objects will become underlined. If an object does not get underlined, you have entered an invalid object.

---

5. Choose OK to return to the Permissions dialog box. The names you entered in the Add Names list will now appear in the Name list, together with a list of permissions that are available for the share.

6. Alter the permissions for each object by checking or unchecking the checkboxes.

7. Remove objects by highlighting the object and then clicking on the Remove button.

Stopping Sharing

In the event that you want to stop sharing a folder, you can quickly remove the share. To stop sharing a folder:

1. Right-click the shared folder in Windows 2000 Explorer.

2. Choose the Sharing command in the context menu.

3. Select Do Not Share This Folder in the Sharing tab of the Properties dialog box.

4. Click OK to stop sharing the folder. If users are connected to this share, a dialog box, shown in Figure 7.11, appears notifying you of the number of users currently attached to that share. Click the OK button to remove the share and disconnect the user(s).

FIGURE 7.11
Disconnecting users from a share.

Administrative Shares

Windows 2000 Server automatically shares some folders. These shares, called *administrative shares*, are not advertised to users who browse the network. In some cases, administrative shares support network functions of the operating system. In other cases, administrative shares are defined for the convenience of administrators.

The following administrative shares are automatically established:

- ADMIN$. An ADMIN$ share is added to each server and is associated with the Windows 2000 Server system directory, which is usually C:\WINNT.

- driveletter$. An administrative share is created for each hard disk. For example, the administrative share for drive C: has the share name C$.

- IPC$. This share supports the named-pipes mechanism that provides interprocess communication between programs. IPC$ supports remote administration of computers.

- PRINT$. This share supports printer sharing.

- REPL$. This share is established when a replication server is configured and is used to support export replication.

The $ in administrative shares

Notice a common thread in administrative share names: they all end with a $. Any share that ends with a $ is not advertised in network browse lists. These are considered *hidden shares.*

Connecting to an Administrative Share

Because administrative shares don't appear in browse lists, you must make an extra effort to connect with them. To connect to an administrative share, do the following:

1. Choose the Map Network Drive command in the Tools menu to open the Map Network Drive dialog box shown in Figure 7.12.

2. The Drive field shows the first available drive letter. You can choose another letter from the drop-down box.

3. In the Path field, enter the UNC name for the desired share. For example, drive C: on server Khan would have the UNC name \\Khan\c$, as shown in Figure 7.12.

4. Click the Finish button to map the drive.

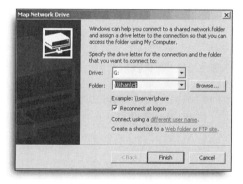

FIGURE 7.12
Mapping a drive to an administrative share.

Creating Your Own Administrative (Hidden) Shares

It is often useful to create shares that are available to administrators but are not advertised to users. To create an unadvertised share, simply include a $ as the last character of the share name. To use an unadvertised share, a user must be aware of the share's existence and must specify the share path name manually.

Understanding Ownership

Ownership is a very important concept in Windows 2000 security. Every object—folder, file, computer, or printer—has an owner who is usually the user who created the object. The owner of an object has a special status, conferred by the CREATOR OWNER special identity, and typically has complete authority over the object.

The owner of an object controls the permissions of all users, even members of the Administrators group. This enables owners to configure home directories that are completely private or to set up directories that can be accessed on a strict need-to-know basis.

The owner of an object cannot give ownership away. Owners can give permission to take ownership, however. This approach prevents a user from creating an object and then making it appear to belong to another user.

Administrators can take ownership of any file directory. This provision is necessary because administrators must have the ability to manage objects owned by users who leave an organization or change departments. An administrator has difficulty abusing this privilege; when taken, a file cannot be given back. An administrator cannot, therefore, take ownership without leaving behind evidence of the action.

Adding Printers to the Network

I spent the first half of the chapter discussing how to manage and share file resources. In the remainder of the chapter I will discuss the other half of a file and print server, the printers.

Types of Network Printers

Creating print queues on your Windows 2000 Server network will probably be one of your first priorities, as network clients are usually anxious to be able to start exercising their ability to print.

Adding printers to the network is one task that you will be able to master very quickly. First you must familiarize yourself with the different types of printers that you can attach to your network. I'm not talking about different brand names or models, but the way that the printer is attached to the network will define how you will need to define the printer to the Add Printer Wizard.

Local Printers

Chances are you've worked with local printers. These are the printers that are attached by parallel cable directly to a computer. These are becoming less common in network situations, mainly because server hardware is usually placed in a secured area, therefore making it difficult to access a locally attached printer. However, there's a great chance that your server has an LPT1 port, or possibly also an LPT2 port. And sometimes you just want to hook up another printer for use on the network.

Network Printers

A printer attached to a workstation can also be made available to the network as a print queue on the server. By sharing the printer that is locally attached to a workstation, you can install the printer onto your server and then share the printer out to your network. The good part of this is that the print jobs get queued to the server and can be managed from the server, even though the printer is attached to another computer. The bad part is that the computer that the printer is attached to must be turned on for the printer to be available. Another drawback is that if someone is using the computer with the printer attached, she will probably feel a slowdown when someone is sending print jobs through her computer.

TCP/IP Printers

Perhaps the most familiar type of network printer is the TCP/IP printer. Over the years this has evolved from print servers using the most notable HP JetDirect series of internal and external network adapters. Many other types of print sharing devices have come and gone. The HP LaserJet printer and its JetDirect counterpart are by far the most popular. In the past, these print servers used the DLC protocol. As TCP/IP became a more mainstream protocol the JetDirect series followed.

Other manufacturers, such as Intel and Lexmark, also make network adapters that printers can plug in to using a standard parallel cable.

Windows 2000 Server connects to any device that can be assigned a TCP/IP address. In the next section, I will step you through creating a print queue on a Windows 2000 Server for such a printer.

Creating a Print Queue for a TCP/IP Printer

You can start the process to create a print queue on your server through the Windows 2000 Configure Your Server program. To create a print queue, do the following:

1. From the Windows 2000 Configure Your Server program, select Print Server.

2. From the Print Server dialog box, choose Start the Add Printer Wizard.

3. The Welcome screen for Add Printer Wizard displays. Click the Next button.

Plug-and-Play Printer Alert!

Do not allow the wizard to automatically detect a plug-and-play printer! Chances are it will not find the printer, and if it does, it might not be the correct printer anyhow. Click the Next button.

---

4. On the Local or Network Printer dialog box, select Local Printer.

5. On the Select a Printer Port dialog box, shown in Figure 7.13, choose Create a New Port. This drop-down box will give you the option to select Standard TCP/IP Port. Select that, and then click the Next button. This starts the Add Standard TCP/IP Printer Port Wizard.

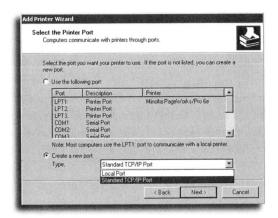

FIGURE 7.13
Select the printer port.

6. Click the Next button to start the Add Standard TCP/IP Printer Port Wizard.

7. The Add Port dialog box, shown in Figure 7.14, prompts you to enter a printer name or IP address for the printer. Click the Next button when you are finished.

Determining the printer's TCP/IP address

If your printer automatically uses DHCP, you can check the DHCP Console to see what address the printer has taken. You can also print a printer test page that should identify the address for the printer. Some printers need to have their IP address set manually. Check the printer manufacturer or print server manual to find out how to set the IP address. After you have entered the IP address, you will see that a port name is automatically generated. You can change this port name to something more descriptive if you want. I have chosen to leave it as is.

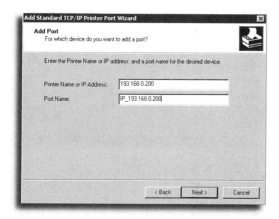

FIGURE 7.14
You need the printer name or IP address to add the port.

8. Select the appropriate device type from the Additional Port Information Required dialog box's Device Type drop-down box. (See Figure 7.15.) If the list does not specify the type of print server you have, click Custom and adjust the settings. The print server manufacturer should provide these settings to you. Click the Next button to continue.

9. The confirmation dialog box, shown in Figure 7.16, will be displayed with a summary of the information that you have provided the wizard. If the information looks correct, click the Finish button to finish creating the print queue.

10. Next, the Add Printer Wizard needs to know what type of printer you are installing, as you can see in Figure 7.17. If your manufacturer has provided a drivers disk or CD-ROM, click the Have Disk button. Click the Next button when you are ready to proceed.

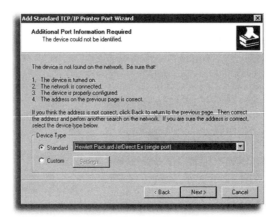

FIGURE 7.15
The port needs additional definition unless it is automatically detected.

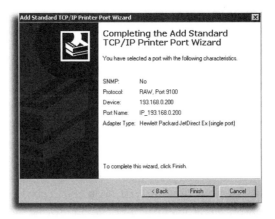

FIGURE 7.16
The Printer Wizard shows you the story so far.

Can't find your printer?

If you cannot find your printer in the list of manufacturers and models, you might want to try the Windows Update button. This feature connects you to Microsoft's Web site and updates the printer lists with any print drivers that have been made available to Microsoft since the release of Windows 2000 Server.

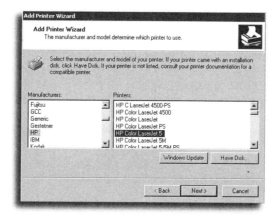

FIGURE 7.17
Define the type of printer you want to install.

11. Now, you need to supply Windows 2000 Server with a name for your printer. (See Figure 7.18.) By default, the Add Printer Wizard supplies a name for your printer. Click Next when you are finished with this dialog box.

Assigning a Default Printer

You can choose to make a particular printer the default for the server. This only assigns the printer as default if you are printing from the server; it will not affect clients on the network.

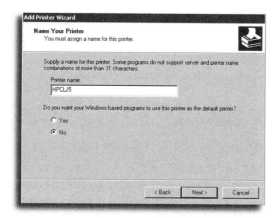

FIGURE 7.18
The printer name should be short but descriptive.

12. The Printer Sharing dialog box lets you make the printer available to the network. Because that was the whole point of getting this print queue installed, click the radio button that is labeled Share As and enter a name that you want network clients to see. Keep it short and sweet, but make it descriptive at the same time. Click Next to move forward.

13. The Location and Comment dialog box, shown in Figure 7.19, lets you enter informational text for the print queue. Click the Next button to move on.

Searching the Active Directory for the right printer

Because the Active Directory schema allows clients to search the network for objects by using keywords, what you enter in the Location and Comment fields might prove to be helpful. Notice that I used the word *color* in the comment. This allows the printer to be found using that keyword. Other attributes for the printer, as defined by the printer driver, allow network clients to easily find a printer on their network that has the capabilities that they are looking for. Whether or not they have permission to use the printer is something else, but I'll cover that later in this chapter.

FIGURE 7.19
The Active Directory schema will retain these entries.

14. The Print Test Page dialog box allows you to test this connection and the printer driver that you installed. I suggest that you choose to run this test now, before your network clients try printing to the queue. Once more, click the Next button.

15. Now you have successfully completed the Add Printer Wizard. Check out the information that the confirmation dialog box, shown in Figure 7.20, shows you. If it looks right to you, click the Finish button to exit the wizard.

FIGURE 7.20
Inspect the information the confirmation screen shows you before you click Finish.

SEE ALSO
➤ *For more information on the DHCP service, see page 390.*
➤ *More detailed information on the TCP/IP protocol can be found in Chapter 9, page 193.*

Creating a Print Queue from a Local Printer

The process for creating a print queue for a local printer is almost the same as the earlier steps; however, in Step 5 you should choose Use the Following Port and select the appropriate port. Click the Next button, and then you can skip to Step 9.

Creating a Print Queue on the Server from a Shared Printer

A printer that is being shared by a workstation can also be shared as a printer object belonging to a server. To add a shared printer as a printer object on the server, do the following:

1. From the Windows 2000 Configure Your Server program, select Print Server.
2. From the Print Server dialog box, choose to Start the Add Printer Wizard.
3. The Welcome screen for Add Printer Wizard appears. Click the Next button.

4. On the Local or Network Printer dialog box, select Network Printer.

5. On the Locate Your Printer dialog box, shown in Figure 7.21, the first option brings up the Active Directory and gives you search capabilities to find another printer object that is stored in the Directory. The second option allows you to specify a printer name, or you can leave this field blank. Click the Next button and you will get a Browse For Printer dialog box to drill down into. The third option is to enter a URL for a printer defined to your intranet or on the Internet. If the printer you choose to add is on Windows NT or Windows 2000 you will not be required to identify the type of printer it is (Step 7) because the drivers will automatically be installed for you.

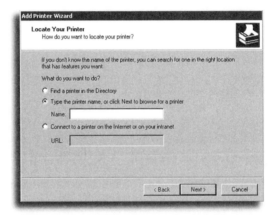

FIGURE 7.21
The Locate Your Printer dialog box.

6. The confirmation dialog box will be displayed with a summary of the information that you have provided the wizard. If the information looks correct, click the Finish button to finish creating the print queue.

7. Next, the Add Printer Wizard needs to know what type of printer you are installing. If your manufacturer has provided a drivers disk or CD-ROM, click the Have Disk button. Click the Next button when you are ready to proceed.

8. Now, you need to supply Windows 2000 Server with a name for your printer. By default, the Add Printer Wizard supplies a name for your printer. Click Next when you are finished with this dialog box.

9. The Printer Sharing dialog box lets you make the printer available to the network. Because that was the whole point of getting this print queue installed,

click the radio button that is labeled Share As and enter a name that you want network clients to see. Keep it short and sweet, but it should be descriptive at the same time. Click Next to move forward.

10. The Location and Comment dialog box lets you enter informational text for the print queue. Click the Next button to move on.

11. The print Test Page dialog box will allow you to test this connection and the printer driver that was installed. I suggest that you choose to run this test now, before your network clients try printing to the queue. Once more click the Next button.

And now you have successfully added a printer object for the shared printer.

Configuring the Permissions for the Print Queue

By default, when you create a printer object, the Everyone group has permission to access this object. If you want to limit the availability of the printer to certain users, do the following:

1. From the Windows 2000 Configure Your Server program, on the Print Server page, click Manage Printers.

2. The Printers page displays icons for each installed printer on your server. Highlight the printer that you want to manage. Notice how a status for the printer is displayed on the left of the dialog box.

3. Bring up the context menu for the printer and select Properties.

4. The Printer Properties dialog box, shown in Figure 7.22, displays the information that you provided when you set up the print queue. Note that you can change the name of the printer from this General tab. Changing the name of the printer here does not affect the name that you gave the printer for sharing purposes.

5. Click the Sharing tab to display the printer's share name, which you can modify if needed.

Hiding the shared printer in the Directory

On the Sharing panel, you can also choose to not display the shared printer in the Directory. You might want to do this if you only want certain clients to know about this printer. By not listing it in the Directory, a client won't be able to select it from a list, although they will be able to attach to the printer by manually typing in the name of the printer.

FIGURE 7.22
The Properties dialog box for a printer object offers multiple tabs of information and configuration options.

Installing additional drivers

When you installed your printer, the Windows NT/Windows 2000 drivers were placed on the server for network clients that are also running Windows NT or Windows 2000. If you want to install drivers for other Windows platforms, click the Additional Drivers button, which displays the Additional Drivers dialog box. It is here that you can check the box next to the platform for which you want to store printer drivers onto the server. Click the OK button, and you will be prompted for the location of the respective drivers. When you are finished, click the OK button.

6. The Security tab is available for all print queues you set up on your server. Figure 7.23 shows you the default security settings for a print queue. For my example, I am going to first remove the Everyone group, because I am going to want to specify specific users for this printer. So, click the Add button to display the Select Users, Computers, or Groups dialog box shown in Figure 7.24.

Create a group for each print queue

In my example I selected a number of network clients that will be able to use this printer. I could have first created a group called Color LaserJet Users, added these clients to that group, and then assigned the group permission to the printer. This way I can add users, computers, or other groups to the Color LaserJet Users group to give them permission to use that printer.

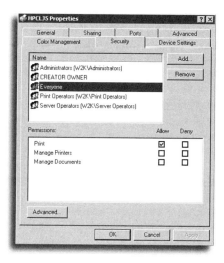

FIGURE 7.23
Security settings for a print queue.

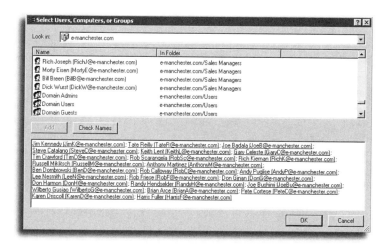

FIGURE 7.24
Select users, computers, or groups to use the print queue.

7. Select the users, computers, or groups that you want to give access to the printer. Click OK to complete the process of setting up print queues on your server.

Networking with Windows 2000

Understanding network protocols ●

Understanding routing protocols ●

Understanding additional network
services ●

Understanding Network Protocols

The odds are pretty good that if you have purchased a copy of Windows 2000 Server, you are going to be connecting it to a network. With Windows 2000, you can use a variety of different protocols, services, and clients to connect and communicate over the network with Windows 2000.

The AppleTalk Protocol

This protocol is used by Windows 2000's Services for the Macintosh. This protocol is required if you want to provide AppleShare-compatible directory authentication and file and printer sharing using Apple's AppleTalk protocol. AppleTalk, taken in the larger context of networking, is an inexpensive local area network (LAN) architecture built into all Apple Macintosh computers and laser printers. Using broadcast-style addressing, AppleTalk is one of the simplest of all network protocols and allows for the Plug and Play network functionality for Apple products. This Plug and Play functionality is not without cost. AppleTalk adds a significant amount of overhead, similar to Microsoft's NetBEUI protocol.

AppleTalk supports Apple's LocalTalk cabling scheme, as well as Ethernet and IBM Token-Ring. It can connect Macintosh computers and printers and even PCs, if they are equipped with special AppleTalk hardware and software. Applications can use AppleTalk protocols across a variety of networks, including LocalTalk, TokenTalk (AppleTalk over Token-Ring), EtherTalk (AppleTalk over Ethernet), and FDDITalk (AppleTalk over FDDI) networks.

The Data Link Control (DLC) Protocol

DLC enables a computer to communicate with other computers, such as IBM mainframes, that use the DLC protocol. Another example of DLC usage are network printing devices. Although TCP/IP printing is rapidly becoming the standard for printers, legacy DLC print devices might still be on your network. Installing this protocol will allow you to set up print queues for DLC-only printers. DLC is slowly becoming an obsolete protocol for microcomputer-only networks.

The NetBEUI (NetBIOS Enhanced User Interface) Protocol

This protocol is also called the NetBIOS Frame (NBF) protocol because it was designed as a basic network protocol that could service NetBIOS network clients. NetBEUI requires no configuration and is fast and efficient. So why not use NetBEUI on every network?

The chief reason is that NetBEUI messages don't include network numbers, which are used to identify network destinations on routed networks. Consequently, it is impossible to route NetBEUI messages through an internetwork, preventing you from constructing NetBEUI networks that have more than a couple hundred computers, all of which must be at the same location. You can't use NetBEUI to build a network that includes a WAN link.

At this stage of computer networking, the NetBEUI protocol is all but dead. The only time you might need to use it is for backward compatibility, but the chances of this happening are very slim because all networking nowadays takes advantage of TCP/IP services.

The IPX/SPX (NWLink) Protocol

NWLink IPX/SPX Compatible Transport is Microsoft's NDIS-compliant version of Novell's IPX protocol. *Internetwork Packet Exchange/Sequenced Packet Exchange (IPX/SPX)* is primarily used for Novell NetWare networks. MS-DOS, OS/2, and all versions of Novell NetWare support communications using IPX/SPX. All versions of Windows also support it. IPX is a connectionless protocol with no guaranteed packet delivery. SPX guarantees delivery through a connection-oriented service. NWLink is a robust, powerful protocol that remains easy to configure. Not much more difficult to configure than NetBEUI, NWLink is routable, allowing you to build internetworks consisting of multiple LAN and WAN elements.

It is important to note that NWLink doesn't enable a Windows 2000 computer to access resources on a Novell NetWare server without other services installed. Microsoft includes Gateway Services for NetWare with Windows 2000 to accomplish this.

SEE ALSO

➤ *For more information on installing Gateway Services for NetWare, see page 301.*

The Streams Protocol

Streams was originally used as a UNIX protocol. It makes it possible for different modules to provide separate interfaces for upstream and downstream traffic. The Streams environment allows the many Streams-based transport protocol drivers that already exist to be plugged in to Windows 2000 with little or no modification. New transport protocol drivers, however, should be written to the newer, more versatile Transport Driver Interface. The OSI-LAN Protocol, which includes the OSI Transport and Network layer drivers, will also be installed if you require the Streams Environment.

TCP/IP

Transmission Control Protocol/Internet Protocol, or TCP/IP is a suite of protocols that includes several service subprotocols, such as FTP, TCP, IP, and UDP (User Datagram Protocol). FTP is a file transfer protocol. TCP is a connection-oriented transport protocol that guarantees delivery. IP is a network layer protocol used to resolve network addresses and negotiate the delivery of messages. It was designed by the U.S. Department of Defense for use during wartime. Soon several major research institutes began developing TCP/IP and it quickly grew. Today it is the most widely used protocol in the world. UDP is a connectionless transport protocol that does not guarantee delivery.

SEE ALSO

➤ *For more information on TCP/IP, see Chapter 9, page 193.*

Understanding Routing Protocols

If you have worked on a computer network or have connected to the Internet, you are probably familiar with the concept of a router. A router is the "traffic cop" for ensuring that your data gets to the proper place after it leaves your network. If you need to send an email message to your friend in California, the data that makes up that message must traverse a number of routers in order to reach your friend. This is true for any data with the exception of data destined for the same network as the one you are connected to. What does this mean to you, the Windows 2000 administrator? Plenty. Your Windows 2000 server can act as a router. Whenever I discuss routers, I mean not only the specialized hardware routers used in large enterprise networks, but also the Windows 2000 server you might be using to route between buildings at your office.

By default, any given router knows only about networks to which it is physically attached. However, you can configure a router to learn about networks that it is not connected to, through either manual configuration or automatic (dynamic) configuration. *Static routers* have all their information about other network entered manually. *Dynamic routers*, on the other hand, use routing protocols that allow routers on the network to share information about routes, as long as they use the same routing protocol. I'll discuss both types in the following sections.

First, I'll look at the most common form of routing: static routing.

Static Routing

Because static routing is a manual process, it should be avoided in all but the simplest of networks. Let's look at a couple of examples to illustrate this process. Say you have three networks, A, B, and C, shown in Figure 8.1, connected by two Windows 2000 servers.

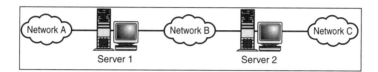

FIGURE 8.1
A simple network suitable for static routing.

Example 1

In this case, a workstation on Network A needs to send a packet to a workstation on Network B. It knows that the destination workstation is not on its own network, so it sends it to Server 1. Because Server 1 is connected to both Network A and Network B, it knows to send the packet to the workstation on Network B.

Example 2

In this case, the workstation on Network A needs to send a packet to a workstation on Network C. Again it knows the destination workstation is not on the local network, so it sends the packet to Server 1. But in this example Server 1 is not connected to Network C, so it doesn't know what to do with the packet, and drops it, unless you tell Server 1 that the route to Network C is through Server 2. In a static environment, you manually tell the router that for traffic destined for Network C, the packets need to be sent to Server 2.

In order to use static routes as shown in Example 2, you need to use the use the ROUTE command.

Using the *ROUTE* Command

The ROUTE command has a number of switches that can be used to statically manage a route table. Up to this point, the ROUTE PRINT command is the only parameter that you have seen. To manage a route table, however, an administrator must be able to add, delete, change, and clear route table entries. Each of these options is available and I discuss them in this section.

The following syntax manipulates network routing tables:

```
ROUTE [-f] [-p] [command [destination]
                [MASK netmask]  [gateway] [METRIC metric]  [IF interface]
```

-f	Clears the routing tables of all gateway entries. If this is used in conjunction with one of the commands, the tables are cleared prior to running the command.
-p	When used with the ADD command, this switch makes a route persistent across boots of the system. By default, routes are not preserved when the system is restarted. Ignored for all other commands, which always affect the appropriate persistent routes. This option is unsupported in Windows 95.
command	One of these:

	PRINT	Prints a route.
	ADD	Adds a route.
	DELETE	Deletes a route.
	CHANGE	Modifies an existing route.

Destination	Specifies the host.
MASK	Specifies that the next parameter is the netmask value.
netmask	Specifies a subnet mask value for this route entry. If not specified, it defaults to 255.255.255.255.
gateway	Specifies a gateway.
interface	The interface number for the specified route.
METRIC	Specifies the metric—that is, cost for the destination.

All symbolic names used for destination are looked up in the network database file NETWORKS. The symbolic names for gateway are looked up in the host name database file HOSTS.

If the command is PRINT or DELETE, destination or gateway can be a wildcard (a wildcard is specified as an asterisk, *), or the gateway argument can be omitted.

If destination contains a * or ?, it is treated as a shell pattern, and only matching destination routes are printed. The * matches any string, and ? matches any one character—for example, 157.*.1, 157.*, 127.*, 224*.

Diagnostic Notes

Invalid MASK generates an error, that is when (Destination & Mask) != DEST.

For example,

```
route ADD 157.0.0.0 MASK 155.0.0.0 157.55.80.1 IF 1
```

The route addition failed: The specified mask parameter is invalid.

```
(Destination & Mask) != Destination.
```

For example,

```
> route PRINT
> route ADD 157.0.0.0 MASK 255.0.0.0 157.55.80.1 METRIC 3 IF 2
destination^ ^mask ^gateway metric^ ^
Interface^
```

If IF is not given, it tries to find the best interface for a given gateway.

```
> route PRINT
> route PRINT 157* .... Only prints those matching 157*
> route DELETE 157.0.0.0
> route PRINT
```

Notice that the -p (persistent) parameter is required to maintain entries after a reboot because the entries in the routing table are normally kept only in memory and are lost if you need to restart your system. The persistent entry switch writes route entries into the Registry so that they become permanent.

Viewing the Routing Table

As you saw in the previous section, you can view the routing table of a Windows NT system using either the NETSTAT -r utility or the ROUTE command. To view the route table using the ROUTE command, type ROUTE PRINT. This provides a display similar to the one shown here:

```
===========================================================
Interface List
0x1 ......................... MS TCP Loopback interface
0x2 ...00 60 08 ea 2e b7 ...... EL574ND4 Ethernet Adapter
===========================================================
===========================================================
```

```
Active Routes:
Network Destination          Netmask         Gateway       Interface Metric
            0.0.0.0          0.0.0.0   10.226.10.185   10.226.10.188       1
      10.226.10.184  255.255.255.248   10.226.10.188   10.226.10.188       1
      10.226.10.188  255.255.255.255       127.0.0.1       127.0.0.1       1
     10.255.255.255  255.255.255.255   10.226.10.188   10.226.10.188       1
          127.0.0.0        255.0.0.0       127.0.0.1       127.0.0.1       1
          224.0.0.0        224.0.0.0   10.226.10.188   10.226.10.188       1
    255.255.255.255  255.255.255.255   10.226.10.188   10.226.10.188       1
Default Gateway:       10.226.10.185
===================================================================
Persistent Routes:
  None
```

Following is an explanation of each:

- 0.0.0.0. If a default gateway is specified, this entry identifies its IP address (10.226.10.185).

- Local host (10.226.10.188). This is the IP address of the host in the example.

- Local network (10.226.10.184). This is the address of the local network. It indicates the gateway and interface and the machine's IP address, and it is used whenever a packet needs to be transmitted to a local destination.

- Network broadcast (10.255.255.255). This is a directed broadcast and is treated as a directed packet by routers. Most routers support the transmission of directed broadcasts: They forward them to the defined network, which broadcasts them to all machines on that network. In this case that network is 10.x.x.x.

- 127.0.0.1. This is the local loopback address and is used for diagnosing problems. It is used to make sure that the IP stack on a machine is properly installed and running and appears by default as soon as IP is installed. This is a reserved address and can't be configured.

- 224.0.0.0. This is the default multicast address. If this machine is a member of any multicast groups, this and other multicast entries indicate to IP the interface used to communicate with the multicast network.

- 255.255.255.255. This is a limited broadcast address for broadcasts destined for any machine on the local network. Routers that receive packets destined for this address can listen to the packet as a normal host, but they do not support transmission of these types of broadcasts to other networks.

- `Default Gateway`. Indicates the configured default gateway (router) the system uses for data destined for other networks.

- `Persistent Routes`. This section indicates any static routes that have been added using the `ROUTE` command with the `-p` (persistent) flag.

Dynamic Routing

The discussion to this point has focused on how to manually edit the route table to notify routers of the existence of networks they are not physically connected to. This would be an enormously difficult task on large networks, where routes and networks can change on a frequent basis. Forget about building any resiliency into the network. If you were to lose a router you would have to manually reconfigure the rest of the network to route around the problem. Imagine trying that on the Internet!

Fortunately, there are routing protocols available that allow routers to "learn" where to send data destined for distant networks. These protocols can be used to notify other routers (assuming the other routers are using the same protocol) about the networks they are attached to and any changes that occur due to outages. A properly designed network can actually route around problems if the routing protocols are set up correctly. Two of the most common protocols used are RIP and OSPF.

RIP

RIP (Routing Information Protocol) is a protocol defined by RFC 1058 that specifies how routers exchange routing table information. With RIP, routers periodically exchange their entire routing tables. This can lead to problems: By default, RIP routers exchange routing information every 30 seconds. The RIP broadcasts, which are sent out on all the routers' interfaces, can report a maximum of 25 entries per RIP message. That means that in a larger network there will be many broadcasts, to the point where the network might never be completely synchronized. So in addition to adding overhead to the network, it's possible in certain situations that even with dynamic routing, a router failure might not be recoverable, if enough routers are out of sync. RIP is also famous for causing RIP broadcast storm, where so much routing information is being broadcast that network performance can be impacted. In addition, any networks more than 15 routers distant are considered unreachable. This limits RIP's utility to small to medium networks.

OSPF

OSPF (Open Shortest Path First) Version 2 is defined in RFC 1583. OSPF is a routing protocol developed for IP networks based on the shortest path first or link-state algorithm. Routers use link-state algorithms to send routing information to all routers on an internetwork by calculating the shortest path to each node based on a map of the network constructed by each node. Each router sends the portion of the routing table that describes the state of its own links (hence "link-state algorithm"), and it also sends the complete routing map. This is far more efficient than RIP, which sends the entire table, and doesn't include link-state information. The advantage of OSPF is that routing updates are smaller and are sent more frequently. This means that in the event of an outage, OSPF will converge (learn new routes) quickly, yielding a more stable, resilient network than the equivalent RIP network. There is a downside to this, however: OSPF uses much greater router resources (CPU and memory) than RIP. Most people consider this an acceptable tradeoff.

IPX Routing

IPX routing can get a little confusing, if only because it also uses RIP, which is a distance vector protocol that servers and routers have traditionally used to propagate and exchange routing information. RIP for IPX is a routing protocol used in many IPX internetworks and is fully supported by Windows 2000. IPX routers use RIP to exchange routing information with neighboring routers on an IPX internetwork. As a router becomes aware of changes in the internetwork, it broadcasts this information immediately to neighboring routers. This mechanism is identical to its TCP/IP counterpart, although addressing is very different.

A newer protocol developed by Novell, NLSP (NetWare Link Services Protocol) is IPX's answer to OSPF. Although not supported by Windows 2000, it is replacing RIP for IPX in a lot of networks, particularly large internetworks.

Network Services

A number of network services available for Windows 2000 are discussed in greater detail in other sections of the book. I discuss them here just to introduce you to them and to direct you to the correct section of the book to find more information.

Domain Name Service

DNS (Domain Name Service) is used on the Internet for resolving fully distinguished domain names to IP addresses. For example, say you want to order a copy of this book to give to your best friend at the office. You need to go out to the Macmillan USA Web site and order it. Which do you think is easier to remember? http://www.mcp.com or http://209.17.55.123. Most people would say http://www.mcp.com, and the Internet community recognized this as they were building the original architecture. And DNS was born. DNS is a hierarchical database containing names and addresses for IP networks and hosts and is used almost universally to provide name resolution. In addition, DNS is now required for all Active Directory Services naming.

SEE ALSO

➤ *For more information on Active Directory Services, see page 26.*

➤ *For more information on DNS, see page 409.*

Dynamic Host Control Protocol

Dynamic Host Control Protocol (DHCP) is the successor to the BOOTP protocol. BOOTP was the first protocol in the TCP/IP suite that allowed a central server to dynamically allocate IP addresses on a network. Although it worked, there were some limitations. DHCP defines a method for dynamically allocating IP addresses on a network segment, while addressing the shortcomings of the BOOTP protocol. Now why would you use DHCP? Let's look at a scenario that explores those uses. You have decided to add TCP/IP to your network and you have 250 end users. Your objective is to get a unique IP address assigned to each workstation. Now you can go to each workstation and manually assign an IP address, and then come up with a spreadsheet or database to track what IPs have been assigned, and what's available, as well as to track who is using that address, in case there's a problem. Keep in mind you will need to set the mask, gateway, and DNS information on each machine as well. Or you could configure each machine to use DHCP for addressing, and set the subnet mask, gateway, and DNS information on the DHCP server instead. Then when TCP/IP is installed on each workstation, you'll just select Use DHCP, and when the system reboots, it's on the network with valid addressing and network information.

SEE ALSO

➤ *For more information on DHCP, see page 389 (Using DHCP Server, Chapter 14)*

SAP Agent

The SAP (Service Access Protocol) Agent is used in conjunction with Gateway Services for NetWare and the NWLink protocol to send service information through the IPX protocol. SAP is used to identify file servers, printers, and numerous other IPX-based services on an IPX network.

File and Print Sharing for Microsoft Networks

This service allows your Windows 2000 server to share files, directories and printers to workstations and servers on the network through TCP/IP, NWLink, or NetBEUI.

SEE ALSO

➤ *For more information on file sharing, see page 154. (File Sharing Basics, Chapter 7)*

Network Load Balancing

This service provides TCP/IP load balancing functionality to Windows 2000. This is a new feature for the Windows product family and is beyond the scope of this book.

QoS Packet Scheduler

Another new feature to the Windows product family, the QoS Packet Scheduler, allows you to ensure Quality of Service for network traffic passing the Windows 2000 server. This is also beyond the scope of this book.

Introduction to TCP/IP

Microsoft's TCP/IP architecture ●

How computer addresses are assigned ●

How computer names work on
Microsoft TCP/IP networks ●

How computer names are managed on
the Internet ●

How TCP/IP handles routing ●

Virtual private networking ●

Essential TCP/IP Concepts

TCP/IP is the common language of the network world. These days, when computers need to talk to computers, it's a safe assumption that they will communicate using TCP/IP.

The TCP/IP protocols did not always display the exalted and omnipresent aura they show today. In the 1980s, TCP/IP was considered by many to be a nonstandard set of informal protocols that were found primarily in the esoteric realm of the Internet, an environment frequented by educators, computer wizards, and defense contractors. International standards bodies were developing official protocols that were expected to put TCP/IP out to pasture before too long.

Today, however, TCP/IP has become the dominant network protocol suite with hardly a viable competitor in sight, the international effort to establish competing protocols having died a quiet death. The difference has been the stodginess of the international standards process versus the vitality of the Internet. Indeed, the success of TCP/IP is a market-driven phenomenon, propelled by consumer demand and the desire to make a buck.

TCP/IP has become so dominant that sooner or later your network is going to need to talk TCP/IP, because sooner or later it is going to need to talk to another network—the Internet or some other—that talks only TCP/IP. That's good and bad; it's good because TCP/IP is an excellent protocol suite, offering good performance and use of network bandwidth. It's bad because until you are used to it, TCP/IP is a lot of trouble to set up and manage.

Until this chapter, you have been working in a Plug-and-Play world where network protocols are concerned. NetBEUI requires no configuration at all, whereas NWLink must be configured only when routing is required. There is so much to configuring TCP/IP, on the other hand, that you need a chapter of background information before you can even begin to set up TCP/IP on a network.

My intention is to keep things as simple and practical as possible. I'll have to give you some theory, but it will be theory that you will immediately put into practice, not theory that you will put into practice "someday."

Microsoft's TCP/IP Architecture

Microsoft has always had a somewhat unique way of organizing protocol suites. The architecture has been organized around two key requirements:

- The need to support TCP/IP alongside NWLink and NetBEUI
- The need to support NetBIOS applications in the TCP/IP environment

Figure 9.1 shows how the pieces of the Microsoft network architecture fit together.

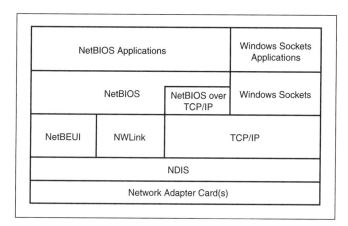

FIGURE 9.1
Microsoft's network protocol architecture.

With the release of Windows 2000 Server, Microsoft has embraced a TCP/IP that does not require NetBIOS. However, this "native" mode for Windows 2000 Server can be used only if there are no legacy applications or clients that still require the NetBIOS layer.

One component of the network protocol architecture is NDIS, the Network Driver Interface Specification, which lets any network protocol communicate with any network adapter. NDIS lets all Windows 2000 protocols communicate through a single network adapter should the need arise.

Microsoft provides application programming interfaces (APIs) that developers use to adapt their programs to the network environment. Notice that Microsoft's architecture supports two APIs:

- NetBIOS is the Network Basic Input/Output System, a fairly old API that has long been the primary API for applications running on Microsoft networks. Most older applications written to network on Microsoft networks have been written to the NetBIOS API.

- Windows Sockets (WinSock) is Microsoft's implementation of the sockets API that has become the primary API for TCP/IP applications. The applications you think of as Internet applications, such as Web browsers and FTP clients, are written for the Windows Sockets interface.

But that leaves a hole. What if I want to run only TCP/IP protocols on my network, but I don't want to abandon my venerable NetBIOS applications? Well, Microsoft has an answer for that as well, called *NetBIOS over TCP/IP* (*NetBT* or *NBT* for short). Thanks to NetBT, any Windows application can network over TCP/IP with no adaptation whatsoever.

Computer Addressing on TCP/IP Networks

TCP/IP predates just about all other networking standards that remain in common use. When the Internet was still a project of the United States Department of Defense and was named ARPAnet (for Advanced Research Projects Agency Network), the idea of a global network that embraced many different brands of computers was as exotic as interstellar travel. No one had formed even a fuzzy vision of how such a network might be implemented. So, the gurus had complete freedom to design a network solution. But freedom brings with it the opportunity to be unique, and some technologies on the Internet are definitely unique.

One unique characteristic of the Internet is the way computers are identified. The designers of the Internet protocols wanted an identification scheme that was independent of any one computer or network equipment design. So they established a scheme of IP addresses. (IP, or Internet Protocol, is one of the two most prominent TCP/IP protocols and is the protocol in the TCP/IP protocol suite that is most intimately concerned with addressing.)

You've almost certainly seen IP addresses—numbers such as 192.168.153.80—while surfing the Web. As you administer TCP/IP on your network, a considerable part of your time will be devoted to IP address assignment, because IP addresses don't just happen. They have to be entered manually into the configuration of each TCP/IP computer on your network. When a computer is added to your network, it needs an IP address. When it moves, it probably needs a new IP address.

So you have to understand how IP addresses work. Unfortunately, IP address rules are a bit subtle, and errors are common. I will hazard a guess that IP address misconfiguration will be the most common cause of difficulty you will experience with TCP/IP networking.

IP Addresses and Dotted-Decimal Notation

An IP address is really a pretty simple thing. It is a 32-bit binary like the following:

11001101101101110010001001101110

Did I say simple? How would you like to remember a few dozen of those? Well, even network gurus blanch at the thought of committing 32-bit numbers to memory, so they devised a system that codes IP addresses in more familiar binary numbers.

To display an IP address in decimal form, the first step is to break the binary address into four eight-bit fields, like this:

11001101 10110111 00100010 01101110

Each of these eight-bit fields—they're usually called octets, incidentally—can be represented by a decimal number in the range of 0 through 255. If you're not comfortable with number conversions, take a look at Figure 9.2. Notice that each digit position corresponds to a power of 2. For example, the third digit from the right corresponds to 22, or 4.

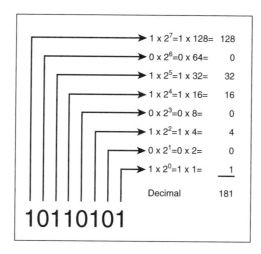

FIGURE 9.2
Converting an eight-bit binary number to decimal.

To convert a binary number to decimal, examine each bit position. If the bit is a 1, the corresponding decimal number is included in the decimal total. If the bit is a 0, that bit does not affect the decimal total. Add up the decimal values corresponding to each 1 bit and you arrive at the decimal equivalent of the eight-bit binary number.

Fortunately, you don't need to convert more than eight bits, because IP addresses are commonly represented in dotted-decimal notation where a decimal number represents each eight-bit group. Figure 9.3 shows an example.

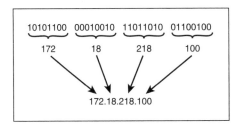

FIGURE 9.3
Converting an IP address to dotted-decimal notation.

Isn't that simple? Well, perhaps not. At least not simple enough to make the head math easy for most of us. Fortunately, Windows includes a shortcut. The Windows Calculator applet has a scientific mode that includes number base conversion functions. Figure 9.4 shows Calculator after it has been placed in scientific mode.

FIGURE 9.4
Converting numbers using Calculator.

To convert a number to another base, do the following:

1. Open the Calculator applet and choose Scientific from the View menu.
2. Select the radio button that matches the base of the number you want to convert (Hexadecimal, Decimal, Octal, or Binary).

3. Enter the number to be converted. (You can paste a number you have copied from another application.)

4. Select the radio button that matches the base you want to convert to (Hexadecimal, Decimal, Octal, or Binary). The result is displayed in the number entry field. (You can copy the results from Calculator and paste them elsewhere if you want.)

Although users see dotted-decimal addresses if they see addresses at all, as an administrator you must be aware of the binary equivalents of IP addresses. This is particularly the case when you get involved with subnet addressing, where the binary bit patterns are crucial information.

Address Classes

Each host on a TCP/IP network—*host* is another term for a device that is attached to a TCP/IP network—must have a unique IP address that distinguishes it from all other hosts on that network. That means that every host that can communicate with the Internet must have an IP address that is unique on the entire Internet.

Actually, a host's IP address contains two pieces of information:

- *netid* is the network to which the host is attached.
- *hostid* is the host's unique ID on its network.

Because the IP address serves two functions, the Internet designers had to decide how many bits of the IP address would serve as the netid and how many bits would serve as the hostid. Did the Internet need a few networks with many hosts per network, or did it need a large number of networks with few hosts per network? Well, the answer was "Both, and we need something in between as well." That answer resulted in the establishment of address classes.

You will encounter three address classes: A, B, and C. Class A defines a few networks, each of which can contain a vast number of hosts. Class C defines many networks, each of which can contain a couple hundred hosts. Class B falls somewhere between A and C.

Figure 9.5 shows how the IP address classes are defined.

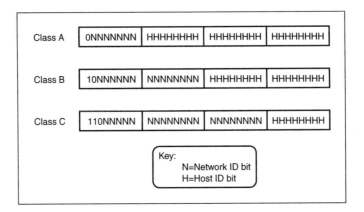

FIGURE 9.5
IP network address classes.

The key differences between the classes are the numbers of bits that are allocated to the netid and hostid portions of the address. Here's how the address classes play out:

- Class A addresses have eight bits in the netid portion and 24 bits in the hostid portion. There are 126 class A networks available, each of which accommodates 16,777,214 hosts. A class A address has a 0 for the initial bit, and the first octet will have a decimal value between 1 and 126. (Networks 0 and 127 have special uses.)

- Class B addresses have 16 bits in the netid portion and 16 bits in the hostid portion. 16,384 class B networks are possible, each supporting 65,534 hosts. A class B address begins with the bits 10, and the value of the first octet falls in the range 128 through 191.

- Class C addresses have 24 bits in the netid portion and eight bits in the hostid portion. Consequently, 2,097,152 class C network addresses are available, each of which can have 254 hosts. A class C address begins with the bits 110, and the value of the first octet falls in the range 192 through 223.

If you take a close look at the bits and try to confirm my totals for netids and hostids, you'll find that the sums aren't what you might expect. That's because some bit patterns aren't available for hosts. Here are some restrictions:

- Address 255 (all 1s in binary) is used to address broadcast messages, which are received by all hosts on a given network. The most common broadcast address is 255.255.255.255, which addresses messages that are to be received by all hosts on the local network.

- The fourth octet cannot be all 1s or all 0s in binary. A hostid that is all 0s refers to this network. So, the IP address 155.38.0.0 refers to the entire network with the netid 155.38. A hostid that is all 1s is a broadcast address, referring to all hosts on a specific network.

- The netid cannot be all 0s because all 0s means "this network." That's why the class A network number 0 is unavailable.

- Netid 127 is a reserved address called the *loopback address*, and is used in testing.

Figure 9.6 shows a network that demonstrates the use of IP addresses. This network consists of four network segments that communicate through routers. Although it is improbable, I have included examples of all three classes of network addresses in the figure. You can freely mix address classes on your networks. The routers will sort things out.

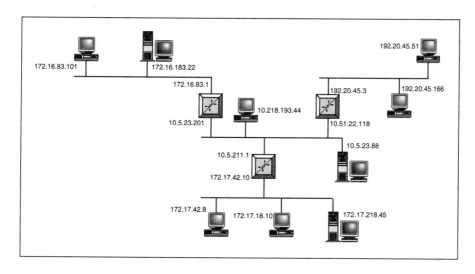

FIGURE 9.6
A TCP/IP network that includes addresses from all IP address classes.

Notice that each network segment is associated with a single netid. All hosts on a given network segment are given IP addresses that share a common netid.

Routers attach to the network as ordinary hosts. A router is assigned an IP address on each network to which it is attached. Actually, and this is an important distinction, the IP address isn't assigned to the router, but to the interface in the router. So, a router has at least two interfaces, each of which is assigned its own IP address.

Networks 172.16.0.0 and 172.17.0.0 were included to illustrate how class B and C netids work. Even though both networks have 172 as the first octet of their IP addresses, these are class B networks (first octet 128 through 192). Therefore, the netid is defined by two octets, and 155.38.0.0 and 155.39.0.0 function as separate network segments. Because a class C netid is defined by three octets, any differences in the first three octets of a class C address refer to different networks.

IP Address Assignment

If you are running a private TCP/IP network, you can choose any IP addresses you want for your hosts. If, on the other hand, your network will be connecting to the Internet, you must use assigned IP addresses that don't conflict with anyone else.

Until fairly recently, organizations requested IP addresses directly from the Internet Network Information Center (InterNIC), but that seldom happens these days because the Internet has simply grown too big for a single point of contact to handle the demand for access. The current practice for most organizations wanting to connect to the Internet is to obtain access from an Internet service provider (ISP) that provides an Internet hookup (for a fee, of course) and assigns a block of IP addresses. The InterNIC has actually been replaced by the Internet Assigned Numbers Authority (IANA), which prefers to work with a relatively few ISPs, assigning them blocks of addresses that they in turn allocate to their customers.

You can no longer obtain a class A or B address. In fact, class C addresses are scarce. Your ISP probably won't assign you a complete class C address unless you really need it. You might be given use of a portion of a class C address. Okay, so how do you use part of an address range? Thanks for asking, because the technique for subdividing address ranges is my next topic.

Subnet Addressing

As you might suspect, a class A or B address is a pretty big thing. It is difficult to imagine a network with 16 million hosts—or even 65,000 hosts—and not a single router, but that is what it would take to use up a class A or B address.

After it had an address space, the Internet community discovered that many of the IP address ranges were too large. A way was needed to subdivide the addresses so that portions of the address space could be allocated to multiple network segments. The mechanism designers arrived at is called subnet addressing.

We come now to one of the most challenging topics in this book. Many TCP/IP newbies find subnet addressing the highest hurdle they must clear, so don't be surprised if you find this material difficult. Just hang in there, and I'll make sure you get a grasp of the concept.

Subnet addressing is a method for "borrowing" bits from the hostid portion of an IP address so that the bits can be applied to the network ID.

Subnetting a Class B Address

Suppose that you have been assigned the Class B address 172.16.0.0. You need to create four separate networks from your one IP address range. The technique is to borrow three bits from the hostid field. These three bits let you configure six separate subnets. (Why not eight? I'll tell you later.)

To see how subnet addressing works, let's first convert the IP address to binary form:

```
10101100 00010000 00000000 00000000
```

Remember, in a class B address, the first 16 bits are the netid and the last 16 bits are the hostid.

To indicate that bits are being borrowed from the hostid, you use a subnet mask, which is also a 32-bit binary number. To make the purpose of the subnet mask clear, you need to examine it beside the binary IP address, like this:

```
10101100 00010000 00000000 00000000
11111111 11111111 11100000 00000000
```

The rules of subnet masking are extremely simple:

- 1 in the network mask indicates that a bit in the IP address is part of the netid.
- 0 in the network mask indicates that a bit in the IP address is part of the hostid.

Because there are 19 bits in the network mask, you now have 19 bits to work with in the netid. This lets you generate the following subnetwork IDs (subnetids) from the class B address:

```
10101100 00010000 00100000 00000000
10101100 00010000 01000000 00000000
10101100 00010000 01100000 00000000
10101100 00010000 10000000 00000000
10101100 00010000 10100000 00000000
10101100 00010000 11000000 00000000
```

Why only six subnets? You have to avoid two "forbidden" subnets (000 and 111), which are explained in an upcoming section.

If you do the math to convert the binary addresses to decimal, you find that the subnet mask 255.255.224.0 lets you construct six subnets with the following address ranges:

172.16.32.1 through 172.16.63.254

through 172.16.95.254

through 172.16.19.254

through 172.16.159.254

through 172.16.191.25

172.16.192.1 through 172.16.223.254

The subnet mask actually becomes part of the configuration of each host on the network, enabling the hosts to discriminate netid, subnetid, and hostid.

Let's put subnetting to work. Figure 9.7 shows an example of a network that is entirely based on the IP address 172.16.0.0. To determine what network segment a host is connected to, you must apply the subnet mask to its IP address.

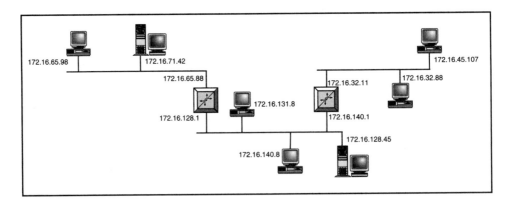

FIGURE 9.7
Subnet addressing with a class B address.

Take host 172.16.89.33, for example. Because this is a class B address, the netid consists of the first two octets and is 172.16. To figure out the subnetid, you need to apply the subnet mask to the third octet, which is binary 1011001. Here's the address octet next to the subnet mask:

```
10110001
```

```
11100000
```

So the subnetid portion is 101 and the hostid portion is 10001.

Which hosts can occupy the same subnet? The third octet for the subnet can have a value between 10100000 and 10111111, or between 160 and 191 decimal. In other words, any host with an IP address between 172.16.160.1 and 172.16.191.254 can be on the same subnet.

Netids, Subnetids, and Routers

To enable two hosts to communicate without a router, four conditions must be met:

- The hosts must be connected to the same network segment
- The host's IP addresses must have the same netid
- The hosts must be configured with the same subnet mask
- The hosts must have the same subnetid

Failing any of these conditions, a router is required to allow the hosts to communicate.

"Forbidden" Subnets

I've alluded a couple of times to the fact that some subnets are not permitted by the Internet standard that defines subnetwork addressing.

The first restriction applies to all TCP/IP implementations: the subnetid cannot consist entirely of 1s because addresses made up entirely of 1s are used to address broadcast messages.

A second restriction is that the subnetid cannot consist entirely of 0s. Actually, there really isn't a good reason to prohibit the all-0s subnet, and avoiding the all-0s subnet wastes valuable address space. So in practice many have chosen to support the all-0s subnets on their products. Windows 2000 permits use of the all-0s subnet, although I have never seen the fact stated in Microsoft documentation.

More Subnet Examples

Because it is so important for you to understand subnet addressing, look at some examples.

Example 1

Problem: For the IP address 10.86.45.3 and subnet mask 255.255.0.0, answer the following questions:

- What is the netid of the IP address?
- What is the subnetid of the IP address?
- What is the hostid of the IP address?
- What host IP addresses permit hosts to communicate directly with this host, assuming all hosts are connected to the same network segment?

Solution: The first step is to determine the class of the IP address. Because the first octet has the value 10, it is a class A address, and the netid consists of the first octet. Therefore, the netid is 10.

The subnet mask reserves 16 bits for the network address. The first eight bits are the netid, so the next eight bits, the entire second octet, make up the subnet ID. Now you know that the subnetid is 86.

The subnet mask leaves 16 bits for host addressing. Consequently, the hostid of this host is 45.3.

This host can communicate with hosts having IP addresses 10.86.0.1 through 10.86.255.254, assuming that all the hosts can communicate without crossing a router.

Example 2

Problem: For the IP address 192.168.45.109 and subnet mask 255.255.255.240, answer the following questions:

- What is the netid of the IP address?
- What is the subnetid of the IP address?
- What is the hostid of the IP address?
- What host IP addresses permit hosts to communicate directly with this host, assuming all hosts are connected to the same network segment?

Solution: Because the first octet has the value 192, this is a class C address, and the netid consists of the first three octets. Therefore, the netid is 192.168.45.

The subnet mask 11110000 reserves four bits for the network address. The fourth octet is 01101101 binary, making the subnetid 0110.

The subnet mask leaves four bits for host addressing. Consequently, the hostid of this host is 1101 decimal.

With this subnet mask, the fourth octet can have binary values 01100000 through 01101111. But a hostid cannot be all 0s or all 1s. Therefore, valid values for the fourth octet are 01100001 through 01101110. Consequently, this host can communicate with hosts having IP addresses 192.168.45.97 through 192.168.45.110, assuming that all the hosts can communicate without crossing a router.

Example 3

Problem: For the IP address 192.168.87.95 and subnet mask 255.255.255.224, answer the following questions:

- What is the netid of the IP address?
- What is the subnetid of the IP address?
- What is the hostid of the IP address?
- What host IP addresses permit hosts to communicate directly with this host, assuming all hosts are connected to the same network segment?

Solution: Because the first octet has the value 192, this is a class C address, and the netid consists of the first three octets. Therefore, the netid is 192.168.87.

The subnet mask 11100000 reserves three bits for the network address. The fourth octet is 01011111 binary, making the subnetid 010.

The subnet mask leaves five bits for host addressing. Consequently, the hostid of this host is 11111 decimal.

Oops, this was a trick question, wasn't it? Given that IP address and subnet mask, the netid is invalid because a netid cannot consist entirely of 1s. Now you can see why it is so important to dig down to the binary bare metal when you assign IP addresses. Unless you do, address errors are inevitable.

Trouble with Subnets

Subnet addressing is one area where network administrators are likely to encounter trouble. Suppose that a subnet contains the following hosts and uses the subnet mask 255.255.234.0:

172.16.161.80

172.16.180.153

172.16.192.209

172.16.177.44

Do you see a problem? Host 172.16.223.153 will be unable to communicate because it has a different subnetid from the other hosts. That isn't extremely obvious until you examine the binary values of the third octets (I've set out the subnet bits in bold type):

10100001

10110100

11000000

10110001

Oh, my! 172.16.192.209 is on another subnet, a fact you could easily miss if you relied on the dotted-decimal addresses.

Default Subnet Masks

A subnet mask is part of every host's configuration. What, even if no subnetting is taking place? Yes, always. When the network address isn't subnetted, the host is configured with a default subnet mask, in which the 1 bits match the standard netid bits for the class of the network class. If the network is using a class A address, for example, the default subnet mask is 255.0.0.0. Here are the default subnet masks:

- Class A: 255.0.0.0
- Class B: 255.255.0.0
- Class C: 255.255.255.0

Subnets: Some Observations

Taking all the rules for subnetting into account, it appears that some subnet masks have more potential than others. After some discussion, I'll give you some tables that make it easy to evaluate the usefulness of various subnet options.

Take the subnet mask 128 (10000000), which in theory ought to permit you to set up two subnets. But one of those subnets would be the all-1s subnet, which is prohibited. So your payoff for giving up a bit of hostid is one subnet, exactly where you started off.

A subnet mask of 196 (11000000) gets you three subnets, not four as you might expect, again because the all-1s subnet isn't permitted. You only get three subnets because Microsoft permits use of the all-0s subnet.

Subnetting a class C address—yes, as small as it is, you might need to subnet a class C address if it is all you've got—has some special concerns because you have so few bits to work with. Suppose you are subnetting a class C address with the subnet mask 255.255.255.248. Here's the binary subnet mask:

11111111 11111111 11111111 11111000

The goal is to create a lot of subnetworks. Although you do in fact make it possible to configure 30 subnets, each subnet accommodates only six hosts! Besides resulting in itty-bitty subnets, you waste a lot of your potential addresses. A class C address can support a maximum of 254 hosts without subnetting. With the subnet mask 255.255.255.248, the same address supports only 180 hosts, 210 if you use the all-0s subnet. It is unfortunate that Internet address space has become so tight that it is necessary to subnet class C addresses, but it is often necessary to do so.

Tables 9.1, 9.2, and 9.3 summarize subnet options for class A, B, and C networks. Some options are marked "invalid" because they don't result in useful subnetwork configurations.

Table 9.1   Class A Subnetting

Subnet Bits	Maximum Subnets	Maximum Number of Hosts Per Subnet	Subnet Mask
0	0	16,777,214	255.0.0.0
1	invalid	invalid	invalid
2	2	4,194,302	255.192.0.0
3	6	2,097,150	255.224.0.0
4	14	1,048,574	255.240.0.0
5	30	524,286	255.248.0.0
6	62	262,142	255.252.0.0
7	126	131,070	255.254.0.0
8	254	65,534	255.255.0.0

Table 9.2   Class B Subnetting

Subnet Bits	Maximum Subnets	Maximum Number of Hosts Per Subnet	Subnet Mask
0	0	65,534	255.255.0.0
1	invalid	invalid	invalid
2	2	16,382	255.255.192.0

continues...

Table 9.2 Continued

Subnet Bits	Maximum Subnets	Maximum Number of Hosts Per Subnet	Subnet Mask
3	6	8,190	255.255.224.0
4	14	4,094	255.255.240.0
5	30	2,046	255.255.248.0
6	62	1,022	255.255.252.0
7	126	510	255.255.254.0
8	254	254	255.255.255.0

Table 9.3 Class C Subnetting

Subnet Bits	Maximum Subnets	Maximum Number of Hosts Per Subnet	Subnet Mask
0	0	254	255.255.255.0
1	invalid	invalid	invalid
2	2	62	255.255.255.192
3	6	30	255.255.255.224
4	14	14	255.255.255.240
5	30	6	255.255.255.248
6	62	2	255.255.255.252
7	invalid	invalid	255.255.255.254
8	invalid	invalid	255.255.255.255

Computer Names on Microsoft TCP/IP Networks

Networked computers are identified by numbers. On TCP/IP networks IP numbers identify them. On NWLink and NetBEUI networks numbers defined by the underlying network such as Ethernet identify them. But the rule is the same: to send a message to another device, a computer must know the numeric ID of the destination device. But people hate referring to computers by numbers, particularly the long numbers commonly used to identify network computers, so it has long been the practice of network designers to provide a mechanism that identifies computers by names. Ideally, computer naming should be completely transparent, requiring no intervention on the part of users and little on the part of network administrators. People use the names, and in the background computers figure out the numbers they require to communicate.

To meet those goals in the past, Microsoft based its network products on NetBIOS names, which were cataloged by a browser service. The NetBIOS name was the name you entered into the computer's configuration when you installed the operating system. The Browser service collected the NetBIOS names of all servers on the network. With the release of Windows 2000 Server, however, Microsoft now offers pure TCP/IP network browsing, using conventions such as Domain Name Service (DNS) and Lightweight Directory Access Protocol (LDAP).

Backward compatibility

For backward compatibility with network clients running earlier versions of Windows that support only NetBIOS naming, Microsoft has retained some services that allow these clients to find resources on the network.

LMHOSTS Files

An LMHOSTS file is a text file, maintained using any text editor, that maps host names to IP addresses. A typical entry in an LMHOSTS file looks like this:

```
192.168.143.8     Drew
```

Each computer must have an LMHOSTS file that contains an entry for each server. That sounds simple, but it turns out to be a significant administrative hassle.

You see, someone must not only update the LMHOSTS file, but also take responsibility for ensuring that a fresh copy is distributed to every computer every time a change takes place in the network configuration. That's fine on small networks that seldom change, but it's a recipe for indigestion on a large or dynamic network.

Windows Internet Naming Service

So Microsoft needed a dynamic service that would keep itself up-to-date, and it came up with the Windows Internet Naming Service or WINS. The WINS system consists of one or more WINS servers that maintain copies of the network name database. Clients register their NetBIOS names and addresses with WINS. And when a client needs to communicate with a server, it queries WINS for the server's address.

WINS appears to solve the NetBIOS-to-TCP/IP translation problem. As clients enter the network, WINS is automatically apprised of any changes. That's better than LMHOSTS files. After WINS is configured, it can be pretty much ignored by the administrator. And, because all WINS communication takes place through directed messages, routers don't interfere with WINS operation.

There's only one problem with WINS. Nobody but Microsoft used it. Everyone else uses Internet-based naming systems, as Windows 2000 Server does natively. So you need to look at the Internet side of things next.

SEE ALSO

➤ *For more information on WINS, see page 372.*

Computer Names on the Internet

The Internet faces a problem much like the problem Microsoft solved with NetBIOS names, LMHOSTS, and WINS. Users cannot remember more than a few IP addresses, so they need names.

As with Microsoft's approach, two techniques have been used to simplify host naming on TCP/IP networks: HOSTS files and the Domain Name Service.

HOSTS Files

HOSTS files works just like LMHOSTS files. They are text files with entries that match host names with IP addresses. An entry in a HOSTS file looks like this:

```
192.168.143.8    drew ws1 blivets99
```

An entry in a HOSTS file isn't that different from an entry in LMHOSTS except that a HOSTS file lets a host have more than one name, called an *alias*. (Also, LMHOSTS files have some special features specific to the Microsoft environment.)

HOSTS files have the same disadvantages cited for LMHOSTS files. They are tedious and, because each host must receive a new copy each time the file is updated, HOSTS files are time-consuming to maintain and distribute. Consequently, most TCP/IP administrators rely on the Domain Name Service to provide name resolution support.

Domain Name Service

Like WINS, the Domain Name Service (DNS) deploys servers that can be queried by network clients to resolve names to IP addresses.

The DNS name database is big, and it can be distributed in chunks across many, many name servers. On a network as big as the Internet, it would be inefficient to maintain the complete database on one computer. For one thing, the computer would be overwhelmed with the data and with servicing name resolution queries. For another, a single database would be impossible to maintain because every organization would need to submit name changes to a central authority, a bureaucratic nightmare when millions of organizations are involved. The Internet needed a naming system that let each organization maintain its own chunk of the database. DNS meets that goal. It is expandable without limit, and it permits local control of portions of the database.

In order to allow Microsoft networks to run as purely DNS-managed, Microsoft has implemented a dynamic DNS, which acts much like its WINS service.

The Microsoft DNS server has three distinct advantages:

- Entries can be modified interactively through a graphic interface.
- It isn't necessary to restart a Microsoft DNS Server to activate database changes.
- The Microsoft DNS Server can obtain names from WINS, allowing it to keep pace with the dynamic Windows naming environment.

SEE ALSO
➤ *For more information on Microsoft's DNS, see page 409.*

TCP/IP Routing

TCP/IP routing is also a bit more involved than anything you have seen so far in the book. The only thing you need to do to configure routing with NWLink is to install RIP for NWLink. With TCP/IP you have two options: static routing and RIP.

SEE ALSO
➤ *For more information on Windows 2000 Routing, see page 422.*

Static Routing

Static routing makes use of a static routing database that resides on each computer. You maintain some entries in the static routing table using entries in the Network applet in the Control Panel. Other entries are managed using the route command-line utility.

Every TCP/IP computer has a static routing table. An important entry in the static routing table is the default router. If a host doesn't know where to send a message, it will send the message to its default router, which is presumed to know how to deliver the message to its final destination.

All TCP/IP routing can be handled through static routing, but it can be a hassle to maintain static routing when the network configuration changes frequently. On large networks it is more common to use a dynamic routing protocol such as the Routing Information Protocol.

Routing Information Protocol

You have already encountered a version of the Routing Information Protocol (RIP) that is used to configure routers for NWLink. Microsoft includes RIP for TCP/IP with Windows 2000 Server.

RIP is a dynamic routing protocol that updates routing tables based on information exchanged with other RIP routers. The dynamic nature of RIP lets routers update their routing tables as the network configuration changes. RIP, or another dynamic routing protocol, is deployed on most large TCP/IP networks because the task of maintaining static routing tables would be overwhelming.

Virtual Private Networking

A *virtual private network (VPN)* is a mechanism for providing secure, encrypted communications in two configurations. First, a user to network configuration, where the remote user connects to the Internet and using a VPN is able to securely become a node on the company network. This is commonly referred to as the "Remote Access" model for a VPN. The other configuration is when a site/office uses the VPN coupled with an Internet connection to securely connect to the network at the other end of the VPN. This is commonly referred to as a site-to-site VPN. The remote access VPN is used to supplant the standard remote access of dial-in or authenticated firewall access to the network. The site-to-site model is being used in places to remove the need for a wide area network. Windows 2000's VPN services can support both models.

Both configurations offer significant cost savings over the more traditional access methods. One downside of the VPN model, however, is during Internet backbone outages. When you are unable to connect to your office because one of the Tier 1 networks has suffered a fiber cut, whom can you call? With a WAN or a remote access solution you always had a vendor you could call for a status or to have a technician dispatched. There is no 1-800-INTERNET number that you can call for technical support. This is the major tradeoff with a VPN solution versus a more traditional approach.

SEE ALSO

➤ *For more information on Windows 2000 VPNs, see page 433.*

part

III

MANAGING YOUR WINDOWS 2000 NETWORK

chapter

10

Managing Drives, Partitions and Volumes

Understanding Windows 2000 File Systems

When Windows NT was created, a high priority was its security architecture. Part of this depended on implementing a file system that would ignore the MS-DOS limitations, and give the operating system a high-performance file system that also had a level of security that would surpass other available file systems.

This chapter explains *NTFS (NT File System)*, contains a history of the *FAT (file allocation table)* file system, and describes how Windows NT provides backward compatibility by offering its own implementations of FAT (FAT16 and FAT32), which differ from the MS-DOS version. Then the chapter looks at managing drives and partitions.

HPFS on Windows 2000 Server

Originally, Windows NT 3.x contained compatibility with the HPFS (High Performance File System) which is used by OS/2. Windows NT 4.0 and Windows 2000 no longer include support for HPFS.

Knowing the different file systems and how to manage them is a very important matter that should be considered before installing Windows 2000 Server.

Usually Windows 2000 Server has been deployed in order to create a secure networking environment for your users. Based on this alone, the NTFS file system should be your obvious choice of file system. In very few cases you might require the backward compatibility of the other file systems offered by Windows 2000 Server.

Choose your file system first

It is advantageous to decide on the file system you will be using on your server in advance of its implementation, because after you choose, it might be difficult to change the file system. In fact, changing the file system can result in data loss.

This chapter reviews the FAT file system in DOS and introduces you to Windows 2000's NTFS, which contains an excellent form of disk compression and security.

Before deciding which file systems to keep or whether NTFS should be implemented, you need to know the background on these file systems. I'll discuss a little history of the file systems and their pros and cons.

Understanding the FAT (File Allocation Table) File System

The FAT file system for personal computers was designed at a time when floppy disks were the most used media, and hard drives had an average capacity of 10MB. Because of this, FAT was not designed with larger capacities in mind; it now requires new operating systems and system BIOSes to allow larger hard drives and directory trees of files that number in the thousands or millions.

Partitions formatted with FAT are broken into *clusters*. The FAT file system is also prone to fragmentation, which is the result of data being written to noncontiguous clusters, which can slow down the read/write process. FAT writes files to the first available cluster it can find and then skips ahead past used clusters to complete writing a file. These clusters are broken down into *sectors*. FAT also tracks a few attributes for each file, including the following:

- The name of the file
- The address of the starting sector
- Whether the file was deemed a system file
- Whether the file has a read-only attribute
- Whether the file has an archive bit (denoting whether the file had been backed up or changed since the last time it was backed up)
- The date of the file's creation or the last time the file was modified

---

Definition of *cluster*

A *cluster* is a group of disk sectors. The operating system (in this case Windows 2000) assigns a unique number to each cluster and then keeps track of files according to which clusters they use.

A *file* is made up of a whole number of possibly noncontiguous clusters. The cluster size is a tradeoff between space efficiency (the bigger is the cluster, the bigger is on the average the wasted space at the end of each file).

Definition of *sector*

Data is transferred to and from a disk in *sectors*, which are subsets of a cluster.

> **FAT16 overhead**
>
> Because the overhead of using the FAT file system grows as partition size increases, it is advisable to not use FAT on partitions that are greater than 400MB.

The two flavors of the FAT file system, FAT16 and FAT32, refer to the number of bits contained in each file allocation table. The advantages of FAT32 over FAT16 far outweigh the advantages of FAT16.

FAT16

The primary advantages of FAT16 over FAT32 are

- *Backward compatibility.* MS-DOS, Windows 9x, some x86 flavors of UNIX, OS/2, Windows NT, and Windows 2000 can all work with FAT16.
- *Utilities.* Many more utilities are available for the recovery of FAT16 partitions.

The major disadvantages of FAT16 are:

- *Boot sector.* The boot sector is located at a specific location on a partition, so if the boot sector becomes corrupted, the system might not boot.
- *Root directory.* The root directory of a FAT16 partition is limited to a certain number of entries. Furthermore, bad (damaged) sectors on a hard drive can limit this number even more.
- *Maximum partition size.* FAT16 partitions are limited to 2GB.
- *Wasted storage.* On hard drive partitions that are greater than 256MB (of which most are nowadays) FAT16 wastes space due to its 32KB cluster size.

FAT32

FAT32 has the ability to support up to two terabytes (2TB), which makes it the format of choice for partitions larger than 2GB (FAT16's limitation) on a Windows 9x system. FAT32 also stores a backup copy of the boot sector, allowing for a system to boot even if the boot sector has corrupted. FAT32 also uses drive space more efficiently, allowing for smaller clusters.

The only real disadvantage to FAT32 is that it does not carry the security attributes that NTFS offers.

Understanding NTFS: The Windows 2000 File System

With the introduction of Windows NT 3.1 in 1993, Microsoft took the advanced capabilities of the High Performance File System (HPFS, previously used in Microsoft/IBM's OS/2) and went many steps further to create NTFS. A major part of the security model that Windows 2000 offers is based on the NTFS file system. Although shared directories can be set up on a Windows 2000 server regardless of the file system used, it is only with NTFS that individual files can be assigned permissions. These rights, which also include rights to a directory, can be assigned permissions whether or not they are shared. Every attribute of the NTFS is kept as a file.

NTFS is the preferred file system for Windows 2000 because it allows the use of all of Windows 2000's security features; however, a system can use both of the natively available file systems at the same time. Of course, only the NTFS partitions have the advantages.

File systems on a floppy disk

Incidentally, whenever Windows 2000 formats a floppy disk, it formats using FAT16 because the overhead of the NTFS file system would create too much extraneous, although important, information making the actual capacity of the floppy disk too small. Therefore, NTFS is not a supported format on floppy disks.

File descriptions on an NTFS volume are stored in a *master file table (MFT)*, which is also a file. Beside several records that contain data about the MFT itself, the MFT contains a record for each file and directory. The MFT also contains a log file. A copy of the MFT is also kept. *Pointers* to the MFT and its copy are stored in the boot sector of the disk. A copy of the boot sector is stored in the logical center of the disk. With this many copies of the MFT, data recovery becomes even easier. That is why NTFS is known as a *recoverable file system*.

When a file is called for on a FAT partition, a pointer to a list of sectors is read. NTFS cuts out one of these steps by having the sector map contained within the MFT. In cases of small files, it is possible that only a single record in the MFT can contain all the information for that one file. Larger files require that additional table records, called *extents*, are read, and directories will require that the *B-tree* structure is read. All in all, this makes for a very speedy file system.

> **Definition of *B-tree***
>
> B-tree stands for *balanced tree*, which is an algorithm. This algorithm is appropriate where the overheads of the reorganization on update are outweighed by the benefits of faster search.

When a partition is formatted as NTFS, numerous system files are created that keep track of certain attributes of that partition.

Choosing FAT over NTFS

FAT16 is handled slightly differently under Windows 2000. Although Windows 2000's FAT16 implementation is entirely backward compatible, Windows 2000 also adds features to the DOS-compatible FAT16 file system. Long filenames are allowed for FAT partitions and are handled the same way as long filenames on a Windows 9x system. That is, the generated *8.3 filename* is stored along with the long filename. FAT partitions can be converted to NTFS.

> **The classic 8.3 filename**
>
> If you used computers before Windows 95, you probably used the DOS 8.3 filenaming convention. This method uses a maximum eight-character filename, followed by a period, followed by a maximum three-character file extension.

One of the few reasons I have come across so far to keep FAT16 or FAT32 partitions on a Windows 2000 Server is for certain DOS-based programs. If these DOS-based programs have not been certified to run on a Windows 2000 server, running them from a FAT partition can give them greater compatibility than running from NTFS. So if you are running any older 16-bit software from your Windows 2000 Server, you should inquire if the manufacturer supports running their software from NTFS.

Better yet, migrate to all 32-bit Windows-based programs.

Another reason to keep a partition as FAT is if it is necessary to dual-boot to DOS or Windows 9x on the server. This is sometimes the case in a test environment, not so much for a production environment.

When booting DOS or the original Windows 95 on a Windows 2000 server, only the FAT16 partitions are recognized. For Windows 95 (OSR2 and up) and Windows 98, only the FAT partitions are recognized. Dual booting with earlier versions of Windows NT will recognize only FAT16, because FAT32 is not compatible with earlier versions of Windows NT, and the Windows 2000 implementation of NTFS is not backward compatible with the earlier versions.

Using Windows 2000 NTFS on Windows NT 4.0

A driver does ship with later service packs for Windows NT 4.0 that allows it to recognize Windows 2000 NTFS partitions.

FAT Filename Concerns

Any long filenames that exist on the FAT partition will be seen with a standard 8.3 filename. Windows 2000 creates an 8.3 filename along with its long filenames the same way that Windows 9x creates 8.3 filenames along with long filenames.

A long filename—for example, My Report—would have MYREPO~1.doc as an 8.3 filename. Note that the embedded space is stripped out, and only the first six characters of the filename are used. The trailing tilde character and the numeral 1 are added in case another filename starts with the same first six characters. If another long filename exists named My Report For September, that file under DOS would be called MYREPO~2.doc, and so on. Spaces are not the only characters that are removed from a long filename. Any other special character that is not supported in 8.3 filenames will be replaced in the conversion by an underscore.

NTFS uses the 16-bit Unicode character set, which contains special characters and support for most international special characters. Because many of these characters are deemed illegal by DOS filenaming standards, these characters are also stripped.

NTFS Filenaming Concerns

As I just mentioned, NTFS uses the 16-bit Unicode character set, which allows some special characters, and includes both uppercase and lowercase letters of the alphabet. Therefore, a filename My Document retains the uppercase characters in its name; however, NTFS does not distinguish between files that use the same characters but different cases.

An NTFS filename anomaly

Interestingly enough, although NTFS can handle filenames of up to 255 characters, files created from the command line can only have filenames up to 253 characters.

The following special characters cannot appear in an NTFS filename:

```
?   "   /   \   <   >   *   ¦   :
```

Copying Files Between NTFS and FAT

When copying files from NTFS to FAT using command-line utilities, such as XCOPY and COPY, you might receive errors because those utilities can handle the long filename, but the receiving file system might choke on embedded spaces among other characters. To get around this, use the /N switch on those commands, and then the short filename will be used. For example, to copy the contents of directory C:\ My Documents from an NTFS partition to the directory D:\DOCS which is located on a FAT partition, use the following syntax:

```
XCOPY "C:\My Documents\*.*" D:\DOCS /N
```

Definition of *syntax*

The word *syntax* refers to a structure of strings in a language. In the example used on this page, the command **XCOPY** is a batch language command, which requires certain parameters to follow it on the command line. This structure defines the syntax of the **XCOPY** command.

Special attention must also be used when creating shortcuts to programs using file associations. If a type of file is associated with a 16-bit program, and the long filename is being used, the 16-bit program will not know how to interpret the filename and will not be able to load the file. This isn't a problem on a system that is running programs compliant with Windows 2000, Windows NT, or Windows 9x.

How to destroy long filenames

Using any 16-bit program, such as the Windows 3.x File Manager, or a DOS utility, such as The Norton Commander, to manipulate files that have long filenames will *wipe out* the long filenames! If this is on an NTFS volume, all the security information will be eliminated as well. Only use 32-bit programs that support long filenames to move or copy files on an NTFS volume.

Choosing NTFS over FAT

The main purpose of file systems is to track data stored on hard drives and facilitate the reading and writing of this data. NTFS's recoverable file system is a great enhancement of FAT's careful-write file system, and the lazy-write file system used by UNIX and FAT as implemented on Windows NT.

FAT's *careful-write file system* allows writes one at a time, and alters its volume information after each write. This is a very secure form of writing, however it is also a very slow process.

The *lazy-write file system* uses a cache. All writes are performed to this cache and the file system intelligently waits for the appropriate time to perform all the writes to disk. This system gives the user faster access to the file system and prevents holdups due to slower disk access. It is also possible that if the same file is being modified more than once, the altered file might never actually be written to disk until the modifications are finished within the cache. Of course, this can also lead to lost data if the system crashes and unwritten modifications are still held in the cache.

NTFS's recoverable file system provides the speed of a lazy-write file system along with recovery features. The recovery features come from a transaction log that tracks which writes to disk have been completed and which ones have not. In the recovery process this log can assure that after only a few moments after a reboot, the file system's integrity is back to 100% without the need of running a utility such as CHKDSK, which requires the scanning of an entire volume. The overhead associated with this recoverable file system is less than the type used by the careful-write file system.

The recoverable file system can also ensure that an NTFS partition will always remain accessible, even if the partition is bootable and the bootstrap has been damaged. In this instance, you can boot from another drive, or boot from disks and still have access to the formerly bootable volume.

NTFS supports *hot fixing* as well. Instead of FAT's notorious "Abort, Retry, Fail?" message, NTFS attempts to move the data in a damaged cluster to a new location in a fashion that is transparent to the user. The damaged cluster is then marked as unusable.

Hot fixing might not always work

Unfortunately, it is possible that the moved data will be unusable anyhow, because the chance of corruption is very likely, unless disk-fault tolerance is enabled, and then the replicated data from the undamaged cluster will be used in its place.

The way that NTFS processes file actions as transactions is the key to its high degree of recoverability. Each write request to an NTFS partition generates redo and undo information. The redo information tells NTFS how to re-create the intended write. The undo information tells NTFS how to rollback the transaction, in case the transaction is incomplete or has an error. After the write transaction is complete, NTFS generates a *file update commit*, which is a log entry that reflects the success of the file change. Otherwise NTFS uses the undo information in order to rollback the request.

The type of commit that NTFS performs is called a *lazy commit*. This is similar to a lazy write in the sense that it will cache these file commits and write them to the transaction log when system resources are high. This feature allows NTFS's high reliability features to have less overhead, overall, on the system.

In the case of system crash, or unexpected shutdown of Windows 2000 (such as someone accidentally powering off the server before a clean shutdown is performed), NTFS will perform a three-pass system check on restarting.

As with most transactional-type logs, checkpoints are created after all log transactions since the last checkpoint have been confirmed. Checkpoint creation occurs every few seconds. The first pass that NTFS makes after a system restart is called the analysis pass. In this pass, NTFS compares items in the transaction log, since the last checkpoint, to the clusters those transactions dealt with. A second pass, called the redo pass, performs all the transaction steps since the last checkpoint. The third pass, which is the undo pass, performs a rollback on any incomplete transactions.

Converting from FAT to NTFS

The CONVERT.EXE utility is a command-line utility that can convert FAT partitions over to NTFS. It will not convert NTFS to FAT.

To use the CONVERT.EXE utility:

1. Open a command prompt, which can be found on the Start menu under Programs, Accessories.
2. Type this command: CONVERT *d: /fs:ntfs* (where *d* is the drive letter for the partition you are converting).
3. The CONVERT.EXE utility will keep you informed of the status of the conversion. When it has completed you will be returned to the command prompt.
4. Type exit to close the command prompt window.

> **Note**
>
> You cannot convert the boot partition while it is active, so if the **CONVERT** command is attempted on the boot partition, an entry is written to the Registry that will initiate the conversion the next time the system is booted.

> **And the winner is...NTFS**
>
> Whenever possible, use NTFS as your file system. Its security and reliability are too good to pass up. Also, the file compression for NTFS is another great advantage. See "Understanding NTFS Disk Compression," later in this chapter, for a discussion on Windows 2000's unique file compression.

The NTFS *CHKSDK* Utility

Whenever you start Windows 2000, the NTFS volumes are checked to see whether they are "dirty". If it detects a potential problem, Windows 2000 will automatically run CHKDSK /F.

If the CHKDSK utility finds orphaned files or directories, they are moved to special directories which are named FOUNDnnn (if no other FOUNDnnn directories exist, the first one created will be FOUND000, the next is FOUND001, and so on). Directories are named DIRnnn.CHK, and if they have files associated with them, those files will be placed within that directory. Orphaned files are named FILEnnn.CHK.

Follow these steps to run CHKDSK manually:

1. Open a command prompt, which can be found on the Start menu under Program, Accessories.

2. Type this command: CHKDSK *d:* (where *d* is the drive letter for the partition you are checking). If no drive letter is entered, the current drive will be checked. (See Figure 10.1.)

3. If you want the CHKDSK utility to automatically fix any problems that it might encounter, use the /F parameter (for example: CHKDSK C: /F).

4. When CHKDSK has completed and returns you to the command prompt, type exit to close the command prompt window.

> **A special consideration when running *CHKDSK /F***
>
> If you want to run CHKDSK /F, run it from a drive other than the one you are checking. For example, to check the C: drive, run CHKDSK C: /F from a D: prompt. If CHKDSK cannot get control of the drive because it is in use, it asks you whether it should run automatically the next time Windows 2000 is booted.

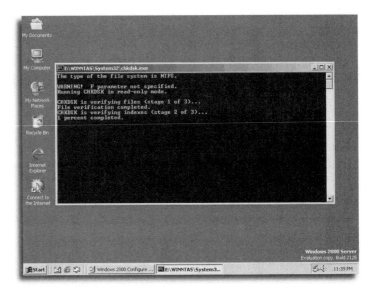

FIGURE 10.1
The CHKDSK utility gives you a running status of the process.

Understanding NTFS Disk Compression

NTFS includes a form of disk compression that is unlike the more familiar Windows 9x DriveSpace.

DriveSpace, which consists of DOS device driver–based programs, creates one large file that contains all the files contained in the drive that you compressed. This single file is a mountable volume that a DOS device driver mounts as its own drive. This drive is then viewed as a standard DOS FAT volume.

Windows 2000 uses Explorer and the COMPACT.EXE utility to individually compress files. These compressed files are then decompressed in real-time when the files are opened.

The type of compression found in Windows 2000 is much safer than the DOS method because it is possible that a corrupted compressed volume on DOS could result in loss of the entire volume. As with all file compression techniques, there is a certain amount of overhead for the decompression and recompression of these files.

With Windows 2000's compression scheme, each file is handled separately; therefore, any corruption affects only that one file.

The algorithm used for NTFS Disk Compression is similar to the DriveSpace one. In DriveSpace, a file is searched for two-byte pieces of data that are redundant throughout the file. NTFS File Compression searches for three bytes of redundant data, thus making NTFS Disk Compression faster, while sacrificing the amount of compression that can be achieved.

Again, this compression is available only for partitions formatted as NTFS.

I personally use Windows 2000's disk compression and haven't had any bad experiences or noticeable lags due to compression. I would advise the following:

- Feel free to use the compression for seldom-used files or archived data.
- Keep in mind that large documents compress very well.
- Do not use file compression for files that are already compressed, such as JPEG graphics, or archive files such as PKZIP or ARJ files.
- Do not use compression on files that are part of a highly critical application (you never know...).
- Back up. Back up. Back up. Whether there are compressed files or not, always keep a current backup.

Setting File and Directory Compression States

Each file and directory on an NTFS partition contains a compression state. This state can be modified by either using the COMPACT.EXE utility, or through the Windows 2000 Explorer.

To compress a folder using Windows Explorer:

1. Select the folder you want to compress, right-click to bring up the pop-up menu and choose Properties. (See Figure 10.2.) This opens the dialog box shown in Figure 10.3.
2. Click the Advanced button to display the advanced attributes for this folder. (See Figure 10.4.)
3. Choose to compress the contents of this folder by checking the Compress Contents to Save Disk Space checkbox.
4. Click the OK button to close the Advanced dialog box.
5. Click the Apply button to apply the changes to compress the folder. In Figure 10.5, you will notice the Inetpub folder is now displayed in blue, indicating it is compressed.

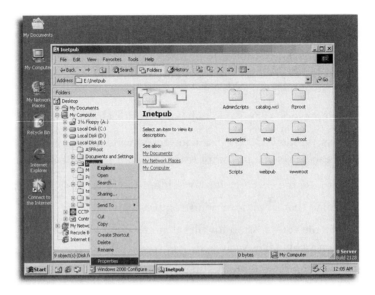

FIGURE 10.2
A context menu can always be opened by right-clicking the folder.

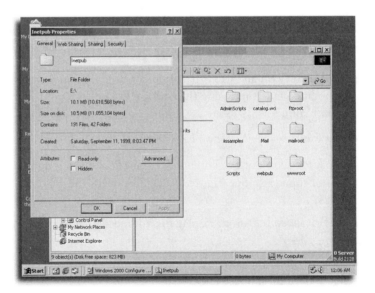

FIGURE 10.3
The Folder properties dialog box allows you to view and configure the folder parameters, including compression.

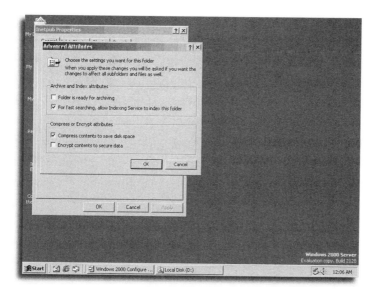

FIGURE 10.4
The Advanced Attributes dialog box allows you to select encryption.

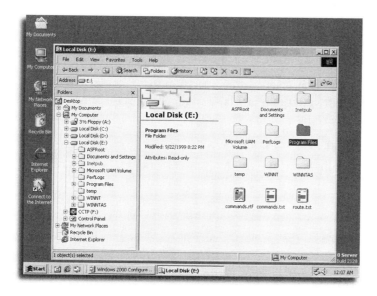

FIGURE 10.5
Windows 2000 shows compressed folders in a different color.

After the Compress Contents to Save Disk Space box has been checked and these changes applied, this folder will have a compression state of compressed.

Other options that are unique to NTFS include the ability to specify a folder for inclusion in Indexing, and whether or not to encrypt the contents of a folder. These advanced attributes can also be applied to individual files. Only compression and indexing can be applied to an entire partition.

Even by changing the attribute for one file within a compressed folder, that does not alter the compression state for the folder. Any new files that are placed in that folder will automatically become compressed.

Using the *COMPACT.EXE* Utility

The COMPACT.EXE utility allows you to set and check compression states through a command line. There are two main reasons to use this method as opposed to using the Windows 2000 Explorer for configuring compression states.

First, you can use COMPACT.EXE to set compression states from a batch file. This can be handy, especially if you are using the COMPACT command along with the /I switch, which allows for open files, which will be skipped during this operation when using this switch. By contrast, when using Windows 2000 Explorer, the compression operation is halted if an open file is encountered.

Second, a compression state–setting operation that fails, due either to a system error or a power failure, can result in a false compression state being reported through Windows 2000 Explorer. Using COMPACT.EXE is the only way to correct this.

The syntax for the COMPACT utility is

```
compact [/c] [/u] [/s[:dir]] [/a] [/i] [/f] [/q] [filename [...]]
```

where

- /c compresses the specified folder or file
- /u uncompresses the specified folder or file
- /s tells COMPACT to apply the operation to all subfolders of the specified folder (dir), or to the current folder if no folder has been specified
- /a displays files with the hidden or system attribute
- /i ignores any errors

- /f forces compression or decompression of the specified folder or file
- /q reduces the amount of data that is reported

Using no parameters with COMPACT simply displays the current compression state of the current folder. filename allows you to specify a file, a folder, or multiple files using the wildcard character. You can also use the COMPACT command along with the /? switch to display an explanation of the syntax for the COMPACT command.

Moving and Copying Files and Folders

When a file is moved to a folder on an NTFS partition, the compression state, encryption state, and indexing state remain unaltered, regardless of the state of the destination folder. This is an attribute of the NTFS file system. If a file is copied to a folder on an NTFS partition, the file inherits the attributes of the destination folder. Whenever files are moved or copied to a FAT partition, these advanced attributes are lost, because these attributes do not exist on FAT.

Windows 2000 has a unique way of handling file systems. Its NTFS file system is certainly leaps and bounds ahead of the FAT file system that you are probably used to and should be properly used to ensure the proper security you'll want for your Windows 2000 servers and domains. Now that you understand how the different file systems work, I'll discuss disk-fault tolerance.

Using RAID to Protect Your Data

RAID stands for Redundant Array of Inexpensive Disks. RAID was originally conceived as a way to use multiple hard drives to provide disk-fault tolerance. This is mainly because hard drives had been the number-one computer component to fail, although as time has passed hard drives have gotten to be more stable.

What exactly is disk-fault tolerance?

Although there are various types of disk-fault tolerance, they all have one thing in common. If a single disk in the system fails, the system will continue to run, and be available to users. If you are the administrator of a production Windows 2000 Server, you will find this invaluable, particularly with older hardware. No one likes to be told the server will be down for three days while the new drive is being shipped.

Using RAID means your data is safe, right?

In a perfect world where drives never fail at the same time, maybe. But in the real world, you should always back up your data to ensure data integrity. RAID is an excellent technology, and can allow your server to continue running when a drive fails, but it should not be considered a replacement for a system backup.

Before I get into the nuts and bolts of RAID, an overview is probably in order. There are several accepted types of RAID around the industry, including

- *Level 0.* Provides data striping (spreading out blocks of each file across multiple disks) but no redundancy. This improves performance but does not deliver disk-fault tolerance.
- *Level 1.* Provides disk mirroring. This is an expensive solution because it involves dual controllers.
- *Level 3.* Same as Level 0 but also reserves one dedicated disk for error correction data. It provides good performance and some level of disk-fault tolerance. This is not supported by Windows 2000 Server.
- *Level 5.* Provides data striping at the byte level and also stripe error correction information. This results in excellent performance and good disk-fault tolerance.

Of these types, the three most common are 0, 1, and 5. Now take a closer look.

Striped Volumes—RAID 0

A Level 0 array is not, strictly speaking, a RAID system because it does not allow for redundant data. It stripes across all drives in the array and can deliver very high performance with none of the overhead needed for writing failure recovery data. Without redundancy, its capacity is the same as the total capacity of the drives in the array. Because RAID 0 offers no data protection, the risk of data loss goes up in proportion to the number of drives in the array. This makes it an acceptable choice only when performance is important and occasional data loss is acceptable.

Mirrored Volumes—RAID 1

RAID 1 arrays use disk mirroring to provide data protection. Each disk in a mirrored pair contains an exact copy of the data on its companion drive. Write performance suffers with mirroring because each write must be performed twice—once for each disk in the pair. Disk duplexing adds a second controller and data path to a mirrored system to enhance reliability. This also improves performance by allowing overlapped I/O on the two sets of disks.

RAID 1 has a number of benefits. It is widely available as an operating system option, either as part of a disk subsystem or as a software package. RAID 1 provides the highest level of redundancy and resiliency of any of the defined RAID architectures. Software mirroring can be configured to take advantage of system resources to move the single point of failure back to the host itself. In addition, a three-way disk mirror configuration available in many disk mirroring packages allows for continued redundant operation even after a single failure.

RAID 1 also has its problems. The principal drawback is the relatively high cost of redundant storage. Although data reliability in RAID 1 systems is very high, usable capacity is only half the total capacity of the disks in the array, making this approach expensive to implement. Standard disk mirroring requires two times the number of drives, and three-way mirroring requires three times the number of drives.

Striping with Parity—RAID 5

RAID 5 performs striping at the block level and distributes parity information evenly across all drives in the array. As a result, RAID 5 can outperform RAID 3 and 4 by processing multiple writes in parallel, while no single drive functions as a bottleneck to disk writes. RAID 5 also performs well in random reads because each disk can function independently to satisfy multiple simultaneous read requests. RAID 5 typically does not equal the performance of RAID 0 or RAID 1 systems because of the overhead required to compute and write error correction data.

What about RAID 2, 3, and 4?

RAID Levels 2, 3, and 4 are not generally used and are considered obsolete types of RAID. Windows 2000 does not support them.

A RAID 5 limitation

One strong limitation of RAID 5 is that if more than one drive fails in a RAID set, all the data is lost. To ameliorate this issue, many hardware vendors allow for the use of online spares with their RAID controllers, so you would need 2 + N (where N is the number of online spares) drives to fail before data loss.

Hardware RAID Versus Software RAID

The type of RAID that is included with Windows 2000 is *software RAID*. Although this type of RAID seems to be more lenient, because it allows for mirroring of logical drives, it actually is not as safe to use as hardware RAID. Software RAID also puts a great deal of additional overhead on the server that should be used to handle user requests instead.

Hardware RAID is available in different forms. The most popular is the Disk Array Controller, a PCI, EISA, or ISA card that has the logic to handle the creation and maintenance of the different RAID levels. One prime example of a RAID card is a Compaq SmartArray II Controller. This card allows you to build a RAID set that is totally operating system independent.

For instance, if you take three 9.1GB hard drives and use the RAID controller create a RAID Level 5 set, a single volume with approximately 18GB of space will be created. When Windows 2000 Server boots, it will see this drive as a single physical drive, which can then be divided into partitions. RAID Level 5 is handled in the background by the hardware.

Another type of hardware RAID is the self-enclosed drive storage unit. An example of this is Compaq's StorageWorks cabinets, which contains 24 hard drives, along with their own controllers. With this product, up to three cabinets can be daisy-chained to offer 72 drives. Using software that runs under Windows, you can create RAID Level 1 and RAID Level 5 sets using any combination of installed drives. This hardware also features other redundancies such as redundant power supplies, fans, and controllers.

So which should you choose?

Whenever possible, you should use hardware RAID for a number of reasons. It is higher performance, keeps RAID overhead off the system, is more flexible (allows for hot spare drives), and is generally more reliable.

Real-Time Mirroring and Clustering

Although not officially a RAID solution, there are other options for keeping user data available to the network. One such solution is *real-time server mirroring*. Made popular by companies such as Vinca and Octopus, real-time mirroring allows you to have two or more servers that replicate data in real-time. A provision allows one server to take over for another server in the case of a downed server (whether intentional, for maintenance, or due to a hardware failure). There are even solutions that allow for multiple servers to be mirrored to one server, with the latter being able to assume the identity of any one of the multiple servers, while continuing to mirror the other "surviving" servers.

A nice feature of this real-time mirroring is that, with the proper equipment, the two mirrored servers can be in two totally different locations, as the mirroring process can occur over a WAN link. This allows this solution to act as a disaster recovery plan too.

Clustering is a concept that has been around for a long time in the world of mainframes, but is only in its infancy for Windows 2000. Hardware vendors have offered their own proprietary solutions for clustering, but it has only been during the last two years that Microsoft has offered an API for Windows NT/Windows 2000 clustering.

Clustering for the mainframes had multiple computers pooling their resources, appearing as one computer to the end user. Clustering for the Windows 2000–based computer is actually fail-over. *Fail-over* is the ability to have resources, such as hard drives, that belong to one server move to another server in the event of a hardware failure. This fail-over is transparent to the end user, who continues to work on the network as if nothing had changed.

At the time of this writing Microsoft only supported two-node fail-over. Greater numbers of nodes in a Microsoft cluster is expected in the very near future.

The Windows 2000 Disk Management Console

FDISK has always been a challenge to me when dealing with a multitude of physical hard drives and partitions. In many instances I've found myself cycling through the hard drives display in FDISK, hoping that the partition I just deleted was the one that I really wanted to delete. And too many times I've found out that I just purged the wrong partition (or the right partition, but from the wrong hard drive).

The Windows 2000 Disk Management Console is a welcome relief because it allows users to view all their physical hard drives and CD-ROM drives all at the same time.

During the installation of Windows 2000, the option of creating, deleting, and formatting partitions is your first exposure to Windows 2000's file systems configuration. The Windows 2000 Disk Management Console is the primary utility for handling your physical and logical hard drives after you have installed Windows 2000. The Disk Management Console is only available to members of the Administrators group in the Windows 2000 domain. Usually the Disk Management Console is used when adding a new physical drive to the server, however it can also be used to modify existing drives and for implementing disk-fault tolerance.

Figure 10.6 shows the Disk Management Console, which represents your physical hard drives and CD-ROM drives. At a glance you can see the different partitions and their size, the volume names, the file systems in use, the drive letter assignments, and the amount of free space that is available for creating new partitions.

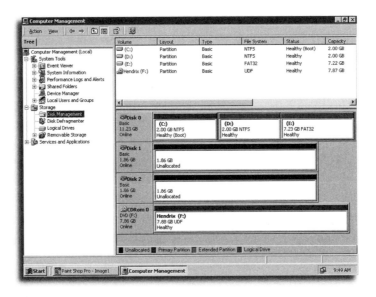

FIGURE 10.6
The Disk Management Console is used to perform all the disk configuration tasks associated with Windows 2000 Server.

Identifying bootable partitions

No matter how you choose to display your drives, a bootable partition is identified by the word *boot* in parentheses next to the partition status, as you can see in Figure 10.6.

To start the Disk Management Console, navigate to the menu selection shown in Figure 10.7.

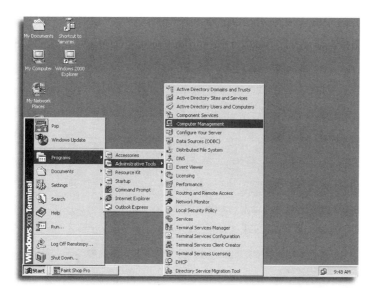

FIGURE 10.7
Navigating to open the Disk Management Console.

To open the Disk Management Console, complete the following steps:

1. From the Start menu, select Programs.

2. From Programs, select Administrator Tools.

3. In Administrator Tools, choose Computer Management.

4. In the Computer Management Console, select Disk Management, located under Storage.

Configuring the Disk Management Console

The Disk Management Console uses visual cues to allow you to easily identify the size and type of partitions on your hard drives. Different colors are used as a legend to identify a primary partition, a logical drive, a stripe set, a mirror set, and a spanned volume. You can customize this legend by choosing Settings from the View menu.

Changing the View

Besides the standard graphical partition representation of hard drives, removable media, and CD-ROM drives, the View menu item allows you to switch the view for the top pane and the bottom pane. To change the look and feel of this application, do the following:

1. Open the Disk Management folder in the Computer Management application.

2. From the menu, select View.

3. From the View drop down menu, you can select what will be displayed in the top and bottom panes of the application. You choices include the following:

   - *Disk List.* This view shows all drives in an Explorer-like list.
   - *Volume List.* The default view for the top pane, this view shows all volumes in an Explorer-like list.
   - *Graphical View.* The default view for the bottom pane, this view shows the partitions in a stacked graphical format.

4. These changes go into effect immediately after selection.

Working with Partitions

I spent the first half of this chapter discussing how the Disk Management Console works. Now you'll learn how to actually use it to manage partitions.

Working with Existing Partitions

In the case of a new server, where no partitions existed on the hard drives prior to the installation of Windows 2000, there should be no problem for Disk Management Console to recognize all your server's partitions. However, if you are installing Windows 2000 on top of a hard drive that already has MS-DOS or another operating system installed, there are cases where Windows 2000 will not be able to understand the existing partitioning of a disk. This happens when a partition table does not comply with the strict requirements that Windows 2000 enforces. When this occurs you must first boot from the operating system that created the disk partition. Then, back up any information that you would like to retain from those partitions. After it is completed, delete the partitions by using FDISK for MS-DOS or the appropriate utility for that particular operating system.

To re-create the partitions, use either a recent version of MS-DOS or the Windows 2000 installation program if you have deleted the partition that contained Windows 2000. Otherwise, you can boot Windows 2000 and use the Disk Management Console to re-create the partitions.

Notice in Figure 10.8 that Disk 0, Disk 1, and Disk 2 show the word *Basic* above their capacities. A *basic disk* is one that has not been optimized for use with Windows 2000. It is still usable under Windows 2000, but you be unable to take advantage of the advanced features of Dynamic Disks if you are working with a basic disk.

SEE ALSO

➤ *For information on converting a basic disk to a Dynamic Disk, see page 255.*

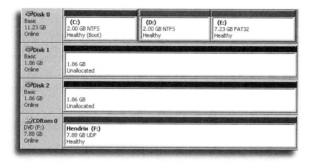

FIGURE 10.8
All hard drives are currently basic disks.

Dynamic Disks break the limitation that Windows 2000 has for volumes. With a Dynamic Disk you can create spanned volumes, formerly known as volume sets; striped volumes, or RAID-0; mirrored volumes, or RAID-1; simple volumes, or just a plain partition; and striping-with-parity volumes, or RAID-5. The various types of RAID are discussed in "Using RAID to Protect Your Data," earlier in this chapter.

Creating a Primary Partition

When creating a partition, you need to first decide on the type of partition you want to use. Windows 2000 allows any number of partitions on a hard drive. You are only limited by free space. MS-DOS allows only two types of partitions: a primary partition that is usually used for the operating system files, and an extended partition. An extended partition, which is compatible with pre–Windows 2000 operating systems, can contain one or more logical partitions. If you create a primary partition that is formatted as FAT, MS-DOS will be able to recognize this as a MS-DOS drive. Any extended partition containing logical drives, which are also formatted as FAT, will also be recognized by MS-DOS as valid drives. Non-extended partitions beyond the first FAT drive will not be recognized as a valid drive, nor will any partitions that are formatted as NTFS. Be sure to keep this in mind if you are planning to dual-boot the server as both Windows 2000 and Windows 9x/MS-DOS. Even FAT partitions might not be recognized by MS-DOS if the partitioning scheme is not one that is MS-DOS compliant. Complete the following steps to create a partition:

1. Open the Disk Management Console.

2. Select the hard drive by clicking the representation of the drive that is noted as Unallocated Space, as shown in Figure 10.9.

FIGURE 10.9
Select the free space that you want to work with.

3. Choose Create Partition from the context menu, which starts the Create Partition Wizard.

4. Click Next. In the dialog box that appears you can select the type of partition you want to make (Figure 10.10). Because you are working in free space, the only choices are Primary and Extended. If this were an extended partition, the only option available would be Logical, which is grayed out. Select Primary, and then click the Next button.

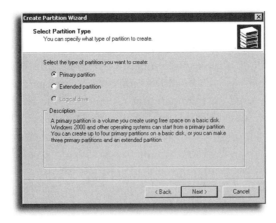

FIGURE 10.10
As you did with FDISK, choose the type of partition you want to create.

5. Now select the size for the partition you want to create (see Figure 10.11). In this example I am taking the full amount of free space on the drive. Click Next to continue.

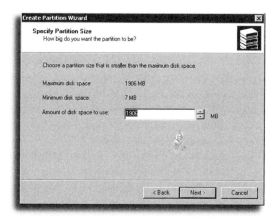

FIGURE 10.11
Select the amount of space you want to use for this new partition.

6. The Assign Drive Letter or Path dialog box, shown in Figure 10.12, lets you choose to assign the partition an available drive letter or no drive letter, or you can mount this partition as a folder in an existing partition. The latter option can create some interesting results, which I will demonstrate later, but for now I have assigned the partition the next available drive letter. Click the Next button.

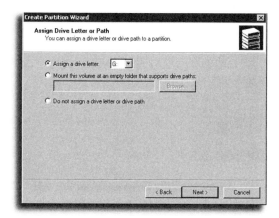

FIGURE 10.12
You can assign a drive letter or a path.

7. Next you choose the format for the partition (Figure 10.13). If you want to format as anything but NTFS, you will not have the option to enable compression. You do not have to format the partition now if you only want to create it. Otherwise, select the file system and click Next.

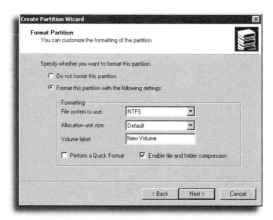

FIGURE 10.13
Partitions can be formatted as FAT16, FAT32, or NTFS.

8. The Create Partition Wizard displays a summary (shown in Figure 10.14) of the choices you made regarding the creation of this partition. Click the Finish button to complete the process.

FIGURE 10.14
Before clicking the Finish button, check your selections.

9. Notice that in Figure 10.15 the new partition, Drive G, is shown with a status of Formatting. This formatting occurs in the background. After it has completed, the status changes to Healthy.

FIGURE 10.15
The newly created G drive is formatting.

Formatting a Partition

After creating a partition, if you choose not to format the volume, you can always follow this procedure to format an existing partition. Complete the following steps to format a partition:

1. Open the Disk Management Console.

2. Bring up the context menu for the partition that you want to format.

3. Select Format from the context menu.

4. Make your selections and click OK to start the format.

Other methods of formatting

You can format an existing partition using Windows 2000 Explorer. And you can still use the **FORMAT** and **LABEL** commands from the command prompt for formatting and labeling a volume.

Canceling a format

You can cancel the format from the context menu for the partition, but be aware that if the partition was formerly formatted, canceling this format would not restore the partition to its former state.

Changing a Drive Letter

If you would like to change the drive letter for any partition, select the partition and then choose Change Drive Letter and Path. Click Edit and fill in the appropriate information then click OK.

A new feature of Windows 2000 is the ability to mount a volume within a folder. Here is how you do it:

1. Display the context menu for an existing volume. In this example I am using a CD with the label Hendrix (see Figure 10.16).

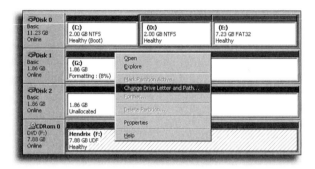

FIGURE 10.16
The context menu for an existing volume.

2. Select Change Drive Letter and Path.

3. The next dialog box, shown in Figure 10.17, displays the current drive letters and paths for the chosen partition. At this point, the CD drive is only accessed through the drive letter F.

FIGURE 10.17
A path for the volume can be added, edited, or removed.

4. Click the Add button to add another method of accessing this partition.

5. Choose the Mount in NTFS Folder option and specify a folder name on an existing partition (Figure 10.18). I created a folder named Hendrix on my D: drive. The name of the folder has nothing to do with the volume label for the CD, but I named them the same for easy identification. Click OK to add this path.

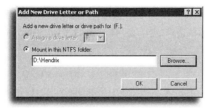

FIGURE 10.18
The selected volume is now accessible by the entered path.

Notice in Figure 10.19 that the CD drive icon appears in the D: drive. Now, using the path D:\HENDRIX, I can access this CD.

FIGURE 10.19
The D: drive with an icon for the CD-ROM drive.

Creating an Extended Partition

Creating an extended partition is similar to creating a primary partition; however, you have the option afterward to create logical partitions within the extended partition. This allows the partitions to remain DOS-compatible, if that is a concern of yours. Complete the following steps to create an extended partition:

1. Open the Disk Management Console.
2. Select a free space on a hard drive that already has an existing primary partition.

3. Right-click the space and choose Create Partition from the context menu.

4. The Create Partition Wizard starts. Click the Next button.

5. The Create Partition Wizard recognizes that this is a basic disk and allows you to choose to create either a primary partition or an extended partition (see Figure 10.20). Select Extended Partition and click the Next button.

FIGURE 10.20
Choose Extended Partition to create a host for logical drives.

6. Now enter the amount of disk space you want to use for the Extended Partition. As shown in Figure 10.21, I have chosen to use all available disk space. Click Next.

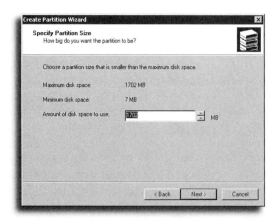

FIGURE 10.21
The amount of disk space held for logical volumes.

7. The Create Partition Wizard displays a summary (see Figure 10.22). Click Finish to create the extended partition. The newly created partition (shown in Figure 10.23) is shown as Free Space.

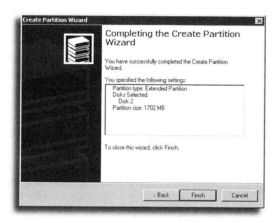

FIGURE 10.22
The summary for the creation of an extended partition.

FIGURE 10.23
An extended partition is seen as free space but is required for creating logical drives.

What about formatting?

The Create Partition Wizard does not ask about formatting the partition. That is because an extended partition does not get assigned a drive letter. It can host logical drives that will be formatted and assigned a drive letter, if you choose.

Creating Logical Partitions

The following steps enable you to create a logical partition within the extended partition:

1. Open the Disk Management Console and select the extended partition. Display its context menu by right-clicking. (See Figure 10.24.)

FIGURE 10.24
The context menu for an extended partition.

2. Select Create Logical Drive from the menu.

3. The Create Partition Wizard restarts.

4. The only choice for the type of partition is a Logical Drive. Click Next.

5. Choose the amount of space you want to use for this drive (Figure 10.25).

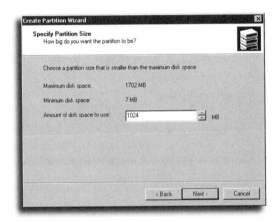

FIGURE 10.25
Because there can be more than one logical drive within the extended partition, size the drive as needed.

6. Assign a drive letter or a drive path. Click Next.

7. Choose the format you want to use for this logical drive (Figure 10.26). Click Next.

8. The summary (Figure 10.27) is displayed, and you can click Finish to create the logical drive.

In Figure 10.28 the logical drive (I:) is color-coded as a logical drive, and the remaining space is still marked as free space.

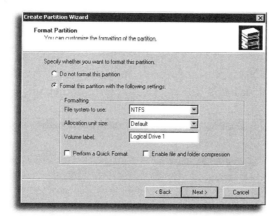

FIGURE 10.26
The format of the logical drive can be FAT, FAT32, or NTFS.

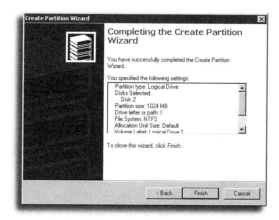

FIGURE 10.27
This summary gives the detail on the logical drive that was just created.

FIGURE 10.28
Drive I is a logical drive within an extended partition.

Deleting Partitions

Complete the following steps to delete a partition:

1. Open the Disk Management Console and select the partition you want to delete. Display its context menu (Figure 10.29) by right-clicking.

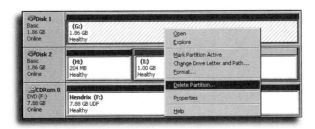

FIGURE 10.29
Select Delete Partition from the context menu to remove a partition.

2. Choose Delete Partition from the context menu.

3. A confirmation dialog box prompts you to confirm the partition deletion. Click the Yes button and the partition is removed.

A deleted partition cannot be recovered

Be sure to back up all the information on the partition before you proceed with the deletion. After the partition is deleted, that information is gone, unless you are willing to pay a lot of money to a data reclamation company. These companies specialize in restoring data from inadvertent deletion, head crashes, or other data loss issues where the data might still be on the drive.

Partition Properties and Tools

The Disk Management Console allows you to check your partitions for errors, defragment your drives, and display other information regarding the drives. Using the following steps, you can display these properties:

1. Open the Disk Management Console and highlight the partition you want to work with.

2. Bring up the context menu by right-clicking and select Properties (see Figure 10.30).

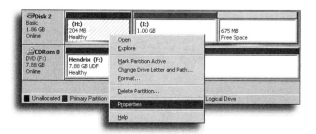

FIGURE 10.30
The Properties of a partition offers tools and information about the partition.

I will run through these options in the "Options Available Through the Properties Dialog Box" section later in this chapter because many more options are available after you make the drive a Dynamic Disk.

Converting a Drive to a Dynamic Disk

Having a drive as a Dynamic Disk gives you many more options for the creation of volumes. It also changes the way you can maintain those volumes, such as the ability to limit the amount of drive space that a particular user may use.

The conversion process from a basic disk to a Dynamic Disk does not erase any data. It is a safe process and only requires 1MB of free space on the drive you are converting. When you upgrade a system drive, the computer requires a restart to complete the conversion process. If the computer is turned off during the conversion process, you will probably lose all the data on that drive and have to re-create a partition.

Dynamic Volumes versus partitions

Dynamic Volumes are created on Dynamic Disks. These are no longer called "partitions" when they exist on a Dynamic Disk.

First, I'll show you how to convert some disks to Dynamic Disks and then I'll take you through the different procedures you can use for working with these.

The following steps enable you to convert a basic disk to a Dynamic Disk:

1. Open the Disk Management Console and open the context menu for the basic disk you want to convert by right-clicking.

2. As shown in Figure 10.31, select Upgrade To Dynamic Disk from the context menu.

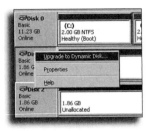

FIGURE 10.31
A context menu for a basic disk.

3. A dialog box prompts you to select the basic disks that you want to convert. For this example, shown in Figure 10.32, I'm converting the second and third drive I have installed. Click OK.

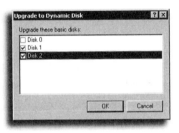

FIGURE 10.32
Select the basic disks that you want to convert to a Dynamic Disk.

4. The Disks to Upgrade list (shown in Figure 10.33) shows properties for these disks to help you determine whether you have chosen the correct disks. The Details button allows you to view further information about the chosen disks. Click OK when you are finished.

5. A confirmation box lets you know that after the conversion process is finished, these disks will be unusable by any other operating system. If you accept that, click the OK button.

6. The next dialog box lets you know that any partitions on these disks will be dismounted. In other words, if you are running any applications from the disks, close the application as the drives will become inaccessible during the conversion process. Click Yes to continue.

7. Figure 10.34 shows the newly upgraded Disk 1 and Disk 2 as Dynamic Disks.

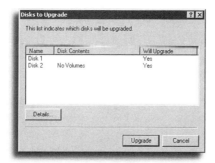

FIGURE 10.33
The Disks to Upgrade dialog box shows basic information about the disks.

FIGURE 10.34
Disk1 and Disk2 have been converted to Dynamic Disks.

To view the Properties on a Dynamic Volume, use the same process that you do for a partition, which is to select Properties from the context menu.

Options Available Through the Properties Dialog Box

The General tab shown in Figure 10.35 will show you the label for drive (which you can change) along with free space information.

Why can't I compress a folder or index the drive?

It's probably because you are trying to compress and index on a basic disk. These features are available only on Dynamic Volumes.

The next tab, Tools (Figure 10.36), is available to both basic disks and Dynamic Volumes.

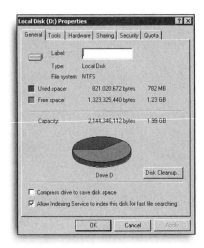

FIGURE 10.35
General information and configuration for a drive.

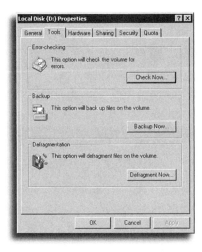

FIGURE 10.36
These three tools are available to both partitions and dynamic volumes.

The first button on the Tools tab, Check Now, scans your partition for defects in the file system. You can also choose to have the drive media checked for defects. To check a drive for errors, follow these steps:

1. Open the Disk Management Console and select the disk you want to check. Open the disk properties by right-clicking the disk and selecting Properties from the context menu.

2. Select the Tools tab and click the Check Now button.

3. You can choose to have this process automatically fix any errors it finds in the file table, and you can also choose to have a thorough scan performed that will look for defects in the drive (see Figure 10.37).

FIGURE 10.37
Choose the options you want to turn on for the disk check.

4. Click Start to begin the checking process.

5. When finished you will either have a message that Disk Check is complete, or you will be given a summary of errors with the ability to view a log of the errors.

Checking a busy disk

If you select a volume, such as the system partition, that is busy with a process and cannot be locked for inspection, you will receive a message that asks whether you want to check the volume the next time the system is started. You can choose to allow this, or you can choose to cancel the Check Now option. If you allow it, the next time you boot Windows 2000, a character-based version of the disk checker will run before the GUI loads.

The next button invokes the Windows 2000 Server Backup program.

SEE ALSO

➤ *For information on Backup, see page 305 ("Backing Up Files" Chapter 12)*

The third button brings up the Windows 2000 Disk Defragmenter program. Disk defragmentation is often overlooked for NTFS; however, it is necessary. Although NTFS resists fragmentation, it does not prevent it. Follow these steps to defragment your drive:

1. Open the Disk Management Console and select the disk you want to check. Open the disk properties by right-clicking the disk and selecting Properties from the context menu.

2. Select the Tools tab and click the Defragment Now button.

3. Select the drive you want to defragment (see Figure 10.38).

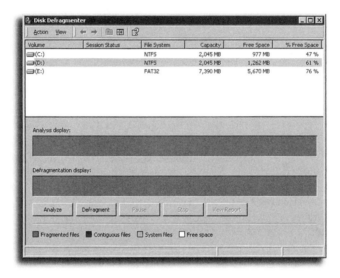

FIGURE 10.38
The Windows 2000 Disk Defragmenter is used to optimize the storage of data on the specified partition.

4. You have the option to analyze the disk for fragmentation before you start the defragmenter, or you can jump right into the defragmenter.

5. Select the appropriate action: analyze or defragment.

6. If you choose to analyze, you will see a display similar to the one in Figure 10.39. After the analysis is finished, the program will make a recommendation to you.

7. If you choose to defragment the drive, click the Defragment button.

8. A display similar to the one shown in Figure 10.40 will be shown.

Defragmentation can take a long time

Depending on the condition of your drive and how much fragmentation needs to be processed, this process can take a very long time—possibly hours. Luckily this process can run in the background.

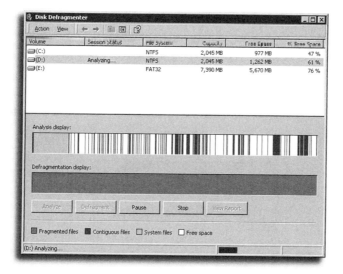

FIGURE 10.39
A drive being analyzed for fragmentation.

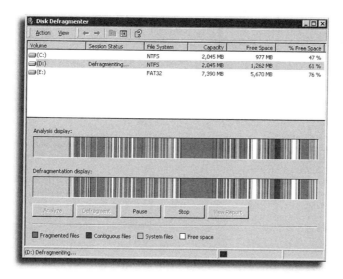

FIGURE 10.40
The defragmenting process in action.

The next tab is the Hardware tab, shown in Figure 10.41. This tab displays a list of the actual hardware that is installed in your computer. You can view additional information about the devices by clicking the Properties button.

The Sharing tab shown in Figure 10.42 displays any information regarding the drive and if it is shared. By default, an administrative share appears. The Share Name drop-down box displays any other shares that might have been made for this drive at the root level.

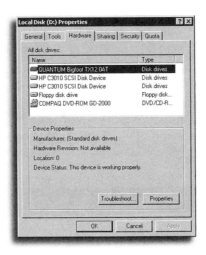

FIGURE 10.41
These are the physical hard drives installed in your server.

SEE ALSO
➤ *For more information on file sharing, see page 153.*

On NTFS drives, the Security tab allows for the setting of permissions at the file system level.

Disk Quotas

The final tab, Quota, is only available on drives that have been formatted as NTFS. I'm sure any Windows NT Server users will rejoice when they realize that quotas are now available with an upgrade to Windows 2000. By default, Disk Quotas are turned off (see Figure 10.43).

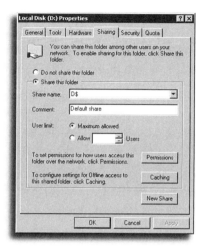

FIGURE 10.42
Add, modify, or remove shares for the drive through the Sharing tab.

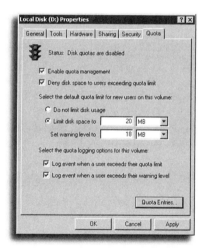

FIGURE 10.43
The Quota tab shows the service turned off by default.

To configure Disk Quotas, do the following:

1. To enable Disk Quotas, check the box next to Enable Quota Management.

2. In the confirmation dialog box that appears, click OK to continue.

3. As the disk is scanned, the traffic light changes from red to yellow. After it finishes, the traffic light is green, indicating that Quotas are now enabled.

You can choose to limit space to a certain number of kilobytes, megabytes, or gigabytes, among other space measurements. You can also specify a limit at which time users are notified that usage is creeping toward the limit. You can choose to log events when users reach their limit, and when they reach their warning limit.

Click the Quota Entries button to view information about the usage of the current drive (see Figure 10.44).

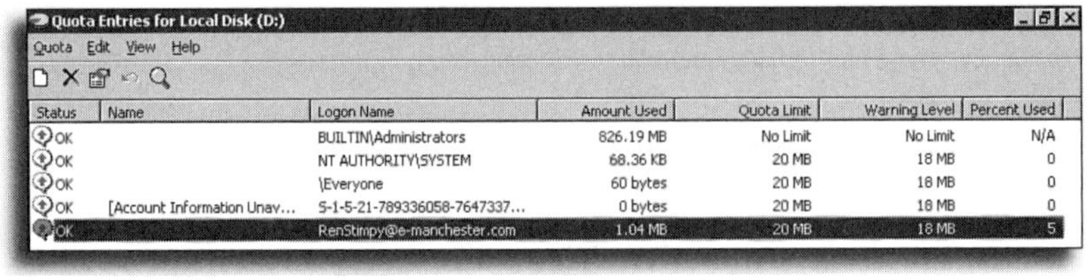

FIGURE 10.44
The list of entries for usage of the selected drive.

You can choose to view the Properties for a selected user that is using drive space on that volume by choosing Properties from the context menu (see Figure 10.45).

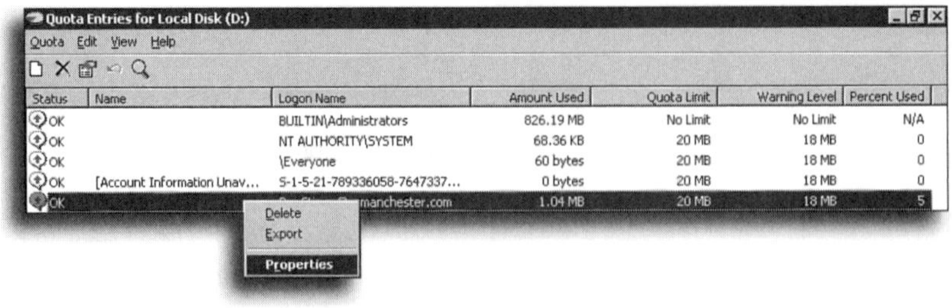

FIGURE 10.45
The context menu for a selected user.

The resulting dialog box, shown in Figure 10.46, allows you to modify the quota limits for that user or eliminate the quota altogether.

FIGURE 10.46
Individual users can have their quotas adjusted.

Dynamic Volumes

A Windows 2000 Server disk volume is composed of one or more partitions on one or more hard drives that are formatted with a file system and can be assigned a drive letter.

With MS-DOS, a volume was simply a partition on one hard drive, but with Windows 2000 Server, on a Dynamic Disk you can create different types of volumes that offer greater flexibility and disk-fault tolerance.

Working with Spanned Volume

You can combine free space from one or more hard drives to create a spanned volume. A *spanned volume* is a logical volume that is seen by the operating system as one volume. In reality, after the first segment of a spanned volume is used, the file system continues on the next segment of the spanned volume. One advantage of using a spanned volume is that you can save drive letters by combining areas on different hard drives, as opposed to assigning a drive letter to each individual area (volume).

Disk I/O can also improve because it is possible that data from the same program is being read from multiple physical drives at the same time, instead of queuing instructions for one physical drive. You might also run across a partitioning scheme that ends up with small empty areas at the end of multiple hard drives. These can easily be combined to form one volume.

Spanned volumes and Dynamic Disks

Spanned volumes can only be created using space from Dynamic Disks.

Follow these steps to create a spanned volume:

1. Open the Disk Management Console and bring up the context menu for the first area you want to use in the spanned volume.

2. Select Create Volume (see Figure 10.47). This starts the Create Volume Wizard.

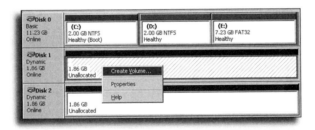

FIGURE 10.47
The selected free space starts the spanned volume.

3. Click the Next button.

4. From the list of available volume types, choose Spanned Volume.

5. Click the Next button.

6. The Select Disks dialog box, shown in Figure 10.48, has the first disk already selected. Add any other disks you want to include in this volume. Figure 10.49 shows both Disk1 and Disk2 selected. Click a Dynamic Disk and then alter the size that will be used on that particular disk.

7. Click the Next button after you have selected what disks you will use.

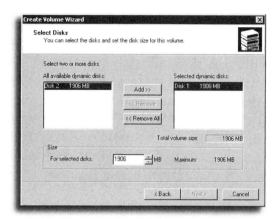

FIGURE 10.48
A disk that can be added to the spanned volume appears on the left.

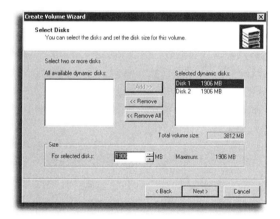

FIGURE 10.49
Now both drives have been added to participate in the spanned volume.

8. Next, assign a drive letter or path for the spanned volume (see Figure 10.50).

9. Click Next after you finish.

10. Specify the file system and format options, as shown in Figure 10.51. Click the Next button.

11. A summary will be displayed such as the one in Figure 10.52. If this is what you want the wizard to create, click the Finish button.

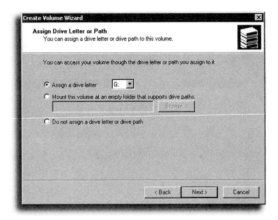

FIGURE 10.50
The spanned volume can be assigned a drive letter or a path.

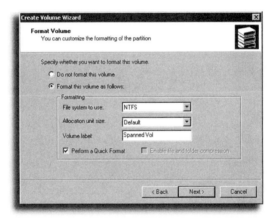

FIGURE 10.51
The file system for a spanned volume.

Working with Mirrored Partitions

Mirroring allows you to create a mirror image of a dynamic volume on another drive. This form of disk-fault tolerance is also known as RAID-1. Usually you should mirror all the dynamic volumes on a server, so that in case of a drive failure you can easily install a working drive that contains all the information from the faulty drive.

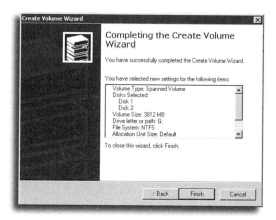

FIGURE 10.52
Click the Finish button to have the wizard create the volume shown in the summary.

Follow these steps to mirror a dynamic volume:

1. Open the Disk Management Console and select the dynamic volume that you would like to mirror.

2. Select Create Volume from the dynamic volume's context menu (see Figure 10.53).

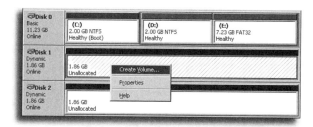

FIGURE 10.53
The context menu for a dynamic volume.

3. The Create Volume Wizard starts.

4. From the list of available volume types, choose Mirrored volume (shown in Figure 10.54).

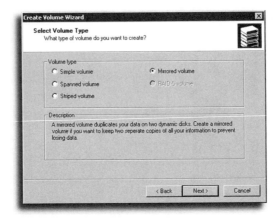

FIGURE 10.54
Select Mirrored volume for a fault-tolerant duplicate of the selected volume.

> **5.** Click the Next button. The first disk is already selected on the right side of the screen. Add any other disks you want to include in this volume. Click a Dynamic Disk and then alter the size that is used on that particular disk. Figure 10.55 shows both drives that are used in the mirror set.

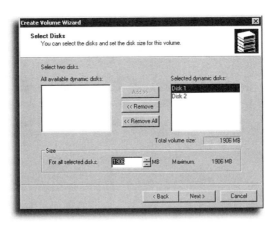

FIGURE 10.55
After the second disk is selected, the pair for the mirror is complete.

6. Click the Next button after you have selected what disks you will use.

7. Next, assign a drive letter or path for the Mirrored volume (see Figure 10.56).

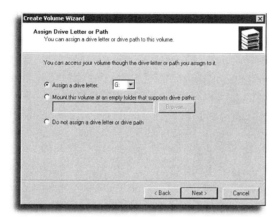

FIGURE 10.56
A drive letter or path can be assigned to the mirrored volume.

8. Click Next after you have finished. Specify the file system and format options (see Figure 10.57).

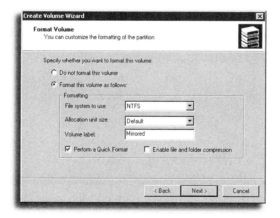

FIGURE 10.57
Select the file system for the mirrored volume.

9. Click the Next button. A summary is displayed, much like the one in Figure 10.58. If this is what you want the wizard to create, click the Finish button.

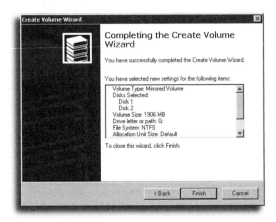

FIGURE 10.58
If the summary correctly reflects what you want to create, click the Finish button.

Working with Stripe Sets

In general, disk striping is a way to evenly distribute data across two or more hard drives, thus increasing performance.

There are two types of disk striping: RAID-0, or striped volumes; and striping with parity, or RAID-5. In both cases, data is written across multiple drives, which can allow data to be written in a faster manner, especially if you are using more than one disk controller.

Stripe Sets Without Parity

Although offering no disk-fault tolerance, disk striping offers increased performance. In fact, the highest performance disk configuration for Windows 2000 Server is a stripe set without parity. This is because you have multiple read/write heads available for disk I/O, without the parity overhead of a stripe set with parity. Disk striping will evenly distribute a volume across multiple physical hard drives. This is also known as RAID 0.

> **One problem with striping without parity**
>
> Although a striped volume is a cost-efficient way to increase disk performance, the entire volume can be lost if any of the hard drives that contains part of the striped volume has a failure.

Creating a Striped Volume

Select a dynamic volume that you would like to include in your striped volume and then follow these steps to continue the process:

1. Select Create Volume from the dynamic volume's context menu.

2. The Create Volume Wizard starts.

3. Click Next.

4. From the list of available volume types, choose striped volume.

5. Click the Next button. The first disk is already selected. Add any other disks you want to include in this volume. Click a Dynamic Disk and then you can alter the size that is used on that particular disk.

6. Click the Next button after you select what disks you will use.

7. Next, assign a drive letter or path for the striped volume.

8. Click Next after you finish. Specify the file system and format options.

9. Click the Next button. A summary is displayed. If this is what you want the wizard to create, click the Finish button.

> **The smallest calls the shots with striping**
>
> Because all the regions used for the stripe set must be the same size, the smallest free space region determines the size of the stripe-set volume.

To remove a striped volume, select one member of the striped volume. Then select Delete from the context menu. After confirming that you want to remove the entire striped volume, those regions are then marked as available.

Back up, back up, back up
Be sure to back up all the information on the striped volume before you proceed with the deletion.

Disk Striping with Parity

Of Windows 2000 Server's choices for a software disk-fault tolerance solution, disk striping with parity, or RAID-5, is the most secure and robust form of disk-fault tolerance available. This form of disk striping is very similar to disk striping without parity, but it also involves one more hard drive. Data is written across two or more hard drives, whereas another hard drive holds the parity information. This way, if one hard drive fails, the two remaining drives can recalculate the lost information and place this information back onto a newly installed working hard drive. This then brings the minimum number of hard drives involved in disk striping with parity to three, with a maximum number of 32 hard drives.

Follow these steps to create a RAID-5 (striped with parity) volume:

1. Open the Disk Management Console and select a dynamic volume that you would like to include in the RAID-5 volume.

2. Select Create Volume from dynamic volume's context menu (shown in Figure 10.59).

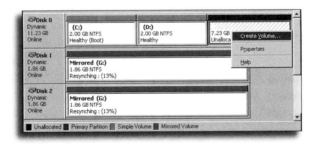

FIGURE 10.59
Select the first disk to be part of the RAID-5 volume.

3. The Create Volume Wizard starts. Click Next.

4. From the list of available volume types, choose RAID-5 Volume.

5. Click the Next button.

6. The first disk is already selected. Add at least two other disks you want to include in this volume. The smallest amount of space used on one volume is the amount that is used on the other volumes. Figure 10.60 shows all three selected disks.

7. Click the Next button after you select what disks you will use. Next, assign a drive letter or path for the RAID-5 volume (see Figure 10.61).

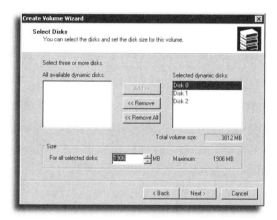

FIGURE 10.60
These three disks will have data and parity striped across them.

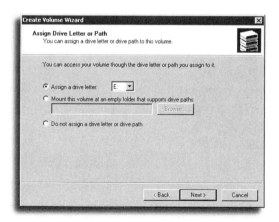

FIGURE 10.61
A drive letter or path can be assigned to the RAID-5 volume.

8. Click Next after you have finished. Specify the file system and format options (see Figure 10.62). Click the Next button.

9. A summary is displayed (as seen in Figure 10.63). If this is what you want the wizard to create, click the Finish button.

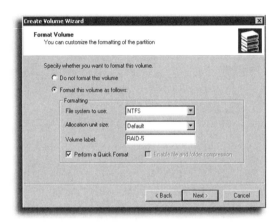

FIGURE 10.62
Specify the file system for the RAID-5 volume.

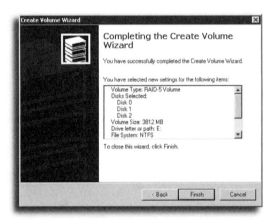

FIGURE 10.63
The summary is the last step before the RAID-5 volume is created.

RAID-5 is not an option

Windows 2000 makes it very easy to determine whether you can create a RAID 5 configuration or not. If you don't have enough disk space, or you have not selected enough drives, the option for creating a stripe set with parity is not available.

To remove a RAID-5 volume, select one of the members of the RAID-5 volume. Then select Delete from the context menu. After confirming that you want to remove the entire RAID-5 volume, those regions are then marked as available.

Working with the Windows 2000 Server Registry

Examining the Registry's Structure

The Registry is structured as a hierarchy consisting of containers that hold data. The containers are called Registry keys, and the data is called value entries. Registry keys are represented as folders in the Registry Editor, and value entries appear in the right-hand pane of the Registry Editor as keys are selected.

Registry Subtrees

Entries in the Registry are grouped under five keys, each of which comprises a sub-tree of the overall Registry:

- HKEY_LOCAL_MACHINE. Contains computer hardware information and configuration information for software installed on the computer. Part of this subtree is recon-structed each time the computer is started to reflect the current hardware con-figuration.

- HKEY_CURRENT_CONFIG. Contains the current hardware configuration, derived from the configuration used to boot Windows 2000.

- HKEY_CLASSES_ROOT. Contains object linking and embedding (OLE) and file-class association data. Information in this subtree is duplicated in HKEY_LOCAL_MACHINE.

- HKEY_CURRENT_USER. Contains user-profile data for the currently logged-on user.

- HKEY_USERS. Contains all actively loaded user profiles, including the default pro-file and a duplicate of information in HKEY_CURRENT_USER. Profiles for remotely logged-on users are stored in the Registries of their local computers.

You will become most acquainted with HKEY_LOCAL_MACHINE, which contains most of the parameters you will want to configure. So let's dig deeper into the Registry, using HKEY_LOCAL_MACHINE as the vehicle for discussion.

In Figure 11.1, the HKEY_LOCAL_MACHINE key is expanded and drilled down to reveal some content details. The technique is identical to that of browsing the file system in Windows 2000 Explorer, so I won't go into the details of how I arrived here.

As you can see, keys can contain subkeys, just as folders can contain folders in the file system. Any subkey can contain other subkeys and can also contain values.

FIGURE 11.1
Expanding HKEY_LOCAL_MACHINE.

Assigning Values

Each key and subkey can be assigned one or more values, which are displayed in the right-hand pane of the window. These values have a specific structure. The ComputerName value has only one data entry, but you will see examples of values that have many data entries. As Figure 11.1 illustrates, a value has three fields:

- *Name*. The name of the value entry.

- *Data type*. Programmers are familiar with the concept that data has a type that restricts the information that the data can display. Each data type is discussed in the next section.

- *Data*. The actual data. The type of data stored depends on the data type.

Understanding Hives

The data in the Registry subtrees are derived from six or more sets of files, called *hives*. The term *hive* was coined by a Microsoft systems programmer to reflect the way Registry data is stored in compartmentalized forms. Each hive consists of a data file and a log file. The log file is responsible for the Registry's fault tolerance. The respective log file names can be found in Table 11.1, a little later in the chapter.

Each hive represents a group of keys, subkeys, and values that are rooted at the top of the Registry tree. It's easy to identify the Registry keys that are associated with each hive. Figure 11.2 shows a composite of two windows: the HKEY_LOCAL_MACHINE window from the Registry Editor, and a File Manager window that shows the C:\Winnt\system32\config subdirectory.

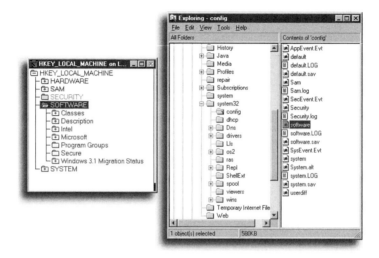

FIGURE 11.2
Hive files in the config subdirectory are related to registry keys.

You can easily identify files in the directory that are related to keys in the Registry. The SOFTWARE key, for example, is associated with the files software and software.LOG.

The Registry hives and files are summarized in Table 11.1.

Table 11.1 Registry Hives and Associated Files

Registry Hive	Associated Files
HKEY_LOCAL_MACHINE\SAM	Sam and Sam.LOG
HKEY_LOCAL_MACHINE\SECURITY	Security and Security.LOG
HKEY_LOCAL_MACHINE\SOFTWARE	software and software.LOG
HKEY_LOCAL_MACHINE\SYSTEM	system, system.LOG, and System.ALT
HKEY_USERS\DEFAULT	default and default.LOG
HKEY_CURRENT_USER	Ntuser.dat and ntuser.dat.LOG

Beginning with Windows NT 4.0, the user part of the Registry, corresponding to HKEY_CURRENT_USER, has been stored in the files Ntuser.dat and ntuser.dat.LOG in the user's profile directory. In prior versions of Windows NT, the user profile files were stored in the `config` subdirectory. Notice that in Figure 11.2, hives are associated with all the subtrees in `HKEY_ LOCAL_MACHINE` except `HARDWARE`. The information in the `HARDWARE` subtree is regenerated each time the computer is booted and therefore is not stored permanently in hives. On Intel x86 computers, the information is gathered by the `NTDETECT` program. On Advanced RISC computers, the information is gathered by the ARC configuration database.

The hives are responsible for storing the following categories of information:

- `HKEY_LOCAL_MACHINE\SAM`. Stores security information for user and group accounts. This information is used by the Windows 2000 Server Security Account Manager (SAM).

- `HKEY_LOCAL_MACHINE\SECURITY`. Security information regarding local account policy, used by the Windows 2000 security subsystem.

- `HKEY_LOCAL_MACHINE\SOFTWARE`. The configuration database for locally installed software. Serves the same purpose as application `.INI` files for Windows 2000 applications.

- `HKEY_LOCAL_MACHINE\SYSTEM`. The system startup database. Data is configured during installation and when the computer is reconfigured. The computer can't start without this information.

- `HKEY_USERS\DEFAULT`. The default user profile.

- `HKEY_CURRENT_USER`. The profile for the current user of the computer. This information is duplicated in the `HKEY_LOCAL_MACHINE\SYSTEM` hive. If entries in the hives disagree, `HKEY_CURRENT_USER` takes precedence.

Viewing the Registry

With Windows 2000 Server you get two Registry viewers: One is window oriented, and the other is tree oriented. Let's take a quick look at the Registry in each viewer.

First is the old-style Registry Editor, shown in Figure 11.1, which has changed very little since Windows NT 3.5x. To start the original Registry Editor:

1. Click the Start button.
2. Select Run.
3. Enter the command `regedt32`.
4. Click OK.

Initially, the windows cascade, but in Figure 11.3 I have moved the windows so that you can see each window.

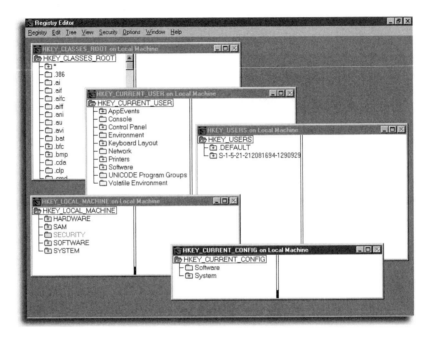

FIGURE 11.3
The Registry Editor started by the command `regedt32`.

Windows 2000 also includes a tree-oriented Registry Editor. To run the newer Registry Editor:

1. Click the Start button.

2. Select Run.

3. Enter the command `regedit`.

This editor, shown in Figure 11.4, works a lot more like Windows 2000 Explorer. I have expanded one branch so that you can see what the data entries look like. The data entries shown aren't particularly significant, but I had to find values that weren't too deep in the tree so that you could see a variety of values as well as the overall tree structure.

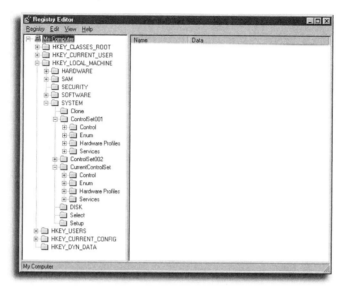

FIGURE 11.4
The Registry Editor started by the command `regedit`.

Unfortunately, neither Registry Editor has a corner on features. Regedit has better search capabilities and unifies the Registry into a single tree, so on the surface it appears superior. It also allows for running in Read Only mode, which is a safer way to investigate the registry. But Regedt32 makes it easier to edit data values, and its entries look more like the entries you will encounter in reference books. So, despite my general preference for the user interface of Regedit, I will use Regedt32 to illustrate Registry concepts in this chapter.

Editing the Registry

The Registry is a database that records most of the parameters that configure Windows 2000 and applications designed for Microsoft 32-bit operating systems. Windows 2000 still supports .INI files for the sake of compatibility with 16-bit Windows applications written for Windows 3.x environments, but with Windows 2000, Windows NT, and Windows 9x, the emphasis is on storing configuration data in the Registry.

The Registry is designed to be more robust than older text-file configuration files. It is difficult to damage Registry files because changes are recorded in log files, enabling Windows 2000 to back out of incomplete changes and repair damage.

Perhaps the chief disadvantage of the Registry is that it is big, and it takes a bit of time to become oriented so that you can find the parameters you need. Consequently, the bulk of this chapter will be devoted to exploring the Registry structure. After you locate what you require, the mechanics of editing the Registry contents are not difficult at all.

Editing a Remote Registry

If you need to, you can edit the Registry of a remote Windows 2000 or Windows NT computer. The command Select Computer on the Registry menu opens a dialog box where you can select another Windows 2000/NT computer. After you do so, two keys of the remote computer's Registry will be loaded into windows in the Registry Editor.

In Figure 11.5, Registry Editor is running on computer MALAPROP2.

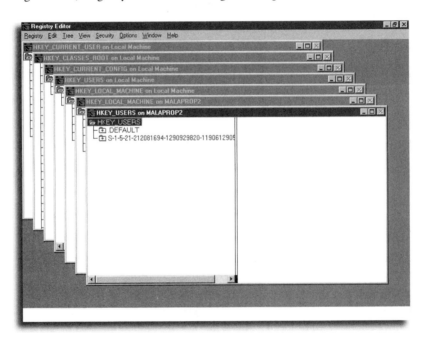

FIGURE 11.5
Editing Registry keys on the remote computer MALAPROP2.

I have selected the Registry of MALAPROP2 with the result that two windows are added to the Registry Editor:

- HKEY_LOCAL_MACHINE on MALAPROP2

- HKEY_USERS on MALAPROP2

HKEY_LOCAL_MACHINE and HKEY_USERS are the only keys you can access in this way, but then again, they are the only keys you are ever likely to edit.

When you have finished viewing or editing data in a window, select the window and choose Close from the Registry menu.

The ability to edit a remote Registry is of occasional value. In some cases, it can save you a trip to the user's computer. In other cases, it can help you repair damage to the user's environment that prevents you from working on the user's computer directly.

Assigning Values

Each key and subkey can be assigned one or more values, which are displayed in the right-hand pane of the window. These values have a specific structure. The ComputerName value has only one data entry, but you will see examples of values that have many data entries.

Editing Registry Value Entries

In several places in this book you will encounter settings that can only be changed by editing Registry values. You will encounter many other settings in the Windows 2000 documentation, magazine articles, and elsewhere. All Windows 2000 Server administrators should be familiar with the procedures for adding and editing Registry values.

Let's try something harmless by making a change to the desktop. The current user's personal environment settings are stored in HKEY_CURRENT_USER. Let's make a simple change by modifying the current user's wallpaper. Follow these steps to edit a Registry value entry:

1. Start the Registry Editor. Choose the Run command from the Start menu. Enter regedt32 in the Open field and click OK.

2. After the Registry Editor starts, check the Options menu. If the Read Only Mode option is checked, remove the check mark. Otherwise, you will be unable to save changes.

3. If the HKEY_CURRENT_USER window isn't open, open it by doing one of the following:

   - Choose HKEY_CURRENT_USER from the Window menu.

   - Double-click the HKEY_CURRENT_USER icon.

   - Double-click the Control Panel key. After this key opens, you see the subkeys shown in Figure 11.6. In this figure, the Desktop subkey has been selected. It contains the field you will be editing.

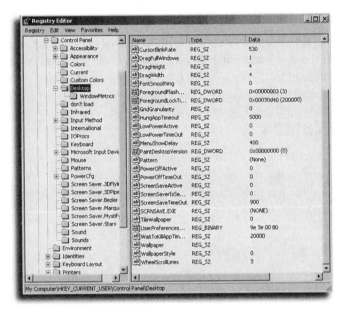

FIGURE 11.6
Subkeys for the Control Panel key.

4. Click the Desktop key to display its values.

5. Double-click the entry named Wallpaper. A dialog box opens that contains the value of the current wallpaper file. Figure 11.7 shows an example of a Registry value editor—in this case, the editor for a REG_SZ data type. Edit this entry to read greenstone.bmp, which will configure the wallpaper file to a file that should exist on your system. (The change has already been made in Figure 11.7.)

FIGURE 11.7
The Registry Editor dialog box for a REG_SZ entry.

6. Click OK to save the entry.

7. Quit Registry Editor. The wallpaper should now change.

Other Registry entries are edited in a similar fashion, although you will be shown different dialog boxes depending on the data type of the value entry.

Identifying Data Types

A data type describing the types of values that can be stored classifies each data entry. You'll encounter some other data types if you browse around, but these five types are the ones that most concern you:

- REG_BINARY. This data type describes raw binary data, the form used to store most hardware data, which can be viewed in more readable form in WinMSD, the Windows 2000 diagnostics utility. An example of such an entry follows:
  Video:REG_BINARY:00 00 00 00

- REG_DWORD. Data represented by a number up to four bytes long. This data can be displayed in binary, hexadecimal, or decimal form. An example follows:
  ErrorMode:REG_DWORD:0

- REG_EXPAND_SZ. Data represented in an expandable data string, which contains a system variable. The following example makes use of the %SystemRoot% variable:

  `SystemDirectory:REG_EXPAND_SZ:%SystemRoot%\system32`

- REG_MULTI_SZ. Data represented in a multiple string, consisting of lists or multiple values. Most human-readable text is of this type. Here is an example that has three values (autocheck, autochk, and *):

  `BootExecute:REG_MULTI_SZ:autocheck autochk *`

- REG_SZ. Character data used to store human-readable text. For example:

  `DaylightName:REG_SZ:US Eastern Standard Time`

WinMSD: The Windows 2000 Version of Microsoft Diagnostics

The WinMSD utility that comes with Windows 2000 Server allows you to quickly take a snapshot of your server and identify most the important settings for your server, all in one place.

Especially handy is the ability to print out a report from WinMSD.

Finding Registry Entries

The Registry is a big place, and you might be wondering how you can locate specific keys. After you become familiar with the Registry structure, you can find a great deal by browsing, but the Registry Editor does have a Find Key command. The catch is that you need to know which subtree to look in. After that, it's pretty straightforward.

As an example, look for entries regarding installed printers. Because this is hardware, the keys appear in the HKEY_LOCAL_MACHINE subtree. To find a Registry key:

1. Open the HKEY_LOCAL_MACHINE window.

2. Select the root key of the tree HKEY_LOCAL_MACHINE.

3. Choose Find Key from the View menu. You can see the Find dialog box shown in Figure 11.8.

4. Type printer in the Find What box.

5. Do not check the Match Whole Word Only box, because many key names are compound words, and printer might be only part of the key name.

6. Don't check Match Case unless you're trying to find a specific entry for which the case of the letters is known.

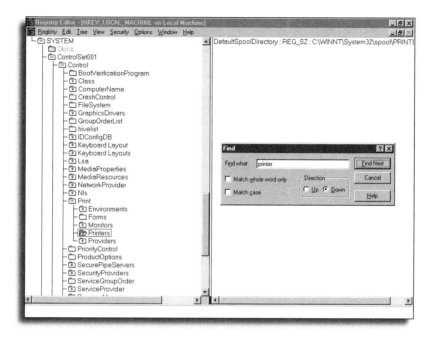

FIGURE 11.8
An example of a registry search.

7. Select Down if it is not already selected.

8. Click Find Next to initiate the search.

9. The search result is shown in Figure 11.9. (I opened the Printers key after it was found to ensure that it held the information I wanted.) The specific printer information probably differs on your computer, but the key under which the information is located should be found without trouble.

The beauty of searching

Searches are one area where the tree-oriented Regedit editor excels. For one thing, you don't need to know which subtree holds the object you're searching for, because you can start searching from the top of the Registry tree. For another thing, you can search for keys, values, and data. Figure 11.8 shows the Find dialog box for Regedit. In many cases, you will use Regedit to find the data you want and then use Regedt32 to make the desired changes.

FIGURE 11.9
Search options in Regedit.

chapter 12

Protecting Your Data

Why Back Up Your Data?

Performing file backups is about as glamorous as paying for life insurance. Ninety-nine percent of the time, you make your nightly backup, or send off your hard-earned cash, and you get nothing in return. It's only when disaster strikes that there is a payoff. At least if you have been making good backups, you will be around when the beneficiary thanks you for retrieving a critical file from the nether regions. On the other hand, if the McKenzie Proposal is lost (the day before it is due, of course) because you botched the backups, you might be banished to the nether-regions yourself. It's easy to get lazy about backups, but nothing a LAN administrator does is more important than archiving data. When you think about it, the LAN is data. The hardware and software are just there so that the data has a place to be. LANs typically have a lot of data, and critical data at that. Backup involves planning, execution, and testing. You need to have an effective backup plan for your organization; you need to execute the plan faithfully; and you need to run frequent tests to ensure that the backups you are making are functional.

So you want to back up your server. In order to accomplish this, you need to make three decisions:

- Choose backup software.
- Choose backup hardware.
- Choose a type of backup to perform.

You'll also want to set up a backup schedule. The following sections will help you make these choices.

Selecting Backup Software

This chapter doesn't spend much time covering backup software selection. Instead, it focuses on the Windows 2000 Backup program. Nevertheless, you should take the time to evaluate other products that can back up Windows 2000 because of additional features, such as client backup, additional hardware support, special software for backing up databases and other types of open files, and the ability to back up additional servers, even in a cross-platform environment. Windows 2000 Backup can back up clients through shares, but you must share the root directory of a share to back up an entire volume. In a large organization with many clients, backing up through shares is complex and trouble-prone. There are also security implications in requiring that all the data that is being backed up be shared on the network.

Third-party backup products include client backup software that makes the process much more convenient and reliable. Here are a few products you might want to examine, with their Web sites:

- *Backup Exec, from Seagate Software.* http://www.seagatesoftware.com
- *ARCserveIT, from Computer Associates.* http://www.cai.com
- *UltraBac, from UltraBac.* http://www.ultrabac.com

These are just a few of the dozens of products available, and should in no way be considered a comprehensive list or a product recommendation. When you evaluate any product, you need to take your requirements into account. But if your budget is tight, Microsoft has got a deal for you. Windows 2000 Backup is free, it is reliable, and it meets the needs of many organizations. It might be a permanent or temporary solution for you. I'll leave it up to you to decide which backup product best meets your needs. That leaves hardware and scheduling as planning considerations.

Selecting Backup Hardware

The Windows 2000 Backup program allows you to back up to both tape drives and logical drives, which might be local hard drives, networked hard drives, or another type of storage, such as optical storage. Given the size of today's hard disks, tape is the backup medium of choice for the vast majority of organizations. No other backup medium offers the combination of capacity and low cost that is available with tape.

LANs have backup needs that are distinctly different from user workstations. For one thing, there is more data on a LAN. For another, LANs are in use for a greater portion of the day. When an individual user goes home, he or she can start a backup job that can run for 12 hours if necessary. If you run a LAN, you might have trouble scheduling two hours a day for backup.

Therefore LAN backup hardware needs to be big and it needs to be fast. Before you buy any tape hardware, you need to carefully plan the capacity and speed you require. When you buy into a particular type of tape hardware, you are making a long-term commitment. In some cases, new generations of tape drives are not backward compatible.

How to select a drive?

Before you go shopping for a tape drive, there are a couple of things you should be sure to take into account. Capacity and speed are two of the major requirements. Another factor is compatibility. Be sure to check the Microsoft Hardware Compatibility List (HCL) before buying any hardware for your server.

In your search for tape hardware, you will encounter four technologies:

- *Quarter-Inch Cartridge (QIC)*. This format derives from work at 3M and uses a quarter-inch wide tape that shuttles back and forth through the cartridge as the head moves from track to track. The latest generation of QIC cartridges is called Travan, with the most recent drives having capacities in excess of 10GB per cartridge (uncompressed). Some QIC drives are designed to connect to parallel ports or high-speed parallel interfaces, but these are far too slow to consider for LAN backups. SCSI devices are available and offer better speed, but lag behind other options. In general QIC hardware is too slow to consider for backing up LAN servers.

- *Digital Audio Tape (DAT)*. This format is derived from the DAT format originally developed for audio recording. DAT uses a technology called *helical scan* to record data, a method similar to that of a video recorder, to write data at high density on 4mm-wide tape. The tape moves past the heads at a relatively slow pace, yielding a relatively slow backup speed. A DAT cartridge is slightly larger than a credit card in width and height and contains a magnetic tape that can hold 2–24GB of data. It can support data transfer rates of about 2MB per second (MBps). It is important to note that DATs are considered sequential-access media. That means that they access the data in sequential order. If the data you need to retrieve was written to the tape last, the drive needs to scan the entire tape before it can restore the data, yielding potentially slow restores. DAT is faster than QIC, but slower than 8mm or Digital Linear Tape (DLT).

- *8mm*. This format also uses technology derived from video recording to store data on 8mm-wide tapes. 8mm helical-scan cartridges have great capacity but they require relatively expensive tape drives. They also have relatively slow data transfer rates. 8mm is a proprietary technology of Exabyte Corporation, which makes all 8mm drive hardware. Capacity of 8mm is very high, currently about 40GB per cartridge, and comparatively fast data transfer rates (up to 3MBps) are supported.

- *Digital Linear Tape (DLT).* DLT is a type of magnetic tape storage device originally developed by DEC and now marketed by several companies. DLT uses a half-inch tape in a unique cartridge that has a single take-up reel (the other reel is in the drive) and the cartridges come in several sizes ranging from 20GB to over 40GB. DLT drives are faster than most other types of tape drives, achieving transfer rates of 2.5Mbps.)

For quite a while, DAT held an edge as best compromise of capacity and throughput at moderate cost, but other technologies are beginning to chip away at DAT's lead in the marketplace. Exabyte offers 8mm drives that compare very favorably to the cost of DAT drives. Perhaps the chief disadvantage of DAT, 8mm, and DLT is that you can't trot down to CompUSA and buy one off the shelf. You need to do your research, find a qualified vendor, and order the hardware you need.

Because research is required, here are some Web sites that will get you started:

- `http://www.compaq.com/` For Compaq's extensive line of storage solutions.

- `http://www.iomega.com/` For information about Iomega's line of QIC tape systems.

- `http://www.hp.com/tape/` HP now the Colorado line of QIC tape backup devices. They also produce the SureStore line of DAT and DLT drives.

- `http://www.exabyte.com/` For information about 8mm technology and descriptions of Exabyte's products.

Limitations of Tape Backup

Notice that none of these backup types protects you against loss of data in files that have been modified since the most recent backup. What if you cannot afford to lose a single change that is made to any file, regardless of when the last backup was made? If you are running computers for a bank, how do you ensure that not a single transaction is lost? There is no such thing as continuous backup, and open files can't be backed up. If your data is so critical that nothing can be lost, you need to be looking into one or more of the following options:

- RAID disk storage, so that a single hard drive failure will not cause a loss of data.

SEE ALSO
➤ *For information on RAID, see page 235 ("Using RAID to Protect Your Data" Chapter 10)*

- Fault-tolerant hardware that has redundant power supplies, error-correcting memory, and other goodies that keep you from losing data.

- Real-time mirroring solutions, such as Vinca Co-Standby Server.

- Microsoft Cluster Services for redundant application servers.

- Fault-tolerant software that can rebuild damaged files. A good database system keeps a log file that can reconstruct all transactions that take place. As long as the hard drives that contain the log file survive a disaster, you can restore last night's backup and roll the log forward to reconstruct the database to the point of failure.

Other Tape Backup Considerations

Tape backup can be a fairly involved process. Here are several miscellaneous topics you should consider when planning your backup strategy:

- *Open files.* Many applications and services keep files open at all times, and open files cannot be backed up because they are in a constant state of being modified. Windows 2000 Backup waits a bit to see whether an open file will be closed, skipping the file and reporting an error in the Backup log if the file cannot be backed up. Some software packages, such as SQL database servers, have their own backup software. Other software packages, such as WINS, automatically create backup copies of their active data files so that the backup copies can be archived to tape. As you plan your backup strategy, identify the applications that maintain perpetually open files and ensure that you have taken them into account. Most third-party solutions offer "open files agents" that will handle backing up open files.

- *Multi-tape backups.* In many cases, the data to be backed up exceed the capacity of a single tape, forcing you to either have multiple tape drives or to resort to spanning, the practice of continuing backup jobs on multiple tapes. All tape backup software packages support spanning. But spanning means someone needs to be there to change the tape. Is someone in your LAN room during the night? If not, you can't span backup jobs. Unless, that is, you have a tape autoloader. These wonderful gadgets accept eight or more tapes and change them as required.

  If, that is, your tape backup software supports autoloaders, which Windows 2000 Backup doesn't. If you have serious amounts of data to back up, you will need a very big tape drive or several tape drives.

- *Backing up clients and multiple servers.* Ideally, all critical files should be stored on a LAN server where they can be backed up easily. Often, however, users store critical files on their network clients, files that should be included in your backup plan. Windows 2000 Backup has only a limited capability to back up network clients and remote servers. To back up a remote computer—the computer that isn't running Windows 2000 Backup—you must map a network drive to a share on the remote computer and back up the network drive. That means, of course, that a suitable share must exist on the remote computer, typically a share at the root directory. On Windows 2000 computers, you could use the administrative share that is assigned to each volume, but by default only administrators have access to the administrative shares. If backups will be executed by members of the Backup Operators group, that group must be enabled to connect with administrative shares. As you can see, backing up a large number of remote computers quickly becomes complex, what with assigning share permissions, mapping drive letters, and running the backups. And then, because backups are identified by drive letters, you need to remember which network drive was used to back up which computer. The record keeping can get complex indeed.

- *Backing up remote registries.* There's another problem with Windows 2000 Backup. It cannot back up the Registry on a remote Windows 2000 computer. If you can't back up the Registry, you are missing most of the computer's configuration data. I'll show you a workaround later in the chapter, but it is just a workaround, not a slick solution to the problem.

What if you need to back up multiple computers, including the Registry?

If you are committed to backing up several computers from a central server, you have an excellent justification to investigate the third-party backup products mentioned earlier. All provide software that runs on the client and simplifies the process of performing remote backups. And all make it easier to track what files came from which computer.

- *Automation.* You probably don't want to spend your evenings and weekends in the computer room running backups. If your company doesn't have an overnight computer staff, it would be nice to be able to automate the process so that it starts in the wee small hours when everyone has gone home.

Planning Tape Rotations

Tape rotation seeks to meet several goals:

- To spread wear across all your tapes
- To store data on and off site
- To have several copies of files where possible
- To retain files for a required minimum period

There are many different approaches to tape rotation, some of which are very complex. This chapter considers two approaches that are easy to manage manually:

- *Two-set rotation*. If you don't need to archive files for extended periods of time, this is an easy-to-manage, simple rotation schedule. Essentially, you create two sets of five tapes and use each set in alternate weeks. Figure 12.1 illustrates the process.

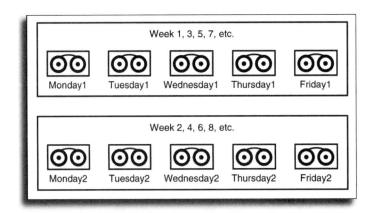

FIGURE 12.1
A two-set rotation backup schedule.

The tape labels in the figure assume that one tape will be required for each day. If your file volume requires spanning, you will need to create a set of tapes for each night—labeled, for example, Friday1A, Friday1B, Friday1C, and so forth.

- *Grandfather-Father-Son*. The grandfather-father-son (GFS; or grandmother-mother-daughter, if you prefer) is a compromise between simplicity and the goal of establishing a long-term file archive. I will show you one variation on the GFS rotation concept, after which you might want to customize the schedules to more closely meet your needs.

For the GFS rotation shown in Figure 12.2, you need the following tapes:

- Four tapes for each weekday: Monday through Thursday

- Five Friday tapes, one for each Friday of the month, labeled Friday1 through Friday5 (because some months have five Fridays)

- One tape for each month

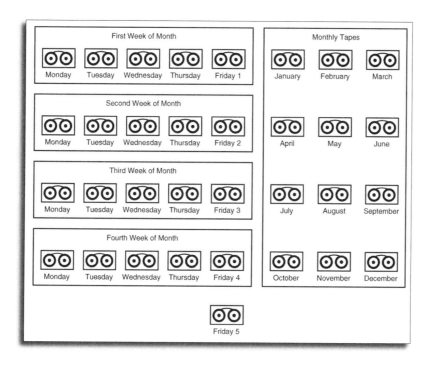

FIGURE 12.2
A grandfather-father-son tape rotation schedule.

Monday through Thursday, a backup is performed using the tape for that night. These tapes are reused each week. You can perform a normal, differential, or incremental backup, depending on your needs and backup time window.

The first Friday of the month, the Friday1 tape is used to perform a normal backup. These tapes are rotated each week. Except for the tape required for the current week, these tapes are stored off-site, preferably in a facility specifically designed for the storage of data tapes.

On the last day of each month, a normal backup is performed on that month's tape. These tapes are stored off-site for at least one year. Legal requirements in certain industries might require a longer tape-retention schedule.

If you own two tape drives, you can make on-site and off-site copies of the Friday and monthly tapes, enabling you to immediately access each night's backup in the event of an emergency.

Planning Your Backup Schedule

Tape backups can be performed according to a variety of schedules, depending on your needs and goals. Before you buy any backup products, consider your options and your needs. Know how you want to back up files before you buy the products necessary to do the job.

Types of Backups

Windows 2000 Backup can perform five types of backups. To understand how the backup types differ, you need to understand the *file archive bit* (also called the archive attribute). The archive bit is a marker on a file that can be turned on and off to indicate whether the file has been backed up since it was last modified. Whenever a file is modified in Windows 2000, the archive bit is set. Some backup operations look only for files for which the archive bit has been set. Backup operations do one of two things to the archive bit when the file has been backed up: They leave the bit in its current state, or they clear the bit to indicate that the file has been backed up.

The five types of backups are as follows:

- *Normal.* A *normal backup* does two things: It backs up all files that have been selected, regardless of the setting of the archive bit, and it clears the archive bit to indicate that the files have been backed up. Obviously, a normal backup performs a thorough backup of the selected files. By clearing the archive bit, a normal backup indicates that all files have been backed up.

- *Copy.* A *copy backup* does the following: It backs up all files that have been selected, regardless of the setting of the archive bit and leaves the archive bit in its pre-backup state. In other words, a copy backup does not alter the files that are backed up in any way, including changing the archive bit.

- *Differential.* *Differential backups* are so named because they record all the differences that have taken place since the last normal backup. A differential backup does the following: It backs up only files that have the archive bit set to show that the file has been modified and leaves the archive bit in its pre-backup state. Differential backups often are used in combination with normal backups. A normal backup of all files is performed each weekend to archive all files on the

LAN, for example. Then a differential backup is performed each night of the week to back up all files that have been modified since the weekend. Figure 12.3 shows how this schedule works.

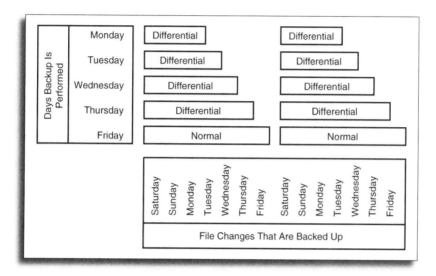

FIGURE 12.3
A weekly backup schedule using differential backups.

To restore all files on the LAN, you need to restore two sets of tapes:

- The normal backup for the preceding weekend
- The differential backup for the previous night

Differential backups commonly are used to reduce the amount of time in which backup jobs must run during the week. If you can schedule a normal (full) backup for the weekend but have limited time during the week, a differential backup still might fit into the weekday backup window.

- *Incremental. Incremental backups* record only the changes that have taken place during a preceding interval of time—often one day. An incremental backup does the following: It backs up only files that have the archive bit set to show that the file has been modified, and it clears the archive bit to indicate that the file has been backed up. Figure 12.4 shows how a combination of normal and incremental backups would work. The figure assumes that a normal backup is performed during the weekend, and an incremental backup takes place each weeknight. Notice that each incremental backup only records files that have been modified since the previous backup took place.

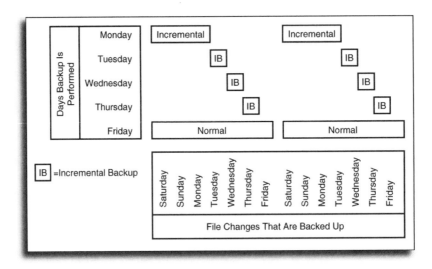

FIGURE 12.4
A weekly backup schedule using incremental backups.

Incremental backups are used to further reduce the time interval required to back up networks. If your LAN includes critical data, you might want to run incremental backups more than once a day so that an entire day's worth of work cannot be lost. The disadvantage of incremental backups is that several tapes can be required to restore the network. If the LAN fails on Thursday, you must restore the last normal backup and the incremental backups for Monday, Tuesday, and Wednesday.

■ *Daily. Daily backups* identify files to be backed up by examining the date stamp. If a file has been modified on the same day the backup is being made, the file will be backed up. A particularly useful application for daily backups is to make checkpoint backups during the working day to capture changes at intervals shorter than 24 hours.

Backing Up and Restoring Files

Now that you have an idea of the planning issues involved in establishing your backup strategy, let's get real and see how Windows 2000 Backup works. Despite the limitations noted earlier in the chapter, Windows 2000 Backup is quite a solid program. It is easy to use and reliable, and it might be all your organization requires. Unless you know that you are going to select another software package, try working

PART III

Backing Up and Restoring Files **CHAPTER 12**

with Windows 2000 Backup for a while. It will help you get comfortable with the backup process and experiment with some strategies before you plunk down big bucks for a third-party backup package.

Before you can back up files, you need to install the drivers that enable Windows 2000 Backup to work with your tape drive. After looking at tape driver setup, I'll dig into the Backup program.

Installing Tape Drivers

Like every other hardware device, tape drives need drivers. Your first stop, therefore, is the Add/Remove Hardware applet in the Control Panel. You might want to first check the Device Manager to see whether Windows 2000 had already spotted your tape drive and installed the drivers for it.

Backing Up Files

Figure 12.5 shows the Windows 2000 Backup program. You will find its shortcut in the Accessories/System Tools program group (see Figure 12.6).

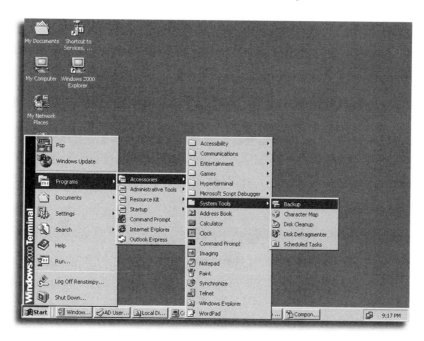

FIGURE 12.5
Execute the Backup program from the Start menu.

305

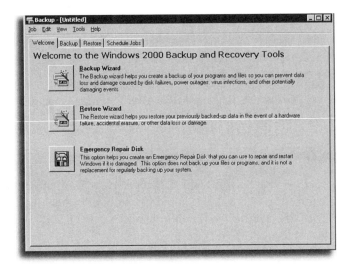

FIGURE 12.6
The Windows 2000 Backup program Welcome tab.

The Windows 2000 Backup program gives you three choices for running a wizard, or, you can manually specify the action you want to take by selecting the appropriate tab.

Selecting Files for Backup

The Backup Wizard makes it very easy to create a backup job. To run the Backup Wizard, do the following:

1. Click the Backup Wizard button. The Welcome screen is displayed.

2. Click the Next button. The What to Back Up screen (Figure 12.7) gives you three choices that are shown in Table 12.1. For this example I have chosen the second option so that I can be selective.

Table 12.1 The Choices for What to Back Up

Option	Description
Back Up Everything on My Computer	Creates a full backup. This includes all hard drives and the System State.
Back Up Selected Files, Drives, or Network Data	Presents a list of drives and shares that you can choose from. The System State is also an option that you can choose.

Option	Description
Only Back Up the System State Data	The System State creates a back up of all crucial system files and settings, including the registry, the COM+ Class registration database, and the system boot files. On a domain controller the Active Directory and SYSVOL folders are also backed up. If the server is a Certificate Server, the Certificate database is backed up as well.

FIGURE 12.7
What to Back Up offers three easy options.

> **3.** After clicking on the Next button, the Items to Back Up screen is shown (see Figure 12.8).

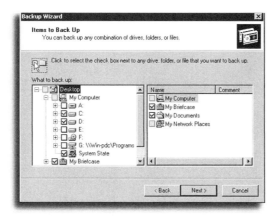

FIGURE 12.8
Choose the items to back up by checking boxes.

4. To select entire volumes, just enable the check boxes of the desired volumes in the Items to Back Up window. There are a number of different methods for selecting the data to be backed up. They include the following:

   - To back up an entire drive, check the check box next to a logical drive or network drive that you have attached to.

   - To back up specific files or folders, double-click a drive to open a drive tree window. The drive tree window works much like trees in utilities such as Windows 2000 Explorer. You double-click a directory icon labeled with a plus sign (+) to open the directory to the next level, for example.

   - Choose the files or directories to back up by checking the associated box. Checking a folder selects all subfolders of that folder. You can, if you want, open the subfolders and remove the check marks from specific subfolders or files.

   Notice that a folder check box is filled with gray if any files or subfolders under that folder are unchecked. This indicates a partial backup of that folder.

5. Click the Next button to bring up the Where to Store the Backup screen (see Figure 12.9). If you have a tape drive installed, the Backup Media Type drop-down box will list a tape device. You also have the option to back up to a file. In this example I am backing up to another drive, therefore I have entered the name of the file as `E:\Total Backup.bkf`.

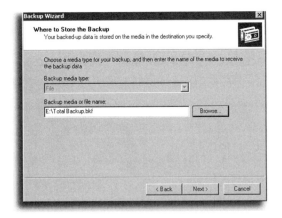

FIGURE 12.9
Where to store the backup can be a tape drive or other media with a logical drive letter.

6. Clicking the Next button brings the Backup Wizard to the end (see Figure 12.10). You can click the Next button or can specify additional options by clicking the Advanced button. If you click the Next button, the backup operation starts immediately using default settings.

FIGURE 12.10
Verify the options you have chosen for backup in this dialog box.

7. After clicking on the Advanced button, the Backup Wizard first allows you to choose the type of backup you want to perform. By default the backup would be a Normal backup. The choices are shown in Figure 12.11.

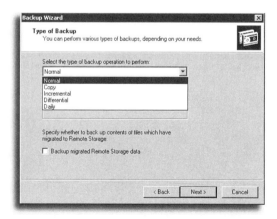

FIGURE 12.11
These are the choices for the type of backup that can be performed.

8. After you click the Next button, the option appears to tell Windows 2000 Backup to perform a verify after the backup has completed (Figure 12.12). The verify reads the backup media and compare it to the actual data, therefore insuring that the backed up data is identical to the actual data. This same screen allows you to choose compression if the hardware you are using supports compression.

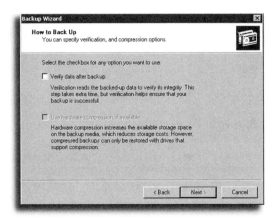

FIGURE 12.12
You can choose to run a verify after the backup and enable hardware compression if your hardware supports it.

9. Click Next to choose whether to append to existing data (default) or overwrite existing data on the backup media (Figure 12.13). If you have chosen to overwrite the media, you can also set security on the backup media.

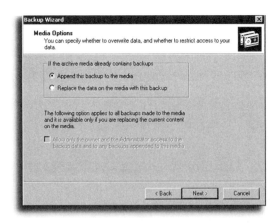

FIGURE 12.13
You can either overwrite or append to your backup media.

10. Proceed to the next screen, Backup Label (Figure 12.14), which gives you a default label for the backup. You can accept that or you can type your own descriptive label for the backup media and for the backup itself. These labels are helpful to let you find the right backup when you need to perform a restore.

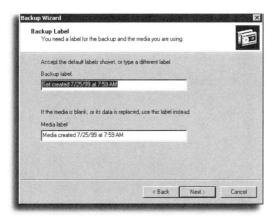

FIGURE 12.14
Providing a descriptive Backup Label makes finding files to restore easier.

11. The When to Back Up screen (Figure 12.15) permits you to leave the default setting of running the job immediately, or you can click the radio button named Later and then specify a Job Name.

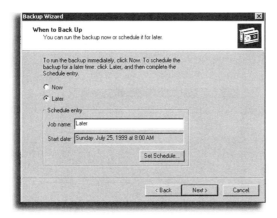

FIGURE 12.15
Either run the job immediately or choose to schedule it for a later time.

12. Click the Set Schedule button to define when "Later" is. By default the job is set to run once immediately. The Schedule Job dialog box (shown in Figure 12.16) is now displayed.

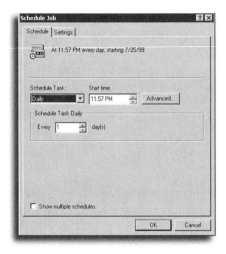

FIGURE 12.16
A backup can be scheduled at regular intervals or only once.

13. Options you can choose are to run the job once or at regular intervals. In my example I have set up the job to run once a day just before midnight.

14. Click the Advanced button to display the Advanced Schedule Options (see Figure 12.17). These options include setting an end date for the defined interval and additional repeat times during that interval. Click OK when you are finished with this dialog box.

FIGURE 12.17
Advanced schedule options permit you to further define the right type of backup for your environment.

15. On the Settings tab (see Figure 12.18) you have other options to customize how the backup job will proceed. You can specify a time limit for the backup to run. For instance, if you have a time window because you do not want the overhead of the backup running on the server while people are working, you can limit the length of time that the backup runs. Of course, you might not have a full backup. But the option is available to you.

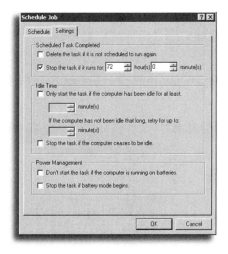

FIGURE 12.18
The Settings tab permits you to force a time to end your backup.

16. After you are finished specifying the schedule, click the OK button.

17. Then click the Next button to view the Completing the Backup Wizard dialog box (Figure 12.19). This dialog box confirms your choices for setting up the backup job. If it looks good to you, click the Finish button.

Verifying the Backup

The Backup Status box displays a running commentary that informs you of the backup progress (see Figure 12.20).

When the backup has finished, a dialog box similar to the one shown in Figure 12.21 is displayed. You can either click Close to exit or click Report to see a detailed report on the backup. Note in Figure 12.22 the report shows that certain files were not backed up due to the fact that they were in use (open). I recommend that you check this report so that you can see whether the backup was successful.

FIGURE 12.19
The Backup Wizard has completed.

FIGURE 12.20
Monitoring the status of a backup.

FIGURE 12.21
The backup has completed.

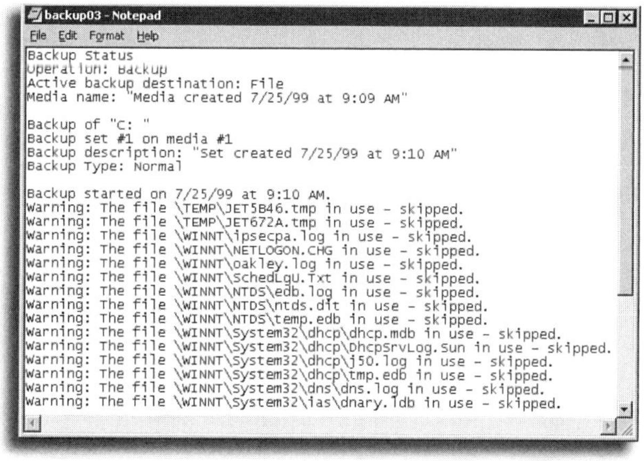

FIGURE 12.22
The Backup report shows if files have been skipped.

Restoring Files with the Restore Wizard

After you have successfully completed a backup, you can follow these steps in order to restore files.

1. Click the Restore Wizard button from the Welcome tab.

2. The Welcome To The Restore Wizard dialog box prompts you to click the Next button to proceed.

3. First, you need to choose what you want to restore. The backups that you had previously created will be shown in the What to Restore dialog box (see Figure 12.23). Select the media you want to restore from, and then select the drives or individual files you want to restore. This selection process is much like the process used to select files and folders for backup.

4. By default, the Restore Wizard restores the selected files to their original location and does not overwrite existing files. This is stated clearly in the Completing the Restore Wizard dialog box (see Figure 12.24). If you want to change any of these default options, click the Advanced button. Otherwise you can click the Finish button.

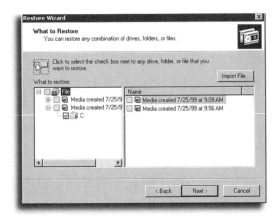

FIGURE 12.23
What to Restore shows you a list of backups that have been done on this computer.

FIGURE 12.24
The Restore Wizard displays the default settings for the restore process.

5. If you click the Advanced button, you are presented with the Where to Restore dialog box (see Figure 12.25). You can choose to leave the default, or you can change it to an alternative location. Click the Next button when you have finished your selection.

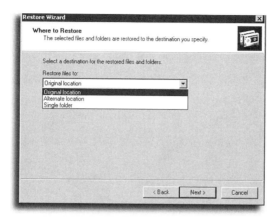

FIGURE 12.25
You can choose to restore files to a folder different from the original folder.

6. The How to Restore dialog box (shown in Figure 12.26) lets you choose to not overwrite files, to overwrite if the restored files are newer, or to unconditionally overwrite files. Click the Next button.

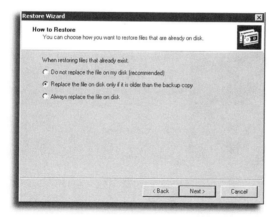

FIGURE 12.26
Select the option to overwrite existing files.

7. The Advanced Restore Options, shown in Figure 12.27, give even greater flexibility in how to handle the restoration process.

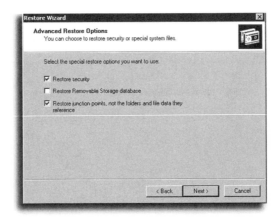

FIGURE 12.27
These granular options permit you to choose, among other settings, whether to restore security settings.

8. Clicking Next on this dialog box returns you to the Completing the Restore Wizard dialog box, but this time the options reflect any changes that you made (see Figure 12.28).

FIGURE 12.28
Check the settings you might have changed before you initiate the restore from this dialog box.

9. The Restore Wizard will now prompt you to load the appropriate tape. If you back up a file, the Restore Wizard confirms the filename for the Backup file (see Figure 12.29). When you are ready, having specified the correct media, click the OK button to start the restore process.

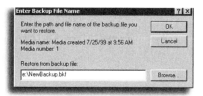

FIGURE 12.29
Confirm that you will be restoring from the proper media.

10. A dialog box displays the status of the restore process. When the restore has finished, a dialog box like the one shown in Figure 12.30 is displayed. From this dialog box you can choose to exit the Restore Wizard or you can first view a log for the restore process.

FIGURE 12.30
The Restore process is complete. Click Report to see the results.

11. If you click Report, you see a report much like the one shown in Figure 12.31. In this report, no files were processed because all the files in the backup were older than the files currently on disk.

Setting Default Options

The default options for both the backup and restore processes can be changed to suit your requirements. Access these by selecting Options from the Tools menu. The resulting dialog box is shown in Figure 12.32.

FIGURE 12.31
This restore report shows that no files were restored. This was due to the files on disk being newer.

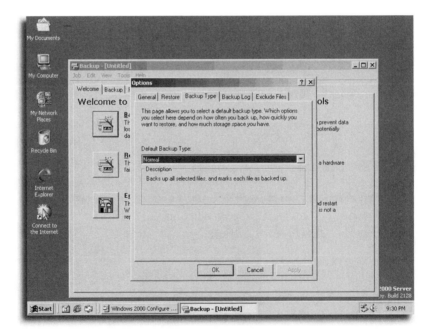

FIGURE 12.32
Set default backup and restore options from this menu item.

Test Your Tapes

Don't take your backup procedures for granted. Test your tapes to ensure that files can be restored properly. If possible, try the procedure discussed at the end of this chapter and try to restore an entire server from tape backups. It's better to practice before you have a real emergency because emergencies mean pressure. And who needs pressure when trying something for the first time?

Another good idea is to run small restore jobs on a weekly basis to ensure that your files, directory structures, and security settings are being archived and can be recovered properly.

Recovering a Server

If you experience total failure of a server's boot hard drive, the hardest part of recovery is restoring the system directory. You cannot just reinstall Windows 2000 and then restore the \Winnt directory tree because the running copy of Windows 2000 holds files open that prevent the restoration of critical files. Often, attempting to restore the system directory just results in a nonworking system.

I'm going to describe a procedure that works. The procedure assumes that you are backing up the Registry each time you run a backup job. To recover a server from a backup, do the following:

1. Reinstall Windows 2000, specifying a different system directory than the one used previously. The normal system root directory is the default c\Winnt. In this example, I assume that Windows 2000 is installed in the directory c:\Win2K.

2. Configure the tape drive.

3. Start the Backup program and get your most recent backup tape that includes the system directory.

4. Restore the most recent normal backup to the original file locations. Because the original system root directory is not being used, Backup can restore all files to that directory without conflicting with open files. Check Restore Local Registry and Restore File Permissions when restoring the files.

5. Restore any incremental or differential backups that were made since the last normal backup.

6. When prompted, select Yes to All to restore all files on the tapes, replacing existing files if necessary.

7. When satisfied the server is operating properly, delete the temporary system directory (`C:\Win2K`).

The preceding procedure assumes that you are restoring the following files:

* The entire system directory (`C:\Winnt`)
* The System State
* A `boot.ini` file that boots the operating system in `C:\Winnt`

If you are not restoring a `boot.ini` file that boots Windows 2000 from the system directory you are restoring, you will need to edit `boot.ini` to boot the restored copy of Windows 2000.

Here's Your Security Blanket

Reliable backups are among the best security blankets a network administrator can have. Nothing builds your credibility with users like the magic of pulling a lost file out of oblivion. Establishing good, tested backup procedures is a lot of work, but the reward will come. Sooner or later it will come. And you will be glad of every minute you spent on file backups.

Protecting Your Server with a UPS

I have spent a lot of time discussing how to protect the data on your server by making sure you have good backups. Now I will explain how to ensure your data isn't corrupted due to power issues. I'll discuss the hows and whys of using an Uninterruptible Power Supply (UPS).

Identifying Power Problems

Power problems create havoc on computers. Here are just a few of the problems a computer must contend with:

* *Power outages.* Complete losses of power.
* *Voltage variations.* You know how the lights in your house dim when you start the vacuum cleaner? Power-hungry systems can cause the voltage at an AC outlet to vary by a surprising degree. I've seen more than one server problem caused by these periodic "brownouts." Brownouts are also stressful for equipment. Repeated brownouts can burn out power supplies.

- *Voltage spikes and surges.* A voltage spike so short that you might not even notice it can damage equipment. Lightning is a prime cause of voltage spikes.

- *Line Noise.* Radio frequency noise on the AC line might get past the filtering in your computer power supply, which is really only designed to cope with the 50–60Hz frequency of line current. Noise can also cause computers to act erratically.

Any of these issues could have a serious impact on your computers ability to maintain data integrity and remain available to your users. What should you do?

Defending Against Power Problems

The Uninterruptible Power Supply (UPS) utility lets Windows 2000 monitor an uninterruptible power supply and undertake a smooth shutdown in the event of a power failure. However, depending on your equipment, you might need more than one device to deal with all the problems cited in the previous section. Many UPS units don't provide spike protection or filtering, and most can't protect against voltage variations in the AC line.

At a minimum, every computer should be plugged into a surge and spike protector, and you need to plug your UPS into one unless the UPS provides surge and spike protection. Don't even think about using a $10 special. Expect to spend about $50 for a surge and spike suppressor—particularly one that also filters out high-frequency noise.

A surge and spike suppressor is designed to eliminate relatively short voltage changes. If your power line experiences periodic brownouts or over-voltages, you need a power-line conditioner. These devices can level off low and high voltages, maintaining a constant output voltage within a reasonable range of line fluctuations. Expect to spend about $300 for a power-line conditioner. If possible, have an electrician install a dedicated conditioned power line for your server. I used to think that power-line conditioning was seldom required, but the proliferation of electronic equipment (copiers and laser printers are particular culprits) connected to the power lines of a typical office often results in a dirty power system that must be shared by a server. A server is an expensive investment and a few hundred dollars for a power-line conditioner seems a small added cost.

Uninterruptible Power Supplies

All UPS devices work by charging a battery during normal operation. The power in the battery can be converted to AC current that can be used to power a computer.

A UPS can be designed to operate with the battery either online or offline. Figure 12.33 shows how the two types of UPS devices work.

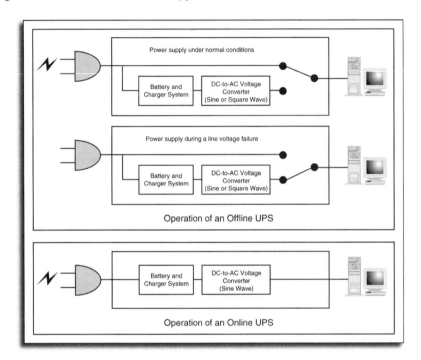

FIGURE 12.33
Offline and online UPS Systems.

The majority of UPSes use the *offline* approach. Under normal conditions, the AC line is switched directly to the outlets that service the computer. AC power is also directed to the battery system, which is kept constantly charged. When power fails, an electronic switch connects the UPS outlets to the inverter circuits that convert DC power from the battery into AC power that can run the computer.

The most significant problem with an offline UPS is the period of time that is required to switch from direct AC power to the inverter. Most UPS devices are now designed to make the switch rapidly enough that few computers are bothered, but this was once a common problem.

The *online* UPS makes it unnecessary to switch power because the computer is always connected to the battery/inverter system. The outside AC power runs the charging circuits that keep the battery topped off, but it is never directly connected to the computer. Because there is no switch-over, a power outage is handled much more smoothly. Because the AC line voltages are never connected to the computer, an offline UPS inherently functions as a surge, spike, and power-line conditioner.

Every battery-powered UPS must be capable of converting battery-direct current (DC) into the alternating current (AC) required by the protected computer. In the majority of UPS devices, the AC voltage produced is not a true sine wave, such as the AC current you get from the wall. Most UPS devices produce a square wave that can cause problems with some computer equipment. Some manufacturers design their equipment to produce a simulated sine wave, which is a stepped-square wave. Simulated sine waves are acceptable to most equipment. Figure 12.34 illustrates the various waveforms.

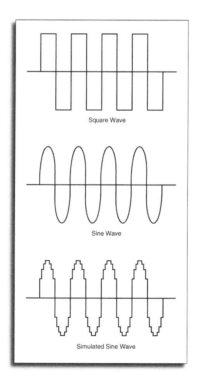

FIGURE 12.34
Waveforms produced by a UPS system.

Because an online UPS is constantly supplying the computer with remanufactured AC, it must produce a true sine wave. Equipment operating too long on a square-wave AC will be damaged.

Most offline UPS systems produce square-wave voltages, which can be used to operate the majority of computers for relatively short periods of time, such as the few minutes it takes to shut down the server properly in the event of a long power failure.

UPS systems can power a server for only a limited time before their batteries are depleted. Therefore, it's desirable to have a means of automatically monitoring the UPS and shutting down the server before the UPS can no longer sustain the required operating voltage. Windows NT includes a UPS service that can provide UPS monitoring with many UPS systems.

Connecting the UPS to the Server

To use the UPS service, your UPS must be equipped with a monitoring interface—usually a DB-9 connector that uses RS-232 serial interface signaling. A cable is used to connect the UPS to a serial port on the computer.

Unfortunately, there are no standards for how UPS monitoring should be done, and every manufacturer seems to have a different way of configuring the monitoring port. Therefore, it's always best to obtain a cable that is designed to match your UPS to Windows 2000 Server. Contact the manufacturer of the UPS to obtain cables or cable specifications.

After you connect the UPS to your server with a suitable cable, you can configure the UPS service.

Configuring the UPS Service and the UPS Monitor

You access the UPS configuration dialog box from the UPS tab in the Power applet in the Control Panel.

Configuring the UPS Monitor

Follow these steps to configure Windows 2000 to use a UPS:

1. Open the Power applet in the Control Panel and click the UPS tab (See Figure 12.35.)

2. Click the Select button to open the UPS Selection dialog box shown in Figure 12.36.

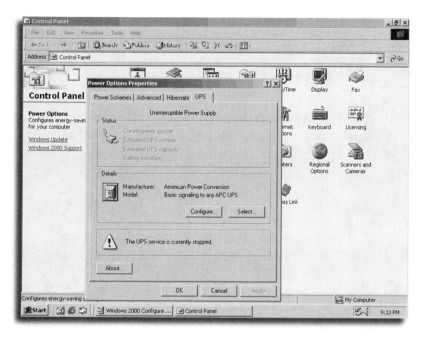

FIGURE 12.35
The UPS tab is used to configure all your UPS settings.

3. Select the appropriate UPS manufacturer, model, and COM port. Click OK to return to the UPS tab of the Power applet.

4. Click Configure to open the UPS Configuration dialog box (Figure 12.37).

    From here you can configure the following options:

    • *Enable All Notifications.* You can tell the application to notify users and administrators of a power outage. You can also configure the time interval for those notifications. They will be sent as Windows broadcast messages.

    • *Critical Alarm.* A critical alarm is generated when the UPS is almost exhausted, or at a specified time interval after the power outage. You can configure this interval, configure an application to run when this alarm is reached (such as a paging application) and configure the action to be taken (Shutdown, for example.)

    Click OK to return to the UPS tab of the Power applet.

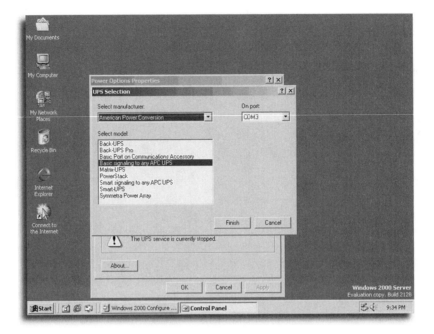

FIGURE 12.36
The UPS Selection dialog box is used to select the make and model of the UPS to be managed, as well as the appropriate communications port.

Use the UPS manufacturers recommended settings

The manufacturer of your UPS is the best source of information for the values to put in these fields. Because the UPS can't signal a low-battery condition, the UPS service uses these values to estimate when a low battery condition is likely.

In your UPS configuration, allow for short outages

Most UPSes send a power failure warning immediately, even for a very short loss of service. If the UPS service interprets such a short loss as the start of a serious outage, it often notifies network users to log off when logging off is unnecessary.

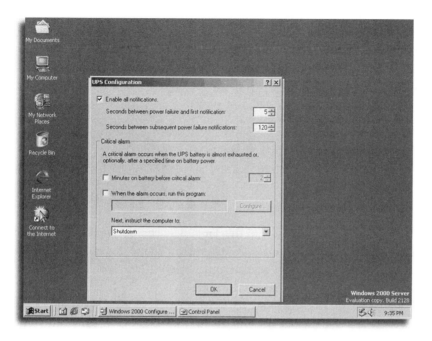

FIGURE 12.37
The UPS Configuration dialog box allows you to configure the actions the UPS service should take in the event of an outage.

Behind the scenes: When the UPS service is activated

When you activate the UPS service, it automatically configures its own startup parameters so that it starts automatically when the server boots. The UPS service configuration also ensures that the Alerter, Messenger, and EventLog services are started.

When the UPS service starts up, it tests the interface to the UPS hardware by assuming that normal power conditions prevail. If you specify a positive voltage at the CTS pin to signal a power failure, the UPS service assumes that a negative voltage will be found at the pin. Each pin you activate in the UPS Control Panel is tested. If the expected voltages aren't found, the UPS service won't start.

Testing the UPS

Never assume that your UPS works. After you have configured the UPS service, plan a test. If the server is being used, schedule the test for after hours.

Follow these steps to test your configuration for the UPS Service:

1. You can use the Send Message command in Server Manager to notify users that a test will take place. Users must log out for the duration of the test.

2. Pull the plug on your UPS and see what happens.

Some UPSes have their own configuration software

If you have a UPS with software that will allow you to do a scheduled self-test, that is a better method for testing than just unplugging the UPS.

---

3. After the delay you specified (in the Time Between Power Failure and Initial Warning Message box), a message is broadcast to the domain letting it know the power status. This message repeats at the intervals you specified. During this period, new users can't attach to the server.

4. At this time, the server can resume normal function if power is restored. When power comes back up and the UPS hardware clears the power failure signal to the UPS service, users receive a message alerting them of the updated status. Users can reconnect to the server and resume their work.

5. The next step is initiated in one of two ways:
   - If you configured the UPS service to expect a low battery signal, the UPS initiates the next phase of the shutdown.
   - If you configured the UPS service to use a timed shutdown (Expected battery life), the next phase starts when the shutdown timer expires.

6. After a low-battery condition occurs, UPS executes any command you specified in the UPS command screen. This command must execute in 30 seconds or less if the server is to be shut down smoothly within two minutes.

7. After executing the command, the UPS service starts a controlled shutdown of the server. After it begins, the shutdown process can't be aborted.

8. You should let your test continue until the UPS service shuts down the server.

chapter

13

Monitoring Windows 2000

Why Monitor Performance on Your Server?

When you are setting up a Windows 2000 server, you're creating a system that will be capable of handling a variety of tasks, such as print serving, file serving, and possibly email, antivirus, communications (data, faxing, gateways), among the many other uses for a network server. These used to be called file servers, but nowadays they are usually much more than that.

It is relatively easy to set up a Windows 2000 server and get users connecting to it. Oddly enough, most administrators do not spend every day installing Windows 2000 servers. A large part of their job, beyond user management and support, is maintaining the servers. It's very easy to say an administrator maintains the server, but what does that mean? In large part, it means an administrator must be proactive and monitor the server. An administrator should be the first person to know when the server is almost out of disk space, or when processor utilization is spiking to 100% at 11:00 every morning, or even if the network is being flooded with errors from a failing Ethernet adapter.

In a perfect world, when a user sits down at her computer and she needs to access a file or a service that is running on the server, she's going to get a quick response, as if she were running software directly from her hard drive. But sometimes a user will notice a delay or possibly be disconnected from an application due to a timeout or a system error, or worse, an unknown problem. And you, as the administrator, will receive an irate phone call or many phone calls, as users call to let you know that the network isn't working. This inevitably means you need to get on the job and troubleshoot the problem. But wouldn't it be nice if you knew there was a problem or, even better, that there was going to be a problem before the user called? That's what System Monitoring is used for and why you need to be familiar with the best way to monitor your Windows 2000 server.

Isn't Windows 2000 Server self-tuning?

Even though Microsoft touts Windows 2000 as self-tuning, there are many instances when a Windows 2000 computer can require manual tuning. For this reason, Microsoft includes System Monitor as a part of Windows 2000. Although some users view it as a nuisance, System Monitor can help you pinpoint bottlenecks and identify hardware and software that might cause a bottleneck or poor performance on your Windows 2000 computer. Its data-gathering features can also help you when it comes time to justify the need for upgrading hardware. Capacity planning is a key component of being a successful Windows 2000 administrator.

Server Bottlenecks

Generally, if you are suffering a performance problem, you should look for a *bottleneck*. A bottleneck occurs when hardware or software is performing so poorly that it prevents other components from running at optimum speed. This can be on the server, the network, or the local workstation. Finding and diagnosing these bottlenecks are among the most important tasks of a network or system administrator. If you can find the bottleneck, you can usually fix the problem by upgrading a component, offloading processes, tuning system resources, or replacing a failing component.

SEE ALSO

➤ *For information about planning your hardware for a Windows 2000 server, see page 22. (Chapter 2, Number of Processors)*

Before you explore System Monitor, you should look at the most common resources you need to monitor:

- Processor
- Memory
- Disk
- Network

Before you jump into the monitoring utilities, take a closer look at what you need to watch out for in each of these areas.

Processor

The processor can be considered the heart of the system. Processor performance is critical to everything the system does, and ensuring that the processor isn't overused is one of the first things to check when you have a server that appears to be running slowly.

Windows 2000 supports *symmetric multiprocessing*, which means you can have multiple CPUs processing system requests. Windows 2000 can have up to 32 processors. If you have a *multithreaded application*, you can even have different application threads being processed by different CPUs. The monitoring utilities of Windows 2000 allow you to monitor each individual processor, as well as some aggregate statistics.

Memory

There are two sorts of memory to be monitored in a Windows 2000 server: *Random Access Memory (RAM)*, which is the physical memory in the server, and *Virtual Memory*, which is the cache memory for the system's paging file. The *paging file* is used to store information from RAM when RAM is full. A general rule of thumb for memory in a server is to install as much as you can afford. Few applications function poorly with too much memory. On the other hand, memory tends to be the first place you find bottlenecks because many of today's applications are extremely memory intensive. You might have noticed that loading Microsoft Office 2000 on a workstation with 32MB RAM pretty much ensures you cannot run any additional applications. Magnify this by a factor of 10 for some of the larger server applications such as Systems Management Server or SQL Server.

One thing that can affect the performance of virtual memory is the location of the paging file. If you place the paging file on a slow hard drive, system performance will be slow. If you either spread the paging file across multiple hard drives, or place it on a striped disk array, you will see better performance for your virtual memory.

SEE ALSO
➤ *For more information on RAID arrays, see page 235.*

Disk

Enabling disk statistics

In order to monitor disk statistics, you must issue the command `diskperf -y` and then reboot the server. When you finish monitoring, be sure to turn off disk monitoring with `diskperf -n`. This feature adds a significant amount of overhead to the system and should only be active when needed for monitoring.

Disk performance can be one of the most complicated areas of performance monitoring and optimization. That's because hard drives are generally the slowest component on the system. Compared to RAM, disk access is an order of magnitude slower. A number of other things affect disk performance:

- Drive type
- Controller type
- Number of controllers/disks
- Type of disk usage

Drive Type

Hard drives are always measured by access time. A year ago an access time of 10ms was considered fast, where 2–3ms drives are now increasingly common. IDE drives are usually slower than SCSI drives, and there are a number of different types of SCSI formats: SCSI-1, SCSI-2, Fast SCSI-2, and SCSI-3 are the common SCSI formats for hard drives.

A couple of metrics gaining popularity are the revolutions per minute (RPM) and the maximum data transfer rate. It is becoming more common to see the RPMs listed as part of the drive description. The key to drive types is to match the drive technology to the rest of the system. You wouldn't run a slow SCSI-1 drive on a SCSI-3 controller because it would slow the entire system down.

Controller Type

A number of different controllers are available on the market today, at a variety of transfer speeds. Table 13.1 lists some of the common controller types.

Table 13.1   Common Disk Controller Types

Drive Type	Maximum Transfer Rate
IDE	Approx. 2.5 megabytes per second (MBps)
SCSI-1	Approx. 3.0MBps
SCSI-2	Approx. 5.0MBps
Fast SCSI-2	Approx. 10.0MBps
Ultra Wide SCSI / SCSI-3	Approx. 40.0MBps

One other feature of controllers is whether they support RAID. RAID-5 (disk striping with parity) provides higher performance than a standard hard drive, due to the additional read/write heads in the additional drives. Additionally, a hardware RAID implementation is much faster than a Windows 2000 software implementation because the processing associated with maintaining the array is offloaded to the controller's processor and removed from the operating system and the CPU.

Number of Controllers/Disks

Another factor when considering disk controllers and performance is the number of drive controllers installed. The more disk controllers you have installed, the more aggregate throughput you have available to the system. If you can get 5MBps from one SCSI-2 controller, you can get up to 10MBps with two SCSI-2 controllers. There is certainly a point of diminished returns, especially when you begin to reach the throughput levels of the system bus; in a lot of cases, however, an additional controller can significantly improve performance.

If additional controllers improve performance, additional hard drives can also improve performance. Each hard drive on the system adds an additional read/write head to disk operations. As discussed in Chapter 12, "Protecting Your Data," disk striping (multiple drives in a single array) is the highest performance drive configuration because of the array's capability to perform concurrent reads and writes. Therefore, if you have four drives in an array, theoretically you can move four times as much data written to or read from the hard drives. As with the controllers, there is a point of diminished returns, but additional drives can improve system performance.

Disk Usage

When we say disk usage, what we are really saying is the implementation of the server. In other words, a database server with a large number of records affects disk performance more heavily than a file and print server, where users are just storing word processing documents and printing memos. The size of database records or files being stored can also affect performance. If you are designing a high-end database server, you should be looking at the fastest drives possible, preferably in a hardware RAID configuration, and with multiple controllers, if possible.

For single-processor servers, Microsoft recommends using a SCSI-2 controller as the minimum.

Network

The final piece of the performance puzzle is the network. Like the disk performance, there are a number of factors to take into account when you assess network performance. The most significant factors include

- Network adapter type
- Number of adapters
- Number of protocols
- Additional network services
- Amount of network traffic
- Network infrastructure

Network Adapter Type

This might be obvious, but it is important to remember that an Arcnet adapter, which runs at 2MBps, offers slower performance then a gigabit Ethernet connection, offering 1 gigabyte per second (GBps) throughput. In the middle of that mix is 10MB Ethernet, 100MB Ethernet, 4MB Token-Ring, 16MB Token-Ring, and even 100MB ARCnet, if you can still find the adapters. The medium that a network interface card offers is very important to performance metrics. The speed of the adapter affects the server's network performance.

The bus type of the adapter is also important to performance calculations. An 8-bit ISA adapter is going to be significantly slower than a 32-bit PCI adapter. A good rule of thumb for this is to try to use 32-bit PCI adapters whenever possible. If you have an EISA bus, try to use 32-bit cards there as well. With ISA, you are limited to 16-bit, but that is still better than an 8-bit card because you have twice as wide a data path to the CPU and the other components.

Network adapters are also available with their own processors. This is useful because it offloads a lot of the traffic processing from the system CPU and leaves it on the network adapter. In a high-traffic environment where the server is forced to process a large number of packets, a processor on the network adapter can mean the difference between a functional server and a paperweight with hard drives.

Number of Adapters

The number of adapters can actually be a two-edged sword. Like the disk controllers discussed earlier, additional network interface cards can provide additional throughput to the system. On the other hand, if the additional cards are being used in conjunction with routing activities, the additional processing required by the routing function (discussed in "Additional Network Services," later in this chapter) could offset the advantage of multiple cards.

Number of Protocols

This is an easy one. Just remember that protocol equals overhead. For every protocol the system is using, additional system resources must be dedicated to communications. For example, if you have IPX and TCP/IP loaded on the system, the system must advertise itself for both protocols. On a busy system the overhead can become substantial.

Where possible, try to limit the number of protocols used by the system. If you can't limit the protocols, try to disable any unneeded services using both protocols.

Additional Network Services

Services such as routing, Active Directory, DNS, DHCP, WINS, and others all add overhead to the network processing. As with the additional protocols, any additional network services add overhead to the system. Where possible, limit the number of additional services running on a server. Generally, DNS is not required on every Windows 2000 server in your enterprise. Be especially careful when you are using your server as a LAN or WAN router. Not only does it add overhead to your server, but software routing is also generally less efficient than a hardware implementation. This can induce latency in network communications.

Amount of Network Traffic

There are two ways to look at network traffic and its impact on performance. First, a highly congested network gives the appearance of slow server performance because the congestion requires many packet rebroadcasts. The second problem with a highly congested network is the fact that the server needs to process all those packets. Although network interface cards are available with on-board processors, which can significantly reduce the load on the server CPU, you must be aware of what your traffic levels should normally be, what sort of card you have, and what the impact of the traffic will be on the server. Large amounts of traffic directed to the server can even cause the server to stop running.

Network Infrastructure

The final piece of the network puzzle is not really part of the server at all, but can have a significant impact on the server's performance. What does this mean to an administrator? Well, be aware of where your routers are. Know what path users must take in order to access the server. If you are running an application server for the Accounting Department, make sure it's not six network hops away from the users. Also, be aware that older routers don't handle traffic as efficiently as newer ones. Switches generally yield a faster network response time than hubs or router-based local area networks. You also need to know how the routers are configured. Do your routers forward NetBIOS traffic? If so, they can add to the broadcast traffic on your network. Are the switches on your network Layer 2 or Layer 3? Although this section won't teach you everything you need to know about networking, it's a good thing for you to become familiar with as you progress in your career.

All right, now that I've covered the basics of what to look for, take a look at how to monitor the critical pieces of your Windows 2000 server.

The Windows 2000 System Monitor

The Windows 2000 System Monitor, also known as the Performance Console, is a tool that allows you to pick apart individual components on a computer (including hardware and software), record statistics, graph those statistics, and view real-time statistics. Right out of the box, System Monitor offers over 350 statistics for your Windows 2000 system. Use the following steps to open the Performance Console:

1. Click the Start button.
2. Select Programs from the Start menu.
3. Select Administrative Tools.
4. Click Performance.

After you open the Performance Console, the System Monitor opens up by default into Chart View (see Figure 13.1).

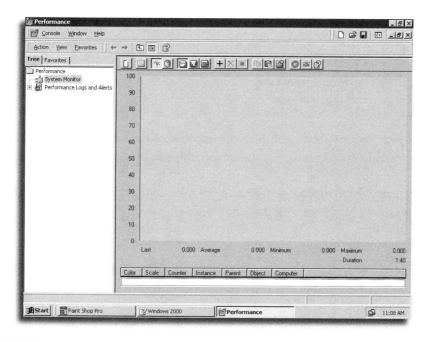

FIGURE 13.1
The Performance Console opens with the System Monitor in chart view. It is here that you need to add counters in order to view useful information.

This is the view you'll use the most; it allows you to view statistics in real time. Note the numbers that run along the left side of the chart. By default these values show the range 0–100. For some counters these represent a percentage, and for others they indicate a count. When setting up your counters you have the option to change the range that is shown.

System Monitor can be used for a number of tasks, including the following:

- *Create a baseline.* A baseline is a measurement of the server performance over time during normal operation. This information can be used later to determine how much the server's workload has been increased and is an important tool in determining system upgrades.

- *Identify bottlenecks.* You can monitor your server to find out whether you are approaching bottlenecks on any of the system's components. This is particularly useful when you are trying to justify upgrades to the system. Management loves to see facts when justifying spending several thousand dollars on upgrades.

- *Monitor resource usage over a period of time.* Not only can you do spot checks from time to time to identify bottlenecks, but you can also run Performance Monitor to see how resources are used over a period of time. This can be useful if you need to prove you are meeting service-level agreements, to verify that applications perform as advertised, and to compare usage to other systems performing similar tasks.

- *Perform capacity planning.* You can collect information with set parameters, and by altering the parameters, you can determine future resource requirements. For example, if you have 10 typical users connecting to a Web server, you can take the data related to their system usage and determine the requirements (approximately, of course) for a thousand users. This type of proactive capacity planning is something that many organizations lack these days and is a very useful skill for any administrator.

- *Troubleshoot.* System Monitor can provide valuable information if you are having problems with the system. It can quickly identify abnormal resource utilization and can help reduce the time needed to track down problems in a system.

All these things are critical to your ability to administer a Windows 2000 server effectively. There is nothing more embarrassing than going to management with a rush purchase order for a larger hard disk because suddenly the database has filled the volume and you didn't know it.

Performance Objects and Counters

System Monitor can monitor many Windows 2000 functions. Table 13.2 lists some items that can affect how well your Windows 2000 computer and your network is running. In System Monitor you refer to the entity that is being monitored as a performance object and the statistic that it captures as a counter.

Table 13.2 System Monitor Performance Objects and Counters

Performance Object	Counter
Processor (CPU)	Percent of processor time used Interrupts per second
Hard Drive (physical)	Average disk queue length Disk reads per second Disk writes per second
Paging File	Percent of usage
System	System uptime File write operations per second File read operations per second
Server	Bytes received per second Bytes transmitted per second File open Files opened total Logons per second Total logons
Cache	Copy reads per second Copy read hits percentage
Network Segment	Network utilization percentage Broadcast frames received per second Total bytes received per second
Process	Processor time percentage Counter set

This is only a small subset of the objects that System Monitor can monitor. The objects that can be monitored by System Monitor are extensible, so developers can create their own objects to be monitored. All the Microsoft BackOffice products add performance objects to System Monitor. Microsoft has provided an API (Application Programming Interface) to allow developers to add performance objects to System Monitor that relate to their applications.

Analyzing the Data

What you really need to know is what data is necessary to capture when you're trying to detect bottlenecks or other adverse conditions. System Monitor is a great tool just to get a good idea of how your Windows 2000 computers are running and to analyze network segment traffic. But the primary reason to use the System Monitor tool lies in monitoring the performance objects and counters that are shown in Table 13.2, as well as the other available performance objects and counters.

Analyzing Memory

To monitor the memory usage of a particular program, you can have System Monitor look at the Process performance object. The counter Working Set can tell you the amount of memory that the program has reserved for its use. This can be handy for spotting applications that are using excessive amounts of memory, or for evaluating what impact an applications is having on the system.

When there is not enough physical memory installed, the paging file (PAGEFILE.SYS) is used as virtual memory. To determine the usage of the paging file, look at the Physical Disk performance object for the disk, or disks, that contain a paging file. When added together, the counters Avg. Disk Transfer/sec and Pages/sec counter values should not exceed 0.1. If they do, that means that at least 10% of disk access time is being used for writing to a paging file, which is not acceptable. This means you should really consider adding memory to the computer.

When to resize the paging file

If the maximum paging file size, as defined in the System applet in Control Panel, is close to the actual size of the paging file, you should increase the size of the paging file.

Analyzing Processor Activity

The Processor performance object can allow you to monitor activity on a CPU, and in the case of multiprocessor computers, there will be multiple instances for the Processor performance object.

The % Processor Time counter allows you to view a percentage of elapsed time that a processor is executing a process. When this number is up near the 100% limit, you know that a faster processor can help the computer handle these processes more efficiently. Even more important, though, is also checking the Processor Queue Length counter for the System performance object. This queue tells you how many processes are sitting idle waiting for the processor to be freed up. If this queue is low, your processors might be sufficient.

General I/O Monitoring

You can diagnose a hardware problem by looking at the Processor performance object's Interrupts/sec counter. This counter tells you the number of I/O requests that are waiting for processing. If this number rises without processor utilization rising, it might mean that there is another bottleneck in an I/O device, or for that matter, possibly a malfunctioning I/O device.

Disk Drive Monitoring

System Monitor gives you counters that can help you look at each drive in your Windows 2000 computer and see whether they are operating properly and efficiently.

The Physical Disk performance object has counters that allow you to observe each hard drive in your system. The % Disk Time counter can let you identify the usage of each of your hard drives. The Current Disk Queue Length counter reports the number of waiting I/O requests for a hard drive.

If the % Disk Time is over 90%, which is high, the Current Disk Queue Length tells you whether the drive is handling requests efficiently. Disk Queue Lengths that are over twice the number of spindles making up the hard drive (which is usually one spindle, although RAID drives can have more) can be a symptom of a faulty controller, the need for faster disks, of even just a bad drive cable. Resolving these performance problems might involve buying new drives, adding drives, adding or replacing controllers, and possibly moving data to another computer.

You can look at these statistics for each individual drive, and there is an instance that is called _Total, which will give you an overview of all your disks.

Network Monitoring with System Monitor

Although System Monitor is not a replacement for advanced network monitoring tools such as Hewlett Packard Open View, or network packet analyzers such as Network Associate's Sniffer, you can get statistics that let you evaluate and analyze how specific computers and network segments are handling network traffic.

The Redirector performance object monitors transmissions from the computer, and the Server performance object monitors requests to the computer. Using the counters associated with these performance objects can tell you how well the computer is handling the task of operating as a server. Monitor the Processor performance object at the same time, and you will be able to tell whether problems stem from an overused CPU. The same holds true for monitoring the Physical Disk performance object in conjunction with the Redirector and Server performance objects.

Network Monitor is another tool that comes with Windows 2000

The Network Monitor application, which ships with Windows 2000 Server, is a subset of the Network Monitor that ships with Microsoft Systems Management Server. Used in conjunction with System Monitor, the Network Monitor can help you evaluate your computer's overall performance and identify bottlenecks on your network, which includes identifying network adapter cards out on the network that might be malfunctioning. This is discussed in detail in the section "Using Windows 2000 Server Network Monitor," later in the chapter.

Displaying Views for System Monitor

The System Monitor can be displayed in any of three ways. The buttons on the toolbar, shown in Figure 13.2, represent these different views.

Each view can be displayed in real time or displayed from a saved log file. To choose between real-time data and logged data, use the buttons shown in Figure 13.3.

These different views are explained later.

FIGURE 13.2
These three buttons change
the System Monitor view.

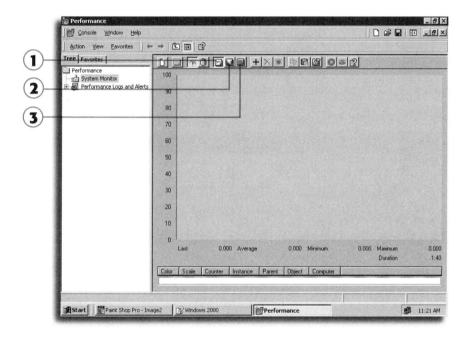

① Chart view

② Histogram view

③ Report view

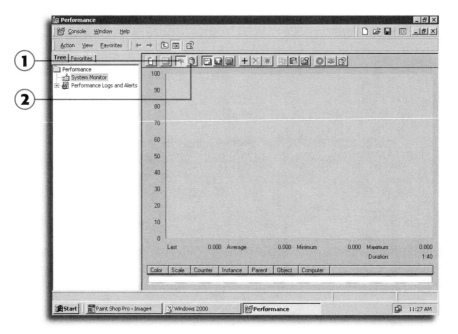

FIGURE 13.3
Choose between real-time data and logged data using these two buttons.

(1) Click this button to view real-time data (default)

(2) This button lets you view saved data from a log file

Charting in System Monitor

When you view the System Monitor, the data area is blank. That is because no default counters are chosen. The counters need to be added manually, unless you open a previously saved group of counters. Saving System Monitor with counters already loaded is described later in the section "Additional Ways to Change the Chart Display."

Follow these steps to create a chart in System Monitor:

1. Click the toolbar button with the plus sign. This displays the Add Counters dialog box. The Add Counters dialog box, shown in Figure 13.4, presents many options for adding monitored performance objects to the System Monitor display.

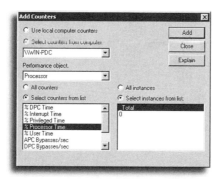

FIGURE 13.4
The Add Counters dialog box allows you to select performance counters.

2. The first item that can be chosen is the computer that will be monitored. By default, the local computer is the chosen computer. You can enter the name of another computer to monitor as well. You can enter any computer that is running Windows 2000 or Windows NT for remote monitoring. After you enter a valid computer name in the entry field, that computer name is added to a list that is accessible from the drop-down box.

3. Choose the appropriate performance object you want to monitor from the Performance Object drop-down box. By default, Processor is already chosen.

4. Select the counter that you want to monitor for the performance object you just chose. Under the performance object list is the Counter list. If you click the button labeled Explain, the Explain Text, shown under the Add Counters dialog box, explains the counter's purpose. As you highlight counters, the Explain Text continues to show you information. You can close the Explain Text dialog box by clicking the close button in the upper-right corner of the dialog box.

5. If applicable, select a value from the Instance list. The Instance list shows values only for selected performance objects. For instance, in Figure 13.5, the Instance list shows the value _Total and the value 0. This is because there could be multiple processors in a computer, and in this case, only processor 0 exists, so the value _Total is the equivalent of selecting 0.

6. When you have made your choices for the particular counter, click the Add button to add the counter to System monitor.

7. Repeat steps 2–6 until you are finished adding counters to the current System monitor.

8. Click the Close button to exit the Add Counters dialog box.

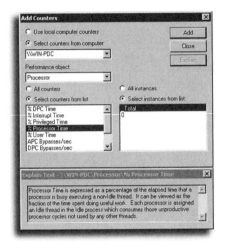

FIGURE 13.5
The Explain Text gives you quick information about the selected counter.

Choosing a Counter for System Monitor That Includes an Instance List

Figure 13.6 shows Physical Disk as the chosen performance object, and the Instance list has two values: _Total and 0 C: D:. The first is a total of all physical drives, and the other value represents the one hard drive currently installed in the computer. The 0 indicates it is the first drive installed on the system (they number 0, 1, 2, and so on as they are installed) and C: D: represents partitions on the drive. If additional drives had been installed, this list would be longer.

> **Specifying attributes**
>
> Because the System Monitor chart can track multiple counters at the same time, you need to specify the attributes for each line that will occupy the chart, in order to tell them apart.

By bringing up the context menu on the chart (Figure 13.7), you can select many options for the display of the System Monitor.

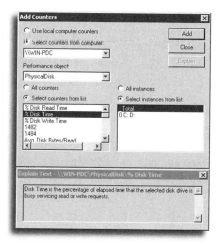

FIGURE 13.6
The Physical Disk Performance Object has one instance for each physical drive.

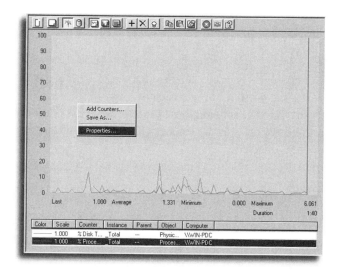

FIGURE 13.7
The context menu for the System Monitor.

Follow these steps to change the look of the System Monitor:

1. Display the context menu for System Monitor.
2. Select Properties from the menu.

3. On the Properties dialog box, select the Data tab.

4. Highlight the performance object you want to modify.

5. You can change the width, style, scale, and color of the line that is representing the performance object in the System Monitor.

6. Click the Apply button to make the change immediately and select another performance object to modify, or click the OK button to close the Properties dialog box.

7. Click the Add button to add another performance object to the graph. You can also remove performance objects from here.

Don't clutter the System Monitor

You might want to limit the number of counters in a chart to a minimum so that the display does not get too crowded. You can run multiple instances of System Monitor and have a few performance objects represented in each instance of System Monitor.

Viewing a Chart

After you have selected the counters for the chart, a real-time display of these counters is displayed. At the bottom of the screen is a legend showing the different counters and the type of line that is being drawn to represent the counter. By highlighting one of these counters in the legend, you can display statistics in a status line that is directly below the chart.

Changing the Look of a Chart

Additional tabs in the System Monitor Properties dialog box allow you to change the way the chart is displayed. As you can see on the General tab shown in Figure 13.8, you can choose to display a graph, a histogram, or a report. The legend, toolbar, and value bar are optional but turned on by default. The update schedule for real-time monitoring can be changed here, as can the overall look of the display.

The data source can be changed from the Source tab (see Figure 13.9).

FIGURE 13.8
You can modify the way that a histogram or report shows its values.

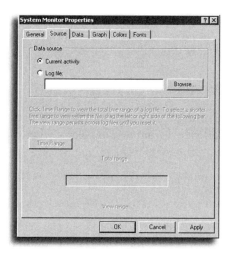

FIGURE 13.9
The Source tab allows you to select whether real-time data or data from a log file is displayed.

The Graph tab, shown in Figure 13.10, allows you to enter a title to be displayed in System Monitor, for both the x- and y-axes. You can enable grids, and you can also specify the range of values that will be shown in the display.

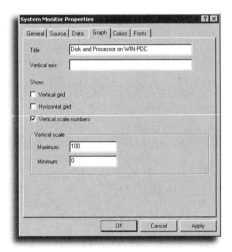

FIGURE 13.10
The Graph tab lets you further modify the look of the display.

The Colors tab gives you the ability to change the background and foreground color of the System Monitor display, and the Fonts tab lets you change the type of font used in the labels and report text.

Additional Ways to Change the Chart Display

After counters have been selected for the chart and you are in Chart View, you have the option to remove individual counters, or clear all the counters without going into the System Monitor properties page.

Follow these steps to remove an individual counter:

1. Highlight the counter you want to remove by selecting it from the legend at the bottom of the System Monitor display.

2. Either press the Delete key, or click the Delete button on the toolbar.

To remove all the counters, click the Clear Counter Set button on the toolbar.

Follow these steps to save your System Monitor settings:

1. Choose Save As from the Console menu.

2. You can save an unlimited number of different settings and you can name your settings in a descriptive manner. Your settings are saved into a file with the .MSC extension, which you have the option to name in a descriptive manner. In this

example, I have named the file disk and pagefile. Click the OK button to save the file.

3. The resulting file, shown in Figure 13.11, can have a shortcut created for you to have easy access to the file.

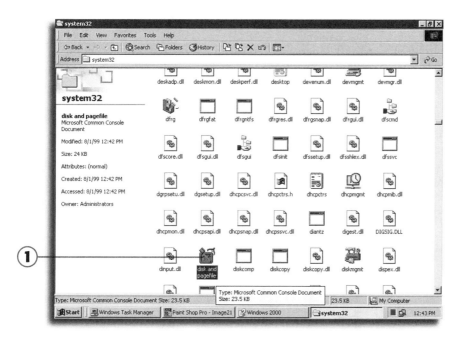

FIGURE 13.11
You can copy the saved file or create a shortcut to give easy access to the saved settings.

① Here's your shortcut

A saved MSC file can be copied to another computer

Administrators can share their saved Performance Console settings simply by copying the MSC file, or attaching it to email.

Saving a Performance Console to an HTML file

As an alternative method of saving a Performance Console's settings, you can right-click anywhere on the System Monitor and select Save As from the menu. You are then prompted for a filename, which will have the extension of .HTM. These saved settings can be used whenever a dialog box gives the option of Load Settings From when creating a new set of settings anywhere within Performance Console.

Using System Monitor Data for Reporting

A Performance Log can be created so that you can chart data that has been collected over a period of time. This data can be saved into a text file or binary file. It can be especially helpful if you compare one log to another created at a different time.

Follow these steps to creating a Performance Log:

1. Select Counter Logs under the Performance Logs and Alerts from the Performance tree.
2. Bring up the context menu from any blank area on the log file list.
3. Select New Log Settings from the context menu.
4. Provide a name for the new log settings you want to capture.
5. Click OK.
6. Add the performance counters that you want to include in this log (see Figure 13.12).

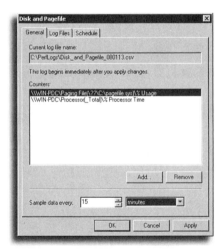

FIGURE 13.12
The General tab lets you select counters and a data capture interval.

7. Set the interval for the collection of data.
8. Click the Log Files tab, shown in Figure 13.13.

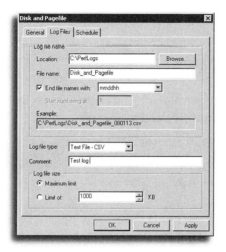

FIGURE 13.13
Set the name and type of log file you want to create.

9. You can change the default location for the log file and the log filename. If you are going to be creating multiple logs, you might want to select a suffix for the log filename.

10. Choose the log file type. This can be a text file or a binary file.

11. Limit the size of the log.

12. Select the Schedule tab (Figure 13.14).

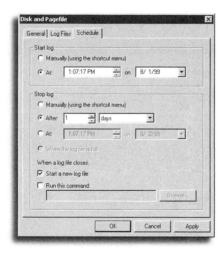

FIGURE 13.14
The Schedule tab lets you set the time to start and stop the data capture.

13. By default, the data capture starts immediately. You can choose to delay the logging by entering a data and time.

14. The log can be stopped at a particular time, or you can choose to manually stop the log through the Performance Console.

15. Select whether to create a new log after the current log closes. You can also execute a command at the time the log closes.

16. Click the OK button to save the log settings.

The types of files that System Monitor can save can be imported into Microsoft Excel or almost any other data analysis tool.

Starting and stopping data capture manually

You can start and stop data capture by bringing up the context menu for the particular Performance Log settings and choosing Start or Stop from the context menu.

Capturing Alerts in the Performance Console

An *alert* is a threshold that you can set for any performance counter. When the threshold is met, you can trigger an event, such as writing to the event log, or notifying a user.

Follow these steps to set up an alert from scratch:

1. Select Alerts under the Performance Logs and Alerts from the Performance tree.

2. Bring up the context menu from any blank area on the Alerts list.

3. Select New Alert Settings from the context menu.

4. Provide a name for the new alert settings you want to set.

5. Click OK.

6. Add the performance counters that you want to monitor for this alert (see Figure 13.15).

7. Set the threshold for each counter you selected.

8. Set the interval for which this counter will be checked.

9. Click the Action tab, shown in Figure 13.16.

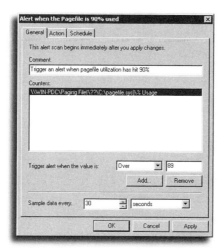

FIGURE 13.15
The General tab lets you select counters and set a threshold.

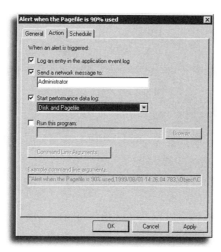

FIGURE 13.16
The Action tab lets you choose how to respond when a threshold is met.

10. Select the Schedule tab (see Figure 13.17).

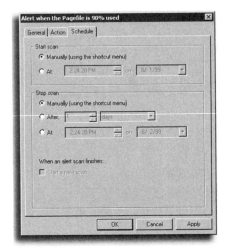

FIGURE 13.17
The Schedule tab lets you set the time to start and stop monitoring the counters for an alert.

11. By default, the alert monitor starts immediately. You can choose to delay the start by entering a date and time.

12. The alert settings can be stopped at a particular time, or you can choose to manually stop it through the Performance Console.

13. Select whether to create start a new alert scan when the first one is finished.

14. Click the OK button to save the alert settings.

If you save the Console with Alerts or Counter logs, these settings will be saved along with the file.

About trace logs

Trace logs are not covered in this book, as they should only be used for advanced troubleshooting because of their high overhead on the system.

Using Windows 2000 Server Network Monitor

The Windows 2000 Network Monitor gives you a method of capturing and displaying network data from your server. This can come in handy if you are having any problems communicating with the network. Incoming and outgoing network packets can be captured to a file for examination. Filters allow you to concentrate on the type of packets that you want to examine.

Microsoft's Systems Management Server offers an enhanced version of Network Monitor that allows for capture and examination of network packets from any computer on the network that has the Network Monitor Driver installed.

In order to run Windows 2000 Server's Network Monitor, you must install the Network Monitor from the Add/Remove Programs applet in Control Panel. When you install this program, the Network Monitor Driver is also installed. Figure 13.18 shows a local area network connection's properties sheet with the Network Monitor Driver installed.

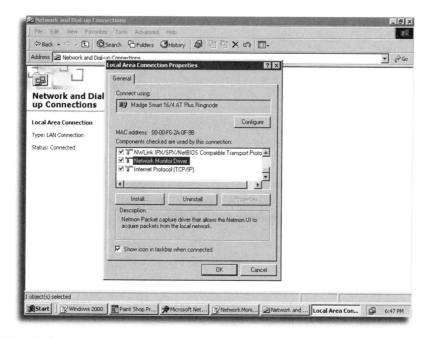

FIGURE 13.18
This local area network connection includes the Network Monitor Driver.

To run the Network Monitor, go to the Administrative Tools program group (shown in Figure 13.19) and select Network Monitor.

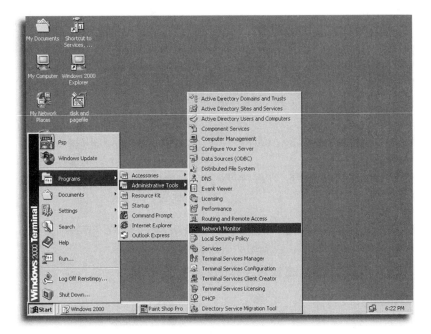

FIGURE 13.19
Navigating to the Network Monitor shortcut on the Start menu.

The Network Monitor interface is divided up into four sections (see Figure 13.20). Each of these sections can be resized to allow you to view the data that is most important to you. These sections are

- *The Graph pane.* This pane shows a graphical representation of the data being captured.

- *The Statistics pane.* This pane shows the network statistics, including number of frames, number of broadcasts, number of bytes, and several other network statistics on both network and captured packets.

- *The Session Statistics pane.* This pane shows all the statistics relating to different sessions on the network. This will show the paired machines communicating.

- *The Station Statistics pane.* Shows all station related statistics, including network address, Frames Sent, Frames Received, and so on.

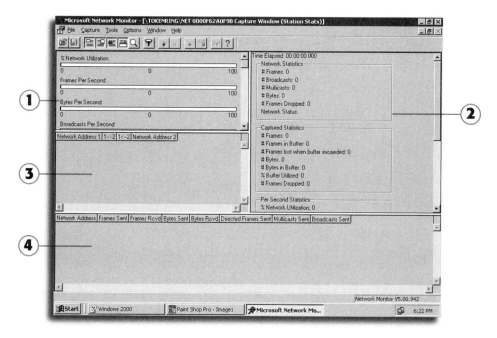

FIGURE 13.20
The Network Monitor is divided into four sections.

(**1**) The Graph pane

(**2**) The Total Statistics pane

(**3**) The Session Statistics pane

(**4**) The Station Statistics pane

Follow these steps to capture network data:

1. Open Network Monitor by going to the Administrative Tools program group and selecting Network Monitor.

2. Go to the Capture menu and select Start, or press the F10 key (Figure 13.21) to start capturing data for analysis. In real time you will see counts for numbers of frames, broadcasts, utilization, and a host of other statistics.

3. Stop the capture by selecting Stop from Capture menu or press F11.

FIGURE 13.21
Start capturing network data from the Capture menu.

   4. To display the captured data, select Display Captured Data from the Capture
   menu or press the F12 key. The Capture display will look like the one in
   Figure 13.22.

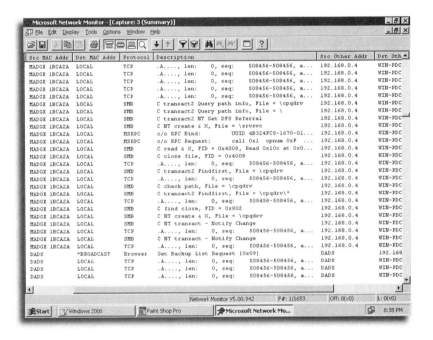

FIGURE 13.22
A screen of captured data.

The data shown in this part of the capture shows a portion of communication between the server, WIN-PDC, and a client, DADS. The DADS computer has made a request to see the contents of a directory on the server. These are shown as SMB packets. If the DADS computer had difficulty viewing this directory, this log would come in handy to help diagnose the problem. The in-depth analysis of packet captures and decodes would take several books and at least a couple days of hands-on training. For this book you should simply be familiar with the capabilities of Network Monitor. It will probably be a while before you are ready for decoding traffic captures.

Capturing Addresses

When you first start Network Monitor, it doesn't really know anything about your network. In order to be able to start limiting your captures to certain protocols, addresses, or types of broadcast, you need to know a little about the type of traffic you have on your network and where it's coming from. It is a good idea to run a capture just to populate the Address database. The Address database can be used if you are looking for data that has been sent to or received from a specific computer on the network.

Follow these steps to view and save the captured addresses:

1. Go to the Administrative Tools program group and select Network Monitor.

2. Select Addresses from the Capture menu. The list of captured addresses, shown in Figure 13.23, can be saved to a file. You have the option to manually add addresses, delete entries, or edit existing entries by adding comments.

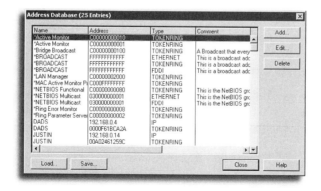

FIGURE 13.23
The Address database shows the name and address of every machine the server sees on the network.

4. Click the Save button to save the file. By default the file is saved in the NETMON folder (shown in Figure 13.24).

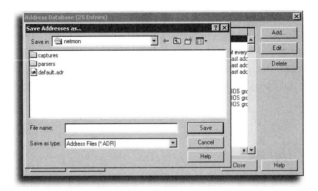

FIGURE 13.24
Saving the Address database as default.adr automatically loads it the next time you start Network Monitor.

During a new capture you can choose to load the address file you had saved. In this example I saved the file as default.adr which is automatically loaded when Network Monitor is started.

Using a Capture Filter

The data that you capture through Network Monitor can be filtered based on protocol, type of broadcast, or network address. To create a filter, click the toolbar button that looks like a funnel.

The Capture Filter dialog box allows you to specify what data you want to capture. For instance, in this example, I will set up a filter that will only capture traffic between two computers. One is named DADS and the other is my server, WIN-PDC.

Follow these steps to capture data between two computers:

1. Open Network Monitor.

You need addresses to make this work

You must have the addresses already defined in the Address database. To do this, see the section "Capturing Addresses," earlier in this chapter.

---

2. Click the funnel button.

3. Highlight Address Pairs and click the Address button (see Figure 13.25). This opens the Address Expression dialog box, where you can select the addresses for the capture expression.

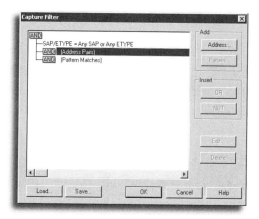

FIGURE 13.25
The Capture Filter dialog box allows you to build the capture criteria.

2. Select both computers. Notice in Figure 13.26 I have chosen the entry for the computers where the IP address is shown, not the MAC address. Also, I have chosen to capture data going both ways.

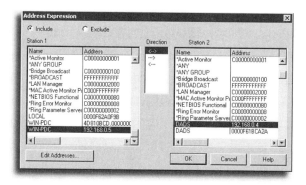

FIGURE 13.26
Select the two computers you want to capture data for.

3. Click OK and the filter will show the chosen Address Pair (see Figure 13.27). You can save this filter to a file if you want.

4. Click the OK button and the filter will be in place.

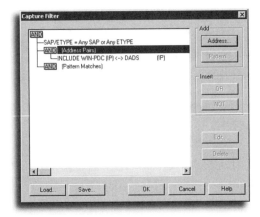

FIGURE 13.27
A capture defined to limit to one Address Pair.

5. Start the capture again to capture data only from those two computers. When you start the capture you will be asked whether you want to save your last capture. You can save the capture for use at a later time.

The capture in Figure 13.28 is part of the result of using the capture filter.

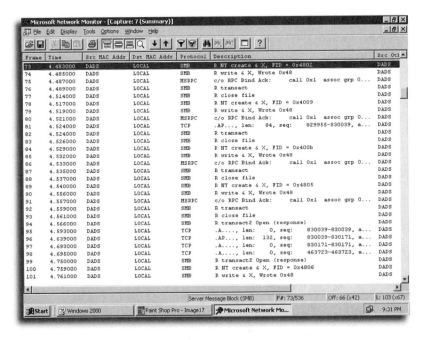

FIGURE 13.28
A capture that has been limited to two computers.

If you double-click one of the captured frames, you will see the display split into three panes, as shown in Figure 13.29: the summary windows, detail view, and hex view. It is within this latter view that you can actually see the real data within the frame, not just a description of the frame.

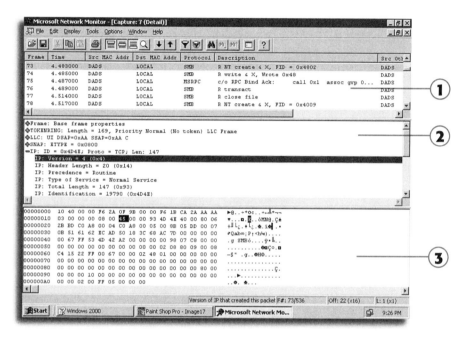

FIGURE 13.29
The Detail pane shows what's actually within the packet.

① Summary window

② Detail view

③ Hex view

part

IV

EXPANDING YOUR WINDOWS NETWORK

chapter

14

Advanced TCP/IP Concepts

WINS (Windows Internet Name Service) and Windows 2000

If you have spent any time working in the Windows NT Server 4 world, you are undoubtedly aware of how difficult it can be to set up and maintain an infrastructure for Windows Internet Name Service (WINS). You also are undoubtedly wondering why Microsoft didn't get rid of WINS with Windows 2000. Well, the good news is that with Windows 2000, WINS is for backward compatibility only. Windows 2000 Server running in native mode knows nothing about WINS. The Active Directory (AD) and Domain Name Service (DNS) are used to perform the functionality that WINS had been providing for Microsoft networking clients: resolving names into addresses.

But what if you still have clients on your network that are not AD-enabled? What if you still have servers on your network that are also pre–Windows 2000?

In order for them to function on a TCP/IP network, they will use either WINS or LMHOSTS. LMHOSTS is discussed later in this chapter. WINS is the clear winner for providing this service. It is because of that that you might consider running a Windows NT Server 4.0 WINS server on your network. This chapter provides information on how to enable WINS on a Windows NT Server 4.0 server.

Why Is There WINS?

These days, TCP/IP is rapidly approaching ubiquity on networks worldwide, due almost entirely to the popularity of the Internet. It's difficult to even consider functioning in today's connected world without TCP/IP. But when Microsoft began to add TCP/IP support to its LAN server products, it had a problem because the naming system used on Microsoft networks doesn't function on routed TCP/IP networks.

Microsoft network computers are known by their NetBIOS names. From the administrator's perspective, NetBIOS names are pretty cool because they automatically advertise servers' identities on the network with no effort on the part of the administrator. Simply install a server and, presto, it shows up in users' browse lists.

But NetBIOS has a design limitation that shows up in routed networks because NetBIOS relies heavily on broadcast messages to spread the word about servers and their shared resources. Broadcast messages are messages that are received by every computer within earshot, rather than by a specific computer. Broadcasting is a lot like shouting in a restaurant—everyone else must stop talking to listen to one loud person. That's fine if the message is important ("Fire!") but not if it's just someone complaining about his clam chowder.

To confine the impact of broadcast messages, networks typically don't forward broadcast messages through routers. If they did, the broadcast message could echo throughout the internetwork and take over the whole thing. Microsoft specifically designed its NWLink routing protocol to forward NetBIOS messages, but TCP/IP is another matter. TCP/IP is standardized, and Microsoft's TCP/IP router has to be like everyone else's TCP/IP router. So Microsoft had to find a way to make NetBIOS naming work in a standard TCP/IP network.

Microsoft's first solution, introduced in its older LAN Manager server, was to use files named LMHOSTS, which consisted of records matching NetBIOS names to IP addresses. When a computer couldn't find a particular NetBIOS computer on the local network it would consult its LMHOSTS file to see whether the computer could be found elsewhere.

LMHOSTS files fall in the category of "static name databases" and are similar in use and format to the HOSTS file used for name resolution, originally in conjunction with UNIX hosts. An LMHOSTS file is a text file that must be edited manually. After creating a master LMHOSTS file, an administrator must copy the file to every computer on the network. Every time a computer was installed or removed, the master LMHOSTS file had to be updated and redistributed. Doesn't that sound like fun? (You will briefly examine the structure of the LMHOSTS file later in this chapter, but I doubt that LMHOSTS will be your chief naming mechanism.)

So Microsoft needed a dynamic name service that would keep itself current on computers on the network, and that could work in routed TCP/IP environments. Microsoft dubbed it the Windows Internet Name Service (WINS). Although you can support naming on your TCP/IP network using LMHOSTS, you don't want to unless you have lots of free time. It is far better to set up WINS and let it do the work for you. And that's what this chapter teaches you to do.

NetBIOS Node Types

There are two ways computers can communicate on a network:

- Through broadcast messages, which every computer receives
- Through directed messages, which are sent to a specific computer

Whenever possible, it is preferable to communicate through directed messages. Also, directed messages will propagate across routers. So, Microsoft needed a name service that relied primarily on directed messages. It took a while to arrive at that goal, however, and you need to examine the various naming methods that can be used on Microsoft networks.

These naming methods are referred to as *node types*. A node, you will recall, is simply a device on a network. Every computer on a Microsoft computer is configured with one of four node types that determines whether the computer will learn names through broadcast messages, directed messages, or some combination of broadcast and directed messages. Before you can work with WINS, you need to know what the node types are and when they are used:

- B-node (broadcast node) relies exclusively on broadcast messages and is the oldest name resolution mode. A host needing to resolve a name request sends a message to every host within earshot, requesting the address associated with a hostname. B-node has two shortcomings: Broadcast traffic is undesirable and becomes a significant user of network bandwidths, and TCP/IP routers don't forward broadcast messages, which restricts b-node operation to a single network segment.

- P-node (point-to-point node) relies on WINS servers. Clients register themselves with a WINS server and contact the WINS server with name resolution requests. WINS servers communicate using directed messages, which can cross routers, so P-node can operate on large networks. Unfortunately, if the WINS server is unavailable, or if a node isn't configured to contact a WINS server, p-node name resolution fails.

- M-node (modified node) is a hybrid mode that first attempts to resolve names using b-node. If that fails, an attempt is made to use p-node name resolution. M-node was historically the first hybrid mode put into operation, but it has the disadvantage of favoring b-node operation, which is associated with high levels of broadcast traffic.

- H-node (hybrid node) is also a hybrid mode that favors WINS. First, an attempt is made to use p-node to resolve a name via WINS. Only if WINS resolution fails does the host resort to b-node to resolve the name via broadcasts. Because it typically results in the best network utilization, h-node is the default mode of operation for Microsoft TCP/IP clients configured to use WINS for name resolution. Microsoft recommends leaving TCP/IP clients in the default, h-node configuration.

Although networks can be organized using a mixture of node types, Microsoft recommends against it. B-node clients ignore p-node directed messages, and p-node clients ignore b-node broadcasts. Therefore, it is conceivable that two clients could separately be established with the same NetBIOS name.

Elements of a WINS Network

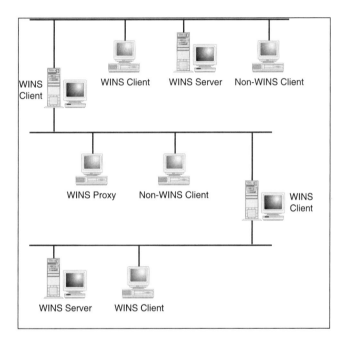

FIGURE 14.1
A routed network that uses WINS.

Figure 14.1 illustrates clients and WINS servers on a routed network. Four types of computers appear in the figure:

- *WINS servers.* When WINS clients enter the network, they contact a WINS server using a directed message. The client registers its name with the WINS server, and uses the WINS server to resolve NetBIOS names to IP addresses.

- *WINS clients.* WINS clients use directed (p-node) messages to communicate with WINS servers, and are typically configured to use h-node communication. Windows NT, Windows 95 and 98, and Windows for Workgroups computers can be WINS clients.

- *Non-WINS clients.* Older Microsoft network clients that can't use p-node can still benefit from WINS. Their broadcast messages are intercepted by WINS proxy computers that act as intermediaries between the b-node clients and WINS servers. MS-DOS and Windows 3.1 clients function as non-WINS clients.

- *WINS proxies.* Windows NT, Windows 95 and 98, and Windows for Workgroups clients can function as WINS proxies. They intercept b-node broadcasts on their local subnet and communicate with a WINS server on behalf of the b-node client.

Notice that two WINS servers are found on the sample network. Both WINS servers can register client names when a client enters the network. Periodically, the WINS servers replicate their databases so that each WINS server comprehends the entire network. Whenever possible it is desirable to have at least two WINS servers. This lets name resolution take place when one name server is down. It also lets administrators distribute WINS activity across multiple servers to balance the processing loads.

Installing the WINS Service

Any Windows NT Server computer can be configured as a WINS server. To install the WINS service, do the following:

1. Open the Network and Dial-up Connections applet in the Control Panel (or right-click My Network Places and select Properties). Click Add Network Components at the bottom of the left pane (see Figure 14.2). This starts the Windows Optional Networking Components Wizard, shown in Figure 14.3.

2. Select Networking Services and click Details. The Networking Services details dialog box is shown in Figure 14.4. WINS is at the bottom of the list of available services.

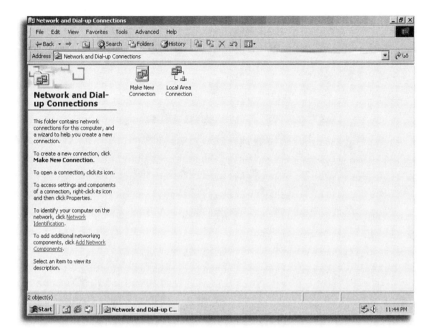

FIGURE 14.2
The Network and Dial-up Connections Applet manages all network services.

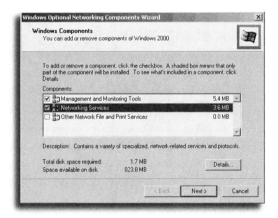

FIGURE 14.3
As with most Windows 2000 management functions, adding WINS is completely driven by the wizard.

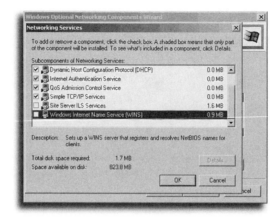

FIGURE 14.4
There are a large variety of optional Network Services included with Windows 2000.

3. Click the open check box to the left of the Windows Internet Name Service. Click OK to return to the Windows Optional Networking Components Wizard dialog box.

4. Click Next to continue. This opens the Configuring Components dialog box, shown in Figure 14.5. If you are using a dynamic address, at this point you will be asked if you want to change to a static address.

FIGURE 14.5
The Configuring Components dialog box gives you a running status of the installation.

5. After the Configuring Components process is complete, the Local Area Network Properties dialog box will open. Click OK to complete the installation of the service. You will not need to reboot the server.

Managing WINS

When the WINS service is installed, a shortcut to the WINS management application is added to the Administrative Tools program group in the Start menu. This is another Microsoft Management Console snap-in, so it should look familiar. This application is used to monitor and manage all WINS functions. Figure 14.6 shows the WINS management snap-in.

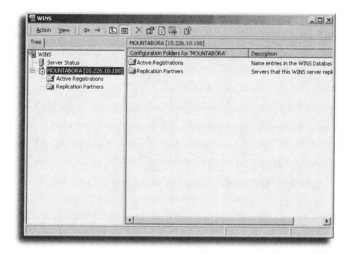

FIGURE 14.6
The WINS Snap-in for the Microsoft Management Console.

To Add WINS servers to the WINS application, do the following:

1. Open the WINS management application.

2. Select WINS at the top of the left-hand pane and click Action, Add Server. The Add Server dialog box shown in Figure 14.7 will open.

3. Enter the NetBIOS name or IP address of the server you want to add. You can also browse the network to find the server.

4. Click OK after the server has been entered. In this example, the WINS server RIVERALPH has been added in Figure 14.8.

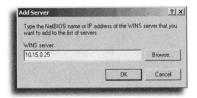

FIGURE 14.7
Adding a WINS server is as easy as entering the server's NetBIOS name or IP address.

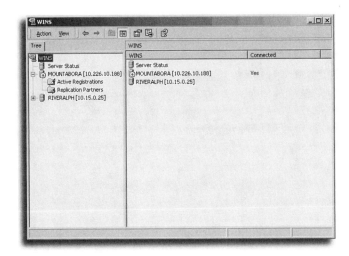

FIGURE 14.8
The new WINS server has been added to the server list.

Configuring WINS

Several properties on a WINS server can be adjusted. To configure a WINS server, do the following:

1. Select a server in the Tree pane of the WINS management snap-in.

2. Right-click the server and from the context menu, select Properties. The Properties dialog box (shown in Figure 14.9) will open.

3. The General tab shown in Figure 14.9 can be used to configure how often the server statistics are updated, as well as where and when to back up the WINS database. The statistics referenced on this tab can be seen in Figure 14.10, and can be viewed by selecting Display Server Statistics from the server's context menu. Click in the Intervals tab to see the dialog box shown in Figure 14.11.

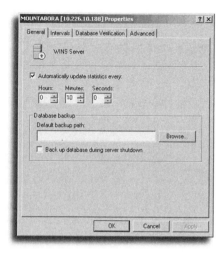

FIGURE 14.9
The General tab of the WINS Server Properties is used for configuring the statistics and database backup
parameters.

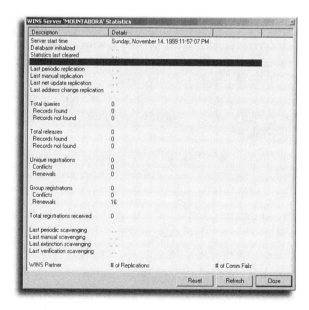

FIGURE 14.10
All the statistics for the WINS server are shown in this dialog box.

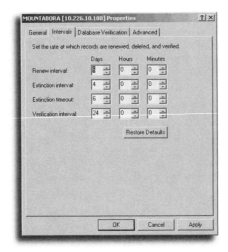

FIGURE 14.11
The Intervals Tab allows you to set the four key intervals used in maintaining the WINS database.

4. The WINS Intervals tab includes four properties that affect WINS client name resolution:

- Renewal Interval specifies the intervals at which a WINS client must reregister its name. A name that isn't reregistered is marked as released in the WINS database. A good renewal interval value is four days (96 hours), which ensures a client retains its registration over a long weekend. If clients are forced to renew very frequently (more often than three days), network traffic is increased.

- Extinction Interval specifies the interval between the time a name is marked released and when it is marked extinct. Extinct records are eligible to be purged. Try setting this value to four times the renewal interval.

- Extinction Timeout specifies the interval between the time a name is marked extinct and when the name is actually purged from the database. The minimum value is one day.

- Verification Interval specifies the interval after which a WINS server must verify that names it doesn't own are still active. The maximum value is 24 days (576 hours).

5. Click the Database Verification tab to see the dialog box shown in Figure 14.12. Selecting Verify Database Consistency Every X Hours causes Windows 2000 to check the database for consistency using the configuration you specify. (This is a new feature with Windows 2000.) Click the Advanced tab to see the final set of configuration parameters (see Figure 14.13).

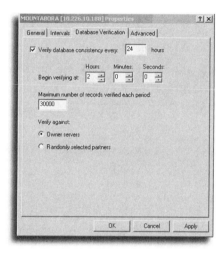

FIGURE 14.12
The Database Verification tab allows you to configure database consistency checks for the WINS database.

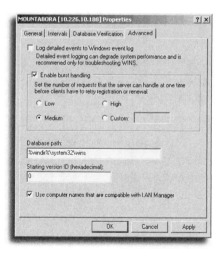

FIGURE 14.13
The Advanced tab allows you to configure logging, number of WINS requests, database path, and backwards compatibility.

6. The following Advanced properties are available:

- Log Detailed Events to Windows Event Log turns on detailed logging. Because verbose logging can consume considerable resources, it should be turned on only during performance tuning.

- Enable Burst Handling is used to set the number of concurrent requests the server can handle before clients have to retry. This can be set to Low, Medium, High, or Custom. The higher the setting, the more resources consumed by the WINS service.

- Database Path sets the path for the WINS database file. By default this path is `%windir%\system32\wins`.

- Starting Version ID (Hexadecimal) is used to specify the database version. This is seldom used.

- Use Computer Names That Are Compatible with LAN Manager is used to ensure complete backward compatibility.

What about replicating my WINS database?

If you're already at the point where you need to set up WINS replication, you've exceeded the scope of this book. There are several advanced titles available that cover WINS in greater detail. If you are relying on that large a WINS infrastructure, it is probably worth accelerating your migration to a pure Windows 2000 network and phasing out WINS as quickly as is practical.

Backing Up and Restoring the WINS Database

One potential problem with WINS is that WINS keeps its database open whenever it is running, and open files can't be backed up. As a result, if there is a system crash, you will lose the WINS database file. This forces WINS clients to reregister and could result in some clients being unable to use their accustomed names.

To avoid this problem, the WINS database is backed up automatically every 24 hours, creating files that can be backed up to tape. The backup directory is specified in the WINS Server Configuration dialog box.

SEE ALSO

➤ *The WINS Server Configuration dialog box is discussed in this chapter, page 379.*

You might want to force a backup of the database to take place, for insurance or to capture the WINS database at a particular point in time. And you certainly need to know how to restore the database from its backup in case you ever need to restore an entire server from tape.

Where should the backup be run?

Backing up a WINS database must be performed on the computer running the WINS Server service.

To back up the WINS database, do the following:

1. Open the WINS management application. Right-click the server to be backed up and from the context menu select the Back Up Database command, which will prompt you to select a folder for the backup in the Browse for Folder dialog box (see Figure 14.14).

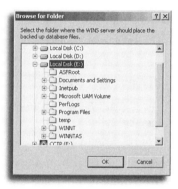

FIGURE 14.14
The standard Browse dialog box is used to select the location for the backup.

2. Select the location for the backup. The best location is another hard disk so that the database files remain available if the primary hard disk fails.

3. Specify the drive and directory in which backup files should be stored. WINS management snap-in proposes the directory you specify in the WINS Server Configuration dialog box. If desired, you can also specify a new directory name to be created in the directory chosen in Step 3. By default, a subdirectory named wins_bak is created to store the backup files.

4. Click OK to make the backup. When the message shown in Figure 14.15 appears, after the backup completes, click OK.

FIGURE 14.15
The WINS database backup has been completed successfully.

Restoring the WINS Database

If users can't connect to a server running the WINS Server service, the WINS database probably has become corrupted. In that case, you might need to restore the database from a backup copy. You can do this manually or using menu commands. The procedure must be performed on the computer running the WINS service. To restore the WINS database using menu commands, do the following:

1. Stop the WINS Service using one of these methods:
   - Stop the Windows Internet Server Service using the Services tool in the Control Panel.
   - Open a command prompt and enter the command net stop wins.

2. Start the WINS management snap-in. Ignore any warning message that says The Windows Internet Name Service is not running on the target machine or The target machine is not accessible.

3. Choose the Restore Database command from the Mappings menu.

4. In the Select Directory to Restore From dialog box, specify the directory from which to restore.

5. Click OK to restore the database.

6. Start the WINS service using one of the following methods:
   - Start the Windows Internet Server Service using the Services tool in the Control Panel.
   - Open a command prompt and enter the command net start wins.

Configuring WINS Clients

Each Microsoft client can be configured with the IP addresses of two WINS servers. On Windows 2000 servers, the WINS server properties are on the WINS tab of the Advanced TCP/IP Settings dialog box, shown in Figure 14.16. You can specify multiple WINS server IP addresses and order them as primary, secondary, and so on.

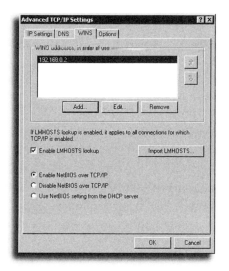

FIGURE 14.16
You can add as many WINS servers as are on your network.

The client prefers the primary WINS server. If your network has two or more WINS servers, you should configure clients so that all WINS servers are used about equally.

Configuring Name Resolution with *LMHOSTS*

If for some reason you don't want to configure WINS on your network, or if you want to have a backup in case a single WINS server fails, you can use LMHOSTS files to provide naming support for Microsoft network clients.

An LMHOSTS file has a very simple structure, as shown in the following:

```
172.16.0.1      MALAPROP1
172.16.0.50     ISAAC
172.17.0.25     ALBERT
172.17.0.100    MARIE
```

Each entry in LMHOSTS appears on a separate line and consists of two fields: an IP address and a name. The fields must be separated with at least one space or tab character. You will find a sample LMHOSTS file in the directory C:\Winnt\system32\etc.

LMHOSTS Files Keywords

Several keywords can appear in LMHOSTS files. Here is an example of a file with keywords:

```
172.16.0.1    MALAPROP1    #PRE    #DOM:MALAPROP
172.16.0.5    MALAPROP2    #PRE
#BEGIN_ALTERNATE
#INCLUDE \\MALAPROP1\PUBLIC\LMHOSTS
#INCLUDE \\MALAPROP2\PUBLIC\LMHOSTS
#END_ALTERNATE
```

The #PRE keyword specifies that the entry should be preloaded into the name cache. Ordinarily, LMHOSTS is consulted for name resolution only after WINS and b-node broadcasts have failed. Preloading the entry ensures that the mapping will be available at the start of the name-resolution process.

The #DOM: keyword associates an entry with a domain. This might be useful in determining how browsers and logon services behave on a routed TCP/IP network. #DOM entries can be preloaded in cache by including the #PRE keyword.

The #INCLUDE keyword makes it possible to load mappings from a remote file. One use for #INCLUDE is to support a master LMHOSTS file that is stored on logon servers and is accessed by TCP/IP clients when they start up. Entries in the remote LMHOSTS file are examined only when TCP/IP is started. Therefore, entries in the remote LMHOSTS file must be tagged with the #PRE keyword to force them to be loaded into cache.

If several copies of the included LMHOSTS file are available on different servers, you can force the computer to search several locations until a file is successfully loaded. This is accomplished by bracketing #INCLUDE keywords between the keywords #BEGIN_ALTERNATE and #END_ALTERNATE, as was done in the preceding sample file. Any successful #INCLUDE causes the group to succeed.

SEE ALSO

➤ *For a more detailed discussion of Registry concepts see Chapter 11, page 279.*

Enabling Clients to Use *LMHOSTS* Files

Generally speaking, LMHOSTS files are unnecessary on networks that have a properly functioning WINS name service. If an internetwork will not be using WINS, LMHOSTS lookups should be enabled and LMHOSTS files should be configured to help computers find critical hosts.

Any TCP/IP client can be enabled to use LMHOSTS files by checking the Enable LMHOSTS Lookup check box in the WINS tab of the Advanced TCP/IP Settings dialog box (see Figure 14.16).

Guidelines for Establishing *LMHOSTS* Name Resolution

B-node computers that are not configured to use WINS name resolution can use LMHOSTS to resolve names on remote networks. If the majority of name queries are on the local network, it isn't generally necessary to preload mappings in the LMHOSTS file. Frequently accessed hosts on remote networks can be preloaded with the #PRE keyword.

#DOM keywords should be used to help non-WINS clients locate domain controllers on remote networks. The LMHOSTS file for every computer in the domain should include #DOM entries for all domain controllers that don't reside on the local network. This ensures that domain activities such as logon authentication continue to function.

To browse a domain other than the logon domain, LMHOSTS must include the name and IP address of the primary domain controller of the domain to be browsed. Include backup domain controllers in case the primary fails or in case a backup domain controller is promoted to primary.

LMHOSTS files on backup domain controllers should include mappings to the primary domain controller name and IP address, as well as mappings to all other backup domain controllers.

All domain controllers in trusted domains should be included in the local LMHOSTS file.

That wraps up our discussion of Microsoft's name resolution methods. Let's move on to some of the other IP services available under Windows 2000.

Using DHCP Server

As a fledgling TCP/IP administrator, you might be freaking out about the amount of configuration required to keep your network clients happy. Move a WINS server, and you have to reconfigure every client. Move a client to a new subnet, and you have to update its IP address—and the manager who plugs his notebook into a new location every day definitely won't be in your good graces. Every change to the network requires a visit to one or more computers to update configuration properties. As if running a LAN isn't tough enough, you're too busy swatting mosquitoes to take aim at that grizzly that's charging out of the bushes.

Well, the Internet community has long been aware of the hassles of host configuration, so it came up with the Dynamic Host Configuration Protocol (DHCP). DHCP can save a tremendous amount of wear and tear on you and on your shoes. It takes a bit of time to set things up at first, but not all that much, and the rewards can be generous.

How DHCP Works

Figure 14.17 shows a DHCP network that has two DHCP servers.

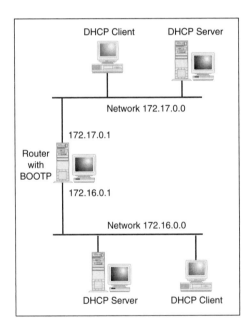

FIGURE 14.17
A network with two DHCP servers.

Although a single DHCP server can support a network of any size, it is often useful to have two. Here's what happens when a DHCP client enters the network:

1. The client broadcasts a DHCP discover message that is forwarded to DHCP servers on the network.

2. Each DHCP server that receives the discover message responds with a DHCP offer message that includes an IP address that is appropriate for the subnet where the client is attached.

3. The client considers the offer message and selects one. It sends a request to use that address to the DHCP server that originated the offer.

4. The DHCP server acknowledges the request and grants the client a lease to use the address.

5. The client uses the IP address to bind to the network. If the IP address is associated with any configuration parameters, the parameters are incorporated into the client's TCP/IP configuration.

In step 1 I told you that DHCP clients request their addresses using broadcast messages. The preceding chapters have pointed out several times that broadcast messages don't cross TCP/IP routers. Does that mean that a DHCP client can't obtain an IP address from a DHCP server on another subnet?

No, not if you configure routers with the BOOTP protocol. BOOTP is an older protocol that assigns IP addresses, and it remains in use to allow DHCP broadcasts to propagate across routers. Thanks to BOOTP, a DHCP server can service clients on any number of subnets.

In Figure 14.17, BOOTP is enabled on the router, which must, of course, be configured to route TCP/IP traffic. When the client broadcasts a request for an IP address, BOOTP receives the request and sends a directed message to any DHCP server that it knows about. This allows a DHCP server on a remote subnet to receive the request. The DHCP server responds through a directed message, so there is no problem with routing the response back to the client.

Installing DHCP

DHCP is installed as a Windows 2000 Server networking service. After installing the DHCP service, you need to configure BOOTP on any routers and then define subnet configurations on the DHCP server.

To support DHCP on a network, one or more computers must be running the DHCP service. A DHCP server can't also be a DHCP client. Therefore, computers running the DHCP Server service must be configured with static IP addresses. To install the DHCP server service, follow these steps:

1. From the Windows 2000 Configure Your Server application, choose Networking, and then select DHCP (see Figure 14.18).

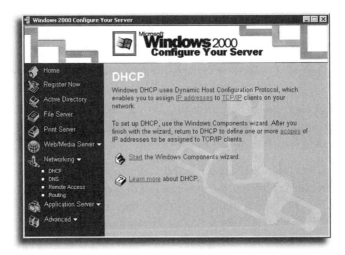

FIGURE 14.18
The DHCP page in Configure Your Server.

2. Click the hyperlink <u>Start</u> within the Windows Component Wizard.

3. In the Windows Component Wizard, scroll down until you see Networking Services (see Figure 14.19).

4. Click the Details button.

5. From the list of Networking Services, check the box next to Dynamic Host Configuration Protocol (DHCP), as shown in Figure 14.20.

A DHCP server cannot also be a DHCP client

If you currently have your server configured as a DHCP client, the DHCP installation prompts you to enter a static IP address for your server because a DHCP server cannot be a DHCP client.

6. Click the OK button, and DHCP services will be installed.

7. After this is completed, click the Finish button from the dialog box that lets you know that you have successfully completed the Windows Components Wizard.

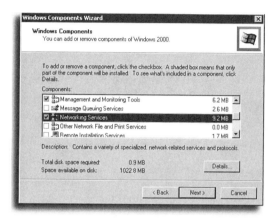

FIGURE 14.19
Select Networking Services from the Windows Components Wizard.

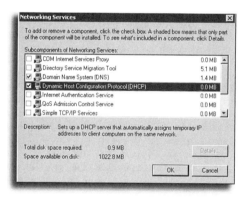

FIGURE 14.20
Choose to install DHCP.

Managing DHCP Scope

A scope is a range of IP addresses that can be assigned to clients on a given subnet. A scope can also include a set of configuration parameters that are assigned to clients that obtain their IP addresses from the scope. After installing the DHCP service, you must define at least one scope on the server. To create a DHCP scope, do the following:

1. Using the Windows 2000 Configure Your Server program (Figure 14.21), click the hyperlink within Open the DHCP Manager.

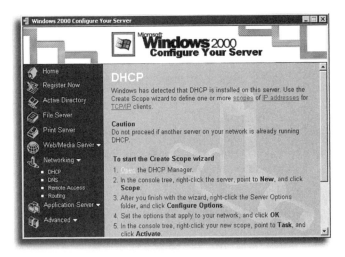

FIGURE 14.21
Click the word Open to bring up the DHCP Manager.

2. The DHCP Manager, shown in Figure 14.22, displays the newly created DHCP Server service.

3. Right-click the DHCP server name to show its context menu. From the context menu select New Scope (Figure 14.23).

4. The New Scope Wizard now starts. Click the Next button to start defining your scope.

5. The first thing you will do is name your scope, preferably, in a descriptive manner (see Figure 14.24). Click the Next button when you have finished entering the name.

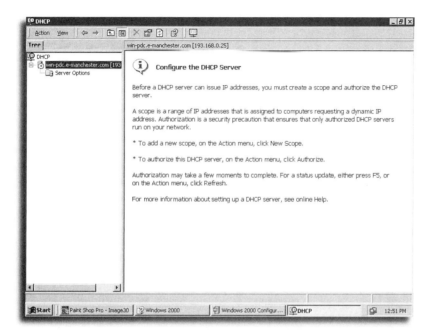

FIGURE 14.22
A brand-new DHCP server.

FIGURE 14.23
Add a scope to the DHCP server.

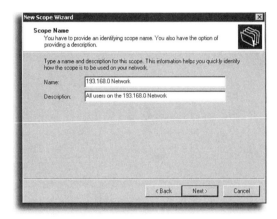

FIGURE 14.24
The name makes it obvious that all users on the 193.168.0 subnet will use this scope.

6. Now you can define the IP address range that you will use. In a later step you will be able to exclude addresses from this scope, so you should make it as large as you can. You also have the option to define reservations for particular addresses that exist within the scope, so those will not require exclusion. In Figure 14.25 I have defined the scope from 100 to 253.

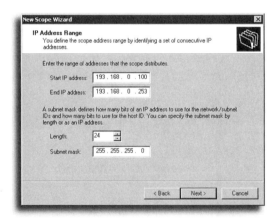

FIGURE 14.25
A range of addresses is needed to define the scope.

7. The Lease Duration, as shown in Figure 14.26, is the amount of time that must elapse before an IP address is automatically placed back into the DHCP pool. Usually this is only used in cases where there are more computers than IP

addresses. In that type of environment it is important that DHCP relinquish their address so that others can get onto the network. In a lot of cases, the IP addresses used in a DHCP scope are not legal addresses; therefore, there should be more than enough addresses for everyone. If a lease duration is not needed, just specify 0. Click the Next button to continue.

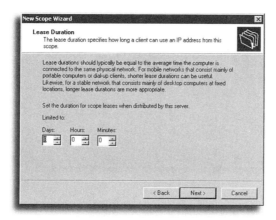

FIGURE 14.26
Setting the proper lease duration can help free up unused IP addresses.

Legal IP addresses

When I refer to a legal IP address, I am talking about addresses that have been registered with the IANA (Internet Assigned Numbers Authority), the organization that registers IP addresses used on the Internet. In many cases a network will not be connected to the Internet, therefore it is unnecessary to use registered addresses. Also, even if a network is connected to the Internet, firewall hardware/software or proxy hardware/software can be configured to allow the network to use illegal addresses, using address translations.

You don't necessarily have to lose your lease

Any DHCP client that had been assigned an address will automatically try to extend the lease after half of the lease has passed. If it is unable to do so it will continue to try to do so for the duration of the lease.

8. DHCP Options are other TCP/IP settings that you can assign to DHCP clients at the time that they are getting an address from the server. These can include IP addresses for routers and WINS servers (the most frequently used choices). If you want to define these options now, choose Yes, as shown in Figure 14.27.

You will be able to configure more options after the scope has been created, but if you want basic options enabled for this scope, you should start here. Click the Next button to continue.

FIGURE 14.27
By choosing to define options, you can also distribute other IP information.

9. The first option you can configure is the Router, or Default Gateway, as it is more commonly called. Here you have the option to enter as many paths out of your local network as you need. You can order them according to priority too. Figure 14.28 shows a single address being declared as the default gateway address. Now click the Next button.

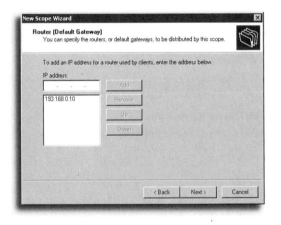

FIGURE 14.28
A default gateway will enable the client to pass data to hosts on other networks.

10. The next option, shown in Figure 14.29, is the DNS server address. As with the previous option, you can specify as many addresses as you want. In fact, in this option (and the next) you can enter a server name and have the address resolved for you. Click Next when you have finished adding your DNS server(s).

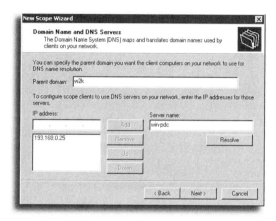

FIGURE 14.29
In this case, the DNS server is the same as the DHCP server.

11. You only need to define a WINS server if clients or servers on the network can still use WINS services. Obviously you also need to have a WINS server on your network. Type the name of one or more WINS servers if you want to be able to give your DHCP clients this information. One WINS server has been defined in Figure 14.30. Then click the Next button.

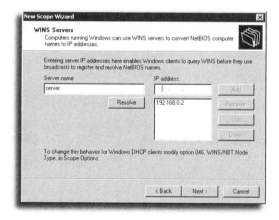

FIGURE 14.30
WINS is only necessary for pre–Windows 2000 computers.

12. At this point the scope has been created. If you want to be able to have your clients use it, you must activate the scope first (Figure 14.31). Make your choice, and then click Next to complete the process.

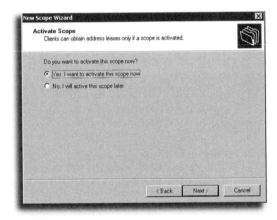

FIGURE 14.31
In order to make the range of addresses available to DHCP clients, the scope must be activated.

Authorizing the Server

If you just installed DHCP services on your computer, the DHCP Server still needs to be Authorized. You can do this by simply bringing up the context menu for the DHCP Server and then selecting Authorize. Notice in Figure 14.32 that there is a little down-arrow icon next to the server name. This shows that the server is unauthorized.

When the server is authorized you will see the down arrow change to an up arrow, as shown in Figure 14.33.

Setting Global Options

During the Create a Scope Wizard you were able to set certain options for that particular DHCP scope. This included a default gateway, DNS server, and WINS server addresses. If you find that you will be defining additional scopes, you might just want to set these options for the server. This way these options will automatically be carried over into any scope you define. Figure 14.34 shows the context menu and option to select to configure these global options.

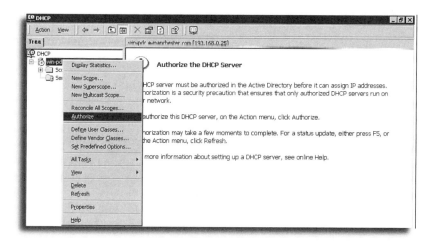

FIGURE 14.32
How to authorize a DHCP server.

FIGURE 14.33
The DHCP server is now authorized.

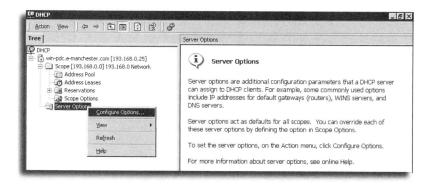

FIGURE 14.34
The menu item to choose to set options for the DHCP server.

Reviewing the Options Already Configured for a Scope

To review or modify the options that you have already set for an individual scope, do the following:

1. Select the Scope in DHCP Manager and click the plus sign.

2. Click Scope Options (shown in Figure 14.35).

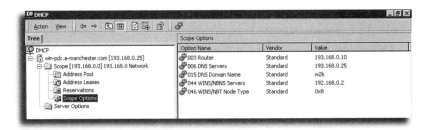

FIGURE 14.35
The Scope Options object.

3. To alter an existing option, double-click that option. To add a new option, bring up the context menu for Scope Options and select Configure Options.

Deactivating a Scope

If you need to temporarily deactivate a scope, perhaps because you do not want any more clients leasing from it while you make modifications to the options, just bring up the context menu for the scope (shown in Figure 14.36) and choose Deactivate. The little down-arrow icon will appear next to the scope after it's deactivated (see Figure 14.37).

Guidelines for Defining Scopes

You must define at least one scope, on at least one DHCP server, for each subnet that contains DHCP clients. You might wonder how the DHCP server knows which subnet a client is attached to. After all, the client doesn't know its IP address, so it can't very well know its subnet.

We can thank BOOTP forwarding for sorting out this mess. When BOOTP forwards a DHCP discover message, it tags the message with the address information of the subnet from which the request was received. This lets the DHCP server assign an IP address for the correct subnet.

FIGURE 14.36
Deactivating a DHCP scope.

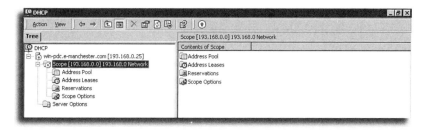

FIGURE 14.37
This shows a scope as a deactivated scope.

On a network, it is always useful to have two of anything important so that life goes on if one thing fails. Because you can have multiple DHCP servers, you might be tempted to assign two DHCP servers scopes for the same subnet. Then clients from the subnet can obtain their leases even if one DHCP server goes down.

Suppose that you configure two DHCP servers to support subnet 192.168.48.0, for example. You create scopes on both DHCP servers that offer IP addresses in the range 192.168.48.1 through 192.168.48.254. How does that work out?

Pretty badly. The design of DHCP doesn't let the DHCP servers exchange information about active leases. Therefore, it's possible for each DHCP server to assign the same IP address. If you want disaster on a network, having two hosts with the same IP address is a good start.

To avoid this, you need to assign different IP address ranges to the scopes on each server. One server could assign IP addresses 192.168.48.1 through 192.168.48.127, for example, while the other server offers 192.168.48.128 through 192.168.48.254. It doesn't matter how you divvy up the addresses, so long as the ranges don't overlap.

It might look as if you're wasting addresses if you choose this approach, but you aren't. Both servers respond to DHCP requests for the subnet and offer IP address leases. All the IP addresses remain available for assignment. Only when one server is down does part of the address range become unavailable.

Setting up a Reservation

A reservation can be very useful if you want to use DHCP to keep track of your IP address assignment, but you want certain computers or printers to always use the same address. You might be thinking: Why not use a static IP address? Well, if you use static addresses, the only way to change the address is by going to the computer and changing it manually. By using a reservation, you can revoke the lease and make a change at the server. Also, it allows you to view the status of the computer/printer.

To add a reservation you will need the MAC address for the computer or printer.

What's a MAC address?

A MAC (Media Access Control) address is a hardware address that uniquely identifies each node of a network. This address is assigned to the network interface card, and each is completely unique. A MAC address has the format 00-80-5F-7D-B2-FA, or 00805F7DB2FA. This is also known as the *physical address*.

How do I find my MAC address?

That's an easy one. If you are running Windows NT or Windows 2000, go to the command prompt and type IPCONFIG /ALL. The physical address listed is your MAC address.

For Windows 9x, go to Start, Run and type WINIPCFG. This gives you all the statistics on your network interface, including the MAC address.

For a printer, or a print server, read the manual to find out how to print a test page. If the printer or print server has a network interface, the MAC address will be on the test page.

1. Right-click Reservations. Select New Reservation from the Reservations context menu (shown in Figure 14.38).

FIGURE 14.38
Add a new reservation to the DHCP scope.

2. In the New Reservation dialog box (shown in Figure 14.39), enter a name for the reservation, the address that you want to reserve, the MAC address for the network adapter, and an optional description for the reservation.

FIGURE 14.39
Defining the address reservation.

3. Click the Add button.

4. To add more reservations, repeat steps 2 and 3.

5. Click the Close button and the DHCP Manager (shown in Figure 14.40) will reflect the new reservation.

6. Highlight the reservation to see the options that have been assigned to it (see Figure 14.41).

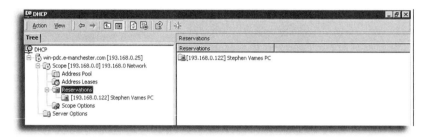

FIGURE 14.40
A defined reservation in the DHCP Manager.

FIGURE 14.41
This reservation inherited these options from the global options settings.

Is that reservation in use?

Notice that you can check the status of the reservation when you view Address Leases (see Figure 14.42).

FIGURE 14.42
This reservation has a status of inactive.

Backing Up and Restoring the DHCP Database

After clients are registered with DHCP, the contents of the DHCP database become quite valuable. To preserve its contents, Windows 2000 Server periodically makes a backup copy of the database in the directory C:\Winnt\system32\dhcp\backup\jet\new. The copy of the database can be backed up to tape.

SEE ALSO

➤ *For more information on backing up your server, see page 305.*

If the DHCP service is started but clients can't obtain leases, it's possible that the DHCP database might have been corrupted, in which case it might be possible to restore the backup database.

The first thing to try is to simply stop and start the DHCP service. If DHCP attempts to start and discovers that its database is corrupted, it will automatically attempt to recover the backup database.

If that fails, try the following:

1. Stop the Microsoft DHCP Server service using the Services Console.
2. Copy all files in C:\Winnt\system32\dhcp\backup\jet\new to C:\Winnt\system32\dhcp.
3. Start the Microsoft DHCP Server service using the Services Console.

After you restore the database, you need to make it current on active leases that have been recorded since the backup was made—a procedure called reconciling the DHCP database.

To reconcile the DHCP database, do the following:

1. Start DHCP Manager.
2. Select a scope from the DHCP Scopes pane.
3. Bring up the context menu and choose Reconcile
4. Repeat steps 2 through 4 for each scope.

Managing DHCP Clients

There might be times when you need to visit a client and review or renew its DHCP configuration manually. The tool you use is actually a general-purpose TCP/IP client tool named ipconfig.

If you want to know a client's TCP/IP configuration, you can go for the short form by opening a command prompt on the client and entering the command `ipconfig`. But I'm going to show you the long form. Enter the command `ipconfig /all` to see all the intimate details of a client's configuration. A sample configuration looks like this:

```
Windows 2000 IP Configuration
        Host Name . . . . . . . . . : mountabora
        DNS Servers . . . . . . . . : 172.17.0.27
        Node Type . . . . . . . . . : Hybrid
        NetBIOS Scope ID. . . . . . :
        IP Routing Enabled. . . . . : No
        WINS Proxy Enabled. . . . . : No
        NetBIOS Resolution Uses DNS : No
Ethernet adapter E100B1:
        Description . . . . . . . . : Intel 82557-based
Ethernet PCI Adapter
        Physical Address. . . . . . : 00-A0-C9-22-E8-D9
        DHCP Enabled. . . . . . . . : Yes
        IP Address. . . . . . . . . : 172.16.0.225
        Subnet Mask . . . . . . . . : 255.255.0.0
        Default Gateway . . . . . . : 172.16.0.254
        DHCP Server . . . . . . . . : 172.16.0.1
        Primary WINS Server . . . . : 172.17.0.10
        Secondary WINS Server . . . : 172.16.0.10
        Lease Obtained. . . . . . . : Tuesday, November 15,    1999 11:00:50 PM
        Lease Expires . . . . . . . : Thursday, November 17,   1999 11:00:50 PM
```

This listing reports just about anything you would want to know about a client's TCP/IP settings. It sure beats visiting all the TCP/IP property tabs!

Here are a couple of other useful things to do with `ipconfig`:

- To force a DHCP client to give up its lease on an IP address, enter the command `ipconfig /release`.
- To force a DHCP client to renew its lease or to obtain one if it doesn't have one, enter the command `ipconfig /renew`.

DHCP can be one of the biggest time and frustration savers you can add to your network, but you have to design your DHCP support carefully. Be sure clients can communicate with the DHCP servers through routers. And plan your scopes carefully so that DHCP servers can't assign conflicting IP addresses. It takes a bit of work, but there is a significant payoff for your effort.

Supporting the Domain Name System

The Domain Name Service is used on the Internet for resolving fully distinguished domain names to IP addresses. You might remember the example from Chapter 8, "Networking With Windows 2000," in which I asked which you think is easier to remember: `http://www.mcp.com` or `http://209.17.55.123`. DNS enables a Web site creator to use `http://www.mcp.com`. And so DNS was born. DNS is a hierarchical database containing names and addresses for IP networks and hosts and is used almost universally to provide name resolution. Domain Name Services are invisible but essential components of user-friendly networks. Users cannot be expected to remember dozens of IP addresses.

I thought you said *Domain Name System*!

You might have noticed that the acronym DNS stands for two different things in this section: *Domain Name System* and *Domain Name Service*. These names are interchangeable, although Microsoft tends to use *Service*, whereas most Internet users use *System*. From here on out we will use System for consistency.

DNS was designed with the capability of naming every computer on the Internet, and that's a lot of computers—potentially four billion! No single computer now in existence could handle that number of hostnames, particularly given that every minute millions of users are querying the name database. Consequently, DNS was designed as a distributed database. Parts of the overall name database are placed on separate computers so that the data storage and query loads are distributed throughout the Internet. Hundreds of thousands of computers share the responsibility of providing naming support on the Internet. It is also important to keep in mind that DNS was designed for power and flexibility, not for easy administration.

To administer DNS, you must understand DNS theory. You must understand the DNS name space architecture and how individual DNS servers support their portions of the overall name space. After you have a picture of DNS as a whole, you'll be ready to look at the specifics of supporting DNS with the Windows 2000 DNS server. Windows 2000 Server includes a DNS server service that is reasonably easy to administer because it uses the familiar Microsoft GUI. Because Microsoft's new implementation of DNS is dynamic DNS, you might not even have the need to administer it. See "Introduction to Dynamic DNS," later in this chapter for details.

How the Domain Name System Works

If you have ever used the Internet, you have seen DNS names. In most cases, a Web URL contains a domain name, as in http://www.microsoft.com. You don't need to learn a foreign language here. Domain names are the stuff of everyday experience. However, the DNS name space is complex. DNS names compose a hierarchical database that functions much like the directories in a file system. Hierarchies are powerful database structures because they can store tremendous amounts of data while making it easy to search for specific bits of information. Before examining the specifics of the DNS name space hierarchy, I'll review some rules about hierarchies in general.

The Structure of Hierarchies

You are intimately acquainted with hierarchies if you have been working with computers for more than a few days; all modern computers use hierarchical structures for organizing file storage. It's too chaotic to store all files together on a homogenous hard drive. Files need to be stored in related groups. The best approach is the hierarchical one, and PCs have been using hierarchical file systems since MS-DOS version 2.

Figure 14.43 illustrates a common file system hierarchy. You have undoubtedly seen hierarchies referred to as trees. I commonly refer to a directory tree, for example. Technically, the tree in Figure 14.43 is an inverted tree because it is oriented with the branches pointing down, but inverted trees have become so commonplace that one seldom thinks of their unusual orientation. Well before computers were invented, genealogies were referred to as family trees, even though the root ancestor is typically at the top of the diagram.

In file systems, the intersections of the branches are called directories or folders, of course. A directory can contain files and other directories. The capability of placing directories in directories allows you to extend the file system nearly without limit, adding categories and subcategories as the application demands.

In practical terms, hierarchies become unwieldy if they sprout too many levels. There are no hard and fast rules to this. A lot depends on whether applications or users must cope with the levels. A computer program can remember a file pathname of indefinite length, but humans have difficulty remembering more than four or five levels.

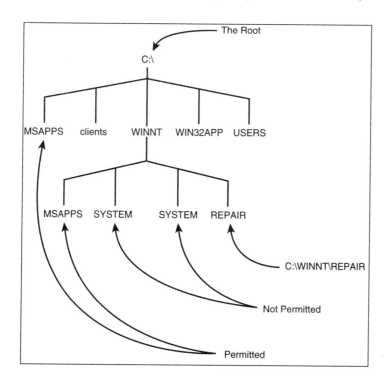

FIGURE 14.43
Directory trees illustrate the rules for constructing hierarchies.

There are several rules for constructing hierarchies:

- Every hierarchy has exactly one top container, usually called the root. On a file system, this is the root directory. All other containers are subcontainers of the root container.

- Every item within a container must have a unique name within the container.

- The full name of an item includes its own name as well as the names of all the containers that connect it with the root. This full name is often referred to as a fully qualified name.

- Items in different containers can have the same name because they will have different fully qualified names.

Now that you've reviewed the rules for constructing hierarchies, you will now see how they apply to DNS.

The DNS Name Space Hierarchy

Figure 14.44 illustrates a small part of the DNS name hierarchy.

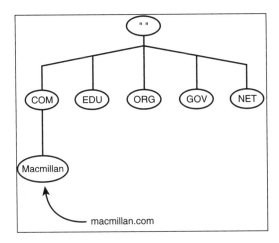

FIGURE 14.44
Part of the DNS name hierarchy.

The containers in the DNS hierarchy are called domains. The hierarchy starts with a root container, of course, referred to as the root domain. The root domain doesn't have a name, so it is typically represented by a single period.

Directly below the root domain are the top-level or first-level domains. Lower-level domains are second-level, third-level, and so on.

Figure 14.44 depicts the most common top-level domains, the ones you are most likely to encounter, but the list is only partial. For one thing, each country is assigned a top-level domain name, and there are too many of those to list. Also, there are specialized top-level domains such as MIL (reserved for the United States military) that few of us will encounter. Finally, new general-purpose domain names are being added because some domains are becoming so full that it is difficult to invent new names within the domains. For this discussion, though, you'll stick with the most common top-level domains:

- *COM.* Originally, the COM domain was supposed to contain commercial entities, but COM has become the overwhelming favorite top-level domain, and everyone wants his personal subdomains to be in COM. Because COM has been overused and abused, it's nearly impossible to come up with a sensible new name for a COM subdomain. Crowding in COM is the main impetus behind the definition of new top-level domains (Example: `mcp.com`).

- *ORG.* This domain is supposed to accommodate organizations that are noncommercial in nature. Although many noncommercial organizations have registered in the COM domain, most have respected the intent of this domain. This is a good place for nonprofit organizations, professional groups, churches, and other such organizations (Example: `npr.org`).

- *EDU.* This domain was originally supposed to embrace all types of educational institutions, but it began to fill up quickly as schools gained access to the Internet. Now it is primarily reserved for higher education institutions. Primary and secondary schools are supposed to register in their state domains, which are subdomains of their country domains (Example: `berkeley.edu`).

- *GOV.* This domain contains agencies of the United States Federal government, apart from the military, which has the MIL domain (Example: `whitehouse.gov`).

- *NET.* This domain supports Internet service providers and Internet administrative computers (Example: `ibm.net`).

Every host named on the Internet will have a hostname in the Internet DNS name hierarchy. Typically, hostnames are listed to include every domain that connects the host with the root—for example, `isaac.widgets.urwrite.net`. A domain name that includes all domains between the host and the root is a fully qualified domain name (FQDN).

When an organization wants to establish a domain name on the Internet, the domain name must be registered with the one of the authorized registration authority. One that many people are familiar with is Network Solutions, formerly the InterNIC. You can research new domain names and access registration forms at `http://www.networksolutions.com`. You can also contact your Internet Service Provider for assistance.

To register a domain name at Network Solutions, do the following:

1. Search the Internet directory to identify a domain name that isn't already in use.

2. Determine the IP addresses of two domain name servers—a master (Also known as the Start of Authority or SOA) and a backup (or secondary) name server—that will be authoritative for your domain. If your ISP will be providing your name servers, obtain the IP addresses from your ISP.

3. Register the domain name with Network Solutions. The Web site includes online forms for registering and changing domain names.

4. Pay the registration fees, which currently include $70 per domain name for the first two years and then an annual fee to keep the name.

At some point, you'll need to host your domain on the name servers you have identified. Before you learn how to do that, I'll explain how your name servers will fit into the overall process of name resolution on the Internet.

Resolving Hostnames Through DNS

Many computers provide DNS name services, each supporting a small portion of the overall DNS name space. A name server that resolves names for a domain is said to be authoritative for the domain. A name server can be authoritative for one or many domains located anywhere in the DNS hierarchy.

Of special interest are the root name servers that support the root of the name space hierarchy. At present, there are ten computers supporting the root domain. As you'll see in a moment, the root name servers are critical to the name resolution process. When a local name server can't resolve a name, it refers the name to a root name server, which begins the process of searching for a name server that can resolve the name.

Every client is configured with the IP address of at least one DNS server. When the client needs to send data to a host, it must learn the IP address of the host. To resolve the hostname to an IP address, the client sends the hostname to its name server, as shown in Figure 14.45.

The DNS name server resolves a name to an IP address using the following process:

1. The name server looks in a local memory cache for names it has recently resolved. If the name is found in the local cache, the name server can provide the IP address the client requires.

2. The name server looks in local static tables to see whether the administrator has added an entry that maps the hostname to an IP address. If a static entry exists, the name server forwards the IP address to the client.

3. The name server refers the request to a root name server.

4. The root name server refers the request to a name server for the first-level domain in the hostname. The first-level domain name server refers the request to a name server for the second-level domain in the hostname, and so on, until a name server is encountered that can resolve the complete hostname.

5. The first name server that can resolve the hostname to an IP address reports the IP address to the client.

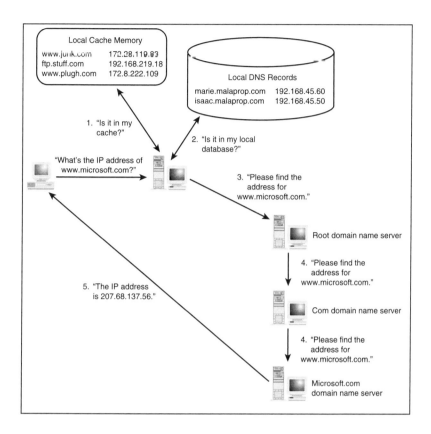

FIGURE 14.45
The process of resolving a DNS name.

As the administrator of a TCP/IP network, you must ensure that your local users have access to at least one, and preferably more, DNS name servers. These name servers can include your Windows 2000 Server DNS server, other private ones you configure on your own network, or name servers provided by your ISP. Which should you choose?

If you elect to use DNS name servers provided by your ISP, this relieves you of the responsibility for maintaining a DNS server, as a Windows 2000 Server running DNS can dynamically maintain itself for local traffic. An ISP will always offer at least two name servers because the registering a domain name requires that every Internet domain be hosted on at least two name servers. Name servers operated by ISPs are typically UNIX servers running BIND, the application that is the overwhelming choice for providing DNS name services in the UNIX environment.

Changes made to the name database on BIND servers are entered in text database files and go into effect only when the name server is stopped and restarted. Consequently, it usually takes 24–48 hours to make a change to the name database of an ISP's DNS servers.

If you elect to operate your own DNS servers using the Microsoft DNS Server service that is included with Windows 2000 Server, you gain two distinct advantages. Hostnames that are entered manually go into effect automatically; there is no need to wait until the name service can be stopped and restarted. Also, the Microsoft DNS Server can communicate with WINS, if needed, so that NetBIOS names are automatically registered in the DNS name space.

Because the Microsoft DNS Server is easy to administer and has particular advantages on Microsoft networks, you'll probably elect to configure your own name servers. In that case, you must have at least two Windows 2000 Server computers on your network so that you can have a master and a backup name server.

Installing Windows 2000 Server's DNS Server

When you install a Windows 2000 Server domain controller and install Active Directory, one task that runs is the installation of Windows 2000 Server's DNS server. Because Active Directory is based on DNS, it uses the DNS extensively. For the most part, you might not have to touch the DNS configuration, unless you want to link external DNS servers, or have other DNS servers on your network that you want to share information with.

If you have a Windows 2000 Server that is not a domain controller, you will need to install DNS manually. To install DNS, do the following:

1. You can install DNS by using the Windows Components Wizard. Access the Windows Component Wizard by opening the Control Panel.

2. Starting the Add/Remove Programs applet.

3. Select Networking Services, shown in Figure 14.46, and then click the Details button.

4. Click Domain Name System (Figure 14.47) so that the checkbox next to it is checked.

5. Click the OK button.

6. The Windows Component Wizard will prompt you for the Windows 2000 Server CD-ROM if it needs to copy files. When it is finished it will display a confirmation.

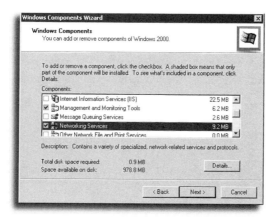

FIGURE 14.46
The Windows 2000 DNS Server is part of the Networking Services component.

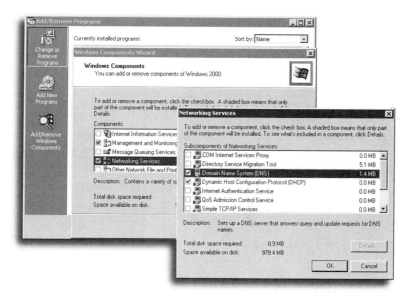

FIGURE 14.47
Selecting Domain Name System installs the service.

Configuring DNS

DNS configuration is handled through a snap-in for the Microsoft Management Console. This can be found in the Administrative Tools program folder (see Figure 14.48).

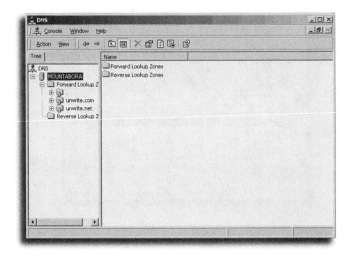

FIGURE 14.48
The DNS Snap-in is used for maintaining DNS.

Although it is possible to manually configure the text files that DNS creates (for all you UNIX fans), the DNS Console makes it much easier to see your DNS name-space configuration, and make modifications. To create a new DNS Zone, do the following:

1. Open the DNS management snap-in using the Administrative Tools entry shown in Figure 14.48. This opens the application shown in Figure 14.49.

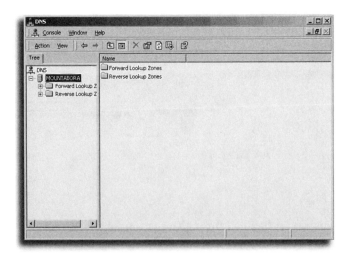

FIGURE 14.49
To manage the DNS table, use the DNS snap-in.

2. Click the Action menu and select New Zone. The New Zone Wizard will guide you through the process. Click Next to continue the process.

3. The Zone Type dialog box (shown in Figure 14.50) allows you to select the type of zone to create. Three types are supported:

   - *Active Directory–Integrated.* This option stores all DNS information in the Active Directory. If your entire domain infrastructure is run on a Windows 2000 platform, this is a good selection.

   - *Standard Primary.* This option stores the information in a text file, like most non–Windows 2000 DNS servers and is useful if you need to transfer information between different types of DNS servers.

   - *Standard Secondary.* This option creates a copy of an existing zone. These are generally used to provide redundancy or load balancing of DNS on a network.

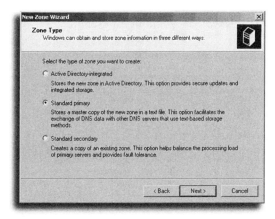

FIGURE 14.50
Choosing the proper zone type is critical to a successful implementation.

If you have any doubts about what to select, choose Standard Primary.

4. Click Next to open the Forward or Reverse Lookup Zone dialog box, shown in Figure 14.51. Choose Forward Lookup Zone. A forward lookup zone resolves names to IP addresses. A reverse lookup zone allows users to resolve an IP address to a system name. Reverse zones are used less often then forward zones and are a bit out of the scope of this discussion.

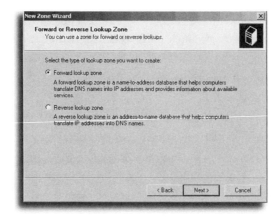

FIGURE 14.51
Forward zones are more commonly used than reverse zones.

   5. In the Zone Name dialog box (shown in Figure 14.52), enter the name of the
   new zone (`newriders.mcp.com` would be an example).

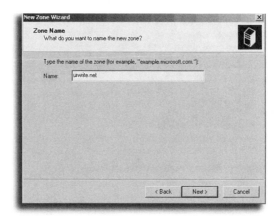

FIGURE 14.52
Zone names can indicate a domain, such as `urwrite.net`, or a subdomain, such as `newriders.mcp.com`.

   6. Click Next to open the Zone file dialog box (see Figure 14.53). This allows you
   to select the name of the zone file, or to load an existing zone file. Zone files are
   stored in `%winroot%\system32\dns`.

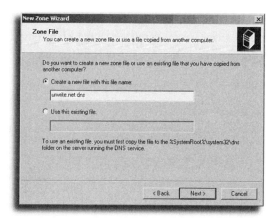

FIGURE 14.53
If this is a new server, select Create New File. If you have a zone file already, select Use This Existing File.

7. Click Next to open the Completing the New Zone Wizard dialog box, shown in Figure 14.54. This gives you a summary of the information you have input.

FIGURE 14.54
Check the information you have input because you can still go back and change it.

8. Click Finish to complete the zone creation.

Introduction to Dynamic DNS

Dynamic DNS (DDNS) is specified in RFC 2136, "Dynamic Updates in the Domain Name System (DNS UPDATE)." It is the foundation of a successful Active

Directory Service implementation. As we have discussed, DNS is used to resolve a name to an IP address, or vice-versa, using a defined hierarchical naming structure to ensure uniformity. Dynamic DNS takes that architecture to the next level.

What is this *RFC* thing, anyway?

Request For Comment (RFC) documents are used to make notes about the Internet and Internet technologies. If an RFC can garner enough interest, it can eventually become a standard. There are RFCs on topics ranging from File Transfer Protocol (RFC 0114, which was updated by RFCs 0141, 0172, and 0171) to the Hitchhikers guide to the Internet (RFC 1118). The first RFC was posted in 1969, by Steve Crocker and the topic was Host Software. You can find listings of all the RFCs at a number of sites throughout the Internet. One place is `http://www.rfc-editor.org/`. At the writing of this book, the highest numbered RFC was 2728 (The Transmission of IP Over the Vertical Blanking Interval of a Television Signal), but will be much higher by the time this book is on the shelves. New RFCs are being published all the time. It is sometimes fun to look at an index of RFCs, where you find memorable ones such as RFC 1882, "The 12-Days of Technology Before Christmas" and RFC 1925, "The Twelve Networking Truths."

Dynamic DNS integrates DHCP and DNS, as described in RFC 2136. Every time a machine requests a new address or renews its address, it sends an option 81 and its fully qualified name to the DHCP server and requests the DHCP server register a entry in the reverse lookup DNS zone on its behalf. The DHCP client also requests an entry in the forward lookup zone on its own behalf. The end result is that every DHCP client has an entry in the DNS zones, both forward and reverse. This information can be used by other Windows 2000 machines in place of WINS, for identifying the names and IP addresses of other hosts.

What is *Option 81*?

Option 81, also known as the Fully Qualified Domain Name (FQDN) option, allows the client to send its FQDN to the DHCP server when it requests an IP address.

Using Your Windows 2000 Server as an Internet Router

If you have a small office and don't want to invest several thousand dollars in a hardware router, you might find that your Windows 2000 server is more than up to the task.

The Routing and Remote Access Services in Windows 2000 Server can allow you to connect your entire network to the Internet. An advantage of the Routing and Remote Access service is integration with the Windows 2000 Server operating system. This service delivers many cost-saving features and works with a variety of hardware platforms and hundreds of network adapters. If it's on the Hardware Compatibility List for Windows 2000, it is supported by RRAS as well. You might ask, "How does this save me any money?" The answer is simple. If you use Windows 2000 as your Internet router, you will not have to go to Cisco, 3Com, Nortel, or any of the other hardware router vendors to buy a router, which can cost anywhere from $500 to $5,000, depending on your requirements.

To connect your network to the Internet, you can create a *translated connection*, which means that the computer running Windows 2000 Server acts as a network address translator. The translator is an IP router that translates addresses for packets being forwarded between the LAN and the Internet.

Configuring Routing and Remote Access

For this example, we will configure Routing and Remote Access to perform Network Address Translation. To enable and configure Routing and Remote Access, do the following:

1. Open Routing and Remote Access, which is located in the Administrative Tools folder in the Start Menu's Programs folder.
2. In the Routing and Remote Access Console, identify the server that you want to configure as an Internet router and bring up its context menu by right-clicking it.
3. Select Configure and Enable Routing and Remote Access. The Routing and Remote Access Configuration Wizard will start.
4. Click the Next button.
5. As you can see in Figure 14.55, there are a number of options for Routing and Remote Access.

   Options include
   - *Internet connection server.* This function allows all the computers on the network to connect to the Internet through the server. Only select this option if you want your Windows 2000 server to act as your Internet router.
   - *Remote Access Server.* This function enables users to dial in to your network. It is the equivalent of the Windows NT 4 Remote Access Server.

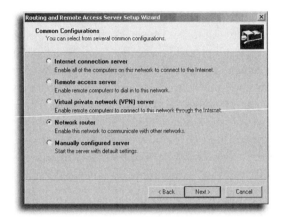

FIGURE 14.55
There are a number of different wizard configurations, or you can configure Routing and Remote Access manually.

- *Virtual Private Network Server.* This option will configure the server to allow secure connectivity to the local network for remote users who are connecting across the Internet.

- *Network Router.* Similar to the first option, this option configures Routing and Remote Access to function as a network router, and to communicate with other networks.

- *Manually Configured Server.* If you really understand routing and your options under Routing and Remote Access, you can manually configure the server.

Enable this computer as a router by checking the appropriate box. You will be configuring the routing capabilities first. Click Next to continue and open the Routed Protocols dialog box (shown in Figure 14.56.)

SEE ALSO
➤ *For more information on supported protocols, see page 182.*

6. Select LAN and WAN as the routing option. Do not allow this computer to accept remote access requests, unless you have multiple LAN adapters or multiple modems, so that you are in the position to dedicate one outgoing adapter for the Internet and another for incoming requests. In this example, I have two LAN adapters and one modem, however this computer will be dedicated to routing Internet traffic.

7. Click the Next button.

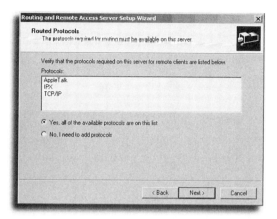

FIGURE 14.56
Routing and Remote Access supports a number of protocols.

8. The Dial-in or Demand Dial Interfaces dialog box (shown in Figure 14.57) appears if you have multiple interfaces. Choose the option that suits your purpose. In this case, I will enable all interfaces for routing.

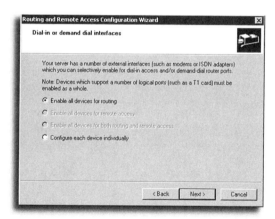

FIGURE 14.57
If you have more than one adapter you will be asked if you want to configure them separately.

9. Click the Next button.

10. The Authentication and Encryption dialog box allows you to specify whether to allow clear text passwords to be sent via the router. I have selected not to allow clear text, but will configure the type of encryption later when I set up the dial on demand entry.

11. Click the Next button.

12. Select the protocols that have been enabled on your Windows 2000 router. For each one, specify whether to allow routing through the router, or have the network traffic stop at the router.

13. Click the Next button.

14. If this connection were being used for dial-in purposes, you could specify whether the client dialing in would be given an IP address from a DHCP server, or you could specify a pool to assign them an address from. I've chosen to use DHCP.

15. Click the Next button.

16. If you have IPX installed on your server, you will be asked if you want to be able to forward IPX file and print sharing requests. For my purpose it is unnecessary.

17. Click the next button and that will complete the Routing and Remote Access Configuration Wizard.

18. Click the Finish button. You will be prompted whether you want to start the Routing and Remote Access service. Click the Yes button to start the service.

Dialing on Demand

The next step to creating your Internet router is setting your connection to the Internet. For dial-up, you need to create a Demand-dial Interface.

This will create what is essentially a phonebook entry for your ISP that will be automatically initiated whenever the Windows 2000 Server Router senses that access to an outside network is required. To create a Demand-dial Interface, do the following:

1. Double-click the server/router in the Routing and Remote Access Console to reveal the Routing Interfaces object.

2. Display the context menu for Routing Interfaces and select New Demand-Dial Interface. This will start the Demand Dial Interface Wizard.

3. Click the Next button.

4. Give the Demand Dial Interface a descriptive name.

5. Click the Next button.

6. Select whether you will use a physical device or are joining a VPN.

7. Click the Next button.

8. The Select a Device dialog box will display the devices that are enabled for routing. Select the appropriate one and click the Next button.

9. Next, enter the phone number that will be used to call this provider. You will have the chance to enter alternative phone numbers after this interface has been established.

10. Click the Next button.

11. The Routing and Remote Access dialog box (shown in Figure 14.58) lets you specify what type of routing will be enabled.

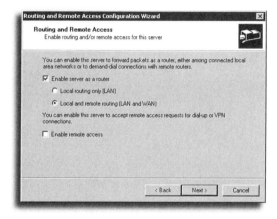

FIGURE 14.58
Determining what type of a router to set up.

12. Click the Next button.

13. Because I have indicated that a script will enable a logon, the Router Scripting dialog box (see Figure 14.59) is displayed.

Showing a terminal window

In the Router Scripting dialog box you can indicate that you want a Terminal Window to be displayed whenever this interface is used to connect. Because I want this to be unattended in my example, I'll pass on having the window open up. Actually, a Terminal Window will come in handy if you are troubleshooting the logon process. The script that I will run is one of the supplied scripts. Other scripts include the capability to perform an unattended logon to CompuServe.

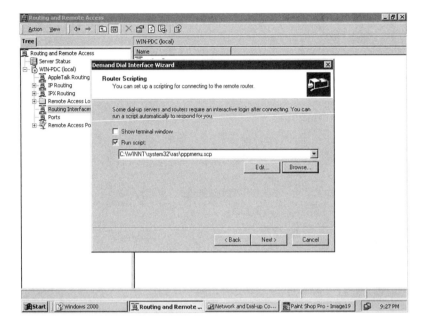

FIGURE 14.59
I have chosen a script from among those supplied with Windows 2000 Server.

14. Click the Next button to enter the dial-out credentials that you want this script to use. If you do not make entries you will be prompted for these items each time this interface is used. Because I am striving for an unattended logon I have filled in the credentials information.

15. Click the Next button to finish this configuration.

16. Click the Finish button to return to the Routing and Remote Access Console. Notice in Figure 14.60 that ISP is now listed as an interface, and its status is disconnected. It will not show connected until a dial connection to your ISP is completed.

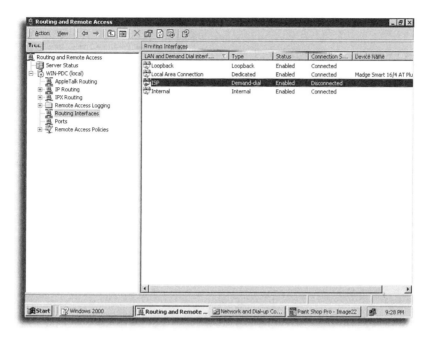

FIGURE 14.60
The new Demand Dial Interface now has its status displayed.

To perform additional configuration on a Routing Interface, do the following:

1. Double-click the Router Interface that you want to modify.

2. The Properties dialog box will be displayed. You can change the configuration for the selected adapter, and you can click the Alternates button to enter additional phone numbers.

3. Click the Options tab (shown in Figure 14.61) to set additional connection options, such as idle time before the connection hangs up and additional dialing properties.

4. If it is required for the connection, you can configure Security options, for instance, to enable other security protocols such as PAP, CHAP, or MS-CHAP.

5. The Networking tab gives you the option to specify the type of server you are dialing into. I have chosen a PPP server. Other options include UNIX servers. You can also configure the protocols, enable or disable network protocols, and make any other configuration changes here, such as specifying a Windows 2000/NT domain that you might be logging in to.

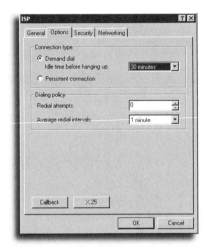

FIGURE 14.61
A connection that is idle can be automatically disconnected.

Understanding Network Address Translation (NAT)

To communicate on the Internet, you must use addresses that have been reserved for your domain by the Internet Network Information Center (InterNIC). A typical company is allocated an IP address, or a range of addresses, from its ISP.

To allow multiple computers in LAN to communicate on the Internet, each computer must have its own public address. The problem is that there are not always enough addresses in a company to go around for each computer. In order to get away with using addresses that do not "legally" belong to you, you can use Network Address Translation (NAT).

In Windows 2000 Server, you can configure a translated connection to the Internet by using the NAT routing protocol provided with the Routing and Remote Access service. Network address translation provides translation, addressing, and name resolution services to LAN hosts.

The concept is simple. A server running NAT is placed between an intranet, which uses private addresses, and the Internet, which uses public addresses. Outgoing packets from the intranet have their private addresses translated by NAT into public addresses. Incoming packets from the Internet have their public addresses translated by the NAT into private addresses.

Reserved private addresses

InterNIC has reserved a number of IP addresses that cannot receive packets from the Internet. These ranges of addresses are

`10.0.0.0` with the subnet mask `255.0.0.0`

`172.16.0.0` with the subnet mask `255.240.0.0`

`192.168.0.0` with the subnet mask `255.255.0.0`

To configure Windows 2000 to support Network Address Translation, do the following:

1. In the Routing and Remote Access Console, display the context menu for General, which is located under IP Routing, shown in Figure 14.62.

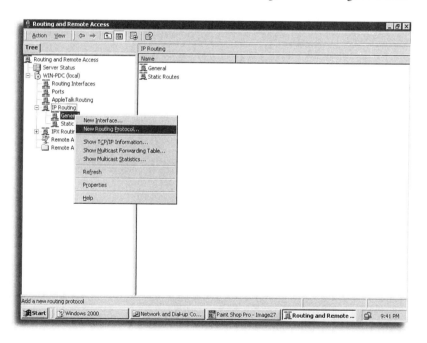

FIGURE 14.62
Navigating to the menu item for installing a new routing protocol.

2. Select New Routing Protocol

3. From the list of New Routing Protocols, select Network Address Translation (NAT).

4. Click OK. NAT will now be added under IP Routing.

5. Display the context menu for NAT (see Figure 14.63).

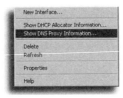

FIGURE 14.63
Use this menu item to add the Demand Dial Interface you created to use NAT.

6. Select New Interface.

7. From the New Interface for Network Address Translation (NAT) dialog box, select the Demand Dial Interface that you have created.

8. Click the OK button.

9. Now, the Network Address Translation Properties page will be displayed (see Figure 14.64).

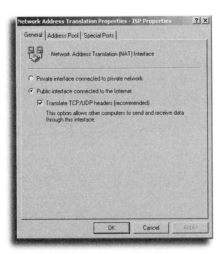

FIGURE 14.64
Advanced settings for NAT.

10. Click the OK button and your new NAT server will be displayed in the right windows of the Routing and Remote Access Console (Figure 14.65). Check this console to see how many users are mapped through NAT, among other statistics.

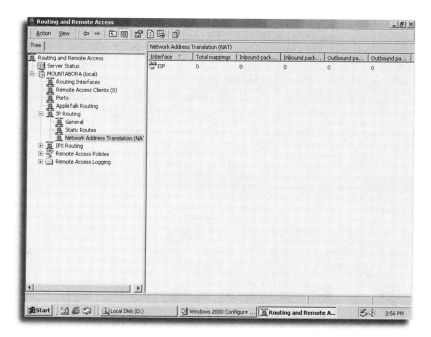

FIGURE 14.65
The Routing and Remote Access Console displays statistics for each interface configured with NAT.

Advanced options for NAT

The Properties page for NAT has other tabs that I didn't discuss. These are used for more advanced situations, such as giving users on your network a public address defined by the ISP. Some applications might require that the user has her own public address, but under normal circumstances this should not be the case.

Enabling Virtual Private Networking

Before you look at how to use Virtual Private Networking (VPN), I should probably briefly define this term. A *VPN* is a mechanism for providing secure, encrypted communications in two configurations. In the first configuration, a user-to-network configuration, the remote user connects to the Internet and uses a VPN to securely become a node on the company network. This is commonly referred to as the Remote Access model for a VPN. The other configuration concerns when a site/office uses VPN coupled with an Internet connection to securely connect to the network at the other end of the VPN. This is commonly referred to as a site-to-site VPN. The remote access VPN is used to supplant the standard remote access of dial-in or authenticated firewall access to the network. The site-to-site model is being used in places to remove the need for a wide area network. Both configurations can offer significant cost savings over the more traditional access methods.

Now how can we use VPNs with Windows 2000? Windows 2000 actually supports two protocols for creating a VPN: the Point-to-Point Tunneling Protocol (PPTP), the only supported VPN protocol under previous versions of Windows, and IPSec, the newer industry-standard protocol. I will look at setting up PPTP and finish with a discussion of what IPSec is, and how it is supported.

Point-to-Point Tunneling Protocol (PPTP)

Microsoft's Point-to-Point Tunneling Protocol (PPTP) is a method of creating a Virtual Private Network. By having two or more computers, both configured with PPTP, communicating over a public network such as the Internet, the computers pass encrypted and secure data between them.

The "tunnel" that PPTP creates actually encapsulates IP, IPX, or the NetBEUI protocols. What this means is that a computer can connect to another computer over a network via IP. By having a Windows 2000 Network and Dial-up Connection, both running PPTP, the computers can continue to communicate via IP, IPX, or NetBEUI. Usually it will be an application that dictates the protocol that is used. More recently IP is the protocol used; however, legacy applications might still rely on IPX or NetBEUI.

> **Secure PPTP connections aren't limited to remote networks**
> Because PPTP can also be used on local area networks, two computers can communicate through PPTP on a LAN and know that their communication is securely encrypted.

To enable a Windows 2000 Server to accept PPTP connections, do the following:

1. Enable Routing and Remote Access (see "Using Your Windows 2000 Server as an Internet Router," earlier in this chapter).

2. Assign the proper privileges to the user or computer account that will be accessing the server through RRAS. By default, when you install RRAS on your server, five PPTP connections will be created. This can be modified by altering the properties for the RRAS ports.

To modify the number of PPTP ports that are available on your server, do the following:

1. Open the Routing and Remote Access Console.

2. Expand the list of properties for the server.

3. Display the context menu for Ports.

4. Select properties.

5. Highlight PPTP and click the Configure button.

6. In the Maximum Ports field, change the number accordingly.

7. Click OK to exit the PPTP port properties.

8. Click OK to exit the Ports properties.

To assign permissions to allow a user PPTP access to the server, do the following:

1. Open Active Directories Users and Computer.

2. Select the Users folder to display the list of user objects.

3. Double-click the user you want to assign permissions to.

4. Click the Dial-in tab.

5. Under Remote Access Permissions, select Allow Access.

6. Click the OK button to apply this permission.

To create a PPTP connection on a client computer, do the following:

1. Display the context menu for My Network Places and select Properties.

2. Double-click Make New Connection, which will start the Network Connection Wizard. Click the Next button to start the process.

3. Select Connect to a private network through the Internet, and then click the Next button.

4. Enter the computer name or IP address for the computer you want to connect to.

5. On the Connection Availability dialog box, select whether this connection will be made available for only the currently logged on user, or for anyone that logs on at the local computer. Click the Next button to continue.

6. The last step is to give a name to this connection which will show up in the My Network places folder. You can also select to create a shortcut on the desktop for this VPN connection.

7. Click the Finish button. You will immediately be presented with a logon dialog box to attach to the remote computer. At this point you can either cancel if you do not want to try the connection, or fill in the necessary fields and click the Connect button.

IPSec (IP Security Protocol)

Microsoft has introduced a new VPN protocol as part of the Windows 2000 Routing and Remote Access services. IPSec is the long-term direction for secure networking. It provides an essential line of defense against private network and Internet attacks, balancing ease of use with security. IPSec is an extension of the existing IP protocol designed to protect IP packets from snooping or modification as well as providing a defense against network attacks. More information on IPSec can be found in RFC 2401. Microsoft implements IPSec a little differently than most other vendors.

How can you access an RFC?

You can find listings of all the RFCs at a number of sites throughout the Internet. One place is `http://www.rfc-editor.org/`.

Microsoft supports IPSec in two different modes:

- *Native.* Native mode is only recommended by Microsoft for interoperability with other IPSec devices. Essentially it supports IPSec according to the specification.

- *L2TP Tunneling Mode.* This mechanism for supporting IPSec uses the IPSec protocol to encrypt the data, but uses L2TP (Layer 2 Tunneling Protocol) as the transport layer. This allows for additional functionality, and potentially increased security.

Because Windows 2000 is so new, neither implementation has been field-tested extensively, so only time will tell how widely they are adopted in the industry.

chapter 15

Integrating Windows 2000 with Other Operating Systems

Configuring Macintosh Services

Windows 2000 comes equipped with the tools you need to enable your Macintosh clients to use resources on your Windows 2000 Server. First you need to install the support required for this function. Follow these steps to install File and Print Services for Macintosh:

1. Start the Windows Component Wizard.
2. Select Other Network File and Print Services (see Figure 15.1).

FIGURE 15.1
The Add Windows Components Wizard allows you to select the components to add.

3. Click the Details button.
4. Place a checkmark in the File Services for Macintosh and Print Services for Macintosh listings (see Figure 15.2).

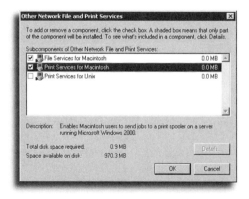

FIGURE 15.2
Select File Services for Macintosh and Print Services for Macintosh.

5. Click OK.

6. Finish the wizard. No additional input is needed from you.

Now that you have finished the installation, look at each of the services you installed.

Using the Windows 2000 File Services for Macintosh

To give Macintosh users access to file shares on a Windows 2000 Server, you must create a Macintosh Accessible Volume. This is a share that is created the same way you would create a standard share; however, this share must reside on an NTFS volume. To create a Macintosh Accessible Volume you need to do the following:

1. Start the Computer Management Console from the Administrative Tools folder.

2. In the System Tools section, select Shares.

3. Display the context menu for Shares, and select New File Share (see Figure 15.3).

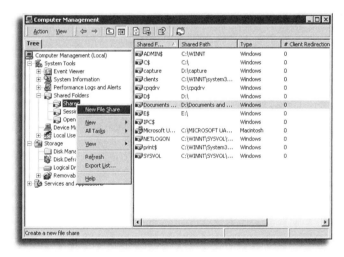

FIGURE 15.3
The context menu for the Shares object.

4. Place a checkmark next to the clients that you want to make this share available to. Don't forget to include Macintosh.

5. Fill in the fields with a folder name, a share name for Windows clients, and a volume name for Macintosh users (see Figure 15.4).

FIGURE 15.4
The Configuration dialog box for creating a new share allows you to identify the share and enable Macintosh users to access it.

6. Click Next.

7. Select the appropriate security option for this share (see Figure 15.5).

FIGURE 15.5
Configure security settings by choosing a standard setting, or choose Custom if you want to be more granular with your security.

8. Click Finish and the share will be created.

In this example I have chosen to make the share accessible to both Windows and Macintosh clients. It is because of this that two shares have been created.

In Figure 15.6 you can see that the Computer Management Console now shows a Captured Picture share for Windows clients and a Captured Picture share for Macintosh users.

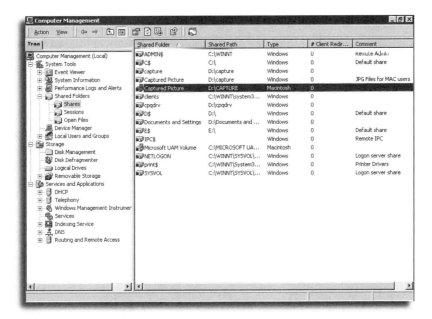

FIGURE 15.6
Notice the Type column shows Windows and Macintosh.

How Windows Filenames Are Translated into Macintosh Filenames

When a Macintosh user creates a file or a folder on the server and gives it a name, File Services for Macintosh checks it for illegal NTFS characters. If the filename contains illegal NTFS characters, File Services for Macintosh replaces the illegal characters. Otherwise, the original Macintosh name is the same as the NTFS name. Macintosh users see the name as it was created. Windows 2000 Server users see the same name with any illegal characters replaced.

After the file server has replaced illegal NTFS characters, Windows 2000 Server takes over the filename translation process. Names that are too long for MS-DOS users are shortened to six characters, a tilde (~), and a unique number. The file extensions are preserved.

Windows 2000 users creating long NTFS filenames (up to 256 characters) should name files with 31 characters (the Macintosh limit) or fewer so that Macintosh users can understand the filenames.

Because MS-DOS users refer to files created by Macintosh users by the translated short names, Macintosh users should give the FAT standard names (eight characters plus an optional period and three-character extension) to files and folders that will also be used by MS-DOS users. This way MS-DOS users won't have to decipher short names. For files that only Macintosh users or Windows 2000 clients will use, Macintosh users can use long file and folder names.

Macintosh File Administration

Macintosh volumes and files are centrally administered through the Microsoft Management Console Shared Folders snap-in. Both Macintosh and non-Macintosh files are administered by using Shared Folders. This improves the integration of Macintosh file management with non-Macintosh files.

You can still use the command-line version of Macfile (`Macfile.exe`) to administer servers, volumes, files, and folders.

Print Services for Macintosh

Print Services for Macintosh is integrated into the Windows 2000 Server Printers folder. Print Services makes printers connected to the computer running Windows 2000 Server available to Macintosh clients, and it makes AppleTalk PostScript printers available to Windows clients.

When Print Services receives print jobs, it sends them to a spooler, which is a portion of the print server hard disk. The spooler then sends the print job to the specified printing device. This enables Macintosh users, as well as Windows users, to submit print jobs and continue working on their computers without waiting for the print job to finish.

The print server also translates all incoming PostScript files if the print request is to a non-PostScript printer attached to the computer running Windows 2000 Server. A Macintosh client (but not a Windows 2000 client) can send a PostScript job to any Windows 2000 Server printer.

Whether printing devices are attached to the computer running Windows 2000 Server or are located elsewhere on the AppleTalk network, the Printers folder displays a list of print jobs for the respective printers you created to represent the devices. By default, each list presents jobs in first-in, first-out (FIFO) order. You can change the priority of jobs, however, and specify permissions for the printer and times for print jobs to run. Follow these steps to connect to a printer on a Macintosh server:

1. Go to Start, Settings and open the Printers menu.
2. Double-click Add Printer to start the Add Printer Wizard, and then click Next.
3. Click Local Printer (see Figure 15.7), and then click Next.

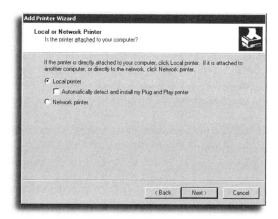

FIGURE 15.7
Select a local printer.

4. When the wizard prompts you to select the port, create a new port from the drop-down list. Choose AppleTalk Printing Devices, and then click Next (see Figure 15.8).

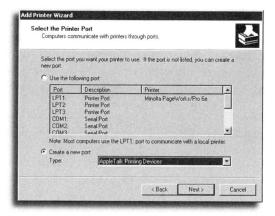

FIGURE 15.8
Create a new port by having the wizard search for AppleTalk printing devices on your network.

5. When you're prompted for available AppleTalk printing devices, select a zone and a printer, and then click OK.

6. When you're asked whether you want to capture the printer, click Yes.

Integrating Windows 2000 with Novell NetWare

Although Microsoft networks have become extremely popular, many of the world's network servers still run Novell NetWare. So it's likely that you will need to make your Windows 2000 Server network coexist with NetWare servers and clients. You can bridge the gap between NetWare and NT in several ways:

- Install both Microsoft and NetWare client components. This enables a client computer to participate on NT and NetWare networks simultaneously.

- Install a gateway that allows users on the Windows 2000 Server network to access files and printers on the NetWare server as if the files and printers were shared by a Windows 2000 server.

Accessing Different Environments with Multiple Client Protocol Stacks

You have seen how easy it is to install more than one protocol on a Windows 2000 computer. It is just as easy to install multiple protocols on other Microsoft clients as well. Clearly, Microsoft has designed a flexible network protocol architecture that can be enhanced just by plugging in new features.

One component required to connect with NetWare is the NWLink protocol, which enables Microsoft clients to converse with NetWare servers running Novell's IPX/SPX protocols. Compatibility with NetWare is the chief reason Microsoft developed NWLink.

In addition to protocol compatibility, a computer needs a NetWare client so that it can log on and communicate with the NetWare server.

On Windows 95 and 98, a NetWare client is installed by default when you set up networking.

On Windows 2000 Server, you install the Windows 2000 Gateway Services for NetWare when you install a network connection that includes the Client Service for NetWare.

Accessing Different Environments with a Gateway

A *gateway* is a protocol translator that allows two very different computer environments to communicate. Windows 2000 Server includes the Gateway Services for NetWare that enables Microsoft network clients to access services on NetWare servers.

The great thing about a gateway is that you don't need to make any changes to the clients. When viewed through the gateway, a NetWare server looks like a Microsoft server. Clients run the same Microsoft network client they are used to, which saves you the trouble of installing client software on network client computers. It also eliminates the need to train your users on the changes they will encounter when logging on to two servers.

Figure 15.9 shows a network that incorporates a Windows 2000 NetWare gateway. On the Windows side of the gateway, clients communicate using any protocol supported by Windows 2000 Server and use Microsoft's techniques for exchanging data between servers. The gateway translates client messages into IPX/SPX format and communicates with the NetWare server using Novell's network conventions.

The interesting thing about the gateway approach is that the NetWare server appears to users as just another shared resource on a Windows 2000 server. No changes to Windows network clients are required to enable them to access the NetWare server through the gateway.

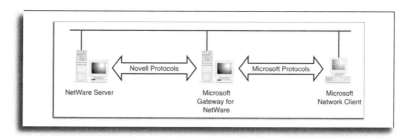

FIGURE 15.9
The Gateway for NetWare translates protocols between Novell and Microsoft environments.

Using a gateway to connect your users with a NetWare server has several attractive features:

- It is easier to set up and maintain users' computers because they require only one network client.

- Users do not need to learn new techniques for accessing network resources.

- Very few changes are required on the NetWare side.

- There is a single point at which the Microsoft network talks to the NetWare network.

But you need to be aware of some disadvantages of gateways:

- The translations the gateway must perform are extensive, and performance is generally slower than a connection with the proper protocols.

- Some features on the NetWare host might not be available.

- Opinions on gateways differ. Operating Windows networks with multiple protocol stacks can work with no real trouble. It is extremely easy to add support for a second network with Windows 2000, Windows NT, Windows 9x, or Windows for Workgroups clients. Performance doesn't take a significant hit with multiple protocols.

Consider using a gateway if your users require fairly casual access to NetWare, particularly if they need to access printers on the NetWare network. Thanks to print queues and spooling, printing performance isn't as critical to most users as application performance. A gateway also is an easy way to enable users to pass files between the two networks.

Setting Up a Gateway

To configure a gateway for NetWare, you must do the following:

1. Prepare NetWare to support the gateway.
2. Install the gateway.
3. Activate the gateway and share NetWare files with users.
4. Share NetWare printers with users.

These steps are discussed in the following sections. To avoid writing another book as large as this one, I'm assuming you are familiar with NetWare techniques and terminology.

Preparing the NetWare Server to Support a Gateway

To set up the NetWare server to support Gateway Services for NetWare, a NetWare administrator must use SYSCON to create the following entities:

- A group named NTGATEWAY. Grant this group the rights that should be available to users who access the server through the gateway. Remember, all users of the gateway access the NetWare server with the same rights.

- A user account with the same username that is used to log on to the Windows 2000 network from the gateway computer. Give this user the appropriate rights. Because I'm logging in as the Windows 2000 Administrator user, I created a user account named ADMINISTRATOR on the NetWare server. Configure passwords so that they are the same on the Windows 2000 Server and the NetWare server. (Several accounts might be necessary if the gateway computer is shared.)

I named my user account GATEWAY. Make this user account a member of the NTGATEWAY group. To create other gateways, create a user account for each gateway and add each account to the NTGATEWAY group. Only one user account is required per gateway computer.

Installing the Gateway Service

When you set up the Gateway Services for NetWare, two components are installed:

- A client service enables the user of the gateway computer to log directly in to the NetWare server, providing the user with a normal NetWare client environment.

- A gateway service enables Microsoft network clients to access shared NetWare resources.

You can configure each of these services to access the NetWare server through a separate NetWare user account.

For the smoothest operation, users should log on to the Windows and NetWare networks with the same username, which should have the same password on each server. After this is finished, Windows can automatically log the user on to each service environment when the username and password are specified.

The Gateway Service for NetWare is installed by modifying an existing Local Area Connection. To install Gateway Service for NetWare, follow these steps:

1. Open the Network and Dial-Up Connections dialog box and right-click Local Area Connection to open the context menu (see Figure 15.10). Select Properties.

2. Select Properties from the context menu of an existing Local Area Connection (see Figure 15.11).

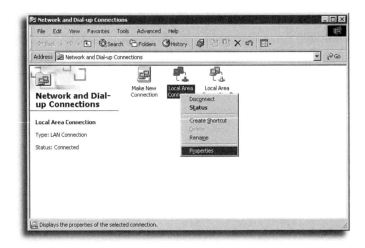

FIGURE 15.10
Use the Network and Dial-Up Connections to add support for NetWare.

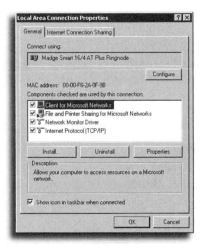

FIGURE 15.11
The General tab shows you what's installed and gives you the ability to install new network services.

3. On the General tab, click the Install button.

4. Select Client, and click the Add button.

5. Select Gateway (and Client) Services For NetWare (see Figure 15.12).

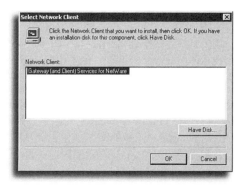

FIGURE 15.12
The Gateway (and Client) Services for Netware will install the service and NWLink (if it is not already installed).

6. Click OK.

7. The Gateway (and Client) Services for NetWare will now appear on the General settings tab, and the GSNW icon will appear in the Control Panel (see Figure 15.13).

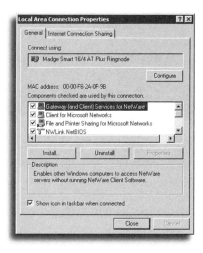

FIGURE 15.13
GSNW is the Gateway Services for NetWare.

Configuring the NetWare User Account Information

When Gateway Service for NetWare (GSNW) is installed, a new GSNW applet is added to the Control Panel. GSNW is used to configure two different things:

- Your preferences for logging directly in to the NetWare server as a NetWare client
- The Gateway Service for NetWare that is used by gateway clients to access the NetWare server

This tool is used to configure NetWare services on the computer and is shown in Figure 15.14. Information in the Gateway Service for NetWare dialog box determines the login preferences for the user whose name is shown after Username. This information is used to configure this user's personal NetWare environment.

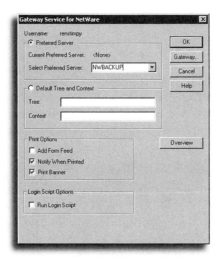

FIGURE 15.14
Configuring the Gateway Service for NetWare.

NetWare Login Preferences

The following fields specify the user's login preferences:

- *Preferred Server.* Click this radio button to establish a Bindery-mode server as the default server. Specify a server name in the Select Preferred Server field. Use this option when connecting to NetWare 3.x or to NetWare 4.x in Bindery mode.

- *Default Tree and Context.* Click this radio button to connect to a Novell Directory Services tree in NDS mode. Specify the tree name in the Tree field and the user context in the Context field.

- *Run Login Script.* Check this if a NetWare login script is to be executed when logging in to NetWare.

The preceding fields are the same that you see when you first log on to Windows 2000 Server after installing Gateway Service for NetWare. The first-time logon process was discussed in the preceding section. You can change these parameters. Changes take effect the next time you log on.

NetWare Printer Preferences

You can also configure your printing preferences in this dialog box. Print options for printing to NetWare printers can be set as follows:

- *Add Form Feed.* Check this box if NetWare should force a form feed at the end of print jobs. Most software sends a form feed, and this option should not be checked in most cases.

- *Notify When Printed.* Check this box if you want to receive a message when a job has been sent to a printer.

- *Print Banner.* When this option is checked, NetWare prints a banner page before each job. Do not check this option if printing to a PostScript printer. Most organizations do not find it necessary to activate banners, but large organizations might find that banners make it easier to identify users' print jobs.

At this point, you have configured your personal preferences for NetWare. These settings do not affect gateway operation. If you will not be configuring a gateway, click OK to exit the utility.

Synchronizing Account Passwords

When the NetWare account was set up for the locally logged-in user, the password was probably not synchronized to the user's password on the Windows network. As a result, the uscr is asked to enter a password each time a connection is established with the NetWare server. For greatest convenience, you should change the password on the NetWare server so that it is the same as the password in Windows 2000.

To change the password on the NetWare server, follow these steps:

1. Open a command prompt.

2. Use the `net use` command to connect a drive to the NetWare SYS volume. For example, if your NetWare server is named NW4, you would enter the following command:

   ```
   net use s: \\nw4\sys
   ```

3. Change to the connected drive.

4. Use `cd` to switch to the \PUBLIC directory.

5. Enter the command `setpass`. Follow the prompts to change the NetWare password.

After passwords match in Windows 2000 and NetWare, you need to enter your password only once when logging on to the network.

Configuring the NetWare Gateway and Sharing Directories

To configure the gateway, click the Gateway button in the Gateway Service for NetWare dialog box, shown in Figure 15.14, to open the Configure Gateway dialog box. At first, the Add, Remove, and Permissions options are inactive because the gateway service has not been started.

To configure a gateway, use these steps:

1. Check Enable Gateway. Checking this option instructs Windows 2000 Server to start the gateway service when the server starts. You can disable the gateway without removing the software by removing the check mark from this box.

2. Enter the NetWare user account name that you created for the gateway server in the Gateway Account box. When an account name has been entered, the Add button is activated.

3. Enter the password for the NetWare user account in the Password and Confirm Password boxes.

4. To make directories on the NetWare server available to gateway users, you must define them as shares. To add a share, click Add to display the New Share dialog box shown in Figure 15.15. Complete the following information for the share you are adding:

   • *Share Name.* Enter the name by which the share will be known to gateway users.

• *Network Path*. Enter the path to the NetWare directory that will be shared. The utility accepts uniform naming convention (UNC) names. For NetWare servers accessed through the gateway, UNC names have the following format:

```
\\server\volume\directory\subdirectory...
```

Figure 15.15 shows the UNC name for the VOL1 volume of the NWBACKUP server.

FIGURE 15.15
Share a NetWare resource.

• *Comment*. You can add a comment to describe the share, if desired. This comment will be shown when the share is listed in users' browse lists.

• *Use Drive*. Select an available drive letter from the list. Drive letters that correspond to physical drives on the computer are not available, and available drives are usually limited to the letters E through Z because a gateway can provide access to, at most, 22 or 23 directory shares.

• *Unlimited*. Choose this option if you do not want to restrict the number of users who can access the share.

• *Allow*. Choose this option and specify a number to restrict the number of users who can access the share. Because performance will suffer if too many users connect to a given share, a limit is desirable.

5. Click OK when you have configured the share. The gateway service will attempt to locate the shared directory on the specified NetWare server. If the share can be validated, it will be added to the Share name list in the Configure Gateway dialog box.

6. By default, the group Everyone is given full control permissions to a newly created gateway share. If you want to change the default permissions, select the entry in the Share name box and choose Permissions. The Access Through Share Permissions dialog box functions like the Share Permissions dialog boxes in File Manager.

7. After you have configured the desired gateway shares, click OK to quit the Gateway Service for NetWare applet.

More About Gateway Shares

The Gateway Service for NetWare applet is used to create gateway shares and assign share permissions. Gateway file shares cannot be managed in Explorer. As a result, you cannot use Explorer to fine-tune directory and file permissions.

You can, however, use NetWare administration tools to assign detailed NetWare rights to the NTGATEWAY group. Directory and file rights will set maximum permissions for all gateway users, regardless of the share permissions that might be assigned by the Gateway Service for NetWare.

As a result, NetWare directories accessed through the gateway should generally be regarded as group directories, not personal directories. You can add a share that grants permissions to only one user, but because you are restricted to 22 gateway shares, assigning private shared directories on the gateway is not very practical.

If any users require personal directories on the NetWare server, you should assign them individual NetWare accounts and equip their computers with NetWare client software.

Sharing NetWare Printers

NetWare users do not print directly to printers. They print to print queue files, from which jobs are printed by a print server. Gateway Service for NetWare enables users on the Windows network to connect to NetWare print queues and print to NetWare-managed printers.

Although NetWare directory sharing is managed with the GSNW utility rather than File Manager, NetWare printers are shared using fairly standard procedures in the Print Manager.

To share a NetWare-based printer, follow these steps:

1. Log on to the NetWare network from the gateway computer. The account you use must have NetWare rights to use the desired print queue.

2. Open the Printers icon in the Control Panel.

3. Double-click Add Printer to open the Add Printer Wizard.

4. Choose Network Printer. Then click Next.

5. Next a Connect to Printer dialog box opens a browse list similar to the one shown in Figure 15.16. Browse the network and select a shared printer. Click Next.

FIGURE 15.16
Connecting to a shared printer.

6. Windows 2000 ordinarily expects to find a suitable printer driver on the computer to which it is connecting. Because NetWare servers don't come equipped with Windows print drivers, you will see the warning The server on which the printer resides does not have a suitable printer driver installed. Before you can print to the NetWare queue, a suitable printer driver must be added to the local computer. Click OK in this message box and go through the steps of selecting and installing a print driver.

7. After the print driver has been installed, the printer is added to the local printer configuration and an icon is added to the Printers window. The locally connected user can now print to the printer. Before gateway users can use the printer, however, it must be shared.

8. To share the printer with the gateway, select the printer in the Printer window. Then choose the Properties command in the Printer menu. Figure 15.17 shows the Sharing tab of the Printer Properties dialog box.

FIGURE 15.17
Configuring properties for a printer shared through the Gateway for NetWare.

9. To share the printer, click Shared. Enter a share name in the Share Name field. Select any additional drivers to be supported in the Alternate Drivers list. You can, if desired, configure the other properties for the share, such as security.

10. Click OK when the share properties are specified.

Windows users can now access this shared printer as if it were directly attached to the gateway computer.

Accessing NetWare Resources from the Gateway Server

Shared printers and directories are advertised in the browse list for the gateway computer, just as if they resided physically on that computer. As a result, most of the NetWare gateway mechanism is invisible to network users.

A user who logs on to the Windows 2000 Server Gateway for NetWare is logged in to the NetWare server as a NetWare client. As a result, resources offered by the NetWare server are available using standard browsing tools.

After gateway shares are established, they appear in your My Computer window as shared volumes. Figure 15.18 shows some examples.

FIGURE 15.18
NetWare gateway shares displayed in My Computer.

Using NetWare Applications Through the Gateway

A wide variety of NetWare MS-DOS utilities can be run through the gateway:

chkvol	grant	pconsole	rights	slist
colorpal	help	psc	security	syscon
dspace	listdir	pstat	send	tlist
flag	map	rconsole	session	userlist
flagdir	ncopy	remove	setpass	volinfo
fconsole	ndir	revoke	settts	whoami
filer				

NetWare menu utilities, such as RCONSOLE, require access to files such as SYS$MSG.DAT, which is installed in the SYS:PUBLIC directory. To access these files, either make SYS:PUBLIC your default directory before running the utility or add SYS:PUBLIC to your search path.

Not all NetWare-aware applications run in a Windows 2000 gateway environment. Consult your program documentation for information about supported environments. Some applications might require that the NWLink (IPX/SPX) protocol be loaded on the client.

Many NetWare-aware applications that are written for 16-bit Windows require DLL files that are provided by Novell. The NWIPXSPX.DLL file is included with the NetWare DOS client software. If the NetWare client software has ever been installed on the client, this file should have been installed. To make the file available to gateway clients, obtain NWIPXSPX.DLL and copy it to the directory C:\Winnt\ system32.

457

Some NetWare-aware applications directly send and receive Novell network proto-col packets. These applications might require a copy of NETWARE.DRV, which is copied to the C:\Winnt\system32 directory when the gateway service is installed. NETWARE.DRV is used in combination with either NWNETAPI.DLL or NWCALLS.DLL, depending on the version of NetWare being used. Consult the NetWare documentation for the correct file to use. Copy these files to the directory C:\Winnt\system32.

Applications do not generally perform as well through the gateway as they would with a direct logon connection. This is particularly true if large amounts of data must flow through the gateway. Gateway translation takes time.

Tape Backup Incompatibilities

One particular area of incompatibility is tape backup. You might be tempted to use the backup program from Windows 2000 Server because it's already included with the product. When backing up NetWare, however, you must use a backup product that is aware of the existence of the NetWare bindery files. Windows 2000 Backup was written for Windows 2000, not for NetWare.

Translation of File Attributes

Gateway Service for NetWare must translate several file system characteristics when users access NetWare files. Among the features that require translation are file attributes. Table 15.1 describes Windows 2000 file attributes and the way they are translated for NetWare files.

Table 15.1 Translation of Windows 2000 Attributes to NetWare Attributes

Windows 2000 Attribute	NetWare Attribute
R (Read Only)	Ro, Di (Delete Inhibit), Ri (Rename Inhibit)
A (Archive)	A
S (System)	Sy
H (Hidden)	H

The NetWare attributes Ci (Copy Inhibit), P (Purge), RW (Read Write), S (Shareable), T (Transactional), Ra (Read Audit), and Wa (Write Audit) are not sup-ported by the gateway, although they do restrict the operations that gateway users can perform on NetWare-based files.

chapter 16

Setting Up Internet Information Server

Introduction to Web Services

Unless you have been living under a rock for the last five years, the Internet has affected your life. You can't watch a TV show or read a magazine without being bombarded with Internet URLs for everything from the products advertised to the show or magazine itself. Everyone wants your email address and it seems like everyone has a Web site to promote home businesses, post pictures of their kids (or pets), or to post resumes because they don't like their present job. It is impossible to overstate the effect of the World Wide Web and the Internet on modern communication. As much as television or radio, the Web promises to revolutionize the way we access information. And as long as the Internet continues to grow in popularity, Microsoft's commitment to providing easy-to-use, robust Internet applications will continue as well.

In this chapter, I will discuss how easy it is to construct a Web server by using Microsoft's Internet Information Server (IIS) 5. IIS is bundled with Windows 2000; it's easy to administer; it's capable; and it has become one of the dominant Web servers on the Internet.

IIS version 5, included with Windows 2000 Server, is a feature-rich application. It includes World Wide Web and File Transfer Protocol (FTP) servers, a Simple Mail Transfer Protocol (SMTP) server, and facilities for using key-based encryption for Internet communication through the Secure Sockets Layer (SSL) protocol. That's too much for this chapter to cover and encompasses some pretty advanced topics that are beyond the scope of this book. Instead, this chapter has a tightly focused agenda, focusing on what will probably be your first use for the IIS application. By the end of it, you'll be able to set up and manage a no-frills World Wide Web server.

Before you jump into building your first Web site, you should at least look at the components of IIS and what they do:

- *Common Files.* Required if any other IIS option is chosen. These are the core files to allow Microsoft Internet Information Server 5 to run on the system.

- *Documentation.* Documentation for all the services, in HTML format for easy reading. If you have never worked with IIS, or you want to make sure you understand the latest version, be sure to select this.

- *File Transfer Protocol (FTP) Server.* Implements the standard FTP protocol, which allows client machines to send and receive files from the server. The File Transfer Protocol (FTP) service provides clients attaching to your server the ability to transmit files to and from your Windows 2000 computer, without the overhead of a network share. A veteran of the TCP/IP protocol suite, FTP has been used as the primary file transfer protocol for the Internet since its inception. Today virtually every operating system bundles an FTP client and there are a number of third-party products available as well. All the Microsoft operating systems since Windows 95 include a character-based FTP client with their TCP/IP protocol stack. If you need to update any drivers on your Windows 2000 Professional computer, the odds are high that the vendor provides patches and updates through FTP.

For the Windows 2000 Professional user, an FTP site might be used to share documents for a virtual team, to trade MP3 files with people on the Internet, to make a new database client available to the field, or even to catalog updates available to a customer.

- *FrontPage 2000 Server Extensions.* These extensions are required in order for the IIS Server to publish webs made with FrontPage 2000. If you are a Web developer or even an aspiring Web developer, FrontPage 2000 Server Extensions can make your life much easier. What server extensions do is allow you to use FrontPage 2000 to develop and deploy your Web designs without going through the tedium of using FTP to upload the files to the server. They also allow you to perform some management functions on the server from within the FrontPage application.

- *Internet Information Services Snap-In.* The IIS Snap-In allows IIS to be managed from within the MMC (Microsoft Management Console). This snap-in is not automatically added to the MMC, and must be added manually. I'll discuss adding the snap-in during the installation section, coming up next.

The Microsoft Management Console

Although not strictly an IIS service, the Microsoft Management Console (MMC) is important when discussing Internet Information Server 5. The MMC is an integral part of the Windows 2000 Professional operating system. This management framework, first introduced as part of Microsoft Internet Information Server 4 and the Windows NT 4.0 Option Pack, provides the next-generation management framework for managing Windows 2000 servers and services. Using management applications known as snap-ins, the MMC provides a single interface for all Windows 2000 management applications. It also provides the main interface for managing your IIS 5 applications. Eventually the MMC will be the standard management interface for all Microsoft's applications, as seen in the latest versions of SQL and SMS.

- *Internet Services Manager (HTML).* This allows all the Internet services to be managed using HTML. If you are not a fan of the Microsoft Management Console interface, or you want to be able to manage Microsoft Internet Information Server 5 remotely from a Web browser, you should install this application. If you are a fan of Microsoft certifications, there was generally one question of remotely managing an IIS installation from the Internet and part of the answer was to load the HTML management application for Microsoft Internet Information Server 4.

Note

Internet Services Manager will only work if the WWW Publishing Service is running.

- *SMTP Service.* Allows the server to provide SMTP services, which is the Internet's standard mail system. This allows mailboxes and forwarding routes to be set up on the system. The Microsoft SMTP Service uses the Simple Mail Transfer Protocol (SMTP) to send and receive email using TCP port 25 for operations. There are a number of clients available for reading SMTP mail, including Microsoft's Outlook Express, included with Internet Explorer 5. These clients allow you to send and receive SMTP mail, which is the primary mail type used on the Internet today. If you want to send mail to Que to tell it how terrific this book is, you will need to send an SMTP mail message. The SMTP Service allows you to turn your Windows 2000 Professional workstation into an inexpensive Internet mail server. One additional feature of having a bundled SMTP service included with Microsoft Internet Information Server 5 is that you can mail-enable Web applications. Let's say you have written a guestbook for your personal Web site and you want it to send you an email message whenever a new entry is added. With the SMTP Service, your application can use the SMTP service to send the email message to you.
- *Visual InterDev RAD Remote Deployment Support.* Allows Visual InterDev to remotely deploy applications (components and ASP pages) to the server. This is for the serious Web developer, and if you are a Visual InterDev expert, you are already familiar with this. If you are not, it's nothing to worry about. Just stick with FrontPage and you'll be fine.

- *World Wide Web Server.* The World Wide Web (WWW) Server enables you to include Hypertext Markup Language (HTML) documents on your Web site and to allow remote clients to reach them using a Web browser. You can also use a variety of other formats for these documents including Active Server Pages, Java applets, Perl scripts, and a variety of graphics formats. The WWW Server allows client machines to access information on the server through a Web browser (such as Internet Explorer 5) using the Hypertext Transfer Protocol (HTTP). HTTP is the protocol that can be credited with the birth and subsequent explosive growth of the Internet and, more specifically, the World Wide Web. The Web Server included with Windows 2000 Professional provides an excellent Web server for application development and testing, workgroup Intranet sites, or hosting small personal Web sites from home. This is not a good application for hosting busy business Web sites.

- *NNTP Service.* The NNTP (Network News Transfer Protocol) Service allows the server to host newsgroups, similar to the ones you might have seen in a Usenet bulletin board. This is a functionality that Microsoft includes only with the server version of the product.

A Few Words About Web Servers

The life of a Web server has become very complicated in recent years, now that Web pages are expected to move, interact, and have sound. These days, a Web site is only as good as its design, and there are an awful lot of really bad Web sites out there. I can't provide you with even a basic tutorial on Web development in this chapter, but you'll have no problem finding scads of material on the topic. In fact, here are a few books from Macmillan that can help you:

- *Teach Yourself Web Publishing with HTML 3.2 in a Week, Third Edition*, by Laura Lemay. Published by Sams.net.

- *Creating Killer Web Sites, Second Edition*, by David Siegel. Published by Hayden Books.

- *Web Designer's Guide to Style Sheets*, by Steven Mulder. Published by Hayden Books.

Despite all the hoopla, a Web server's job is to send documents to user computers, where they are displayed on a Web browser. These documents are somewhat peculiar because they consist of hypertext; that is, they contain more than text. Besides text and text formatting, a hypertext document can contain links to other documents. That's the magic of the World Wide Web: A document's hypertext links can be other hypertext documents, or they can contain sound, graphics, animation, or applications. Name a type of content, and someone is probably working on a way to adapt it to the Web. Can touch and smell be far away for the Web?

For the purposes of this chapter, I am going to keep things simple, relying on documents written in the Hypertext Markup Language (HTML) to illustrate the capabilities of the IIS Web server.

Installing IIS Version 5

Recommendations for installing IIS Version 5 include the following:

- Identify a Windows 2000 Server computer that will host IIS. If you expect IIS to be heavily used, this server should be dedicated to the task of providing IIS services.
- Disable any third-party WWW, FTP, or Gopher servers that might be running on the IIS server. (IIS 5 installation will remove earlier versions of IIS from the host system.)
- Just in case, back up any WWW or FTP content directories currently on the server.
- Format the volumes to be used by IIS with NTFS, or convert them to NTFS. This ensures the highest possible level of security.
- Enable auditing if you feel you need to closely monitor the server for security breaches.
- Set up a name resolution method. You have several choices:
  - DNS is best if you'll be connected to the Internet or if your network includes non-Microsoft hosts.
  - HOSTS files can be used to support Microsoft and non-Microsoft hosts. HOSTS files are static, though, and any change to the network means updating everyone's HOSTS files. Also, HOSTS files won't allow outsiders to access your Web and FTP servers by name.
  - LMHOSTS files can provide static naming for Microsoft hosts.

Complete the following steps to install IIS:

1. Open the Add/Remove Programs applet in Control Panel.

2. Select Add/Remove Windows Components, which will start the Windows Components Wizard.

3. When the list of components are listed, select Internet Information Services, as shown in Figure 16.1.

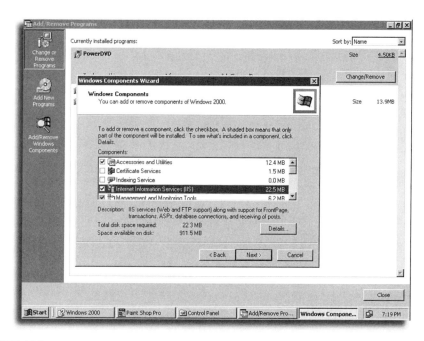

FIGURE 16.1
Adding Components to Windows 2000.

4. If you click Details you will see the individual parts of IIS (shown in Figure 16.2). You can deselect any pieces that you will not use, such as support for FTP, or NNTP.

5. Complete the Windows Component Wizard.

Each product has a product root directory that appears to be the server's root directory to users. For the WWW Service, the default product root directory is C:\Inetpub\wwwroot. The content files that will be published are placed in the WWW Service root directory, but to users of the Web server, they appear to be in a root directory. Users don't see C:\Inetpub\wwwroot at all.

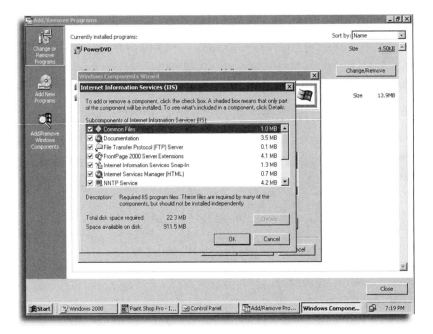

FIGURE 16.2
The individual components of Microsoft Internet Information Services.

It's a good idea to use the default directories during your first installation. You can change the server root directories at a later time if you want.

Testing the Installation

The IIS services that you chose to install should be running as soon as installation is completed.

To test the newly installed Web site with its default pages and home directories, type `http://server_name/postinfo.html` into your browser. Replace *server_name* with your IIS server name.

Configuring Microsoft Internet Information Server 5

To start the Internet Information Services Console and configure your default Web site:

1. From the Administrator Tools folder on the Start Menu, select Internet Services Manager, as shown in Figure 16.3.

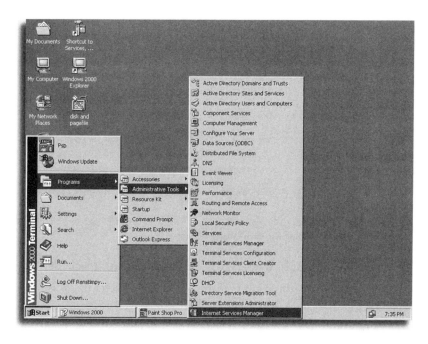

FIGURE 16.3
Opening Internet Services Manager.

2. The Internet Information Services Console will start, as shown in Figure 16.4. Under the Internet Information Services heading in the Internet Information Services Console list are several entries tied to sites. To users, each site is an independent server, but one IIS server can support multiple sites. Initially, a default site is configured for each service supported by IIS. Later in this chapter you'll learn how to create your own Web site. An IIS server can have several Web sites, but all the sites are supported by the same service, which appears in the Services applet as the World Wide Web Publishing Service. You can manage each site individually without affecting other sites. If you stop or start the World Wide Web Publishing Service, however, you affect all sites.

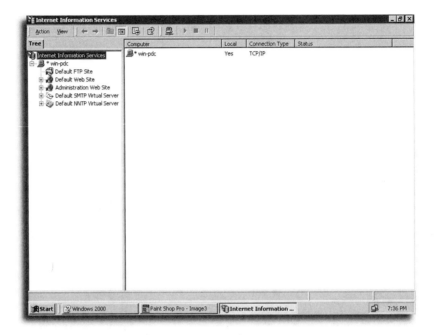

FIGURE 16.4
The individual components of Microsoft Internet Information Services.

3. Click the plus sign next to the server name to view the objects under the server.

4. Select Properties from the context menu for Default Web Site, as shown in Figure 16.5.

5. On the Properties page, shown in Figure 16.6, you can change the name of the Web site, assign an IP address and port, limit the number of connection to the Web site, as well as configure logging. This will be discussed further later in this chapter.

The IIS Toolbar

Three buttons in the Internet Information Services Console toolbar allow you to change the state of a site:

- The Start button starts a service that is paused or stopped. When a service is started, no comment appears beside the service object in the Internet Information Services Console hierarchy.

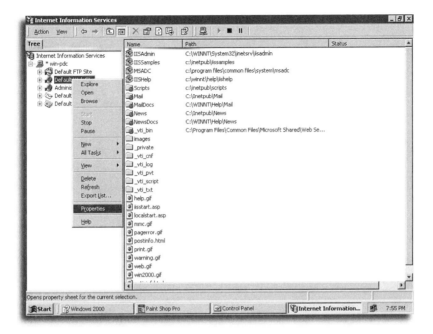

FIGURE 16.5
Opening the Properties of the Default Web Site.

- The Stop button stops the service. When you stop a service, connected users are disconnected, and new users aren't permitted to connect. A stopped service is tagged with the legend (Stopped) beside its entry in the Console hierarchy.

- The Pause button pauses a service. When you pause a service, connected users aren't affected and can continue to access the service. New users, however, aren't permitted to connect with the service. A stopped service is tagged with the legend (Paused) beside its entry in the Internet Information Services Console hierarchy.

In some instances, you must stop a service in order to make configuration changes. You can wait until after hours to stop the service, but you might not have that option. If you don't want to force users off the service, pause the service and wait until all users have disconnected. You can then stop the service without disrupting users.

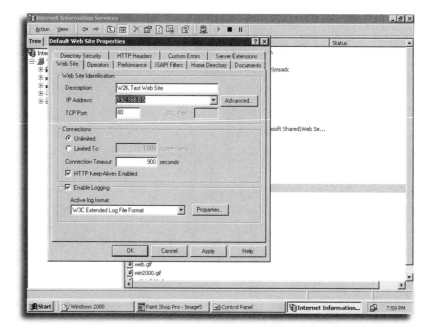

FIGURE 16.6
The Default Web Site Properties page.

You'll find several other buttons on the toolbar:

- Delete removes the object selected in the Internet Information Services Console tree.

- Properties opens dialog boxes for editing the properties of the object selected in the Internet Information Services Console tree.

- Up One Level moves the current context up one level in the Internet Information Services Console tree.

- Add a Computer to the List adds a server to the Internet Information Services Console hierarchy. The Internet Information Services Console can manage more than one server, allowing you to manage several servers from one place.

Creating a Web Site

Now you'll see how easy it is to create a Web site. In doing so, you are going to leave the default Web site intact. That will enable you to examine the technique for supporting multiple Web sites on the same IIS server installation.

In order to create a Web site, you need to perform some high-level steps before you get to the actual IIS configuration process. They are the following:

1. Establish a unique identity for the new Web site.

2. Ensure that existing Web sites don't conflict with the new site's identity.

3. Create the new Web site.

4. Identify the new Web site in DNS.

5. Supply content for the new Web site.

6. Test the new Web site.

I'll expand on each of these subtasks in the following sections.

Identifying the New Web Site

A Web server can support multiple sites, provided each site has a unique identity that consists of one of the following characteristics:

- *A unique IP address.* You can assign multiple IP addresses to the same host, and each IP address can support a distinct Web site.

- *A unique port number.* Each TCP/IP process is identified with a port number. You can enable a new Web site by providing it with a port number that is unique on the computer running IIS.

- *A unique combination of an IP address and port number.* If you want, you can change both the IP address and port.

Configuring a Unique IP Address

The most common technique for distinguishing a site is to provide it with its own IP address. This approach simplifies the user's life because the user must specify a port in the URL if a site is not identified by the default Web port of 80. Fortunately, it is a simple matter to configure more than one IP address for a TCP/IP network adapter. To add an additional IP address to an adapter, you need to do the following:

1. Open Network and Dial-Up Connections as shown in Figure 16.7.

2. Open the Properties for the Local Area Connection that you will use for the Web services (see Figure 16.8).

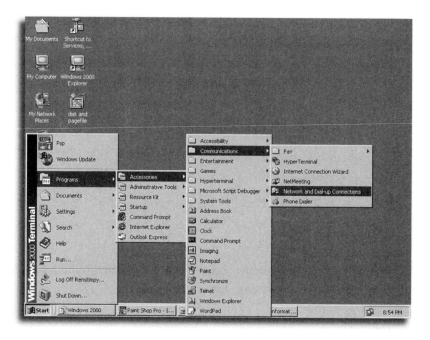

FIGURE 16.7
Opening the Network and Dial-Up Connections dialog box.

3. Select Internet Protocol from the list of Components, and click the Properties button, shown in Figure 16.9. In the Internet Protocol (TCP/IP) Properties page, click the Advanced button, shown in Figure 16.10.

4. The IP settings dialog box lets you add, remove, or edit IP addresses. Choose the Add button and the TCP/IP Address dialog box will be displayed, as you can see in Figure 16.11.

5. Enter a new TCP/IP address and subnet mask to add to the network adapter for this Local Area Connection, and then click the Add button. Add more addresses, if required, by repeating steps 5 and 6. Figure 16.12 shows a total of three TCP/IP addresses for the current Local Area Connection.

6. Click the OK button when you are finished.

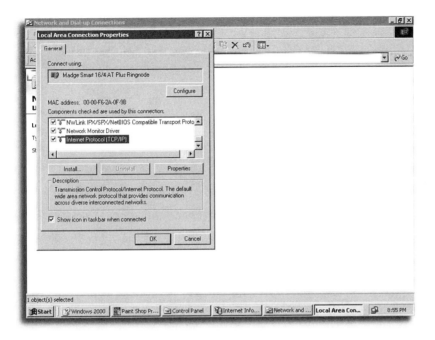

FIGURE 16.8
Opening the Properties for the Local Area Connection.

> **SEE ALSO**
> ➤ *For more information on TCP/IP addressing, see page 196.*

Reconfiguring Conflicting Sites

No two computers can share the same IP address, even if Web servers on those computers are configured with different port numbers. No two Web sites on the same computer can use the IP address that will be assigned to this Web site, unless the sites have different port numbers.

One Web site on an IIS server can be assigned the IP address (All Unassigned), which is the property that establishes the site as the default Web site, not the name. Only the default Web site can have the IP address (All Unassigned).

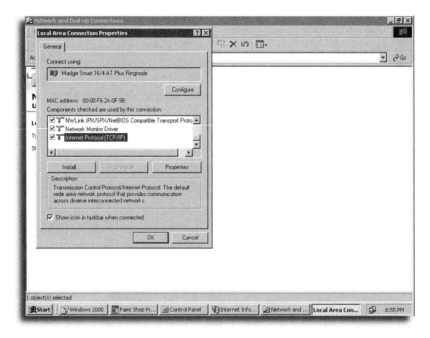

FIGURE 16.9
Under Local Area Connection Properties, you need to select TCP/IP.

The default Web site, the site with the IP address (All Unassigned), will respond to all Web service requests directed to all IP addresses on this computer, unless the IP address is specifically assigned to another Web site. As a result, the default Web site can't conflict with other Web sites that have explicit IP address assignments. Because the default Web site will service all IP addresses that aren't explicitly directed to an operating Web site, you should be careful what you put on the default Web site. ISPs, for example, should use the default Web site as their own so that users will not be directed to another organization's Web site if their intended Web site is not functioning.

Before you install a new Web site, you should review the configurations of existing Web sites running on the IIS server. Reconfigure IP addresses and ports to eliminate conflicts, and identify an IP address/port number combination that can be used to uniquely identify the new Web site.

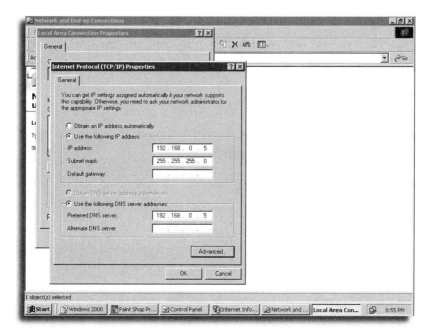

FIGURE 16.10
Clicking Advanced allows you to configure up to 32 total IP addresses on a single card.

Follow these steps to review the IP addresses of existing Web sites:

1. Open the Internet Services Manager and expand the tree to reveal the Web sites.

2. Right-click a Web Site object and choose Properties from the context menu.

3. Note the value of the IP Address field. (You can see the available options in the drop-down selection list.) Ensure that this value doesn't conflict with the IP address of any other site (unless the sites sharing the IP address use different ports). The default Web site created when IIS was initially installed has the value (All Unassigned) for this property. As explained previously, this is the property that defines the default Web site. If you assign the (All Unassigned) address to another Web site, that site becomes the default Web site.

4. Repeat these steps for all Web sites on the server to ensure that no IP addresses conflict with the IP address of the new site.

Not that you are sure that you know what addressing to use, the next step is to create the new Web site. The process is surprisingly simple.

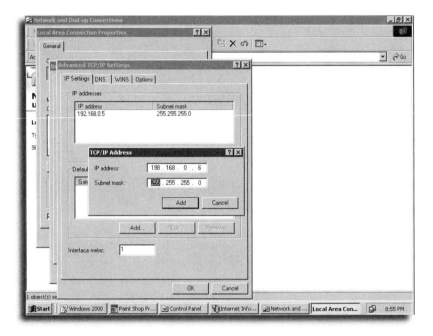

FIGURE 16.11
The TCP/IP Address dialog box allows you to add additional IP addresses to a network interface.

Before you create the site, you should establish its basic characteristics. The Web server must have a DNS name, a root directory, and an IP address. While you plan, you must determine where its root directory will be located. It is often best to add a new subfolder to the \Inetpub folder. On large sites, you should create a separate volume to host your Web site. To improve performance, place the volume on a separate SCSI disk.

The Web site illustrated in this chapter will have the following characteristics:

Web server: MANCHESTER

DNS name: www.manchester.com

Web server root directory: C:\Inetpub\www2root

IP address: 192.168.0.7

Access security: Anonymous connections are permitted.

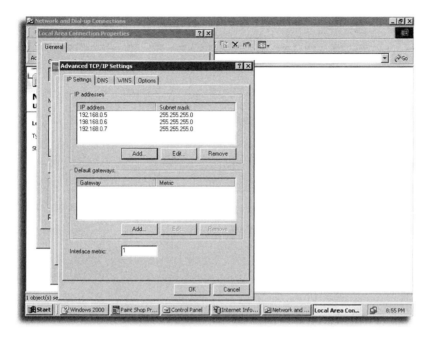

FIGURE 16.12
An adapter with three IP addresses.

Follow these steps to configure the new Web site:

1. Log on as an administrator.

2. Use your favorite file management tool to create the root directory for the new Web site.

3. Open the Internet Services Manager.

4. Right-click the server that will host the new Web site and select New, and then Web Site from the context menu, as shown in Figure 16.13.

5. This will kick off the Web Site Creation Wizard. Click Next to start the wizard.

6. In the first dialog box of the Web Site Creation Wizard shown in Figure 16.14, enter a description of the Web site in the Web Site Description field. Click Next to open the IP Address and Port Settings dialog box, shown in Figure 16.15.

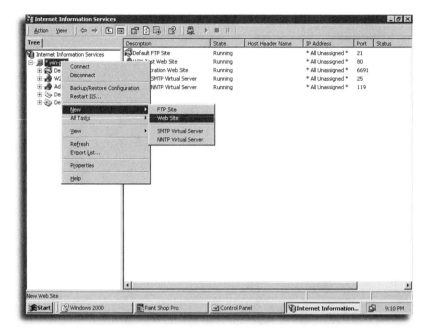

FIGURE 16.13
Creating a new Web site.

7. Select an IP address for this site in the field Enter the IP Address to Use for This Web Site. Remember that the site with the address (All Assigned) is the default Web site. Verify that the port value is correct in the field TCP Port this Web Site should use. This example uses the default Web port of 80.

8. Choose Next to open the Web Site Home Directory dialog box, shown in Figure 16.16. Enter the Web site's root directory in the field.

9. Enter the path for your home directory. The directory must have been previously created, as described in step 2. To permit anonymous access, leave the check mark in the field Allow Anonymous Access to This Web Site.

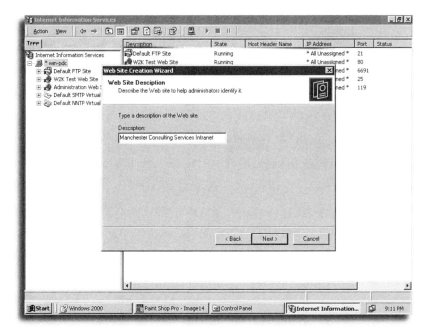

FIGURE 16.14
Enter the Web site description.

10. Click Next to open the Web Site Access Permissions dialog box, shown in Figure 16.17. Check the access permissions to be assigned to IUSR_*servername*. The following permissions are available:

    • *Read.* This option allows users to retrieve documents from the Web server and is enabled by default.

    • *Run Scripts.* This option permits users to execute ASP (Active Server Pages) scripts and is enabled by default.

    • *Execute.* This option permits execution of any executable file, including .dll and .exe files. This option includes script access.

    • *Write.* This option permits users to write to files in the Web server directory.

    • *Browse.* If this option is checked, IIS will generate a browsing document whenever it's asked to serve a directory that doesn't contain the document specified in the URL (or doesn't contain a default document if no document is specified in the URL).

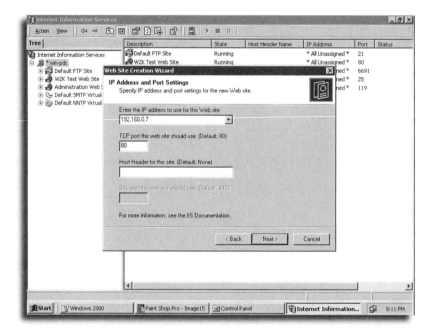

FIGURE 16.15
Configuring the IP address and port settings.

11. Click Next and then, when you get the message that the Web site has been successfully created, click the Finish button to exit the wizard. Figure 16.18 shows the new Web site in the Internet Information Services Console.

Identifying the New Web Site in DNS

Next you must give the new Web site an identity in the DNS name space. Although in some cases you can support basic Web services using NetBIOS names, these names don't permit you to establish multiple Web sites on a Web server. DNS, on the other hand, allows you to define a different host name for each IP address on the computer.

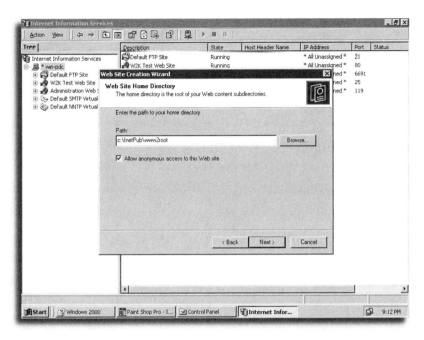

FIGURE 16.16
Entering the home directory path.

Identifying the Web Site with an Address Record

Normally, you'll define an address (A) record for the Web server. You could, for example, add the following A record to the manchester.com domain:

```
www                A        192.168.0.7
```

SEE ALSO

➤ *For more information on DNS, see page 410.*

Identifying the Web Site with an Alias

If you have already established a name for the IP address, however, you might want to create an alias (CNAME) record instead. Suppose that the following resource record was previously added to the manchester.com zone:

```
Manchester2        A        192.168.0.6
```

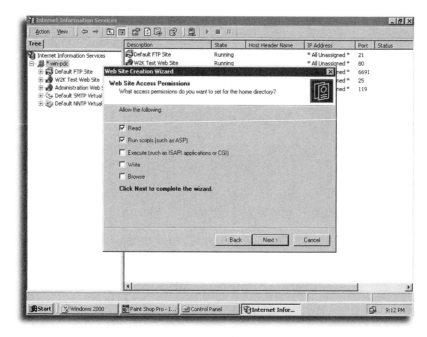

FIGURE 16.17
Setting the Web site access permissions.

This record associates manchester2.manchester.com with the IP address
192.168.0.6. The following CNAME record associates www.manchester.com with
the same IP address by making www.manchester.com an alias for manchester2.
manchester.com:

```
www              CNAME   manchester2.manchester.com
```

Supplying Content for the New Web Site

Web content is a big subject deserving about a dozen books, so I can't explain much
here. Simply put, Web content consists of documents written in the Hypertext
Markup Language (HTML); they are nothing more than text documents you create
with any editor. Here is a simple HTML document you can add to the root directory of your new Web server:

```
<HTML>
<HEAD>
<TITLE>Hello!</TITLE>
</HEAD>
<BODY>Hello! Welcome to my new Web site.<BR></BODY>
</HTML>
```

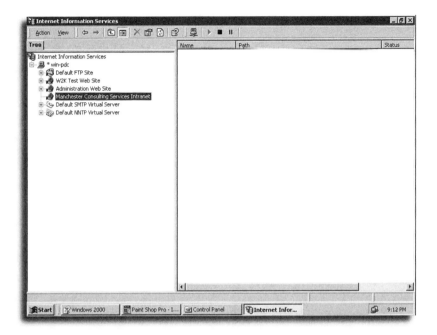

FIGURE 16.18
The new Web site appears under the Web server.

Create this file with any text editor and save it in the Web server's root directory with the filename `default.html`.

After you have created the `default.html` document, it will appear in the Web site contents, as shown in Figure 16.19.

Testing the New Web Site

The first thing to do is test the DNS naming. Start by pinging the Web server by name. For example, enter the command `ping www.manchester.com`. If the ping doesn't succeed, start debugging DNS. Make sure you have added a correct A record for the Web server. Also, check the DNS configuration of the client you are using. Can it ping other hosts by name? If not, visit the DNS tab of the Microsoft TCP/IP Properties page and ensure that the client is properly configured.

SEE ALSO

➤ For more information on TCP/IP testing tools, see page 371.

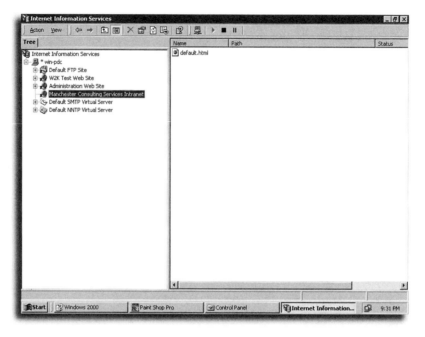

FIGURE 16.19
Notice the newly created `default.html` file.

After you have debugged DNS naming, open a browser and attempt to connect with the Web site. In the case of the sample Web site, you would enter the URL `http://www.manchester.com/`. If you are successful, you'll see a sample Web page.

Configuring Site Properties

There are a great many properties that can be configured to customize a Web site. Some properties address advanced features that are beyond the scope of this chapter, but there are a few that you should review before moving on.

To open the properties page for a site, right-click the site in the Console list and choose Properties from the context menu. Let's selectively examine some of the available properties:

- *Web Site*. Figure 16.20 shows the Properties page with the Web Site tab selected.

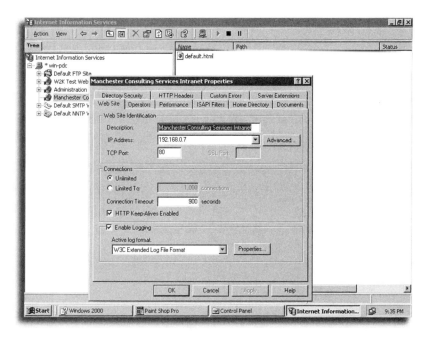

FIGURE 16.20
The Web Site tab of the Properties dialog box.

- *Web Site Identification Properties.* The Web Site tab has three fields that identify the Web site.

- *Description.* This field serves only to identify the Web site in the Internet Information Services Console tree.

- *IP Address.* You can change the IP address associated with the Web site by editing this field.

- *TCP Port.* You can modify the TCP port that is associated with the Web site. This can be used to hide a site from casual surfers.

- *Connection Limit Properties.* Also on the Web Site tab are properties that determine the numbers of users who can connect with the Web site. Although by default the Unlimited option button is selected, it is an unrealistic setting because all server hardware has performance limits. If too many users connect with a server, all users will suffer because of inadequate performance. For this reason, you'll probably want to select the Limited To option button and specify a maximum number of connections. If users complain about performance, you can then reduce the number of connections allowed, until an acceptable performance level is reached.

- *The Connection Timeout Value.* Prevents users no longer actively using the Web site from monopolizing connections. Inactive users will be disconnected when the connection time-out expires.

- *Operators.* The Operators tab, shown in Figure 16.21, allows you to specify which groups and users are permitted to administer the Web server. By default, members of the Administrators local group have access to the Web server administration tools.

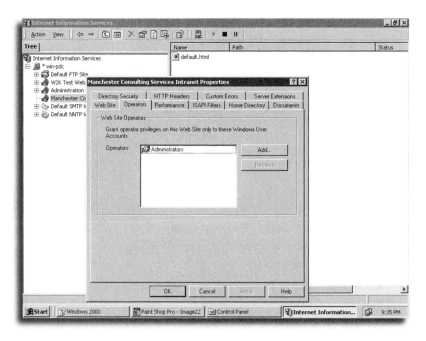

FIGURE 16.21
The Operators tab of the Properties dialog box.

- *Performance.* Figure 16.22 displays the Performance tab. This tab has three settings that you should be aware of:
  - The Performance Tuning slider adjusts the memory that is allocated to the Web server based on the anticipated number of page hits. If memory use is not a concern, set the slider to the More than 100,000 end of the control. Otherwise, adjust the control appropriately to achieve a compromise between performance and memory demand.
  - The Enable Bandwidth Throttling setting allows you to control how much of your available network bandwidth the Web server can use.

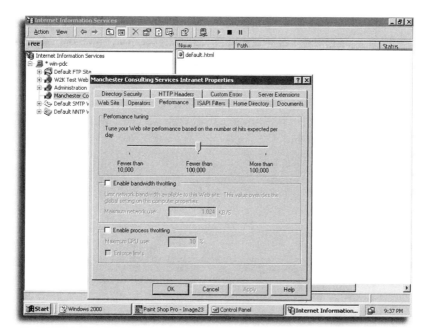

FIGURE 16.22
The Performance tab of the Properties dialog box.

- The Enable Process Throttling setting allows you to control how much of the server's CPU processing time this site will be allowed to use. This can be important if there are other applications running on the server.

- *Home Directory.* The Home Directory tab is shown in Figure 16.23. One option is to modify the source of the home directory (also referred to as the Web server root directory). The Home Directory tab will be modified depending on of the following choices you select as the home directory source:
  - A directory Located on This Computer
  - A share Located on Another Computer
  - A Redirection to a URL

Assuming that the directory is located on this computer, let's review some of the available properties:

- The Read and Write check boxes determine the operations that can be performed by anonymous users.
- Directory browsing is a useful feature in some situations. When a user accesses a directory, several things can happen:

If the URL specifies a particular file and the Web server finds the file, the file is sent to the user's browser.

If the URL doesn't specify a file or specifies a file that isn't present, a default document is presented.

If the URL specifies a file that is not present or doesn't specify a file, and if a default document is not found, the Web site can optionally generate a browsing document.

If you want the Web server to generate a browsing document when the Web server can't provide a requested or default document, check Directory Browsing. The browsing document is essentially a directory listing that shows files and folders in the specified directory. The user can browse the directory by clicking entries in the browser.

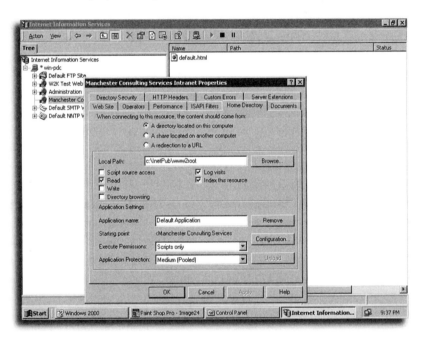

FIGURE 16.23
The Home Directory tab of the Properties dialog box.

The perils of directory browsing

Directory browsing provides a possible back door that allows users to access your Web site content in ways you hadn't anticipated. If you permit directory browsing, carefully review your file and directory security to ensure that browsing users can't perform unwanted actions.

- *Documents.* The Documents tab specifies the names of documents that qualify as default documents. As shown in Figure 16.24, the standard default documents are `default.html` and `default.asp`, in that order. If the Web server encounters several potential default files in a target directory, it serves the one that appears first in the default documents list. You can add or modify the default documents and adjust their order of preference.

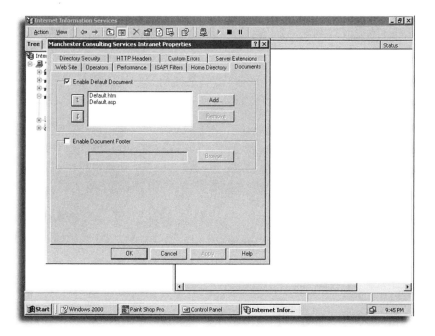

FIGURE 16.24
The Documents tab of the Properties dialog box.

chapter 17

Configuring a Remote Access Server

Features of the Remote Access
Service

Installing and configuring RAS

Managing the Remote Access Server

Dialing out with RAS

Logging RAS events

Introduction to Remote Access Server

More and more workers are spending less and less time in their offices. Executive, sales, and marketing staffs have long been used to traveling to do their jobs. These days, increasing numbers of employees work in virtual offices in their homes, seldom visiting the main office.

Increasingly, remote users are keeping in touch through the Internet. They can, for example, connect to the Internet and receive their email from a company email server. Also, they can connect their browsers to a company Web site and get the latest news. There is little doubt that the Internet has been a prime motivator of the virtual office, providing a worldwide communication infrastructure that didn't exist a few years ago.

However, there remain times when users need to connect directly with the office network. Perhaps they need to retrieve report files from a co-worker's workstation or to leave a spreadsheet where their boss can examine it. In such situations, dial-in access remains a viable method of connecting with the LAN in the home office.

Remote Access Server (RAS) is a dial-in server that is gradually becoming a general communication server. Eventually, you'll be able to use RAS to connect through dial-up lines, conventional Internet connections, or private networks that communicate through the Internet.

This chapter concentrates on the dial-up capabilities of RAS. You'll learn how to set up your own RAS server to let users dial in to your network. You'll also learn how to set up the dial-out capabilities of Windows 2000 to become a dial-in remote client on your organization's network.

Understanding Remote Access Server

RAS enables clients to dial in to a Windows NT Server computer and communicate as remote network nodes. Figure 17.1 shows a computer that has dialed in through a modem. The computer is connected as a remote network node. That means that, although the modem connection is several orders of magnitude slower than a direct network connection, the client functions exactly as though it has a direct connection. Any traffic that would flow through its network adapter when connected directly will flow through its modem when connected through RAS.

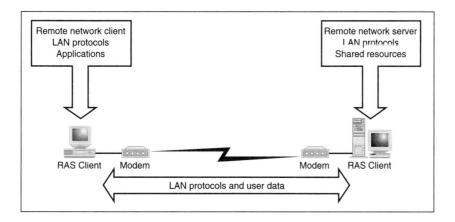

FIGURE 17.1
Operation of a RAS-connected client.

The fact that a client is a remote node means that very little is required to configure the client to operate remotely. It doesn't need to run any special software, other than the dial-out component, and the user works on the dial-in client as if it were directly connected to the network.

Because the dial-in connection is considerably slower than the LAN connection, you need to take certain precautions when setting up the client. It is perfectly reasonable to install applications on a LAN server and let clients access the program files through the network. It is much easier to manage applications that are installed one time on a LAN server than if they are installed a thousand times on a thousand clients. The drawback of running applications from the LAN server is that considerable network traffic is generated.

Unlike LANs, modems are slow, and right now there seems to be no way around it. The new 56Kbps modems help, provided compatible modems are operating at both ends of the connection, but poor line conditions often limit modem performance, particularly on long-distance connections. In addition, the FCC limits the actual speed of a 56Kbps modem to 53Kbps. When you consider that an Ethernet user can frequently pump a burst of data through a LAN at 4–5Mbps, the best modems are slow by comparison.

Because dial-in clients are connected at modem speeds, don't attempt to run applications from the server. All applications should be installed directly on the client so that only data files are transferred through the dial-up connection. The user might copy a .doc file, for example, and edit it locally.

However, all the files required for the Microsoft Word application should be installed directly on the user's workstation. Do everything you can to reduce the data that must be transferred through the dial-up connection.

Even application files are big these days. Excel spreadsheets and documents are frequently larger than 1MB. Document sizes are measured in megabytes, and line speeds are measured in kilobits, so a 1MB document is huge from the perspective of a 33.6Kbps modem. Consequently, it is often useful to use a file compression program to reduce the size of files that are to be transferred through dial-up connections.

When setting up a Remote Access Server, design is everything. Pay careful attention to detail. Keep the traffic levels as low as possible.

Features of the Remote Access Service

RAS consists of two components. The server component is what you usually think of when you use the term *Remote Access Service*. The client component often goes by the name *Dial-Up Networking*. The server and client components are configured separately.

Before looking at RAS configuration, I'll examine some features so that you understand some of the installation questions that face you:

- *Communication technologies.* By far the most common connection method used with RAS is to use modems. However, RAS supports other dial-up technologies as well. I will examine the options listed in the following sections:
  - *Analog modems.* Windows NT can support up to 256 modems. This enables RAS to serve as a powerful dial-up server. RAS supports three modem protocols:
  - *Null modem.* Although it is most common to make serial connections through modems, it is also possible for computers to communicate through two directly wired serial ports, a configuration that is called a *null modem* because the cable that connects the computers fools them into thinking they are communicating through modems. Using null modems, RAS lets two computers communicate without the need for network cards. Null modem cables and adapters are sold in a better computer store near you.

- *X.25.* X.25 is an old, slow, wide area network protocol based on packet switching. X.25 is limited to data rates of 56Kbps and is rapidly being eclipsed by newer technologies such as frame relay. I mention X.25 because you'll see the tabs where RAS can be configured to support X.25. It is unlikely, however, that you'll be implementing a RAS network using X.25.

- *ISDN.* Integrated Services Digital Network (ISDN) is a digital dial-up technology that offers better performance than analog modems. A typical ISDN connection supports two 64Kbps channels and one 16Kbps channel. With the right equipment and software, the 64Kbps channels can be aggregated to provide a total bandwidth of 128Kbps.

Telecommunications providers have been slow to deploy ISDN, and availability remains spotty. ISDN requires end-to-end ISDN capability and special hardware. This is another problem with ISDN. You might be able to obtain ISDN service at one end but not at the other end of a proposed connection.

Gone before it ever arrived?

Just as ISDN is beginning to become readily available, increased competition from new technologies such as cable modems and ADSL threatens ISDN's very existence. It now appears that ISDN will be obsolete before it is fully deployed.

- *Protocols.* RAS supports a number of different connection protocols:
  - *SLIP.* The Serial Line Internet Protocol (SLIP) is an old and basic protocol that operates without error checking, flow control, or security. SLIP has slipped in popularity of late and is less frequently encountered in commercial settings. RAS supports SLIP so that RAS clients can dial in to SLIP servers such as those found in some UNIX environments, but RAS doesn't support SLIP as a dial-in protocol.
  - *PPP.* The Point-to-Point Protocol (PPP) is a significant improvement over SLIP. PPP performs error checking and recovery, enabling it to operate on noisier communication lines than SLIP. Although the extra overhead associated with PPP results in lower performance compared to SLIP, its advantages have gradually made PPP the dominant protocol. RAS supports PPP for dial-in and dial-out functions.
  - *RAS Protocol.* Microsoft has long supported this proprietary protocol and continues to do so in RAS. The RAS Protocol is required to support the NetBEUI protocol.

- *Supported Clients.* Microsoft supports several clients that can dial in to RAS, including the following:

  - *Windows 2000, Windows NT, and Windows 9x.* These clients include RAS server capability and also support the PPP protocol. The clients can dial in and negotiate security with RAS servers supporting RAS, PPP, and SLIP protocols. They can also dial in to UNIX and Internet servers, using PPP or SLIP.

  - *Windows for Workgroups.* Windows for Workgroups includes RAS. You can upgrade the network client software to support TCP/IP, PPP, and SLIP with the TCP/IP client for Windows for Workgroups (WfW).

  - *MS-DOS and Windows 3.1.* The Microsoft Network Client version 3.0 provides RAS support. You must enable the full redirector and access RAS using the rasphone command. RAS for MS-DOS supports only NetBEUI applications and doesn't support TCP/IP or IPX. Given the limitations, you should probably consider Windows for Workgroups the minimum RAS client.

  - *PPP clients.* Any terminal or workstation that supports PPP can dial in to a RAS server. The RAS server will automatically initiate an authentication dialog box. This allows UNIX and other non-Microsoft clients to access files on the RAS server or an attached network.

Installing and Configuring RAS

RAS is configured as a network service. In many ways, installation and configuration procedures resemble the procedures used with a network adapter card, and so much of the material in this chapter will be familiar to you from earlier chapters.

SEE ALSO

➤ *For more information on configuring your network adapter card, see Chapter 8, page 181.*

The RAS installation and configuration procedure involves a number of steps. It is important to note that although there are many orders to the process, the one listed here is the generally accepted method to reduce retracing your steps and reconfiguring software. To install Remote Access Server, you must complete these steps:

1. *Hardware installation.* Before you do anything you need to install your modem hardware.

2. *Configuration of serial ports.* If your modem is external, or uses serial emulation, you will need to set up the ports. This can be combined with the next step if you are using modem cards.

3. *Configuration of the modems.* After the serial ports are configured, you need to configure the modems appropriately.

4. *Installation of the RAS software.* Now that you have modems installed and configured, you can install the RAS software. If there is no modem installed, the RAS installation will start the Modem Installation Wizard to install one. You cannot install RAS without a modem installed first.

5. *Configuration of RAS LAN protocols.* After the software is installed, you need to configure your protocol support.

6. *Configuration of RAS user accounts.* Finally, you need to determine who can connect to the server, and how.

Hardware Installation

Because hardware installation is highly varied, it won't be addressed here; it is beyond the scope of this book. I will mention, however, that the chief limitation of setting up a RAS server on an Intel x86 computer is the limited number of serial ports that the x86 architecture supports. (The limitations I am discussing don't apply to RISC computers.)

Officially, you can add four serial ports to an x86 computer, COM1–COM4. There's a rub, though: COM1 and COM3 ordinarily share IRQ 4, which prevents both ports from being used simultaneously. Similarly, IRQ 3 is shared by COM2 and COM4, and those ports can't be operated at the same time. You must find four free interrupts to have four COM ports. Many serial adapters support only the default IRQs, so even if you can find four free interrupts, your hardware might prevent you from using them.

A variety of vendors have brought out multiport serial communication adapters that allow many serial ports to share a single interrupt. These adapters are your only options if you need to support a RAS solution with more than three or four modems. X.25 PADs are installed as serial devices on RS-232C ports.

ISDN adapters should be installed according to the manufacturer's instructions. Installation of this hardware is beyond the scope of this book.

Configuring Serial Ports

Serial ports are configured using the Device Manager. To start the Device Manager do the following:

1. Bring up the context menu for the My Computer icon by right-clicking. See Figure 17.2.

FIGURE 17.2
The My Computer context menu.

2. Select Properties. This displays the System Properties dialog box, shown in Figure 17.3.

3. Select the Hardware tab and click the Device Manager button.

FIGURE 17.3
The Hardware tab of the System Properties dialog box has a button to click to start Device Manager.

4. In the Device Manager, shown in Figure 17.4, select the Ports entry. Under this entry you should see the LPT and COM ports that have been found on the computer. If you select a port and choose the Properties from its context menu, you access the Com Port Properties dialog box shown in Figure 17.5. This box lets you configure serial communication parameters for the port you selected.

Serial ports must be configured with a variety of parameters, which must match settings in the communications software. These settings follow:

- *Baud Rate*. A measure of the bits-per-second rate at which the port operates. When connecting through a modem, the software negotiates a rate, starting at the value you specify and working toward slower speeds until a compatible rate is found. You should, therefore, set this parameter to the highest value that is supported by your modems.

- *Data Bits*. Serial communication takes place one character at a time. Each character contains 4–8 bits of data. In almost all cases, you'll want to work with 8 data bits, which support advanced character sets and graphics.

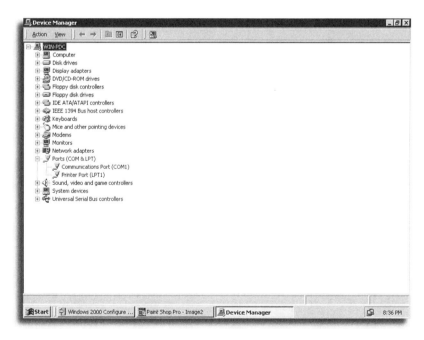

FIGURE 17.4
Device Manager allows you to configure the ports.

- *Parity.* Parity is a rudimentary form of error detection that seldom is employed. In general, you can configure both devices for None. Other options are Even, Odd, Mark, and Space.

- *Stop Bits.* One or more stop bits signal the end of a serial character. It isn't important how many are used, as long as the computers at both ends agree. (However, extra stop bits do waste a bit of the communication bandwidth, and one stop bit will do fine.) One stop bit is by far the most widely used setting.

- *Flow Control.* This parameter determines how the computer and modem inform each other when data is ready to transmit and when the modem's input buffer is full. Options for this setting follow:

    - *Hardware.* The computer and modem communicate through extra wires in the serial cable. This is the most commonly implemented handshaking method.

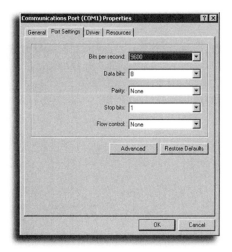

FIGURE 17.5
The Communications Port (COM1) Properties page allows you to configure COM1's settings.

    - *XON/XOFF.* Software handshaking transmits control characters called XON and XOFF to start and stop transmission. This setting is used when flow control must take place between the computers, but it's seldom required.

    - *None.* Risky if the volume of data potentially could overflow the modem's input buffer, which is often the case.

5. Choose OK to save settings. Click Advanced to configure hardware settings for the port.

Configuring Serial Port Resource Settings

Okay, now you're entering a section that you might or might not have to configure. If you are using a single modem with a standard serial port, you should not need to configure the resources for the serial port. However, if you are using internal modems, or you are using a multiport modem card, you will probably need to manually configure computer resources such as IRQ, Base IO, and so on to ensure the card functions properly in your system. In order to configure the resource settings, you need to follow these steps:

1. Click the Resources tab on the Communications Port Properties dialog box to configure additional settings for a serial port. The Resources tab, shown in Figure 17.6, can be used to configure Windows 2000 if your serial ports use nonstandard hardware settings.

FIGURE 17.6
Use the Resources tab to adjust IRQ and IO memory settings.

The settings in the Resources window follow:

- *Base I/O Port Address.* COM ports must be configured with an address in the memory range 2E0H–3FFH. This address supports communication between the OS and the port. Avoid changing the default settings for COM1 through COM4, which have standard and nonconflicting port addresses.

- *Interrupt Request Line (IRQ)*. If your serial port hardware permits you to configure custom interrupts, you can configure Windows 2000 for those interrupts here. To use COM1 and COM3 at the same time (or COM2 and COM4), you need to configure custom, nonconflicting interrupts. Interrupts must be in the range of 2–15, although most of the interrupts in this range are unavailable.

Installing Modems

Before attempting to install RAS, you must install at least one communications device. Modems are installed by using the Modem utility in the Control Panel. Here is the procedure:

1. Open the Phone and Modem Options applet in the Control Panel, shown in Figure 17.7.

FIGURE 17.7
The Phone and Modem Options applet is highlighted in this Control Panel.

2. Select the Modems tab, shown in Figure 17.8. You can use this window to add, remove, and change the properties of modems. Choosing Add starts the Install New Modem Wizard, which can automatically detect most modems.

FIGURE 17.8
There's only one modem here, but if you had multiple modems installed you would have to select the one you wanted to configure.

3. Windows 2000 is adept at detecting modem hardware. In the majority of cases, you should not check Don't Detect My Modem; I Will Select It from a List, which is found in the first window of the installation wizard.

4. Choose Next. The wizard scans your COM ports and attempts to identify a modem. The modem might not be identified by brand. A standard Hayes-compatible modem is identified as a Standard Modem.

5. If you don't like the modem choice, choose Change. You can then select a specific make and model.

6. Choose Next when you're satisfied with the modem choice.

7. Choose Finish when you're informed that your modem has been set up successfully.

Advanced Modem Configuration

To configure the advanced properties of an installed modem, do the following:

1. Select a modem from the Modem tab in the Phone and Modem Options applet in the Control Panel.

2. Choose Properties to open the Modem Properties window.

3. The General properties tab, shown in Figure 17.9, has three settings:

- *Port.* Describes the COM port to which the modem is connected.

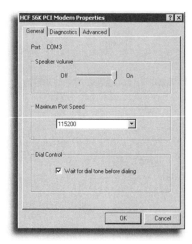

FIGURE 17.9
The General Properties tab for the installed modem.

- *Speaker volume.* Determines the loudness of the modem speaker.
- *Maximum speed.* Specifies the maximum speed at which software should attempt to operate the modem.

4. Select the Diagnostics tab to see information about the modem taken from ROM built into the modem.

5. Click the Query Modem button to execute a number of commands to the modem, and then view the results. (See Figure 17.10.)

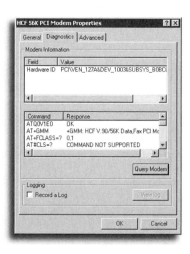

FIGURE 17.10
The Diagnostics tab can reveal the settings stored in a modem's RAM.

6. Choose the Advanced tab, shown in Figure 17.11, to enter additional initialization commands for the modem.

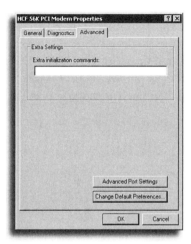

FIGURE 17.11
The Advanced properties for the modem configuration.

7. Click the Advanced Port Settings button to display the Advanced Settings dialog box, shown in Figure 17.12. From here you can

- Enable or disable 16550 FIFO buffers
- Adjust the receive and send buffers
- Change the name for the COM port

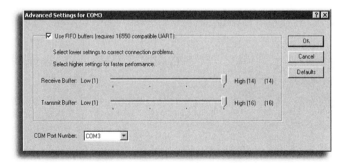

FIGURE 17.12
Advanced Settings lets you set buffer settings and change the COM port name.

Configuring RAS Software

By default, if you have a modem installed in your server, RAS is installed; however, it is not necessarily enabled. Besides configuring the modem for RAS, you also need to grant access to users for RAS. The configuration for RAS occurs in two places. The most important place is in the Routing and Remote Access Console. You can also access this application through the Configure Your Server menu that is available after the initial installation of Windows 2000. It is much easier to get familiar with the Control Panel method, because it is the easiest in the long run.

The Routing and Remote Access Console can be opened by selecting the menu items shown in Figure 17.13.

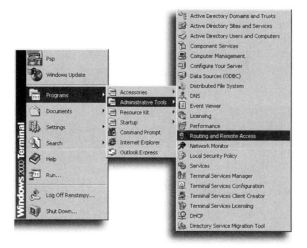

FIGURE 17.13
Opening the Routing and Remote Access Console.

How can I tell where my RAS servers are?
Note that the Routing and Remote Access Console will show an icon for the servers on your network. If the icon next to a server has a green arrow pointing up, the Routing and Remote Access services are active.

To configure RAS you must first configure a modem for RAS. To configure a modem for RAS, do the following:

1. In the Routing and Remote Access Console, select Ports.

2. Bring up the context menu for Ports, and select Properties.

3. From the list of Routing and Remote Access devices, shown in Figure 17.14, select the modem you want to configure.

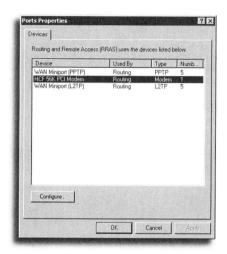

FIGURE 17.14
The Port Properties dialog box includes both physical and logical devices.

4. Click the Configure button.

5. In the Configure Device dialog box, shown in Figure 17.15, you can specify whether the modem will be used for incoming calls only or as a router.

6. Click the OK button to save the configuration.

Now that you have enabled a modem for dial-in, you need to give users access to the modem. Although it is possible to assign RAS options for each individual user through the AD Users and Computers program, the Routing and Remote Access Console allows you to create rules that can apply to everyone, certain groups, certain users, or many other variables.

These are Remote Access Policies, and they really give you control over your remote access solution. You can control who can log on, when they can log on, how they can log on (that is, direct or dial-back), or even what number they can connect from, to name just a few possible actions you can regulate with a policy. It is a good idea to ensure you understand how to make RAS work in the absence of policies, before you start configuring policies. One of the hardest things to troubleshoot with RAS is an issue that could be service-related, or policy-related. If you don't understand the service well, you will have a tough time locating the issue.

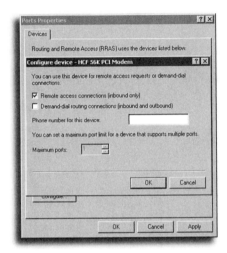

FIGURE 17.15
Specify whether the modem will be used for inbound, or outbound and inbound routing.

To create a Remote Access Policy, do the following:

1. From the Routing and Remote Access Console, bring up the context menu for Remote Access Policies.

2. Select New Remote Access Policy. The Add Remote Access Policy Wizard starts.

3. First, you must give the Policy a name. Enter the Policy friendly name and then click the Next button.

4. The Conditions dialog box allows you to specify the conditions for which this policy will apply. Click the Add button.

5. Add an attribute. For the example shown in Figure 17.16, I will add Day and Time Restriction. Click the Add button.

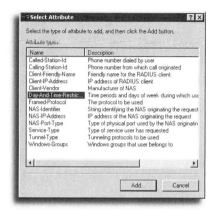

FIGURE 17.16
The Day and Time Restriction is a commonly used condition.

6. I will permit this RAS connection to be used during the hours of 6PM until 8AM, shown in Figure 17.17. Click the OK button.

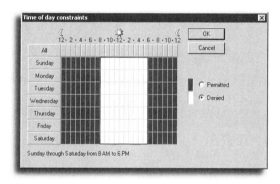

FIGURE 17.17
Select hours and days. Then choose whether to allow dial-in.

7. The Conditions dialog box, shown in Figure 17.18, reflects the Date and Time Restriction.

8. Because I only want a certain group to have this restriction, I will select Windows Groups as a condition and click the Add button.

9. Choose Add in the Groups dialog box.

FIGURE 17.18
After a condition is set, it can be edited.

10. The list of groups is displayed, as shown in Figure 17.19. For this example I am selecting the Remote E-Mail Users group. Click the OK button.

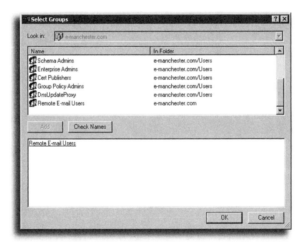

FIGURE 17.19
Select the groups that you want to include in this policy.

11. The Groups dialog box, shown in Figure 17.20, now shows the group I have selected. Click the OK button.

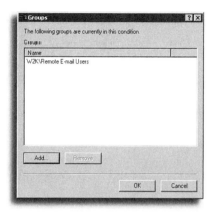

FIGURE 17.20
The Groups dialog box shows the groups that have been selected for this policy.

12. Now the Conditions dialog box shows that this policy will apply to members of the Remote E-Mail Users group and will restrict them from accessing the server through RAS between the hours of 8AM and 6PM, shown in Figure 17.21. Click the Next button.

FIGURE 17.21
Now the combined conditions are displayed.

13. The Permissions dialog box, shown in Figure 17.22, allows you to either permit or deny access. Select the appropriate option and then click the Next button.

FIGURE 17.22
The groups that are in the policy can either be denied or permitted remote access.

14. The User Profile dialog box, shown in Figure 17.23, allows you to further specify options for the users that this policy will apply to. Click the Edit Profile button to bring up these options.

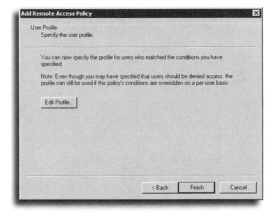

FIGURE 17.23
A profile can be applied to a policy. Otherwise default settings are applied to the policy.

15. Figures 17.24 and 17.25 show the different options available thorough the Edit
Profile dialog box. Click OK to save this policy.

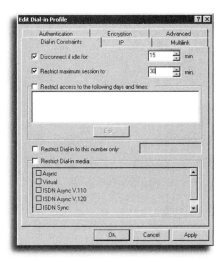

FIGURE 17.24
The Dial-in Constraints tab.

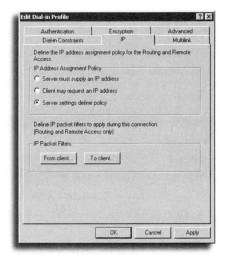

FIGURE 17.25
The IP tab.

Using RAS Multilink

Dial-up multilink capability allows RAS to aggregate multiple physical links into a logical bundle. Bundling is a common technique used with ISDN links. Check Allow Multilink, as shown in Figure 17.26, to support the feature.

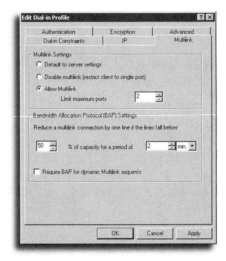

FIGURE 17.26
RAS Multilink settings allow users to increase their bandwidth over regular modem lines.

RAS Authentication Protocols

RAS supports several authentication protocols, and you'll need to select one when you configure a policy, as shown in Figure 17.27.

The supported protocols are the following:

- *CHAP (Challenge Handshake Authentication Protocol).* Adds considerable security to the RAS session. When a connection is being established, the CHAP server sends a random challenge to the client. The challenge is used to encrypt the user's password, which is returned to the server. This has two advantages: The password is encrypted in transit, and an eavesdropper can't forge the authentication and play it back to the server at a later time because the challenge is different for each call.

- *MS-CHAP.* The most secure encryption protocol supported by RAS. MS-CHAP, also known as RSA Message Digest 4 (MD4), uses the RC4 algorithm to encrypt all user data during the RAS session.

- *PAP (Password Authentication Protocol).* A clear-text authentication protocol that is associated with the PPP protocol. PAP authentication should be used only when dialing in to servers that don't support encrypted authentication, such as SLIP and PPP servers.

- *SPAP (Shiva Password Authentication Protocol).* Supported on the RAS server only and is an implementation of PAP on Shiva remote client software.

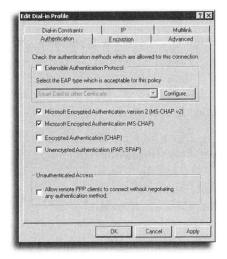

FIGURE 17.27
Various methods of authentication can be accepted for the RAS connection.

What if you want to encrypt the data?

To use the advanced encryption that is included with Windows 2000 Server, you need to connect with a Windows 2000 client. (See Figure 17.28.)

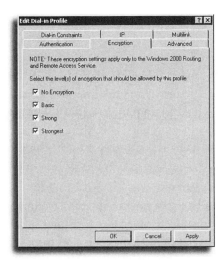

FIGURE 17.28
Encryption options apply only when Windows 2000 users access a Windows 2000 server.

Troubleshooting RAS

By far the most common problems you'll have, at least while you're learning RAS, will result from misconfiguration of the client or the server. Start with a basic setup, get everything working, and then add modem pools and other fancy features. If possible, do your initial testing with two identical modems. If that works and other modems don't, you can be sure the modems are incompatible with RAS.

The Dial-Up Networking Monitor is an extremely useful tool for testing flaky connections; it pops up when dialing commences. The Dial-Up Monitor displays modem status lights during a session, either in a window or as an icon on the taskbar. The window version is more informative, showing the status of the TX (transmit data), RX (receive data), and CD (carrier detect) lines, and whether errors are detected. Especially look for high error rates that might be causing lost connections.

Some other areas that are frequent issues you might want to check include

- *Protocol Mismatches.* If the client is trying to connect using IPX and the server is only set to accept TCP/IP, the user will not be able to connect. Be sure to verify the protocol configurations.
- *Modem Mismatches.* Not only are there issues with certain modems and the RAS service, but there are issues with certain modems talking to other modems. Be sure to set a modem standard and stick to it. That will all but eliminate modem mismatch issues. Failing that, have handy a spare modem you know works, so if you have a user running a modem she bought off the Internet for $18.00, you can determine whether it is the issue.
- *Policy Conflicts.* This issue only crops up if you have policies set, but it is important to be aware of it. If the policy you configured inadvertently prevents a user from connecting, it can be difficult to track down. Some areas where you can run into trouble include restricting the hours for connections, requiring the connection be made from a certain phone (Caller ID might not be working, and the user can't connect), or even requiring RADIUS authentication for a user not in RADIUS. If you use policies and a user is having a problem, check your policies.
- *Hotels.* This doesn't seem to make sense, does it? But you will find that if you have users who spend a lot of time connecting from hotels, they will have problems. Hotel phone lines are famous for their poor quality, and that can cause slow connections or even prevent a connection from being made. This is where

the monitoring tools come in handy, both from a server side and from a client side. Be familiar enough with the Dial-Up Networking Monitor to have an end user check the statistics from their end. Frequently the hotel phone line is to blame.

To try to enumerate every possible scenario or issue you might run into is almost impossible and certainly goes well beyond the scope of this book. But there is one other thing you can do to help narrow down the issue: Look at how to log RAS events.

Logging RAS Events

Logging RAS events can be very helpful in troubleshooting RAS issues. To enable and configure RAS logging, open the Routing and Remote Access Console and do the following:

1. Select Remote Access Logging.

2. Double-click Local File to see its Properties dialog box.

3. Select the items listed on the Settings tab, shown in Figure 17.29, that you would like to log.

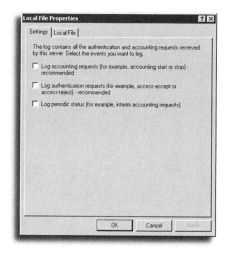

FIGURE 17.29
You can limit the type of events that will be logged.

4. The Local File tab, shown in Figure 17.30, allows you to specify the format, location, and frequency of new log files.

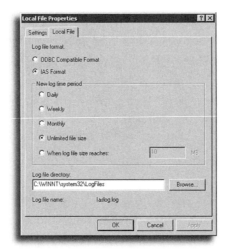

FIGURE 17.30
The type of log file can be text or ODBC. A new log file can be created at regular intervals.

5. Click OK to close the dialog box and effect the change.

By default, the logs are stored in the directory `C:\Winnt\system32\LogFiles`.

GLOSSARY

%SystemRoot% A universal reference to the directory in which the Windows 2000 system files are installed. Typically, %SystemRoot% is C:\Winnt. If multiple copies of Windows 2000 are installed in a multiboot system, each copy will have its own %SystemRoot% directory.

Access Control List (ACL) A list that contains entries defining the levels of access to an object.

Active Directory Service The directory service included with Windows 2000 Server.

Administrative share A hidden share, created by the Windows 2000 installation process. These shares may not be removed and are identified by a trailing $ in the name; for example, C$, D$. Any share name appended with a $ will be a hidden share. Only those shares created at installation are considered Administrative shares.

AppleShare Client software that comes with Macintosh computers and Apple servers.

AppleTalk A network architecture developed by Apple Computer.

archive attribute A file attribute that is set when the file has been modified since it was last backed up.

archive bit See *archive attribute*.

authentication The process of verifying a user's identity on a network.

authoritative When a DNS name server supports the name database for a domain, it is said to be authoritative for that domain.

backup browser A computer that stores a copy of the master browser database. Browse clients can browse the domain or workgroup by querying the backup browser for the browse database.

backup set A collection of files, folders, or other data that have been backed up to a file or tape.

basic disk A physical hard drive that uses the primary partition, extended partition, or logical drive partitioning architecture.

basic volume A logical volume created on a basic disk.

519

binding   A connective relationship between network adapters, drivers, and protocols in a computer's network communication configuration.

browse client   A computer that doesn't store a copy of the domain or workgroup database and must browse the network by querying the browse database on a backup or master browser.

built-in groups   The groups that come predefined by Windows 2000 Server.

certificate   A credential used to authenticate the origin, identity, and purpose of the public half of a public/private key pair.

Certificate Authority   A service (or agency) used to issue, manage and revoke public-key certificates.

certificate services   Software that provides authentication support.

child domain   A Windows 2000 Server domain that exists directly beneath a parent domain in a tree hierarchy.

client   A computer that accesses resources that are shared on a network. Or, the software component of a computer that lets the computer access resources shared on a network.

cluster   a technology that allows for multiple servers to provide fail-over of services.

cryptography   A process that defines a secure method for transmitting data using encryption algorithms.

default router   When a host needs to transmit a packet to a destination not on the local network, it sends the packet to a default router, which is then responsible for routing the packet to its destination network.

DHCP   See *Dynamic Host Configuration Protocol*.

disk drives, duplexing   A configuration of mirrored disk drives in which each disk drive is serviced by a separate drive adapter. This arrangement lets one drive of the pair continue functioning if there is a failure in a disk drive adapter.

disk drives, mirroring   A configuration of two disk drives in which both drives store the same data. A mirrored disk drive set can continue to function when one of the disk drives malfunctions.

disk drives, stripe set   A configuration of three or more disk drives in which data is written in blocks sequentially to each drive. Stripe sets have better storage and retrieval times than single hard disks with comparable specifications but also are more subject to hardware failure.

disk drives, stripe set with parity   A stripe set where one record in each set contains parity data. The parity data can be used to recover data if any one drive in the stripe set fails. A stripe set with parity can continue to function despite the failure of a single disk drive.

disk quota   The amount of space allocated by an administrator for a user or group of users.

Distributed File System (DFS) A service used to present a single directory tree of file shares which can be located on multiple machines and as multiple shares.

DNS   See *Domain Name Service*.

domain   A container in the DNS name hierarchy. Also the network organizational unit for Windows NT networks.

domain local groups   A group object that may only include users or groups from the local domain.

domain master browser A browser on Microsoft TCP/IP networks that collects service announcements from all servers in a domain and creates a master browser database for the domain. Master browsers on other subnets can obtain the domain master browser database for use by browse clients on the local subnets.

Domain Name Service (DNS)   An Internet service used to resolve names to addresses on TCP/IP networks.

duplexing   See *disk drives, duplexing*.

Dynamic DNS (DDNS)   Dynamic DNS is a new addition to Microsoft's DNS implementation. It is a process whereby a workstation's name and address are entered into the DNS table when they obtain an IP address through DHCP.

Dynamic Host Configuration Protocol (DHCP)   A standards-based method of automatically assigning and configuring IP Addresses for DHCP clients.

dynamic volume   A volume that can be created, extended, or deleted without requiring a reboot of this system. This type of volume is new to Windows 2000.

Encrypting File System (EFS) The public key–based service that provides file system encryption for Windows 2000 Servers.

extended partition   A partition that can be configured with one or more logical drives. MS-DOS supports extended partitions as the means of configuring more than one volume on a hard disk.

fail-over   A technology that monitors the "heartbeat" of a server and automatically transfers failing services to another server.

FAT   See *File Allocation Table*.

FAT32   An advanced implementation of FAT that uses smaller clusters.

File Allocation Table (FAT) A list maintained by some operating systems to keep track of file storage on disk.

forest A structure created by domains in more than one Active Directory tree that share the same configuration, but do not share the same DNS namespace.

FQDN See *fully qualified domain name*.

frame One term for a basic unit of network communication, consisting of a message and the information required for delivery. Also referred to as a *packet*.

full backup Copying the entire contents of a computer's hard drives to a medium such as tape, CD-ROM, or another disk.

fully qualified domain name (FQDN) The complete DNS name of a host, including the host name and all domains that connect the host to the root domain. Typically expressed without a trailing period, with the root domain assumed.

fully qualified name The name of a container or data object in a hierarchy, consisting of the object's name and the names of all containers that connect the object to the root container.

Global Catalog A partial replica of every partition in an Active Directory that is used to speed searching.

global group A group object that includes only users or groups from their local domain; however, they can also be defined to access resources outside of their local domain.

group policy Used to configure users' desktops from a Windows 2000 Server computer.

Hardware Compatibility List (HCL) Microsoft's published list of hardware that has passed testing on Windows 2000.

HCL See *Hardware Compatibility List*.

hierarchy A database structure based on the principle of categories and subcategories, typically represented in the form of an inverted tree. Each hierarchy has exactly one master category, typically called the root, and all other categories are subcategories of the root category. Categories can contain subcategories as well as data.

hive Registry data is stored in six or more sets of files called hives. Each hive consists of two files: a data file and a log file.

hop A common metric used with routing protocols, in which one hop is counted for each network that a message traverses on a route.

host A device that is attached to a TCP/IP network.

hostid The portion of an IP address that uniquely identifies a host on its local TCP/IP network.

hosts   A static database file used to resolve names on TCP/IP networks.

IIS   See *Internet Information Server.*

IntelliMirror   A set of technologies included in Windows 2000 to allow a user's desktop configuration to follow him or her to any machine on the network.

internal network number   On IPX networks, each server must have an internal network number, an eight-digit hexadecimal number used to deliver data to the correct process within the server.

Internet   The worldwide network that has evolved out of the ARPAnet developed by the United States Department of Defense.

Internet Information Server (IIS) Microsoft's Internet hosting software.

Internet service provider (ISP)   A vendor that provides network connectivity to the Internet as well as support services such as name, news, and electronic mail.

internetwork   An extended network consisting of discrete networks that communicate through routers. A network of networks. Also called an *internet.*

ISP   See *Internet service provider.*

Kerberos   An identity-based security protocol based on Internet security standards used by Windows 2000 to authenticate users.

LDAP   See *Lightweight Directory Access Protocol.*

Lightweight Directory Access Protocol (LDAP)   A lightweight version of the X.500 directory standard used as the primary access protocol for Active Directory.

lmhosts   A static database file used to resolve names on Microsoft TCP/IP networks.

logical drive   A portion of an extended partition that can be formatted as a volume.

master browser   A computer that collects service announcements from servers and constructs a browse list. Backup browsers periodically contact the master browser to obtain an updated copy of the master browser database.

medium   The vehicle that carries data between a server and a client. Network media include copper cable, optical fiber, microwaves, and light pulses.

metric   Within routing protocols, a number that assigns a preference to a route. The route with the lowest metric is the preferred route.

Microsoft Management Console (MMC)   A framework used for hosting administrative tools.

mirroring   See *disk drives, mirroring.*

Mixed mode   The default mode that Windows 2000 operates in, used to support both Windows 2000 computers and pre–Windows 2000 computers.

MMC   See *Microsoft Management Console*.

name resolution   The process of determining the network address associated with a computer name.

Native Mode   The mode Windows 2000 operates in when supporting Windows 2000 computers only. This mode supports the additional functionality of multimaster replication and nested groups and does not support the ability to replicate with Windows NT 4.0 domain controllers.

netid   The portion of an IP address that identifies the network to which a host is attached.

Network Address Translation   An Internet standard that enables a Windows 2000 Server to use one set of IP addresses on the internal network and a different set of IP addresses on the external network. This can be done to hide the internal addresses or to allow unregistered addresses to be used on the internal network, whereas registered addresses are used externally.

network number   On IPX networks, each network is identified by an eight-digit hexadecimal number that uniquely identifies the computer on an internetwork.

New Technology File System (NTFS)   An advanced file system used in Windows 2000 to offer advanced security features.

node   On networks, a device that communicates on the network and is identified by a unique address. In hierarchies, a container that contains other containers and data.

NTFS   See *New Technology File System*.

null modem   A cable that lets computers communicate through serial ports by simulating a modem connection.

octet   Commonly used to refer to groups of eight bits in network addresses, such as IP addresses. A 32-bit IP address consists of four octets.

paging   The process of swapping data between RAM and disk-based virtual memory.

paging file   A temporary file used to support virtual memory.

parent domain   The topmost domain structure in a Windows 2000 Server domain tree hierarchy.

partition   A physical subdivision of a disk drive that can be formatted with a file system.

Point-to-Point Tunneling Protocol (PPTP)   A protocol used by Microsoft and others to create a virtual private network.

port, hardware A hardware component that lets a computer communicate with other devices. Examples are printer ports, serial ports, and network ports.

port, TCP A software address that lets the TCP/IP protocols deliver messages to the correct process on a computer. Each process running on a TCP/IP computer must be associated with a unique combination of an IP address and a port number. The combination of an IP address and a port number is referred to as a socket.

PPTP See *Point-to-Point Tunneling Protocol*.

primary partition A partition that can be used to boot an operating system.

primary zone A DNS zone that contains the master copies of resource records for a domain.

print server A computer configured to share its printer through the network. Windows 2000 computers become print servers when their printers are shared.

profile See *profile, user*.

profile, local A user profile stored on the user's workstation.

profile, locally cached See *profile, local*.

profile, mandatory A user profile that can be accessed from any workstation on a network. Users can't save changes made to a mandatory profile.

profile, roaming A personal user profile that can be accessed from any workstation on a network. Users can change settings in roaming profiles.

profile, user A database that stores a user's personal computer settings so that the settings are available each time the user logs on.

protocol A standard set of rules for communicating between computers.

Quality of Service (QoS) A set of standards used to ensure a specified quality for data transmissions across a network.

QoS See *Quality of Service*.

Registry key A container for data in the Registry data hierarchy.

resource record A data record in a DNS zone. For example, an address resource record is the data record that describes the address-to-name relationship for a host. Many types of resource records are available.

root In a hierarchy, the container that holds all other containers.

Routing and Remote Access (RRAS) The Windows 2000 Server Routing and Remote Access allows for remote connection to the server.

routing table Each TCP/IP host maintains a routing table that describes routing decisions the host can make. Minimum entries in the routing table include routes to each local network and a default route.

525

RRAS   See *Routing and Remote Access.*

SAM   See *Security Access Manager.*

secondary zone   A DNS zone that obtains copies of the resource records for a domain through a zone transfer from a primary zone.

Security Access Manager (SAM) The component of Windows 2000 that manages the security database and all security functions.

Security ID (SID)   An alphanumeric code used internally by Windows 2000 to identify computers, users, and other objects described in the SAM database.

server   A computer that shares resources on a network.

server mirroring   Real-time replication of a server's data to another server.

SID   See *Security ID.*

site   On an Internet server such as a World Wide Web server, a site is a logical server. Each site must be defined by a unique combination of properties. For example, each Web site running on a given computer must be defined by a unique combination of an IP address and a TCP port.

snap-in   A tool that you can add to a Microsoft Management Console.

socket   The unique combination of an IP address and a TCP port number that identifies a particular process running on a particular TCP/IP computer.

spanned volume   A volume of disk space that resides on more than one physical disk.

Special Permissions   A highly granular type of NTFS permissions that can be assigned to user or group objects.

Standard Permissions   A group of six NTFS permissions that can be assigned to user or group objects.

static route   An item in a routing table that is entered manually and that doesn't change based on information received from a routing protocol.

stripe set   See *disk drives, stripe set.*

stripe set with parity   See *disk drives, stripe set with parity.*

subdomain   A DNS domain located directly beneath another DNS domain in the DNS hierarchy.

subnet   A subdivision of a TCP/IP internetwork that communicates with other subnets through routers.

TCP port   See *port, TCP.*

tree   A logical group of Windows 2000 Server domains that share a common schema.

trusted domain   A domain that allows another domain to share its security database.

trusting domain   A domain that assigns user permissions based on user account and group memberships in another domain that it trusts.

twisted-pair   Cable in which pairs of wires are twisted to reduce sensitivity to electronic noise.

UNC   See *Universal Naming Convention*.

Universal group   A group object that may include any users or groups that are within the same tree or forest.

Universal Naming Convention (UNC)   A naming convention used for defining a resource on a Windows 2000 Server network.

virtual memory   A technique for simulating RAM by swapping memory contents between RAM and disk-based files.

Virtual Private Network (VPN)   A mechanism for providing secure, private communications using a public network (such as the Internet) as the transport method. VPNs use a combination of encryption and authentication technologies to ensure data integrity and security.

volume   A portion of one or more disk drives that can be formatted as a single storage unit. Volumes are usually identified by a drive letter from A: through Z:.

VPN   See *Virtual Private Network*.

Web server   On IIS, a single computer runs one instance of the World Wide Web Server service and functions as one Web server.

Web site   A Web server can support multiple Web sites. Each Web site must be identified by a unique combination of an IP address and port number.

zone   A domain for which a Microsoft DNS server is authoritative.

zone transfer   The process of copying DNS resource records from a primary zone to a secondary zone.

INDEX

F

F10 key (start data capture for Network Monitor), 361

F11 key (stop data capture for Network Monitor), 361

F12 key (display captured data for Network Monitor), 362

fail-over, 239

FAT (File Allocation Table) file system
  choosing over NTFS, 226-228
  converting to NTFS, 228-229
  copying files between NTFS and, 226
  FAT16, 222, 224
  FAT32, 222
  filename concerns, 225
  flavors of, 222
  overview of, 7, 221

FAT partitions, installing from, 55

FAT volume and share permissions, 163

FAT16, 222, 224

FAT32, 222

fault tolerance
  hard drive capacity and, 25
  planning for number of servers and, 22

fault-tolerant hardware, 297

fault-tolerant software, 298

FDISK utility, 13, 239

file administration (Macintosh), 442

File and Print Services for Macintosh, 41, 438-439

File and Print Sharing for Microsoft Networks, 192

File and Printer Sharing dialog box (Windows 95 and 98), 138

file archive bit, 302

file attributes, translation to NetWare, 458

File Server option (Configure Your Server application), 72

File Services for Macintosh
  file administration, 442
  Macintosh Accessible Volume, creating, 439-440
  translating filenames and, 441

file systems
  FAT
    filename concerns, 225
    flavors of, 222
    overview of, 221
  FAT16, 222
  FAT32, 222
  installation and, 35

NTFS
  CHKSDK utility, 229
  choosing over FAT, 226-228
  comparing to FAT, 224
  converting from FAT to, 228-229
  copying files between FAT and, 226
  filename concerns, 225
  moving and copying files and folders, 235
  overview of, 223-224
  NTFS Disk Compression, 230-231
  overview of, 220
  RAID
    hardware versus software types, 238
    Level 0, 236
    Level 1, 236-237
    Level 5, 237
    levels of, 236
    overview of, 235
    real-time mirroring and clustering, 238-239
  See also Disk Management Console; Dynamic Disks; hierarchies

File Transfer Protocol (FTP) Server and IIS, 460

file update commit, 228

filenames, translating Windows into Macintosh, 441

547

partitions
  Active Directory and, 62
  Disk Management
    Console and
      changing drive letters
        for, 247-249
      creating extended,
        249-251
      creating logical within
        extended, 251-252
      creating primary,
        243-246
      deleting, 254
      formatting, 247
      properties and tools,
        overview of, 254
      working with existing,
        242-243
  installation and, 36
  See also Dynamic Disks
Password Authentication
Protocol (PAP), 514
passwords
  selecting, 39
  synchronizing for
    NetWare, 451
  Windows for
    Workgroups 3.11, 143,
    146
paths, specifying, 92
Pause button (IIS tool-
bar), 469
Per Seat mode, 38
Per Server mode, 38
Performance Console. *See*
System Monitor
Performance Log,
354-356

performance monitoring.
  See **monitoring perfor-**
  mance
Performance tab,
Properties dialog box
(IIS), 486
permissions
  administrative shares,
    166-167
  as cumulative, 164
  assigning to shares,
    162-165
  configuring for print
    queues, 177-179
  Everyone group and, 157
  for Web site Access, 479
  overview of, 154
  ownership and, 167-168
  Terminal Services ses-
    sions and, 92
Permissions dialog box
(RAS), 511
Permissions for Programs
dialog box, 157
planning
  disk requirements, 24-25
  identifying goals, 18
  meeting minimum hard-
    ware requirements
      number of servers,
        20-22
      overview of, 18-20
  memory requirements,
    23
  number of processors,
    22-23
  software and Directory
    Services, 25

planning software and
  Active Directory architec-
  ture
  Domains, 27
  Forests, 30
  Organizational Units,
    27-28
  Sites, 26
  Trees, 28-30
Plug-and-Play adapters,
  configuring, 135
plug-and-play printers, 170
Point-to-Point Protocol
  (PPP), 495
Point-to-Point Tunneling
  Protocol (PPTP), 8,
  434-435
pointers to MFT, 223
policy conflicts and trou-
  bleshooting RAS, 516
Port Properties dialog box
  (RAS), 507
power-line conditioners,
  323
PPP (Point-to-Point
  Protocol), 495
PPP clients and RAS, 496
PPTP (Point-to-Point
  Tunneling Protocol), 8,
  434-435
predefined snap-ins,
  10-11
preparing
  for installation, 34
  for upgrade, 52-53
  NetWare Servers to sup-
    port gateways, 446
  to run first time after
    upgrading, 57

Other Related Titles

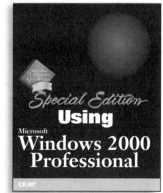

Special Edition Using Microsoft Windows 2000 Professional
By Robert Cowart
ISBN 0-7897-2125-2
$39.99 USA

Practical Windows 2000 Professional
By Ed Bott
ISBN: 0-7897-2124-4
$24.99 USA

Microsoft Windows 2000 Security Handbook
By Jeff Schmidt
ISBN 0-7897-1999-1
$39.99 USA

Windows 2000 Automated Deployment Guide
By Ted Malone
ISBN 0-7897-1749-2
$39.99 USA

Implementing Remote Access Services with Microsoft Windows 2000
By Marcus Goncalves
ISBN 0-7897-2138-4
$39.99 USA

The Multi-Boot and Configuration Handbook
By Roderick Smith
ISBN 0-7897-2283-6
$39.99 USA

Concise Guide to Windows 2000 Dynamic DNS
By Andy Ruth
ISBN 0-7897-2335-2
$34.99 USA

Microsoft Windows 2000 Professional Installation and Configuration Handbook
By Jim Boyce
ISBN: 0-7897-2133-3
$39.99 USA

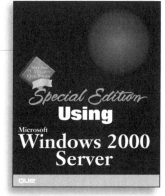

Special Edition Using Microsoft Windows 2000 Server
By Roger Jennings
ISBN 0-7897-2122-8
$39.99 USA

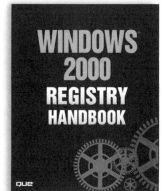

Microsoft Windows 2000 Registry Handbook
By Jerry Honeycutt
ISBN 0-7897-1674-7
$39.99 USA

www.quecorp.com

All prices are subject to change.